THE MINISTRY

OF THE

CHRISTIAN CHURCH

THE MINISTRY

OF THE

CHRISTIAN CHURCH

BY

CHARLES GORE, M.A.

PRINCIPAL OF THE PUSEY HOUSE; FELLOW OF TRINITY COLLEGE, OXFORD,
AND EXAMINING CHAPLAIN TO THE LORD BISHOP OF LINCOLN

SECOND EDITION

WIPF & STOCK · Eugene, Oregon

Wipf and Stock Publishers
199 W 8th Ave, Suite 3
Eugene, OR 97401

The Ministry of the Christian Church
By Gore, Charles
ISBN 13: 978-1-60608-922-4
Publication date 12/8/2009
Previously published by Rivington, 1889

PREFACE.

THERE are two large questions having reference to Christianity which it is important to keep distinct. There is the question whether Christianity is true, and there is the question what, as a fact in history, Christianity has been? It is an indispensable preliminary to all effective dealings with the practical problems, which arise in the attempt to apply and adapt Christianity to current needs and circumstances, that we should study profoundly the genius of Christianity as a continuous historical fact—that we should have a clear answer to the question, what Christianity has been and is. This book, then (assuming broadly the truth of Christianity), attempts to give a partial answer to this second question. It maintains that Christianity is essentially the life of an actual visible society, and that at least one necessary link of connection in this society is the apostolic succession of the ministry. In a word, this book claims on behalf of the apostolic succession that it must be reckoned with as a permanent and essential element of Christianity. It is an 'apology' for the principle of the apostolic succession.

As being an 'apology' for one clause in the Church's practical and theoretical creed, it will be subject to the usual suspicions of prejudice and want of free criticism to which apologetic literature is exposed, and from which the literature of 'free thought' is supposed to be by comparison exempt. But it is, perhaps, only while we are very young that we are inclined to believe dissent from orthodox conclusions to afford any guarantee for a just and critical judgment; in fact, the ambition to form or propagate a new theory gives as strong a bias to the mind as the desire to maintain an old one. At any rate, I have tried to do with my 'prejudices' all that a man can do with those inevitable accompaniments alike of his birth into a continuous society and of the first activities of his own individuality; I have tried to subject them to an exact and free examination in the light of reason and history, and to let it correct or verify them.

A word must be said in explanation of the order and contents of this book. The principle of the apostolic succession has been a formative principle in church history. It seemed, therefore, the best course, after making good the preliminary grounds of this investigation (chap. I), and explaining the idea of the ministry (chap. II), to exhibit the extent to which in church history the principle of the apostolic succession has been postulated and acted upon since the time when the continuous record begins—*i.e.* the latter half of the second century (chap. III). The principle is then examined in the light of the Gospels (chap. IV), of the apostolic documents (chap. V), and of the links of evidence which connect the apostolic age with the continuous history (chap. VI). After this nothing remains but to draw conclusions and make applications (chap. VII). This order treats the question—What has the Church in fact believed about her ministry? as a preliminary to the investigation of her title-deeds, and it was hardly possible for the present writer to treat the question in any other order. Whether or no Mr. Darwin is right in maintaining " that the only object in writing a book is a proof of earnestness, and that you do not form your opinions without undergoing labour" (*Life and Letters*, i. p. 334), it is, at any rate, true that a book had better represent that process of 'labour' by which its writer's opinions have in fact been formed.

The purpose of this book not being primarily or simply archæological, it has been possible to leave out of discussion a good many elements in the history of the ministry which do not, or so far as they do not, affect the principle. It has been necessary to deal largely in quotations from ancient authors, but it has been possible to omit almost all that bears, *e.g.* upon the growth of the metropolitan and patriarchal systems, the relations of the later episcopate to secular society, the history of ecclesiastical discipline or canon law in detail. On all these subjects the student will find a great deal of very valuable material in Dr. Hatch's published works, and in his articles in the *Dictionary of Christian Antiquities*. I very much regret that what seems to me his extraordinary, his most unhistorical, under-estimate of the permanent element of belief and practice in the Christian Church has led to his being mentioned in these pages generally with criticism. I also regret that I had not read till it was too late his article on *Paul the Apostle*, in the *Encyclopædia Britannica*, vol. xviii. If I had done so, I could not have complained, as I have in reference to his Bampton Lectures, of his not plainly stating his position as to certain disputed New Testament documents. In that article he speaks of the Pastoral Epistles as "probably even less defensible," *i.e.* from the point of view of authenticity, than those to the Ephesians and Colossians (p. 422, col. 2; cf. also the remark at the head of the column on the Acts of the Apostles). I might also have noticed that he had already

(*Dict. Chr. Ant.* ii. p. 1481) spoken of the Epistle of Polycarp as "almost contemporary" with the Pastoral Epistles.

I had intended to conclude this book with a discussion of the validity of the episcopal succession in the English Church, but it has seemed better to reserve this, appealing as it would to a different class of readers, for another opportunity.

It remains for me only to express my gratitude for advice and help given me by my friend the Rev. Dr. Paget, and my colleague the Rev. F. E. Brightman—but especially I have to thank another colleague, Mr. R. B. Rackham, who has given ungrudging and continuous labour to preparing this book for publication, and rescuing it from many mistakes. He has also compiled the Table of Contents and the Index of Authors, etc., which will, I hope, render the book more useful for reference. Vallarsius' edition of Jerome has been used throughout, and Hartel's Cyprian, which however follows the Oxford edition in the numbering of the *Epistles*.

PUSEY HOUSE,
St. Peter's Day, 1888.

PREFACE TO THE SECOND EDITION.

IF there are almost no alterations, except verbal corrections, in this Edition, it is not because I have not received valuable suggestions. For instance, I have been advised to enlarge the argument on pp. 34-36, as to the fundamental independence of the Church and the *Collegia*, and in doing so I should have had an opportunity of noticing Professor Ramsay's remarks in the *Expositor* of Dec. 1888, pp. 415 ff., on the use to which he supposes the Church in Phrygia to have put the guild organization, for purposes of concealment. But I have thought that I should do better to wait, before acting on any suggestions that I have received, till I have had the advantage of more criticisms, and till I can myself consider matters again with a fresher mind. Meanwhile, there are three points confirmatory of my argument, by mentioning which, I may perhaps forestall criticism.

1. The newly discovered writings of the Spaniard Priscillian[1] give us, as the sentiment of bishops contemporary with him in Spain, about A.D. 380, a view of the consecration and election of bishops, which falls in with the argument of pp. 100 ff.; "Rescribitur . . . sicut dedicationem sacerdotis in sacerdote, sic electionem consistere petitionis in plebe" (*Tract.* ii. p. 40). The context makes the meaning tolerably plain, viz. that it belongs to a bishop to consecrate a bishop, but to the people to choose and ask for him.

[1] Just edited by their discoverer, Georg Schepps, in the Vienna *Corpus Scriptorum Ecclesiasticorum Latinorum*.

Preface to the Second Edition.

2. Dr. Salmon has kindly pointed out to me that the argument about Colluthus on p. 139 admits of being strengthened by calling attention to the fact that Colluthus *claimed to be a bishop* when he ordained. This appears in the letter of the Mareotic clergy, quoted by Athanasius, *Apol. c. Ar.* c. 76 : "He [Ischyras] was appointed by Colluthus, the presbyter who pretended to the episcopate and was afterwards ordered by the synod of Hosius, and the bishops with him, to be a presbyter as he was before." Thus Colluthus did not even claim to ordain *as a presbyter*.

3. Besides that mentioned on p. 371 of this book, there is another Syriac version of the Canons of Ancyra given by Cardinal Pitrain *Analecta Sacra Spicilegio Solesmensi* iv. 219. The 13th canon in this version is, I am told, inaccurately rendered by the Abbé Martin (p. 447). Translated literally it runs thus: "To chorepiscopi it is not allowed that they should ordain [make ordination] priests and deacons: but again also not that they should consecrate priests of the city, without the permission of the bishop with writings in every one place." I am informed that there is no doubt that 'priests of the city' must be the object of the verb 'consecrate' and not its subject, *i.e.* that it represents πρεσβυτέρους not πρεσβυτέροις. This information I owe to Mr. C. H. Turner of St. John's College, Oxford.

C. G.

Epiphany, 1889.

CONTENTS.

CHAPTER I. THE FOUNDATION OF THE CHURCH.

	PAGE
Preliminary assumptions—	
(1) The genuineness of New Testament documents	1
(2) The truth of the Incarnation	6
Preliminary inquiry: Did Christ found a visible Church?	9
The reasonableness of the idea in itself	9
(1) Witness of the early Christian belief in a visible Church	12
(unanimous in spite of differences in point of view)	13
in the West—Tertullian, Cyprian, Irenaeus, (holding 'nulla salus extra ecclesiam' together with belief in God's wider dealings), the Roman Church	13
in the East—Ignatius, Alexandrian writers	23
the Apologists—Aristides, Justin, Theophilus	28
confirmed by the pagan conception of Christianity	30
(2) The social form of Christianity not due to the secular influence of the 'collegia,' for	31
(a) Christian writers show no trace of such influence	34
(b) Christian terminology was derived from Judaism	35
(3) Witness of the New Testament	36
(a) The Gospels—	
(i) Christ's method,	37
(ii) His institution of social sacraments	40

Contents.

	PAGE
(iii) His Messianic claim	41
(relation of the Church to the 'kingdom of God')	42
(the Church not exclusive, though it makes an exclusive claim)	44
(*b*) The Acts	45
(*c*) St. Paul's Epistles	46

This doctrine is not inconsistent with the doctrines of faith
    and liberty 49
    but agreeable to the principle of all human society . 51
    (Heaven in the Apocalypse a city) . . . 52

Two misconceptions as to the origin of the visible Church—
    (1) That it arose out of a previous condition of individualism 52
    (2) That it was due to Roman influence: difference between the Roman and Catholic conceptions of church unity 56

    Notes on The idea of an invisible Church pp. 19, 49.

CH. II. APOSTOLIC SUCCESSION.

The method of the inquiry 65

The principle of Apostolic Succession expounded . . 69
    It corresponds to the Incarnation, Sacraments, etc. . 71
    The principle more important than the form in which it is embodied 72
    Its importance as—
        (*a*) a bond of union for a universal spiritual society 76
        (*b*) emphasizing men's dependence on God's gifts . 77
        (*c*) satisfying the moral needs of those who minister 81

Answers to objections that—
    (1) 'It is sacerdotal': true and false sacerdotalism . 83
    (2) 'Unspiritual men are thus made to mediate spiritual gifts': distinction of character and office . 95

	PAGE
(3) 'It is opposed to liberty': but liberty is opposed to absolutism, not to authority; the Church not at first or necessarily an imperialist institution .	97
(4) ' It cannot be true in fact ': this objection not tenable	107
(5) 'It unchurches presbyterian bodies': but results must not prevent our facing principles .	109

Note on Morinus' ' de sacris ordinationibus' . p. 68
         Sacramental teaching of the early Fathers 79
         Doctrine of lay-priesthood in catholic theology 89

CH. III. THE WITNESS OF CHURCH HISTORY.

Church history bears witness to certain fixed principles—

1. The principle of apostolic succession through the episcopate (with the requirement for the ministry of episcopal ordination) 116
    appealed to by Irenaeus 116
    accepted by Tertullian 125
    anticipated by Hegesippus 127

A. Further evidence for the East—
    The episcopal successions—
        in Palestine, Syria, Asia, Greece, Macedonia, Thrace, Crete 128
        the supposed exceptional constitution of the Alexandrian Church . . . 134
            (*a*) very doubtful in fact . . . 138
            (*b*) not opposed to the principle of succession 142
    The conception of the ministry in—
        (i) liturgical writings . . . 144
        (ii) canons of councils . . . 152
        (iii) Greek Fathers — Athanasius, Gregory Nazianzen, Chrysostom, Epiphanius . 154

B. Further evidence for the West—
    The episcopal successions undoubted . . 161

The conception of the ministry in—
    (i) Latin Fathers—Cyprian, Lucifer, writers who minimize the distinction of bishop and presbyter, *i.e.* Ambrosiaster, Jerome, etc. 164
    (ii) canons of councils . . . 176
    (iii) liturgies 177

2. Ordination was regarded sacramentally . . 183
    and conferred by laying-on of hands . . 185

3. It was believed to impose an 'indelible character' 187
    though the distinction of 'valid' and 'canonical' was slowly formulated . . . 191

4. The conception of the ministry from the first involved a sacerdotal principle, though the use of sacerdotal terms was of gradual growth . 196

5. The ministry possessed exclusive powers, *e.g.* only a priest could celebrate the Eucharist . . 200
    Tertullian's statement to the contrary due to Montanist views 204
    Montanism—its characteristics . . 207
        not a conservative movement . 211

Summary 213

Note on *The conception of the ministry in the Clementines* p. 130
    ,,   ,,   *Clem. Alex.*   135
    ,,   ,,   *Origen* . 140
The language of Firmilian . . . 155
The early Irish episcopate . . . 162
'One bishop in a community' . . . 165
The primacy of Peter's see . . . 169
Functions of the presbyterate . . . 181
Morinus on the 'tradition of the instruments' . 186
Signification of laying-on of hands . . 187
Reordination . . pp. 189, 192, 193
Sources of sacerdotal language . . 199

CH. IV. THE INSTITUTION OF THE APOSTOLATE.

	PAGE
The postulates of church history to be verified by an appeal to Christ's intention	216
The Gospels generally suggest the institution of a permanent apostolate	219
especially in the commissions to—	
(1) St. Peter—his relation to (*a*) the other Apostles, (*b*) the whole Church	222
(2) All the Apostles after the resurrection . .	226
(the commission in St. John xx to the Apostles rather than the whole Church) . .	229

Note on Sacrificial aspect of the Eucharist p. 226

CH. V. THE MINISTRY IN THE APOSTOLIC AGE.

Evidence of St. Paul's Epistles :

(*a*) The office of an apostle	231
(*b*) The Church an organism with differentiated gifts and functions	238
(*c*) The Pastoral Epistles—their importance ; they show	242
(i) a ministry of presbyter-bishops and deacons, not the chief ministry . . .	244
(ii) an extension of the apostolate to 'apostolic men'	246
(iii) St. Paul's idea of ordination by the laying-on of hands	249
Evidence of the other Epistles	251
Evidence of the Acts :	
(*a*) The apostolate	253
(*b*) A ministry of 'prophets and teachers' . .	260
(*c*) A local ministry of presbyter-bishops and deacons .	262
Summary : (1) The apostolate	265
(2) A subapostolic ministry . . .	266
(3) Presbyter-bishops	267
(4) Deacons	268
(5) Ordination by laying-on of hands . .	268

xvi   *Contents.*

                                                             PAGE
Evidence is lacking as to—
   (*a*) details in the division of functions .   . 269
   (*b*) the form of the future ministry .   .   . 269

      Note on   The Angels of the Apocalypse p. 254

CH. VI. THE MINISTRY IN THE SUBAPOSTOLIC AGE.

Links connecting this apostolic ministry with the episcopate of church history 270

In the East—
  I. St. James originates the 'episcopate' in Jerusalem . 273
 II. The *Didache* shows
     (*a*) a general ministry of 'apostles' and 'prophets' and 'teachers;'
     (*b*) a local ministry of 'bishops and deacons' . 276
III. St. John (with other Apostles) develops 'episcopacy' in Asia   286
    This is confirmed by the testimony of Ignatius to the threefold ministry of bishops, presbyters, and deacons   288
    (in what sense the presbyterate represents the Apostles)   302

In the West—
IV. Clement's Epistle
     (*a*) shows a differentiated ministry having succession from the Apostles;
     (*b*) postulates an order above the presbyter-bishops and deacons   .   .   .   308
 V. Polycarp's Epistle
    implies absence of a bishop at Philippi;
    but this is not inconsistent with a superior ministry not localized there .   .   .   326

Contents.   xvii

                                                   PAGE

VI. The *Shepherd* of Hermas suggests a third order above presbyters and deacons 331

Summary—of possible theories :
1. A college of equal presbyters . . . 333
2. The bishop hidden in the presbyterate . . 334
3. What alone seems to satisfy the evidence—the episcopate derived from a gradual localization of 'prophets,' 'teachers,' and 'apostolic men' . 335

        Note on   *A second apostolic council*   . p. 274
                        The office of reader   .   . 284
                        The Ignatian controversy   . 289

CH. VII. CONCLUSION AND APPLICATIONS.

The verdict of history as to (*a*) the Church, (*b*) sacerdotalism, (*c*) episcopal ordination . . . 337

Is confirmed by the witness of (*a*) the Gospels, (*b*) the apostolic, and (*c*) subapostolic documents . . 340

The cogency of the evidence : it can only be satisfied by the doctrine of the apostolic succession . . 343

This doctrine in its application
    (*a*) invalidates non-episcopal ministries . . 344
    (*b*) recalls episcopal Churches to their true principles . 348

APPENDED NOTES.

A. Dr. Lightfoot's Dissertation on "The Christian Ministry"   353
B. The early history of the Alexandrian ministry .   . 357
C. Rites and prayers of ordination .   .   . 363
D. (i) Canon xiii of Ancyra   .   .   . 370
    (ii) Chorepiscopi   372

	PAGE
E. Supposed ordinations by presbyters in East and West	374
F. The theory of the ministry held by Ambrosiaster, Jerome, etc.	378
G. Laying-on of hands	383
H. Montanism	390
I. Prophecy in the Christian Church	394
K. The origin of the titles 'bishop,' 'presbyter,' and 'deacon,' with reference to recent criticism	399
L. *The Teaching of the Twelve Apostles*	411
Addendum on de Aleatoribus	420

CHAPTER I.

THE FOUNDATION OF THE CHURCH.

THE reader of the history of Christendom cannot fail to be conscious, at each stage of his subject, of the prominent position held in the Church by a Ministry, which is regarded as having a divine authority for its stewardship of Christian mysteries—an authority which is indeed limited in sphere by varying political and ecclesiastical arrangements, but which in itself is believed to be derived not from below but from above, and to represent and perpetuate, by due succession from the Apostles, the institution of Christ. It is this Christian ministry which is to be the subject of the present inquiry. We shall endeavour to ascertain its history, to trace it back through its series of changes to the fountain-head. More than this, we shall endeavour to investigate its authority and search into its title-deeds. Is this ministry, with its claim of an apostolic succession, the mere product of circumstances—valuable just so far as it is found spiritually convenient? As claiming to be a priesthood, does it represent a temporary accommodation of the Christian ideal, more or less necessitated by circumstances, to the Jewish or pagan ideas amidst which the Church spread? Is it a temporary restriction of the free Christian spirit—dangerous, however necessary? Or, on the contrary, is it an original portion of Christ's foundation? Is the episcopal succession, as it meets us in history, simply the fulfilment of Christ's intention, an essential and inviolable element of Christianity till the end?

These are the main questions before us—questions much controverted, yet not on that account incapable of yielding satisfactory solutions. But, like other controverted questions, these which concern the Christian ministry have a tendency to run off their own field and get upon territory foreign to themselves in one direction or another. It will therefore promote clearness if at the beginning the area of the present discussion is carefully marked out.

<small>Prelim. assumptions.</small>

<small>(1) The genuineness of the N. T. records.</small>
1. As an historical inquiry, the investigation of the *origines* of the Christian ministry involves conclusions as to the date and authorship of a number of documents. In regard to the great majority of these there is no division of opinion which is of serious moment for the present inquiry. But this is not the case with regard to some of the documents contained in the New Testament. The genuineness of the Epistles of St. Peter and St. James and of the Epistle of St. Paul to the Ephesians, still more the historical character of the Evangelical records and of the Acts of the Apostles, and the genuineness of St. Paul's Pastoral Epistles, are questions of vital moment in dealing with the history of the ministry. It is well then, in order to narrow the field of inquiry, to make it plain at starting that the genuineness of these

Epistles and the historical character of these records are here generally assumed. True, a considerable part of the inquiry is not affected by the decision in one sense or another of these critical questions. But in the discussion of the ministry in the apostolic age it has great weight.[1] If a certain set of conclusions is here in the main taken for granted, this is not at all because it is desired to exempt the books of Scripture from free criticism. It is done, because no investigation is satisfactory which does not at starting make plain the basis on which it rests, while a discussion of so large a number of critical questions would occupy too much space in preliminaries. It is done, then, to limit the area of inquiry; but, it must be added, with the clearest conviction that the conclusions assumed are those which the facts warrant. There does not seem to the present writer to be any reasonable ground for doubting, for instance, the unity or the genuineness of the Epistles of St. Paul to the Ephesians, to Timothy, and to Titus. The authorship of the Epistle to the Ephesians is guaranteed, not only by the external evidence, not only by its con-

---

[1] Thus Professor Harnack (*Expositor*, May 1887) discusses the origin of the Christian ministry on the assumption that not only the Pastoral Epistles but also the Acts of the Apostles and the Epistle of St. James are second century documents (pp. 334 n.[6], 335 n.[1]), and that the Epistle to the Ephesians was written "a considerable time after the Apostle's death" (p. 331). As he truly says—when he is proceeding "to set forth the chronological data which we possess for the origin and the earliest development of the ecclesiastical constitution"—"This problem would receive the most diverse solutions from those occupying different standpoints regarding the origin of certain New Testament and post-apostolic writings. Any one, for example, who admits the genuineness of the Pastoral Epistles will reach quite different conclusions from one who regards them as non-Pauline, and relegates them to the second century" (p. 322).

nection with the more personal Epistles to the Colossians and to Philemon, but also by the lofty power and richness of thought with which it developes and unifies the fundamental conceptions of predestination and of the Church, which St. Paul had already presented in the Epistles to the Romans and the Corinthians. The Pastoral Epistles are linked together by intense coherence of subject and tone; and there is hardly any writing which can be more certainly pronounced genuine by internal evidence than the second Epistle to Timothy.[1] When we pass to the Acts of the Apostles, there would seem to be scarcely any bit of literary controversy in which, within recent years, we have experienced more completely the reassuring effect of thorough inquiry. The remarkable Christology of the early chapters: the position assigned to the prophets in the earliest Church:[2] the accurate knowledge, as tested by recently-published inscriptions, which the author displays of the titles of local magistrates and the details of local sentiment:[3] the reiterated evidence, which the book affords in its later portions, that the author was an eye-witness of what he records—all this taken together goes to guarantee the substantial accuracy

---

[1] Professor Salmon's vindication of the genuineness of these Epistles will, I think, be considered adequate by a fair-minded and impartial reader. See his *Introduction to the New Testament*, lecture xx. Cf. also Professor Godet on the Pastoral Epistles in the *Expositor*, January 1888.

[2] Harnack selects Acts xiii. 1 f. with vi. 1 f. as passages in which the reader "enters at once upon historical ground . . . which bears the marks of higher credibility."

[3] See Dr. Lightfoot's "Illustrations of the Acts from Recent Discoveries," *Contemp. Review* (May 1878), and Dr. Salmon's *Introd.* p. 339 f.

of the whole record.¹ Further, the position assigned to the Apostles in St. Paul's Epistles and in the Acts suggests or presupposes some such dealings of Christ with them in particular as the Gospels record. Once again, then (for this reason and in virtue of all the body of considerations which make for the trustworthiness of the evangelic records), it is here taken for granted without scruple that Jesus Christ did really give in substance those instructions and commissions to His Apostles and to His Church, both before and after His Resurrection, which He is recorded to have given in the narratives of St. Matthew, St. Mark, St. Luke, and St. John.² It is then from no

---

[1] While we wait for an article on the subject of the Acts by the man who perhaps in all Europe is best qualified for the task, I may refer (1) to Dr. Salmon's *Introd.* lect. xviii; (2) to the discussions on the relation of the Acts to the Epistle to the Galatians in Dr. Lightfoot's Commentary on the latter Epistle, and the appended essay on "St. Paul and the Three"; (3) to the remarkable admissions of one of the last critics amongst those who pay honour to the name of Baur—Dr. Pfleiderer (see his *Hibbert Lectures*, lect. i). Cf. Harnack *Dogmengesch.* i. pp. 62, 63, etc.

[2] The authenticity of St. John's Gospel has been sufficiently vindicated of recent years by Professor Godet and Dr. Westcott.

With reference to a point of some importance for the subject of the ministry in St. Matthew's Gospel—our Lord's commission to St. Peter—Prof. Harnack has recently argued (*Contemp. Review*, Aug. 1886, "The Present State of Research in Early Church History," p. 230) that an earlier version of the narrative is preserved in the text of Tatian's *Diatessaron*. We have in Armenian St. Ephraem's Commentary on this Harmony of the Gospels. In the Latin translation of this (*Evangelii Concordantis Expositio facta a S. Ephraemo*, in Lat. trans. a R. P. Aucher, Mechitarista, pp. 153, 154) the words run: Beatus es Simon, et portæ inferi te non vincent. Afterwards the words Tu es petra are quoted. Here it appears that it is against *St. Peter* that the gates of death are not to prevail, and nothing is said of the foundation of the Church. But we have not the whole text of the *Diatessaron*; St. Ephraem only quotes it to comment on it. Nor does he always quote it fully. In this case he gives no hint of the words Tu es petra till afterwards, out of their order. Elsewhere it is manifest that he does not quote the whole text; see his comments on St. John, as incorporated in the Harmony (pp. 145-153); and again (p. 66) on the Sermon on the Mount, where the quoted text of St. Matt. v. 22-32

fear of free criticism that the authenticity and trustworthiness of these New Testament documents is here assumed.

(2) The truth of the Incarnation.

2. It will also be taken for granted that the apostolic interpretation of the Person of Christ is the true one —that He was the Incarnate Son of God. It is important to make this plain, because, though little stress will be laid upon this doctrine, yet our rational attitude towards the development of Christian institutions depends to a certain extent upon our relation to it.[1] The Incarnation represents necessarily a climax in the divine self-revelation. It represents this necessarily, because no closer relation of God to man is conceivable than that involved in the "Word—Who is God—made flesh" in the historical Person, Christ Jesus, in such sense that "he who hath seen Him hath seen the

---

runs thus: "Sed ego dico vobis: qui dicit fratri suo, fatue . . . qui dicit fratri suo, vilis aut stulte. . . . Audistis quia dictum est: non adulterabis, sed ego dico vobis: quicunque aspicit et concupiscit, adulterat. Si manus tua vel pes tua scandalizet te . . ." St. Ephraem does not by any means quote the whole text; but he refers to more than he quotes. Thus in the passage under discussion, if we reconstruct his text from his commentary (Dominus cum ecclesiam suam aedificaret etc., p. 154), it must have run to this effect: "Blessed art thou, Simon. Thou art Peter, and on this rock I will build My Church, and the gates of hell shall not prevail against thee." The "thee" may be due simply to the "it" (αὐτῆς) being referred to πέτρα and not to ἐκκλησία, a reference which Origen *in loc.* discusses. Probably St. Ephraem accepts this reference and, interpreting the rock of St. Peter, glosses αὐτῆς as equivalent to σοῦ. There are no traces of any such reading as Harnack imagines to have existed in the Greek or in the Syriac versions (either Cureton's or the Peshitto), which have our text. See Zahn's *Diatessaron* p. 163.

[1] For example, it seems a grave critical defect in Dr. Hatch's Bampton Lectures, *The Organization of the Early Christian Churches*, that, as he has not explained his relation to certain most significant New Testament documents, so also he has not made it plain whether he really believes the 'supernatural' character of the Person of Christ. If he does, then his propositions about the merely 'natural' development of Christian institutions will surely want correcting (lecture i. p. 18).

Father." God cannot come any nearer to man, man cannot come any nearer to God than is effected in Him, in Whom "dwelleth all the fulness of the Godhead bodily." This is "the end of the days." As M. Godet strikingly observes: "The history of the world (from the Christian point of view) is summarized in its essence in these three words: He is coming: He is come: He is coming again."[1] The development then of God's revelation of Himself comes to its climax in the Incarnation. Henceforth another sort of development begins. All institutions, all races, all individuals are gradually brought into the light of Christ and judged by their relation to Him. Christ developes Himself as the Second Adam, realizing the capacities of all humanity by bringing it all, age by age, race by race, individual by individual, into relation to Himself, till He can 'come again,' in the revelation of the glory of the sons of God, as the acknowledged centre and head of humanity and of the universe.

It is not here proposed to inquire whether analogies will be found in other departments of evolution to what has taken place in the history of religion. This is a large question, which does not belong to our present subject. But the general theory of evolution must, of course, like every other generalization, mould itself to the facts. It must take account, among other things, of religious facts. Now in the history of religion a term *has*, in a certain sense, been reached in the past. The Christian moral standard, the Christian character claims to be essentially final. The Person-

[1] *Études Bibliques*, N. T. p. 291.

ality of Christ, as it finds expression in His own language and action and in the belief about Him of His earliest disciples,[1] represents finality. Thus also the grace of His Spirit is the fulness of grace, adequate for all ages and all men; and the truth revealed in Him is 'a faith once for all delivered,' simple and universal, which is to mould human character to the end.[2]

Plainly, then, the rational acceptance of this position about Christ gives us certain premises or presuppositions with reference to the institutions which perpetuate the presence, and represent the will and mind, of Christ. A 'once for all delivered' faith and grace associates itself naturally with a once for all instituted society and a once for all established ministry. The question whether "the Christian societies, and the confederation of those societies which we commonly speak of in a single phrase as 'the visible Church of Christ,' were formed without any special interposition of that mysterious and extraordinary action of the divine volition, which, for want of a better term, we speak of as 'supernatural,'"[3] is rationally conditioned by the question whether the manifestation of the Christ is of this order. A supernatural cause sug-

---

[1] I may refer to Dr. Sanday's *What the First Christians thought about Christ* (Oxford House Papers) and to the argument in Mr. Stanton's *Jewish and Christian Messiah* p. 154 f.

[2] See Dr. Westcott's *Christus Consummator* pp. 124 f. 151 f.

[3] Hatch *B. L.* p. 18. On p. 20, the author says the Church "is divine as the solar system is divine." Now inasmuch as the Church is a human society, he must mean that it is divine, as the British constitution or the Roman empire is divine. But if Christ be personally God, if in virtue of a divine life He burst the tomb and rose the third day from the dead, the society to which He gave birth may presumably be divine in another sense—not as exempted from "the universe of law," but because it belongs to that kingdom of law in which effects are relative to causes.

gests supernatural effects. Nothing will be assumed here about the Church and the ministry. The conclusions shall be drawn strictly from the evidence. But belief in the Incarnation opens our eyes to give due weight to the evidence.

Now on the basis of these assumptions a question arises, which must be determined before the proper subject of the present inquiry can be approached. Did Christ found a Church in the sense of a visible society?[1]

Prelim. inquiry.

Did Christ found a visible Church?

That He should have done so is intelligible enough. As it has recently been said,[2] "it is only by becoming embodied in the undoubting convictions of a society, by being, as it were, assimilated with its mind and motives—that is to say, with living human minds and wills—and informing all its actions, that ideas have reality, and possess power, and become more than dry and lifeless thoughts." "As great moral and social and political ideas are preserved in life and force by being embodied in the common and living convictions of the society which we call the State, so great spiritual ideas, which are the offspring of Christianity, are preserved in life and force by becoming the recognised beliefs and motives of the society which we call the

---

[1] "For although it is indisputable that our Lord founded a Church, it is an unproved assumption that that Church is an aggregation of visible or organized societies; and although it is clear that our Lord instituted the rite of Christian baptism, it is an unproved assumption that baptism was at the outset, as it has become since, not merely a sign of discipleship, but also a ceremony of initiation into a divine society" (Hatch *B. L.* pref. sec. ed. p. xii). To the idea that the Church is "a visible society, or aggregation of societies," is opposed the idea that it is "synonymous with the elect."

[2] *The Christian Church* by R. W. Church, Dean of St. Paul's, (Oxford House Papers, No. xvii.) pp. 4, 5, 15.

Church." Christianity would never have done what it has done in the world, if it had been a mere body of abstract truth, like a philosophy, to be apprehended by this or that individual. It would never have done what it has done, if it had been embodied only in a book or collection of books. It has lived on, and worked upon men, as a society or group of societies. This, of course, everybody would admit. The question is whether believers in Christ were left to organize themselves in societies by the natural attraction of sympathy in beliefs and aims, and are, therefore, still at liberty to organize themselves on any model which seems from time to time to promise the best results, or whether the divine Founder of the Christian religion Himself instituted *a* society, *a* brotherhood, to be the home of the grace and truth which He came to bring to men : so that becoming His disciple, meant from the first this—in a real sense this only—incorporation into His society. If this was the case, the Church was not created by men, nor can it be recreated from time to time in view of varying circumstances. It comes upon men from above. It makes the claim of a divine institution. It has the authority of Christ. Christ did not, according to this view, encourage His disciples to form societies; He instituted a society for them to belong to as the means of belonging to Him.[1]

---

[1] Of course this antithesis requires guarding. The supernatural influence in the genesis of the Church did not annihilate "the natural inclination which all men have unto sociable life :" but it controlled and intensified it. This consilience of the natural and supernatural is beautifully expressed by Hooker, *E. P.* i. 15. 2.

Now, as we watch the history of Christendom, we discern "a great number of organized religious bodies owing their existence and their purpose to Christian belief and Christian ideas;" but in the midst of these we discern also something incomparably more permanent and more universal—one great continuous body—the Catholic Church. There it is; none can overlook its visible existence, let us say from the time when Christianity emerges out of the gloom of the sub-apostolic age down to the period of the Reformation. And all down this period of its continuous life this society makes a constant and unmistakeable claim. It claims to have been instituted as the home of the new covenant of salvation by the Incarnate Son of God. Is the claim which this visible Catholic Church has made a just one? This is our present question: we are not asking yet whether the Church has any particular form of polity by divine institution, but whether the thing itself— the visible society—is the handiwork of Christ. This much we premise: that it would be nothing extraordinary if Christ did institute a Church. It is reasonable to think[1] that, if He came to leave among

<small>Intrinsic probabili</small>

---

[1] Cf. the measured words of Butler, *Analogy* pt. II. ch. i: "As Christianity served these ends and purposes, when it was first published, by the miraculous publication itself, so it was intended to serve the same purposes in future ages by means of the settlement of a visible Church; of a society distinguished from common ones and from the rest of the world, by peculiar religious institutions, by an instituted method of instruction and an instituted form of external religion. Miraculous powers were given to the first preachers of Christianity, in order to their introducing it into the world: a visible Church was established in order to continue it, and carry it on successively throughout all ages. . . . To prevent [Christianity being sunk and forgotten in a very few ages], appears to have been one reason why a visible Church was instituted; to be like a city upon a hill, a standing memorial to the

mankind the inestimable treasures of redemptive truth and grace, He would not have cast them abroad among men, but would have given them a stable home in a visible and duly constituted society—a society simple enough in its principles to be capable of adaptation to the varying needs of ages and nations and individuals, simple enough to be catholic, but organized enough to take its place amidst the institutions of the world with a recognisable and permanent character.

<small>Witness of history.</small>

But, as a fact, does history record that He did act thus? The affirmative answer to this question shall be given *first* by exhibiting the impressive unanimity with which the early Christians believed that He did: *secondly*, by making it plain that the existence of the visible Church was not due to external 'secular' influences: *lastly*, by supporting the position from the evidence of the New Testament, especially of the Gospels.

<small>) Early Christian belief—</small>

(1) It is plain that the visible society admits of being differently represented, according as it is regarded as the home of divine grace, uniting men by the Spirit through Christ to God and to one another; or as the kingdom of truth, maintaining the 'witness of Jesus;' or as the organ of divine authority, guiding and disciplining the lives of men. But it is equally plain that such modes of representing the Church

<small>world of the duty which we owe our Maker, to call men continually . . . to attend to it, and by the form of religion ever before their eyes, remind them of the reality; to be the repository of the oracles of God; to hold up the light of revelation . . . and propagate it throughout all generations to the end of the world." Cf. also the general argument of his *Charge to the Clergy of Durham*.</small>

are not at all incompatible with one another, and all of them equally postulate the *visibility* of the Church.

We proceed then to trace up the different lines of tradition in the Church so as to show that the difference of colour put upon Christian truth by the varieties of spiritual temperament and the varying claims of circumstance did not affect this central position. And as, of recent years, considerable originality has been assigned to the "Augustinian theory" of the Church,[1] we will make a beginning with the Church of St. Augustin—the Church of Africa. Now, whatever novelty there may have been in Augustin's presentation of the matter,[2] at least he did not originate the idea of a visible Church. Let us take our earliest representative of African Christianity, Tertullian (at the end of the second century), and listen to what he teaches on the subject, in argument with the Gnostics, giving it as the one thing certain, whatever may be matter for question.

In the West:

Tertullian.

" Christ Jesus our Lord," he says,[3] " so long as He

---

[1] E.g. by Dr. Hatch *l.c.* pp. xii, xiii.

[2] St. Augustin's doctrine of the Church is thus stated by Mr. Cunningham (*St. Austin* p. 116): "The kingdom of God was not a mere hope, but a present reality, not a mere name for a divine idea, but an institution, duly organized among men, subsisting from one generation to another; closely inter-connected with earthly rule, with definite guidance to give, and a definite part to take in all the affairs of actual life. To him the kingdom of God was an actual Polity, just as the Roman Empire was a Polity too: it was 'visible' in just the same way as the earthly State, for it was a real institution with definite organization, with a recognised constitution, with a code of laws and means of enforcing them, with property for its uses, and officers to direct it." This would represent what is meant by "the Augustinian theory." But in fact St. Augustin's relation to the idea of the Church is a complex one. On the whole he intended to spiritualize rather than materialize it: cf. Hermann Reuter *Augustinische Studien*, esp. pp. 101, 150-1, 485 ff.

[3] *de Praescr.* 20: "Christus Iesus, Dominus noster, permittat dicere

was living on earth, spoke Himself either openly to the people or apart to His disciples. From amongst these he had attached to His person twelve especially, who were destined to be the teachers of the nations. Accordingly, when one of these had fallen away, the remaining eleven received His command, as He was departing to the Father after His Resurrection, to go and teach the nations, who were to be baptized into the Father and the Son and the Holy Spirit. At once, then, the Apostles (whose mission this title indicates), after adding Matthias to their number as the twelfth in the place of Judas on the authority of the prophecy in David's psalm, and after receiving the promised strength of the Holy Ghost to enable them to work miracles and preach, first of all bore witness to the faith in Judæa and established Churches, and afterwards going out into the world proclaimed the same teaching of the same faith to the nations, and

interim, quisquis est, cuiuscunque dei filius, cuiuscunque materiae homo et deus, ... quamdiu in terris agebat, ipse pronuntiabat sive populo palam sive discentibus seorsum, ex quibus duodecim praecipuos lateri suo allegerat destinatos nationibus magistros. Itaque uno eorum decusso reliquos undecim digrediens ad Patrem post resurrectionem iussit ire et docere nationes tinguendas in Patrem et in Filium et in Spiritum sanctum. Statim igitur apostoli, quos haec appellatio missos interpretatur, assumpto per sortem duodecimo Matthia in locum Iudae ex auctoritate prophetiae quae est in psalmo David, consecuti promissam vim Spiritus sancti ad virtutes et eloquium, primo per Iudaeam contestata fide in Iesum Christum ecclesiis institutis, dehinc in orbem profecti eandem doctrinam eiusdem fidei nationibus promulgaverunt. Et proinde ecclesias apud unamquamque civitatem condiderunt, a quibus traducem fidei et semina doctrinae ceterae exinde ecclesiae mutuatae sunt, et quotidie mutuantur, ut ecclesiae fiant. Ac per hoc et ipsae apostolicae deputabuntur, ut soboles apostolicarum ecclesiarum. Omne genus ad originem suam censeatur necesse est. Itaque tot ac tantae ecclesiae una est illa ab apostolis prima, ex qua omnes. Sic omnes primae et omnes apostolicae, dum una omnes probant unitatem. Communicatio pacis et appellatio fraternitatis et contesseratio hospitalitatis, quae iura non alia ratio regit, quam eiusdem sacramenti una traditio."

forthwith founded Churches in every city, from which all other Churches in their turn have received the tradition of the faith and the seeds of doctrine; yes, and are daily receiving, that they may become Churches; and it is on this account that they too will be reckoned apostolic, as being the offspring of apostolic Churches. Every kind of thing must be referred to its origin. Accordingly, many and great as are the Churches, yet all is that one first Church which is from the Apostles, that one whence all are derived. So all are the first, and all are apostolic, while all together prove their unity: while the fellowship of peace and the title of brotherhood and the interchange of hospitality remain amongst them—rights which are based on no other principle than the one handing down of the same faith."

Here we have a perfectly clear conception of the one catholic Church,[1] founded in fulfilment of Christ's intentions by His immediate ambassadors, of which every local Church is the representative for a particular area. Behind "the Churches," and prior to them in idea is the one Church which each embodies.[2]

---

[1] Second century writers speak of the Church as *actually* catholic—so strong is their sense that it is meant to be so—i.e. they speak of the Church as having spread universally. Cf. πάντα τὰ ἔθνη τὰ ὑπὸ τὸν οὐρανὸν κατοικοῦντα, ἀκούσαντα καὶ πιστεύσαντα . . . ἐκλήθησαν (Hermas *Sim.* ix. 17); ἡ ἐκκλησία . . . κατὰ τῆς ὅλης οἰκουμένης ἕως περάτων τῆς γῆς διεσπαρμένη (Iren. i. 10. 1); "expansa in universum mundum" (*ib.* iv. 36. 2); ἡ κατὰ τὴν οἰκουμένην καθολικὴ ἐκκλησία (*Mart. Polyc.* 8).

[2] The thought of salvation *in the Church* is so prominent in Tertullian's mind that he finds it in the Lord's Prayer. Speaking of the title "Father," he says (*de Orat.* 2): "Appellatio ista et pietatis et potestatis est. Item in Patre Filius invocatur; Ego enim, inquit, et Pater unum sumus. Ne mater quidem ecclesia praeteritur. Siquidem in filio et patre mater recognoscitur, de qua constat et patris et filii nomen."

Thus the Church is to Tertullian's mind God's institution for man's education and salvation. To the Church belong the Scriptures; so utterly in fact does he refuse to separate the books of the Church from herself that he declines, in theory at least, even to argue as to the meaning of the Scriptures with those outside the Church, because they do not belong to them. So little does he conceive of the Christian religion as an abstract doctrine written in a book![1]

It was, then, through membership in this one apostolic Church, catholic and local, that African Christians believed themselves to inherit the grace of Christ. Communion with God depended on communion with His Church. "He cannot have God for his father," Cyprian is fond of emphasizing,[2] "who has not the Church for his mother." "*Dost thou believe*"—so runs the baptismal interrogation in St. Cyprian's day—"(*in*) *the remission of sins and eternal life through the holy Church?*"[3]

_{Cyprian
c. A.D. 255.}

---

[1] *de Praescr.* 19: "Ergo non ad scripturas provocandum est, nec in his constituendum certamen, in quibus aut nulla aut incerta victoria est, aut parum certa. Nam etsi non ita evaderet collatio scripturarum, ut utramque partem parem sisteret, ordo rerum desiderabat illud prius proponi, quod nunc solum disputandum est: quibus competat fides ipsa, cuius sint scripturae."

[2] *Ep.* lxxiv. 7: "Ubi et ex qua et cui natus est, qui filius ecclesiae non est? ut habere quis possit Deum patrem, habeat ante ecclesiam matrem." Cf. *Ep.* lv. 24: "Quisque ille est et qualiscunque est, Christianus non est qui in Christi ecclesia non est." *Ep.* lxxiii. 21: "Salus extra ecclesiam non est." Cyprian's conception of the bishop constituting the Church will be brought out later.

[3] *Ep.* lxix. 7: "Credis remissionem peccatorum et vitam aeternam per sanctam ecclesiam?" *Ep.* lxx. 2: "Credis in vitam aeternam et remissionem peccatorum per sanctam ecclesiam?"

Dr. Westcott (*Historic Faith*, Note iii. p. 186) does not notice the latter form. Previously (p. 116) he lays stress on the idea that "we do not say we believe in" the Church: we believe only "that it is." This distinction

There is no reason to think that such a question would have startled or shocked the faithful in any part of the Christian Church. Certainly Irenaeus, the bishop of Lyons, who represents the Church of Gaul and the Churches of Asia where he had been brought up, held the same belief in the Church and made the same exclusive claim for it.

Irenaeus c. A.D. 175.

"In the Church," he says, "God placed apostles, prophets, doctors, and the whole operation of the Spirit, and all who do not have recourse to the Church do not participate in Him, but deprive themselves of life.... For where the Church is there is the Spirit of God, and where the Spirit of God is there is the Church and all grace." "God will judge all those who make schisms.... No reformation can be wrought by them which can compensate for the injury of the schism. God will judge all those who are outside the truth—that is, who are outside the Church." "The Church has been planted as the paradise in this world: so then, of every tree of the paradise ye shall eat, says the Spirit of God—that is, of every Scripture of the Lord."[1]

comes from Rufinus; cf. his Commentary on the Creed § 36: "hac itaque praepositionis syllaba Creator a creaturis secernitur et divina separantur ab humanis." Cf. St. Augustin *de Fide et Symbolo* 21. But this would apply neither to all the western Creeds (see, in Heurtley's *Harmonia Symbolica*, Creeds xix, xxvi, xxvii, xxx, xxxvii-viii, and the early Spanish Creed in Priscillian *Tract.* ii. p. 36), nor to the eastern form of the Constantinopolitan Creed (the form of most authority in the Church) with the earlier eastern Creeds (see Pearson *On the Creed* art. ix, notes 52, 53; and Westcott *l.c.* p. 195). It is therefore surely impossible to lay stress on it.

[1] Irenaeus' conception of the organization of the Church is presented later. The passages here quoted are iii. 24. 1 (quoted below, p. 120);

iv. 33. 7: "'Ἀνακρινεῖ δὲ τοὺς τὰ σχίσματα ἐργαζομένους, κενοὺς ὄντας τῆς τοῦ θεοῦ ἀγάπης καὶ τὸ ἴδιον λυσιτελὲς σκοποῦντας, ἀλλὰ μὴ τὴν ἕνωσιν τῆς ἐκκλησίας· καὶ διὰ μικρὰς καὶ τὰς [τυχούσας] αἰτίας τὸ μέγα καὶ ἔνδοξον σῶμα τοῦ Χρισσοῦ

18   *Christian Ministry.*   [CHAP.

(recognition also of God's wider dealings)

It might be asked how St. Irenaeus reconciles this exclusive claim which he makes for the Church with a truth to which he also gives expression—namely, that God's revelation of Himself through His Son, Who is the Eternal Word, 'the Light which lighteneth every man,' is in a sense universal, and that in order to the apprehension of this universal revelation there is a universal capacity for faith which is exhibited in all moral obedience to God wherever found.[1] Irenaeus teaches this, with the Alexandrians and with Justin Martyr.[2] With the last-named father he would,

τέμνοντας καὶ διαιροῦντας καὶ ὅσον τὸ ἐπ᾽ αὐτοῖς ἀναιροῦντας· ... οὐδεμία δὲ τηλικαύτη δύναται πρὸς αὐτῶν κατόρθωσις γενέσθαι, ἡλίκη τοῦ σχίσματός ἐστιν ἡ βλάβη. Iudicabit autem et omnes eos qui sunt extra veritatem, id est qui sunt extra ecclesiam."

v. 20. 2: "Fugere igitur oportet sententias ipsorum [haereticorum]... confugere autem ad ecclesiam, et in eius sinu educari, et dominicis scripturis enutriri. Plantata est enim ecclesia paradisus in hoc mundo. Ab omni ergo ligno paradisi escas manducabitis, ait Spiritus Dei; id est, ab omni scriptura dominica manducate."

The connection in the mind of the early Church between schism and heresy is very close. The fundamental idea of heresy is that of *self-willed separatism* or particularism. Cf. Rothe *Anfänge der christlichen Kirche* § 53 p. 563 f. and pseudo-Athan. *Dict. et Interpret. Parabol. Evang.* qu. 38 (quoted by Rothe *l.c.* p. 566) Πόθεν λέγεται αἵρεσις; ἀπὸ τοῦ αἱρεῖσθαί τι ἴδιον, καὶ τοῦτο ἐξακολουθεῖν. This expresses the primitive idea.

[1] Iren. iv. 6. 5, 7: "Et ad hoc Filium revelavit Pater, ut per eum omnibus manifestetur et eos quidem, qui credunt ei iusti, in incorruptelam et in aeternum refrigerium recipiat; credere autem ei, est facere eius voluntatem.... Nemo cognoscit... Patrem, nisi Filius et quibuscunque Filius revelaverit. Revelaverit enim non solum in futurum dictum est, quasi tunc inceperit Verbum manifestare l'atrem, cum de Maria natus; sed communiter per totum tempus positum est. Ab initio enim assistens Filius suo plasmati, revelat omnibus Patrem, quibus vult et quando vult et quemadmodum vult Pater; et propter hoc in omnibus et per omnia unus Deus Pater et unum Verbum Filius et unus Spiritus et una salus omnibus credentibus in eum."

[2] Justin *Apol.* i. 46: Τὸν Χριστὸν πρωτότοκον τοῦ θεοῦ εἶναι ἐδιδάχθημεν καὶ προεμηνύσαμεν λόγον ὄντα, οὗ πᾶν γένος ἀνθρώπων μετέσχε. καὶ οἱ μετὰ λόγου βιώσαντες Χριστιανοί εἰσι, κἂν ἄθεοι ἐνομίσθησαν, οἷον ἐν Ἕλλησι μὲν Σωκράτης καὶ Ἡράκλειτος καὶ οἱ ὅμοιοι αὐτοῖς, ἐν βαρβάροις δὲ Ἀβραὰμ καὶ Ἀνανίας καὶ Ἀζαρίας καὶ Μισαὴλ καὶ Ἠλίας καὶ ἄλλοι πολλοί, ὧν τὰς πράξεις ἢ τὰ ὀνόματα καταλέγειν μακρὸν εἶναι ἐπιστάμενοι τανῦν παραιτούμεθα. ὥστε καὶ οἱ προγενόμενοι

no doubt, recognise all who, even in heathen lands as well as among the Jews, "lived or live with right reason," as the "friends of Christ" the Eternal Reason, and even as "Christians." How would he reconcile such a position with the exclusive claim of the Church? Probably by holding that all who had not had the opportunity of becoming members of the Church while on earth would, if they had been true to their light, be received into the Church in Paradise. At any rate the reconciliation was not effected by the idea of an *invisible Church* to which they belonged— an invisible Church containing the true servants of God whether they belonged to the visible Church or not. Neither the existence of good men outside the Church, nor the presence of bad men inside it, ever drove the Christian Fathers, whether eastern or western, to this hypothesis.[1]

ἄνευ λόγου βιώσαντες ἄχρηστοι καὶ ἐχθροὶ τῷ Χριστῷ ἦσαν καὶ φονεῖς τῶν μετὰ λόγου βιούντων· οἱ δὲ μετὰ λόγου βιώσαντες καὶ βιοῦντες Χριστιανοὶ καὶ ἄφοβοι καὶ ἀτάραχοι ὑπάρχουσιν.

[1] The Church on earth was regarded as subdivided into false and true members—the latter constituting the κυρίως ἐκκλησία of Origen, the corpus Christi verum of Jerome and Augustin. Neither of these (as Rothe, *Anfänge etc.* p. 618 n. 44, remarks) "agrees with the invisible Church of the Protestants." The point of difference is specially this, that, whereas the members of the 'invisible Church' are regarded as belonging indifferently to any or no ecclesiastical unity, with Origen and Augustin the conception is the opposite. The membership in the 'true Church' depends upon membership in the one visible Church on earth. The true Church is a subdivision of the actual Church—its genuine members. For "non omnes qui tenent ecclesiam, tenent et vitam aeternam" (Augustin *de Bapt.* v. 20); "multi ... sunt in sacramentorum communione cum ecclesia, et iam non sunt in ecclesia" (*de Unit. Eccl.* 74). See further Rothe *Anfänge* § 61, esp. pp. 612 ff. and Stanton's *Jewish and Christian Messiah* p. 230: "Let me premise that I think the distinction cannot be maintained, which was first introduced by the theology of the sixteenth century ['the idea appears pretty fully developed in Wiklif,' footnote], between a visible and invisible Church in this world, the latter consisting only of the truly godly. Not only is such a distinction uncountenanced by Scripture,

The Roman Church

Victor c. A.D. 190.

From Africa and Gaul we come to the great western centre—Rome. Certainly the idea of the visible Church and its unity was prominent there at the time when Victor, the bishop, attempted to excommunicate the Churches of Asia for keeping Easter after their own specially Johannine tradition. He endeavoured, says Eusebius,[1] "to cut them off from the common unity" and make them "utterly excommunicate." He was reproved by Irenaeus for introducing into the Church the idea of a rigid uniformity, in place of the common faith, as the bond of union. He is reminded how, in the middle of the century, his predecessor Anicetus had kept his fellowship with the Asiatic Polycarp, in spite of their difference as to this

but the very idea of a Church is that of a Society which has its officers and its organisation. It is a contradiction in terms to call a number of individuals a Church who are not united together in a body. The moment they do begin to unite, by virtue of their common supposed characteristic of genuine godliness, they cease to be invisible. There have been such attempts to form a pure Church; but history and the warnings of our Lord Himself have taught us what to think of them." Of course the greater part of the Church is to us invisible, but that is because its members are no longer on earth, and they enjoy "perfect fellowship with one another, as well as with their Lord." Cf. also William Law's *Third Letter to the Bishop of Bangor*, at the beginning—a powerful and racy passage. Of course the truth that the Church is a visible society, containing evil as well as good, is involved in our Lord's language in the parables of the Net gathering of every kind and the Field of wheat and tares: it is involved also in St. Paul's whole conception of the Church and of 'the saints,' that is the Christians as *bound to holiness* by the consecration laid upon them in virtue of being baptized members of Christ, but not necessarily actually holy. Still it was only when the long repose of the last parts of the second century and the first half of the third made the Christian profession popular and easy, that the full weight of the problem came upon the Church. In part there was a disposition to meet it by rigorous discipline, passing into an impatient refusal to tolerate the 'mixed' condition of the Church; and this was a fruitful source of schism. In part stress was laid upon the Church on earth being only an outpost of a celestial society (cf. Tertull. *de Bapt.* 15 una ecclesia in caelis), an earthly image of it (cf. Clem. Alex. *Strom.* iv. 8. 66 εἰκὼν τῆς οὐρανίου ἐκκλησίας ἡ ἐπίγειος), or a preparation-ground for it: and thus necessarily imperfect.

[1] Euseb. *H. E.* v. 2.

particular custom—"those who observed it, and those who did not, keeping the peace of the whole Church."

But we may go back in the same Church at least [1] to the earlier part of the second century, to the days of Hermas, the seer of the *Shepherd*. In his visions the Church is represented as an aged lady, who appears to Hermas, and "through whom he receives visions and revelations." She is aged, it is explained to him, because "she is the first creation of God, on whose account the world was made."[2] The Church is here thought of as in a way existing from the beginning in the purpose of God, in the ideal world. But this divine Idea has become a fact. The actual Church, made up of those yet alive and of some who have departed in the faith of Christ, is represented to Hermas under the figure of a tower with a marvellous unity, which is being built by the angels of God upon the waters of baptism, the stones which are used for the tower, and those which are rejected, representing all sorts of men.[3] This actual Church which is in process of being constructed is declared to be identical with the ideal Church. What existed before in idea is now real.[4] And this real, visible Church is the only way

Hermas.

---

[1] See further on the date, in chap. VI.

[2] *Vis.* ii. 4 : Τὴν πρεσβυτέραν, παρ' ἧς ἔλαβες τὸ βιβλίδιον, τίνα δοκεῖς εἶναι ; ἐγώ φημι· Τὴν Σίβυλλαν· Πλανᾶσαι, φησίν, οὐκ ἔστιν. Τίς οὖν ἐστίν ; φημί. Ἡ ἐκκλησία, φησίν. εἶπον αὐτῷ· Διατί οὖν πρεσβυτέρα ; Ὅτι, φησίν, πάντων πρώτη ἐκτίσθη· διὰ τοῦτο πρεσβυτέρα, καὶ διὰ ταύτην ὁ κόσμος κατηρτίσθη. Cf. *Vis.* iv. 1 : αἱ ἀποκαλύψεις καὶ τὰ ὁράματα ἅ μοι ἔδειξεν διὰ τῆς ἁγίας ἐκκλησίας αὐτοῦ.

[3] *Vis.* iii. 2-8.

[4] The tower which is the visible Church on earth *is* the ideal Church which appeared to Hermas, Ὁ μὲν πύργος ὃν βλέπεις οἰκοδομούμενον, ἐγώ εἰμι, ἡ ἐκκλησία, ἡ ὀφθεῖσά σοι καὶ νῦν καὶ τὸ πρότερον (*Vis.* iii. 3). Cf. [pseudo] Clem. *ad Cor.* 14. If Hermas' Church of the divine Idea is spoken of "as a sort of Aeon" (Rothe *Anfänge* p. 612 n. 42) it must be remembered that the Idea is

of salvation. "When the tower is finished, those who have not yet repented can no longer find place, but will be cast out."¹ There is another vision of the building of the tower to the same effect.² In this it is made plain that the Church in its present state is imperfect. Many, who had been gathered out of all nations "into the one body," have fallen away and been cast out for awhile or for ever. Those who are members of the Church at present are evil as well as good; many will have to be cast out; and thus the Church as a whole will at the last be purified into complete holiness and unity. Still, as it is, the Church represents God's will, God's purpose of redemption; and those who separate themselves from it, separate themselves from the hope of salvation—like the covetous or the extortionate. They are represented as men diseased: "they who are covered with scabs are they who denied their Lord and turned not to Him, but have become dry and desert-like, and cleave not to the saints of God, but isolating themselves, lose their own souls."³ How could imagery express more strongly the idea of salvation through the Church?⁴

We may go back in the same Church to a yet

actualized to Hermas, as the Word is made flesh. This differentiates the Church's system from the Gnostic; the Valentinian Aeon ἐκκλησία is (by contrast) only ideal. For the Jewish form of the doctrine of the eternal Church see *Book of Enoch* c. 39.

[1] *Vis.* iii. 5. There is, however, an inferior salvation implied for some who do not find place in the tower, if they repent, and after a purgatorial purification (*ib.* 7).

[2] *Sim.* ix. This tower is built upon the great Rock, Christ.

[3] *Sim.* ix. 26.

[4] The commission to Clement to send the book to *the other cities* (εἰς τὰς ἔξω πόλεις) implies the sense that the local Churches are essentially connected (*Vis.* ii. 4).

earlier date, and still in the Epistle of Clement we shall find, without poetry or vision, the sense of the Church as vivid as possible. The Church in that Epistle is a visible society, with the divine principle of order stamped upon her, as upon the Church of the old covenant, by God's authority,[1] and there is a common tradition over the different local Churches, for neglecting which that at Rome is bound to take her sister at Corinth to task. The western temper no doubt tended later (as will be seen) to colour the idea of the Church. As the Church at Rome became Latinized and came to inherit the secular prerogatives of the Roman name in addition to her own spiritual privileges, no doubt her influence gave a new tone—the tone of secular empire—to Christian institutions. Thus the doctrine of the Church becomes materialized, but it is a complete mistake to suppose that the conception of the Church, or of the visible unity of the Church, was at all western in origin.

Ignatius of Antioch was a thorough oriental; and he writes to Churches which inherit the fruits of the last years of apostolic influence when that influence had its centre at Ephesus. Yet it is impossible to conceive a teaching about the Church as a visible society more intense, more passionate, than that of Ignatius. Christ's authority is perpetuated in visible societies with a visible organization, and each of these societies, each Church, with its bishop

Clement c. A.D. 96.

In the East: Ignatius c. A.D. 110.

---

[1] Clem. *ad Cor.* 40-44; see further chap. vi. "The new law of the Church" Clement "most characteristically connected with the two models of the political and military organization of the Roman state and the sacerdotal hierarchy of the Jewish theocracy" (Pfleiderer *Hibbert Lectures* p. 252).

and priests and deacons, is an embodiment of what is not local, but catholic.¹ "Where the bishop appears, there let the people be, as where is Christ Jesus, there is the catholic Church." "He who is within the sanctuary is pure, he who is outside is impure, that is to say, he who does anything apart from bishop and presbytery and deacons is not pure in his conscience." "If any one follows a separatist he does not inherit the kingdom of God."²

The Church may be represented from different points of view. It may be emphasized, as was said above, as the home of a divine grace covenanted to its members alone; this is perhaps the thought specially suggested by the scriptural metaphors of the body of Christ and the branches of the Vine. It may be emphasized from the side of authority, the Church being the mistress of men to subdue and to rule them; and this is the thought specially dear to the Roman genius. It may be emphasized also from the side of the revelation of truth, the Church being the school of truth to train human characters under its discipline; and no doubt to the Alexandrians it is from this point of view that Christianity is mostly, though not of course exclusively,³ thought of and loved. Christ is the Truth. It is on the Church's truth that the minds of Athanasius and Didymus are mainly

The Alexandrians—

---

¹ *ad Smyrn.* 8. "The bishop is the centre of each individual Church, as Jesus Christ is the centre of the universal Church" (Lightfoot's note). For further quotations and discussion see chap. VI.

² *ad Trall.* 7: *ad Philad.* 3.

³ See, e.g., a fine passage in Origen (*c. Cels.* vi. 48) where the Church is described as an organism, ensouled by the indwelling Word—ὑπὸ τοῦ υἱοῦ τοῦ θεοῦ ψυχουμένην τὴν πᾶσαν τοῦ θεοῦ ἐκκλησίαν.

The Foundation of the Church.

fixed;[1] it is the divine philosophy—superseding all the fragmentary truth possible to the world apart from Christ by including it in a completer, purer whole—that Clement and Origen love. But it is quite an error to suppose that they were the less *churchmen* on this account. We have in St. Augustin's Confessions an account of an old Platonic philosopher, Marius Victorinus, trying to induce a simple-hearted bishop to consider him a Christian on account of his convictions, without requiring him to come into the Church. Did walls, he asked, make Christians? The question was one better left without a direct answer. But at any rate the philosopher was given to understand that he could only become a Christian by being baptized into the Christian body. This 'ecclesiastical temper' was as much that of Clement and Origen as of later Alexandrians.

Clement may indeed have had an idea of a "Church within a Church," a Church of the men of knowledge who get beyond mere faith; but men of faith and men of knowledge are at one in common church membership, in common use of the sacraments, in common obedience to "the Church's rule," "the apostolic and ecclesiastical right rule of beliefs."[2] The faith is not

Clement c. A.D. 190-200.

---

[1] This is very beautifully illustrated by Didymus' commentary on the Psalms. The guidance and food of the soul is mainly the Church's truth, as expressed in her exact dogmas, and his feeling towards this truth is repeatedly expressed with the greatest genuineness and force. Later, in the fifth century, the theology of Cyril has a quite different tone from the theology of Leo. The first thought of the one is Truth, of the other Government.

[2] Men of understanding are described as ὅσοι ὑπ' αὐτοῦ [Χριστοῦ] σαφηνηθεῖσαν τῶν γραφῶν ἐξήγησιν κατὰ τὸν ἐκκλησιαστικὸν κανόνα ἐκδεχόμενοι διασώζουσιν (*Strom.* vi. 15. 125); cf. ἡ ἀποστολικὴ καὶ ἐκκλησιαστικὴ ὀρθοτομία τῶν δογμάτων

a philosophy; it is embodied in the one visible Church, true, ancient, catholic, and apostolic. This only, in contrast to all the late-devised "schools" of heresy which cannot be called Churches, is the home of the elect, the one true virgin mother of human souls.[1] "This being the case," he says, "it is plain that these later-born heresies and those yet subsequent to them are innovations, driven along distorted lines, upon the most ancient and true Church. It has also, I think, been made plain from what has been said that the Church which is true and really ancient is one, and into it the elect according to God's purpose are gathered. . . . The One Church is associated with the nature of the One God. In substance, in conception, in origin, in excellence, we say that the ancient and catholic Church is one only, having nothing like or equal to herself."[2]

Origen.

Just in the same way the truth, which Origen set himself with such noble zeal to expound and to put

(*ib.* vii. 16. 104). The heretic is a man who has "kicked at the tradition of the Church and leaped off to the opinions of human heresies" (*ib.* vii. 16. 95); he neither enters the kingdom of heaven himself, nor allows those whom he deceives to arrive at the truth.

[1] Cf. *Strom.* vii. 17. (quoted below); vii. 15. 92; *Paed.* i. 6. 42 (on the one virgin mother). For further quotations see Rothe *Anfänge* pp. 584 f., 593, 601, etc.; and Dr. Bigg's Bampton Lectures, *The Christian Platonists of Alexandria*, pp. 86, 153 n [2], 98-100, etc.

[2] *Strom.* vii. 17. 107 : Ὧν οὕτως ἐχόντων συμφανὲς ἐκ τῆς προγενεστάτης καὶ ἀληθεστάτης ἐκκλησίας τὰς μεταγενεστέρας ταύτας καὶ τὰς ἔτι τούτων ὑποβεβηκυίας τῷ χρόνῳ κεκαινοτομῆσθαι παραχαραχθείσας αἱρέσεις. ἐκ τῶν εἰρημένων ἄρα φανερὸν οἶμαι γεγενῆσθαι, μίαν εἶναι τὴν ἀληθῆ ἐκκλησίαν τὴν τῷ ὄντι ἀρχαίαν, εἰς ἣν οἱ κατὰ πρόθεσιν δίκαιοι ἐγκαταλέγονται· ἑνὸς γὰρ ὄντος τοῦ θεοῦ καὶ ἑνὸς τοῦ κυρίου, διὰ τοῦτο καὶ τὸ ἄκρως τίμιον κατὰ τὴν μόνωσιν ἐπαινεῖται μίμημα ὂν ἀρχῆς τῆς μιᾶς. τῇ γοῦν τοῦ ἑνὸς φύσει συγκληροῦται ἐκκλησία ἡ μία, ἣν εἰς πολλὰς κατατέμνειν βιάζονται αἱρέσεις. κατά τε οὖν ὑπόστασιν κατά τε ἐπίνοιαν κατά τε ἀρχὴν κατά τε ἐξοχὴν μόνην εἶναί φαμεν τὴν ἀρχαίαν καὶ καθολικὴν ἐκκλησίαν. . . . ἀλλὰ καὶ ἡ ἐξοχὴ τῆς ἐκκλησίας, καθάπερ ἡ ἀρχὴ τῆς συστάσεως, κατὰ τὴν μονάδα ἐστὶν πάντα τὰ ἄλλα ὑπερβάλλουσα καὶ μηδὲν ἔχουσα ὅμοιον ἢ ἴσον ἑαυτῇ.

into relation to the whole of knowledge, was no abstract truth to be thought out by the free action of the individual mind; it was a truth committed to a society and, though the sanctified reason could explain, elucidate, accommodate it, it could not transgress or neglect "the rule of faith" without being self-condemned.[1] "Let the preaching of the Church be preserved," he says at the beginning of the book which most laid him open to accusations of heresy, "handed down through the order of succession from the Apostles, and remaining up to the present time in the Churches: that alone is to be believed as truth which is in no disagreement with the ecclesiastical and apostolical tradition."[2] Origen's teaching upon the Church is full and rich, and when he comments, for instance, on the red cord which marked Rahab's house for safety, he says with equal positiveness that there is no salvation except through the blood of Christ, and no salvation outside the Church.[3] Undoubtedly

A.D. 228-231.

---

[1] See Bigg *B.L.* lecture v. init.

[2] *de Princip.* prooem. 2: "Servetur vero ecclesiastica praedicatio per successionis ordinem ab apostolis tradita et usque ad praesens in ecclesiis permanens; illa sola credenda est veritas, quae in nullo et ecclesiastica et apostolica discordat traditione."

[3] *in Iesu Nave* hom. iii. 5: "Sciebat etenim quia nulli esset salus nisi in sanguine Christi. . . . Si quis ergo salvari vult veniat in hanc domum. . . . Ad hanc veniat domum in qua Christi sanguis in signo redemptionis est . . . Nemo ergo sibi persuadeat, nemo semet ipsum decipiat: extra hanc domum, id est extra ecclesiam, nemo salvatur." *in Matt.* xii. 11: ἥτε ἐκκλησία, ὡς Χριστοῦ οἰκοδομή, τοῦ οἰκοδομήσαντος ἑαυτοῦ τὴν οἰκίαν φρονίμως ἐπὶ τὴν πέτραν, ἀνεπίδεκτός ἐστι πυλῶν ᾅδου, κατισχυουσῶν μὲν παντὸς ἀνθρώπου τοῦ ἔξω τῆς πέτρας καὶ τῆς ἐκκλησίας, οὐδὲν δὲ δυναμένων πρὸς αὐτήν. Cf. his interpretation of St. John i. 29: "He taketh away the sin of the *world*," i.e. "the world of the Church," the world within the world—the true κόσμος (*in Ioann.* vi. ad fin.). It should be added that Origen, like Augustin, recognised that the Church had in some sense begun to exist from the beginning, cf. *in Cant.* i. 11, 12: "prima etenim fundamenta congregationis ecclesiae statim ab initio sunt posita."

Clement and Origen alike endeavoured to mitigate this doctrine of exclusive salvation within the Church, so as to bring it into harmony with God's universal purposes, with His recognised equity and good-will towards all, and with the universal presence of the Word to all men.[1] But with all this it is an undoubted truth that they did, like all the other Fathers, regard God's covenant in Christ as made with a visible society, membership in which was of universal obligation and alienation from which was death.

The apologists—

Nor can it be maintained that the more philosophic apologists of the second century were inclined " to transform the Gospel into a monotheistic moral system." It has been said that in the recently recovered fragment of the Apology of the philosopher Aristides, presented to the Emperor Hadrian about A.D. 125, "Christianity is exhibited as the most absolutely certain philosophy."[2] But an important consideration

Aristides.

---

[1] E.g. (1) By generous recognition of the preparatory discipline of God leading up to the Incarnation all over the world: see above, p. 18.

(2) By drawing a distinction between different points of Christian belief; οἱ εἰς τὰ κυριώτατα παραπίπτοντες are distinguished from οἱ περὶ τῶν ἐν μέρει σφαλλόμενοι. Only the former are ψεῦσται τῷ ὄντι (Clem. *Strom.* vi. 15. 124). Cf. Origen *c. Cels.* v. 63.

(3) By distinguishing grades of salvation, and excluding virtuous disbelievers in Christ only from the highest *eternal life.* Origen *in Rom.* ii. 7: "Iste licet alienus a vita videatur aeterna, quia non credit Christo, et intrare non possit in regnum caelorum, quia renatus non est ex aqua et Spiritu, videtur tamen quod per haec, quae dicuntur ab apostolo, bonorum operum gloriam et honorem et pacem perdere penitus non possit. . . . Sed tamen in arbitrio legentis sit, probare quae dicta sunt."

[2] Harnack, *Contemp. Review* (Aug. 1886), p. 229. The fragments of two *Sermones S. Aristidis Philosophi* have been edited from an early Armenian version, with a Latin translation, by the Mechitarist Fathers. The first Sermo has at least one interpolated word, corresponding to the Latin word *deipara,* but is otherwise apparently genuine. The Emperor Hadrian is assured that there are four stirpes (compertum est nobis quattuor esse humani generis stirpes) or four nationes of men: barbarians, Greeks,

is here left out of account. Christians are spoken of as constituting a new "race" or "kind" of men; side by side with Greeks and barbarians and Hebrews are Christians. The mere adherents of a philosophic school could not be so described; Christians can be (however liable the expression is to be misunderstood), because Christianity is essentially a society, a body. To Justin Martyr Christians are "the genuine high-priestly race of God," and the account of the sacraments which he gives the emperor in his Apology, shows us how completely he conceived of Christianity as a *society*.[1] There is, again, no more beautiful description of the Church than that given by another apologist, Theophilus of Antioch, when he compares the "holy Churches" to fertile and well-inhabited islands in the sea, which have fair harbours of truth to welcome and give security to storm-tossed souls. "To these they flee for refuge who wish to be saved, and who are lovers of the truth, wishing to escape the wrath and judgment of God." And there are other islands, barren and dry and uninhabited

<small>Justin Martyr c. A.D. 148.</small>

<small>Theophilus c. A.D. 180.</small>

Hebrews, and Christians. Hadrian himself, some ten years later, uses similar language (if his letter to Servian is genuine; see Lightfoot's *Ignatius* i. p. 464): "hunc [nummum] Christiani, hunc Iudaei, hunc omnes venerantur et gentes." Cf. Melito's expression for the Christians—τὸ τῶν θεοσεβῶν γένος (ap. Euseb. *H.E.* iv. 26), and the same word in the *Ep. ad Diognet.* 1 (referred to as used by him) καινὸν τοῦτο γένος ἢ ἐπιτήδευμα, also πολιτεία (c. 5), though the author is explaining that Christians remain members of their own different races and are not a people apart. Cf. Justin's ἀρχιερατικὸν τὸ ἀληθινὸν γένος ἐσμὲν τοῦ θεοῦ (*Dial.* 116) and μιᾷ ψυχῇ καὶ μιᾷ συναγωγῇ καὶ μιᾷ ἐκκλησίᾳ (*ib.* 63). It becomes an expression of popular hatred against Christians that they are a genus tertium. See Tertull. *Scorp.* 10: "genus tertium deputamur." *ad. Nat.* i. 8: "Romani, Iudaei, dehinc Christiani; ubi autem Graeci?" Also Origen *c. Cels.* viii. 75: ἡμεῖς ἐν ἑκάστῃ πόλει ἄλλο σύστημα πατρίδος, κτισθὲν λόγῳ Θεοῦ, ἐπιστάμενοι.

[1] *Apol.* i. 65.

save of wild beasts, on whose harbourless coasts ships are only wrecked, and these "are the schools of error, that is of the heresies, which destroy those who approach them."[1]

<small>The heathen idea of the Christians.</small>

Such being the Christian conception of their own body, it was inevitable that the world outside also should have regarded them as members of a society or brotherhood. As a matter of fact it was in this way that they became an object of suspicion. They seemed a sort of secret society, with an unintelligible 'freemasonry' of their own. Men suspected them of all sorts of secret iniquities. And all this was due to the closeness of their corporate life; they seemed a "people of profane conspiracy," "a secret race, avoiding the light, silent in public, chattering in corners," who "recognised one another by secret marks and signs, and loved almost before they knew one another,"[2] calling one another by the suspicious name of "brother."[3] So, like any other guild or sodality, they appeared before the eyes of men as a body whose privileges were conditional on membership. Exact terms of membership were a special feature of contem-

---

[1] Theophilus *ad Autolycum* ii. 14. In order to carry back the evidence of the church conception to the earliest days, outside the area of Christian history covered by the New Testament, it should be mentioned that the *Didache* conceives of Christians as constituting a visible society governed by a common law. The visible society, the Church, knit together by social sacraments (though these sacraments are conceived of in a judaic, meagre spirit), is the home of the revelation of knowledge and immortality given in Christ, and the antechamber to the final kingdom. Cf. x. 5: "Remember Thy Church to deliver her from all evil, and perfect her in Thy love, and gather her from the four winds, the sanctified Church, into Thy kingdom which thou didst prepare for her." Cf. ix. 4.

[2] This vivid picture is given in the *Octavius* of Minucius Felix, cc. 8, 9.

[3] "Sic nos, quod invidetis, fratres vocamus" (*Octav.* 31).

porary guilds. Their members constituted a sort of republic apart.[1] Thus, though Christians might make public explanation of their rites and doctrines to avoid the misconceptions of the outside world, yet these rites and doctrines were admittedly the private property of their society, and no one could have the Christian's God for his father who had not the Christian's Church for his mother.

(2) But it has been suggested that Christianity owed its existence as a visible society to the fact that in the age when it spread there was a special tendency to association 'in the air.' Undoubtedly it was an age of guilds.[2] "The need of association, of the strength which comes of association was, at any rate, as great in antiquity as to-day; and among the peoples of antiquity it is the Romans, perhaps, who had the keenest sense of the need."[3] The religious associations and trade guilds (sodalitates, collegia) were indeed ancient institutions at Rome. But the principle of association had received a great development, beginning with the later years of the Republic and under the early Empire. Thus every trade, every interest, came to have its collegium with its organization more or less elaborate, its officers, its specified terms of membership, its periodical feast. "But it was not necessary, in order to form an association, to be members of the same profession, to be neighbours even, or compatriots;

(2) The social form of Christianity not due to secular influence of the Collegia.

---

[1] See esp. Boissier (as below) p. 261.
[2] See—an admirable account—Boissier *La Religion Romaine* bk. ii. ch. 3: Mommsen *de Collegiis et Sodaliciis Romanorum*: Hatch *B. L.* p. 26 f. My quotations are from Boissier.
[3] Boissier ii. p. 248.

it was enough to experience isolation or weakness, to feel the need of union to fight against misery or 'ennui.' This need was not rare, especially among the working classes."[1] The tendency to use this freedom of association for purposes of political faction led to its being put under restraint. No association might be formed without permission.[2] But notwithstanding such prohibition, associations were formed and spread. "They filled Rome, they spread in the little towns, they penetrated into the country, they covered the richest provinces," they honeycombed all ranks of society.[3] They existed—where the authority to repress should have been strongest—even in the army. Contemporaneously with the early spread of Christianity they developed largely as burial societies—in part, because association in this form was allowed.[4] These burial guilds, in common with perhaps all collegia, had a religious basis more or less nominal, though the real purpose of association was of another sort.[5] With some of the associations the religious object, the promotion of some special cult, was the primary and real bond of union. This had been the case to a very great extent with the Greek guilds.[6]

---

[1] Boissier ii. p. 260.
[2] Hatch *B. L.* p. 27 n².
[3] Boissier ii. p. 250. But the spread was unequal.
[4] This we know to have been the case in the first century. See Boissier ii. p. 280. The inscription from Lanuvium, which is the main evidence of this, is given at the end of Mommsen's *de Collegiis*. There were different classes of burial guilds, some not having the name collegium, but societas (Boissier ii. p. 272).
[5] Boissier ii. p. 268.
[6] θίασοι, ἔρανοι, ὀργεῶνες. See Foucart's *Les Associations Religieuses chez les Grecs*.

They had come into existence in the days before and during the Macedonian supremacy, to cultivate some form of oriental worship with greater freedom than the State religion would tolerate. They had their terms of membership, their priests and officers of various sorts, generally elected annually, their sacred book, their 'immutable law,' their assembly to pass decrees—each one a microcosm of the State organization. These Greek guilds had been much less influential, less respectable, and less prevalent than the Roman. However, they lasted on, and formed an element in that tendency to associate which (since the inscriptions have come to be studied) we know to have been a main characteristic of the otherwise somewhat monotonous life of the early empire.

Such was the character of the period in which Christianity spread. No doubt the Christian Church appeared as one of these multifarious 'collegia.' It was regarded by Pliny in Bithynia as a 'collegium illicitum' whose very existence was illegal. Again, "the first form, in which any Christian body was recognised by the law, was as a benefit-club with special view to the interment of the dead."[1] No doubt, again, the familiarity of the Greek and Roman world with societies, with the idea of incorporation, with terms of membership, its privileges and the loss of them, greatly facilitated the spread of the Christian Church. It was thus an element in what

---

[1] Lightfoot's *Ignatius* i. pp. 17-21. The Jewish communities were also classed with the θίασοι; cf. Joseph. *Ant. Iud.* xiv. 10 : Γάϊος Καῖσαρ, ὁ ἡμέτερος στρατηγὸς καὶ ὕπατος, ἐν τῷ διατάγματι κωλύων θιάσους συνάγεσθαι κατὰ πόλιν, μόνους τούτους οὐκ ἐκώλυσεν οὔτε χρήματα συνεισφέρειν οὔτε συνδεῖπνα ποιεῖν.

we recognise as the 'divine preparation' for the spread of the Gospel; just as the Roman empire itself was another, and the general use of the Greek language, and the diffusion of the religion of the Jews through their dispersion, and the recognition in contemporary philosophy of the idea of the divine Reason or Word. But if the question be asked whether the influence of these contemporary guilds may not have modified the Christian religion in such a way as to be the cause of its assuming the form of an association or system of associations—the Church and the Churches—the answer is a decisive negative.[1]

(a) No trace of such influence in Christian writers.

For, in the first place, any conception of real affinity between the Church and the collegia was, as the quotations above will have shown sufficiently, quite foreign to the minds of the Christian writers. Tertullian indeed suggests a *contrast* between them based on the fact that Christians, and they alone, mutually supported one another and had all things common; but there was no consciousness of resemblance.[2]

[1] In some later developments Christianity may have borrowed in detail from contemporary clubs, e.g. the subdivision of monastic bodies into decuriae and centuriae probably (see Boissier ii. p. 264 with reference to Jerome's letter); again, some customs with reference to the dead and the use of the term memoria in this connection (cf. μεμόριον, μεμορίτης), Boissier ii. p. 290. The term σύνοδος was used for the meetings of guildsmen: cf. σεμνοτάτη σύνοδος Foucart p. 202, sancta synodus (of an actors' guild with immoral reputation) Boissier ii. p. 267 f. But so obvious a term can hardly be said to have been borrowed to express the meetings of bishops. Also ἐκκλησία, but (see next page, note [2]) not in the Christian sense.

[2] The collegia were only very subordinately or slightly charitable associations (see Boissier i. pp. 302, 303); the Greek ἔρανοι probably not at all. "Les Éranes," says Foucart (p. 145), "n'étaient pas des sociétés de secours mutuels." The stipes menstruae were contributions to benefit-clubs, not like the weekly alms of the Christians; see Tertull. *Apol.* 39. The point of closest connection between the Church and the guilds lay in the common meal; the 'love-feast' of the Christians had shown very early its affinities

Nothing in fact was less characteristic of the Christian Church than those natural features of all association which it shared with the guilds, nothing less expressed the sentiments of its members towards their 'mother.' "The resemblances" between the Church and the collegia, says M. Boissier, "are striking at the first glance; as soon as one approaches, the differences are apparent."[1]

Secondly, the nomenclature of the Christian communities suggests the minimum of connection.[2] For in fact the Christian Church had its roots deep in Jewish soil. It derived from Judaism its charac- *(b) Christian forms derived from Judaism.*

---

to the guild suppers (1 Cor. xi. 17 f.). But St. Paul meets this danger by marking the essential difference in origin and aim of the 'Lord's Supper.' Historically, it was a development of the Paschal supper (St. Matt. xxvi. 7).

[1] Boissier ii. p. 302.

[2] In the collegia and sodalicia we should hear of the album, or roll of members: the magistri: the quinquennales: the patroni: the gradus: the schola: the cena: the edituus: the quaestores. In the Greek ἔρανοι or θίασοι we should have the προστάτης, the ἄρχυντες, the ἐπιμελητής, the ζάκοροι, the ἱεροποιοί, the γραμματεύς, the ἀρχιερανιστής, the ταμίας. What an alien atmosphere to this is suggested by the Christian nomenclature! It is the pagan Lucian who speaks of Peregrinus as θιασάρχης of the Christian community.

The characteristic Christian terms are derived from Jewish use; e.g. ἐκκλησία has, primarily at least, the sense of the elect people as such—the Church, rather than the classical sense of the assembly, i.e. the people gathered together for a special purpose, and the former sense is based on Old Testament use. Cf. Acts vii. 38. Thus Vitringa (quoted by Trench *New Testament Synonyms* p. 4): "ἡ ἐκκλησία [=קָהָל] designat multitudinem aliquam quae populum constituit, per leges et vincula inter se iunctam, etsi saepe fiat non sit coacta nec cogi possit." The Hebrew word קָהָל is explained thus (by contrast to עֵדָה, συναγωγή, coetus congregatus): "universam alicuius populi multitudinem vinculis societatis unitam et rempublicam sive civitatem quandam constituentem." Μυστήριον again has (at first) the Old Testament meaning of a divine secret communicated, rather than the pagan sense of a mystery of initiation. So βαπτισμός, εὐχαριστία, τράπεζα Κυρίου, ἐπίθεσις χειρῶν, ἐξομολόγησις, χρῖσμα, ἀδελφοί, καθέδρα, πρεσβύτερος, ποιμήν, προφήτης, εὐαγγελιστής, etc., are all terms of Jewish origin. So perhaps is ἐπίσκοπος, (see App. Note K). The prominent Christian functions of prayer, fasting and almsgiving descend from the Jewish stock, with the whole religious basis of Christianity.

teristic nomenclature—that is to say, from a source much more ancient than the Roman empire or Greek society. The origin of the social form of Christianity is to be sought in the Jewish conception of the Messianic kingdom and in the deliberate intention of Him, who founded the Church, in claiming to be the Messiah.

(3) Witness of N. T. that Christ founded a visible Church.

(3) Does, then, the New Testament bear out the position that Christ appeared as the founder and organizer of a visible society? This question shall be answered from the evidence of (*a*) the Gospels, (β) the Acts, (γ) St. Paul's Epistles.

(*a*) Evidence of the Gospels.

(*a*) The question may be approached with less alarm because there is a remarkable unanimity among men of the keenest historical insight in seeing in Jesus one who above all things came to found a *society*, a *kingdom*. "To deny," says the author of *Ecce Homo*, "that Christ did undertake to found and to legislate for a new theocratic society, and that he did claim the office of judge of mankind, is indeed possible, but only to those who altogether deny the credibility of the extant biographies of Christ. If those biographies be admitted to be generally trustworthy, then Christ undertook to be what we have described; if not, then of course this, but also every other, account of Him falls to the ground." "The city of God, of which the Stoics doubtfully and feebly spoke, was now set up before the eyes of man. It was no unsubstantial city such as we fancy in the clouds, no invisible pattern such as Plato thought might be laid up in heaven, but a visible corporation whose members met together to eat bread and drink wine, and into which they were initiated by bodily immersion in water."[1] There are three lines of evidence which seem to make the truth of this position clear:—

First, there is the method of Christ. Nothing is more remarkable than the refusal of Christ to commit Himself to men as He found them. There is something at first sight repellent in the solemn words of St. John: 'Jesus did not commit Himself to those who first believed in His name, when they saw the miracles, because He knew all men, and needed not that any should testify of man, for He knew what was in man.'[2] That sad secret of human nature—its lamentable untrustworthiness—the secret which in slow, embittering experience has often turned enthusiasts into cynics and made philanthropists mad—Jesus knew it to start with. And, knowing it, He would not build His spiritual edifice on the shifting sands of such a humanity. It was not that He distrusted the capacity of human nature for the highest life. On the contrary, He came to proclaim the brotherhood of all men under the realized fatherhood of God—but not the brotherhood of men as they were. Except

(i) The method of Christ:

---

[1] *Ecce Homo* [18th ed.] pp. 39, 128. On this subject of Christ's institution of a visible Church, I should like to refer (among recent writers) to the Dean of St. Paul's *Advent Sermons* ii and iii, and his Oxford House Paper, No. xvii; Mr. Stanton's *Jewish and Christian Messiah*; Dr. Westcott's Essay on 'The Two Empires' in his *Epp. of St. John*; Mr. Holland's *Creed and Character*; and Dr. Milligan's *Resurrection of our Lord* lecture vi. See also Archbishop Whately *Kingdom of Christ* Essay ii. init. and F. D. Maurice *Kingdom of Christ* i. p. 285 f. These names represent (so far) a remarkable consensus. Among older English writers no one contends more powerfully for the church idea than William Law in his *Letters to the Bishop of Bangor*; see esp. *Letter* iii.

[2] St. John ii. 23-25.

ye be converted, He said, ye shall not enter into the kingdom of heaven. Except a man be born again, he cannot see the kingdom of God.[1] Man must have a fresh start: he must be built upon a new foundation: he must be regenerated, converted, if he is to be fit for sonship and for brotherhood. So Jesus Christ set Himself to give humanity a fresh start from a new centre, and that centre Himself. To do this He withdraws from the many upon the few. To the multitude He speaks in parables, 'that seeing they may not see, and hearing they may not understand.' Only a few, whom He sees capable of earnest self-sacrifice, of perseverance, of enlightenment, are gradually initiated into His secrets. These are 'the disciples.' These He trains with slow and patient care to appreciate His Person. From the most ready of these He elicits, after a time, by solemn questioning a formal confession of His Messiahship—a formal confession that He, the Son of Man, is also the Christ, the Son of the living God.[2] This thorough recognition of His claim gives Him something to depend upon. He has got down to the rock; He can begin to build.[3] 'Blessed art thou, Simon Bar-Jona; and I say unto thee that thou art Rock-Man, and on this rock (the rock of this human character acknowledging My Divine Sonship

---

[1] St. John iii. 3 f.; St. Matt. xviii. 3.
[2] St. Matt. xvi. 16.
[3] Holland *Creed and Character* pp. 46-49. All the idea of this paragraph is admirably expressed in the sermon 'The Rock of the Church.' "Pity, infinite pity, He gave [the crowds]—but Himself He never gave; He could not commit Himself unto them. His work, His mission, His purpose on earth—how could they receive it? how could they understand it?... How can He build [the new house of God] on that loose and shifting rubble, on that blind movement of the crowd, so vague and so undetermined?"

and Mission) I will build My Church.' This gives us the clue to His method. All along Christ had had in view this foundation of the Church, and we see now what He had been waiting for. It was till He had won out of the hearts of His disciples that absolute devotion to His own Person, that complete acknowledgment of His claim, which would enable them to look away from all else and become the stable nucleus of a new society which was to represent His Name. Indeed, the more we study the Gospels, the more clearly we shall recognise that Christ did not cast His Gospel loose upon the world—the world which was so incapable of appreciating it; that would have been indeed to cast His pearls before swine; but He directed all His efforts to making a home for it, and that by organizing a band of men called 'out of the world,' and consecrated into a holy unity, who were destined to draw others in time after them out of all ages and nations.[1] On this 'little flock' He fixed all His hopes. He prayed not for the world, but for these whom God had given Him out of the world. These in wonderful ways He meant to link to Himself in an indissoluble unity, as the branches to the vine, that they might live as an organized body in the world, yet distinct from it—alive with His life, sanctified through His truth, enlightened by His Spirit. Christ then by His whole method declared His intention to found a Church, a visible society of men—which should be distinct from the world and independent of it, even while it should present before the eyes of all men

---

[1] St. John xvii, and the whole of these last discourses.

the spectacle of what their common life might become.

(ii) His institution of social sacraments:

Secondly, the intention of Christ to found a social organization is apparent in the solemn ceremonies which He instituted as tokens of discipleship as well as channels of grace. The sacraments are *social* ceremonies. Baptism had been in Jewish tradition the ceremony of initiation into the ancient Church. As used by John the Baptist, it had been used in distinct relation to the coming of 'the kingdom.' As adopted by Christ, it was no doubt meant to admit into His society, the kingdom which had come, the Church of the new covenant.[1] And whatever possible ambiguity attends the conception of baptism in this respect, is removed by the other sacrament. The Eucharist is nothing if not social. Its whole natural basis as a common meal implies a community. Christ, then, in making baptism and the Eucharist the sacraments of His kingdom, just as in making love of the brethren *the* characteristic of His disciples, emphasized His intention to attach men to Himself not as individuals but as members of a brotherhood.

[1] Dr. Hatch calls this an "unproved assumption" (*B. L.* pref. sec. ed. p. xii). I should have thought that all possible doubt was set at rest by the parallel institution of the Eucharist. That at least is the sacrament of a society. But I cannot understand Dr. Hatch expressing a doubt that baptism had the social significance. It was never an *individual* purification amongst the Jews (see Edersheim's *Life and Times of Jesus the Messiah* i. pp. 272-274); it was always in connection with the covenant which was with a *race*. The baptism of a Jewish proselyte was his incorporation with the race—'his new birth.' See Sabatier *La Didaché* p. 84 f. (an excellent passage on the relation of Christian to Jewish baptism); Taylor *Teaching of the Twelve Apostles* p. 55 f.; and Edersheim ii. app. xii (on the antiquity of the practice). Cf. also 1 Cor. x. 2.

The Foundation of the Church.

Lastly, and perhaps most conspicuously, the intention of Christ to found a society is prominent in His whole claim to be the Messiah. The Messianic king of the Old Testament is the centre of a Messianic kingdom; the suffering Servant of Jehovah, by whose stripes men are healed, is no mere individual, but also the embodiment and representative of the chosen race.[1] Christ, then, when He came as the Messiah, brought the kingdom. 'The kingdom of heaven is at hand'—that is John the Baptist's message, that is the first word of Christ's preaching.[2] But in Him it was more than 'at hand.' It had come *upon* men; it was 'among them.'[3] John the Baptist had been outside it, but now there were those who were inside it, and who, though they were but little, were 'greater' than John the Baptist on that very account.[4] The kingdom had thus a definite limit in time because it was to be a visible institution and not a mere invisible association of good men. Christ had indeed to purify and elevate the conceptions of His disciples so that they might understand its spiritual nature and object; but though it was spiritual, though it was not adapted to the carnal wants of the Jews, though it was not '*of* this

(iii) His claim to be the Messiah.

---

[1] Stanton *Jewish and Christian Messiah* p. 122 f.

[2] But only the *first* word, and then, too, with the addition given by St. Mark—πεπλήρωται ὁ καιρός (Stanton *l.c.* p. 218).

[3] St. Matt. xii. 28; cf. St. Luke xvii. 21. Mr. Stanton seems to be right in interpreting ἐντὸς ὑμῶν, in the midst of you. The kingdom of heaven, our Lord tells the Pharisees, is not to be found by close watching (παρατήρησις). It will not be manifest to those who wait merely on external observation. (Lo, here! or Lo, there!) For it is among you and ye know it not.

[4] St. Matt. xi. 11, 12.

world,'[1] yet it was to be *in* the world—'a net to gather of every kind till the end of the world,' a visible society, that is, in which evil and good should be mixed.[2] Christ then came to establish a 'kingdom of heaven' or a 'kingdom of God.' What does this expression mean? It means an organized society of men in which the old barrier which sin had interposed between heaven and earth has been done away, in which Jacob's ancient dream is a dream no longer, for 'the angels of God ascend and descend' upon the new humanity, and God and man are at one again. It is because Christ's new society is thus heavenly that a divine sanction can attach to its legislative decisions: thus what they bind or loose on earth is to be bound or loosed in heaven, and whose sins they forgive are to be forgiven, whose sins they retain to be retained.[3] Is then Christ's new society, the Church, simply identical with the kingdom of God or of heaven? To

(The relation of the Church to the kingdom of God.)

---

[1] St. John xviii. 36.

[2] St. Matt. xiii. 47. Cf. Stanton *l.c.* p. 220 f. Add Matt. xxii. 2 (the Marriage of the King's Son). "Let us suppose," says William Law (*Letter* iii. pp. 8, 9), "that the Church of Christ was this invisible number of people united to Christ by such internal invisible graces, is it possible that a kingdom consisting of this one particular sort of people invisibly good should be like a net that gathers of every kind of fish? If it was to be compared to a net it ought to be compared to such a net as gathers only of one kind, viz., good fish, and then it might represent to us a Church that has but one sort of members. . . . If any one should tell us that we are to believe invisible scriptures and observe invisible sacraments, he would have just as much reason and Scripture on his side as your Lordship has for this doctrine. And it would be of the same service to the world to talk of these invisibilities if the canon of Scripture was in dispute, as to describe this invisible Church, when the case is with what visible Church we ought to unite."

[3] St. Matt. xviii. 17-20; St. John xx. 22, 23. I am not raising the question yet whether the gift in this latter passage is not given to the *ministry*. See later, chap. iv.

answer this question a distinction must be drawn in view of the double sense in which the kingdom is said to come. In one sense the kingdom is already come; that is, it is established in *spiritual* power and all its forces are at work. But, as St. Augustin has expressed it, "non adhuc regnat hoc regnum;" for it has yet to grow like the mustard-seed, to work its way like the leaven through all the institutions of the world, it has yet to bear its universal witness 'to all the nations';[1] only so at last can the kingdom come *in glory*. Thus in one sense the kingdom already exists, in another sense it has yet to appear.[2] In the first sense, then, the Church *is* the kingdom of heaven, and St. Peter has promised to him the keys—not of 'the Church,' but of 'the kingdom of heaven,' which the Church is; in the second sense, the Church *prepares for* the kingdom rather than *is* it. It represents it in this 'age,' and passes into it with the dawning of the 'age to come.'[3]

---

[1] St. Matt. xiii. 31-34; St. Luke xix. 11; St. Mark xiii. 10, etc.

[2] All this is expressed in the double use of all the characteristic Gospel terms, as (1) of things already being enjoyed; (2) of things hoped for. We *are sons*, yet we "wait for the adoption"; we *are* redeemed, yet we wait for "the redemption of our bodies"; we *are* saved, yet only in the future will "our salvation draw nigh"; it is now only "nearer than when we believed." Here in fact the kingdom is in power—not in glory or final fulfilment. But it is because the present Church is a simple anticipation of the Church as it is to be—the same society at an earlier stage—that even now it is called 'heavenly.' We have been "made to sit in heavenly places": we have "tasted the powers of the world to come": the institutions of the Church are "the heavenly things": and we "*are come*.unto the heavenly Jerusalem" (Eph. i. 3, 20; Heb. vi. 5, ix. 23, xii. 22). So Tertullian has been quoted as speaking of the Church on earth as "in heaven."

[3] Cf. *Didache* ix. 4: "Let Thy Church be gathered together from the ends of the earth into Thy kingdom." Clem. *ad Cor.* 42: οἱ ἀπόστολοι . . . ἐξῆλθον εὐαγγελιζόμενοι τὴν βασιλείαν τοῦ θεοῦ μέλλειν ἔρχεσθαι. Cf. Church's

Christ, then, according to the evidence of the Gospels, founded a community of men, a Church, to be the pillar and ground of the truth which He came to bring, to be the household in which His stewards should dispense the food of God until He came again;[1] and in the great forty days, when He spoke to His disciples of the things concerning the kingdom of God, He spoke to them as the first representatives of that visible society which was to be its earthly counterpart.

(The Church not exclusive.) We must not suppose that the institution by Christ of a Church with a definite limit and an exclusive claim is a narrowing of His love.[2] The claim which the Church makes on every man simply corresponds to his moral needs as Christ interprets them. It is because He loves all that He established a *Civitas Dei*, wide enough for all, in order to their spiritual recovery. The Church would indeed represent a narrowing of the divine love if any were by Christ's will excluded from it. But it is open to all. And as there are those to whom 'the gospel of the kingdom' has never come, or never come with its true appeal, so we are assured that God's purpose is larger than

---

Advent Sermons p. 70 : The kingdom of God "has its witness, its representatives in the universal Church of Christ. Nothing can be an adequate representation of that invisible kingdom of God ; it extends, even on earth, beyond even the bounds of the universal Church. But His Church is the designated and appointed recognition of His kingdom." Ib. p. 72 : 'The Church is "the religious body which He has called into being, to be the shadow and instrument of His kingdom."

[1] St. Luke xii. 41, 42.

[2] See Holland *Creed and Character* serm. iv. 'The Secret of the Church, esp. pp. 59, 60. "God's love in Christ *found itself limited*. . . . How? Not by the Church, but by the crowd, by the block of blind and heedless ignorance."

His Church on earth.¹ There are last in the knowledge of God who shall be first in His acceptance, because they practised all they knew.

(β) When Christ speaks to St. Peter of the foundation of the Church, it is still in the future. The Church only receives its commission to all nations after His Resurrection. It comes into actual corporate life only with the Pentecostal gift. Thus, in the Acts of the Apostles, the Church goes forth for the first time a visible community, vitalized by Christ's Spirit, to be the representative on earth of the risen and ascended Lord.²

(β) Evidence of the Acts.

That Christianity in the Acts is represented by a community, there can surely be no doubt. The souls "who were added" at Jerusalem "continued steadfast in the Apostles' teaching and fellowship." They were members of a society more or less organ-

---

¹ See esp. St. Matt. xxv. 31 f. Cf. Dr. Pusey's *Responsibility of Intellect in Matters of Faith* p. 44 [ed. 1879]: "In those ever-open portals there enter that countless multitude whom the Church knew not how to win . . . or, alas! neglected to win them. . . . In whatever hatred, or contempt, or blasphemy of Christ nurtured, God has His own elect, who ignorantly worship Him, whose ignorant fear or longing He Who inspired it will accept."

² ".To [the Church] alone," says Prof. Milligan (*Resurrection of our Lord*, second thousand, p. 218), "as the representative of the Risen Lord, is the power entrusted by which [His] work may be successfully accomplished. We know that this can be done by no other means than the agency of the Spirit; and it would seem that the gift of the Spirit is bestowed only through the Church as the organ upon earth of the Risen and Glorified Lord in heaven. We dare not indeed restrain the power of the Almighty; but what we have to do with is His *plan*; and of that plan what has now been said appears to be one of the most striking characteristics. . . . It appears to be the teaching of the New Testament that, as it is the prerogative of Christ in His glorified humanity to bestow the Spirit, so it is only through the Church, as the representative of that glorified humanity, that the influences of the Spirit are communicated to the world." He emphasizes earlier the *visible unity* which the Church was meant to have as the representative of the Risen Christ (p. 204).

ized. They had all things common. Salvation was in the community; "the Lord added" to them "day by day those who were being saved."[1] As the new religion spread over Galilee and Samaria it was still "the Church."[2] "The Church at Antioch," where Christians got their new name,[3] is the same society extending itself to a new city. So when St. Paul went abroad, he founded "Churches" to prepare men for the kingdom.[4] And the local Churches are but branches of one stock. Behind the Churches is *the Church* represented by the Apostles. This is the truth which is impressed on the narrative of the Apostolic Conference with its authoritative direction to the Churches—"It seemed good to the Holy Ghost and to us to lay upon you no greater burden than these necessary things."[5] This is only the exhibition in act of the authority given by Jesus Christ to His society over its members, to bind and to loose with heavenly sanction.

(γ) Evidence of St. Paul's Epistles.

(γ) The picture presented in the Acts is the same as that of which we become spectators in St. Paul's Epistles. He writes to "the Church of God which is at Corinth," and that Church is undoubtedly a visible body, containing good and bad members alike. It is a "temple of God," but a temple which sin can

[1] Acts ii. 41-47.
[2] Acts ix. 31: "The Church through the whole of Judaea and Galilee and Samaria had peace." The baptism of the eunuch is an act of an exceptional character.
[3] Acts xiii. 1; xi. 26. On the significance of the exact form Christiani see Simcox's *Early Church History* p. 62: on the analogy of Herodiani, Pompeiani, etc., it suggests, not the disciples of a school, but the adherents of a leader or king.
[4] Acts xiv. 22, 23; xv. 41; xvi. 5.   [5] Acts xv. 28.

destroy;[1] a chosen people, but one like that of the old covenant, capable of like failure;[2] it is "the body of Christ" through sacramental participation in His life, but there may be "schism in the body."[3] St. Paul then conceives of the local Church as a visible community of mixed character, but with unmistakeable limits. The distinction between 'those within' and 'those without' is very marked.[4] But each local Church is only one representative of *the Church* which is general. St. Paul governs each particular Church in accordance with the evangelical tradition of truth and life, which is common to all and to which he is himself subject.[5] He passes back imperceptibly, without any break in thought, from the Churches to the Church;[6] the Church in fact simply (as far as this world is concerned) *consists of* the Churches. Thus, when in the Epistle to the Ephesians he is drawing out the spiritual significance of the Church as "the body of Christ, the fulness of Him who filleth all in all"—when he is declaring it to be one, in virtue alike of the one life which it

---

[1] 1 Cor. iii. 17.   [2] 1 Cor. x. 1-13.
[3] 1 Cor. x. 16; xii. 12-28. It is of course plain why the *imperfections* of the Church are dwelt on in connection with the local societies: they are naturally matters of specially local concern and local treatment.
[4] 1 Cor. v. 9-13; cf. xiv. 23; 2 Cor. vi. 14 f. Of course the brethren at a particular place, as at Rome, when St. Paul wrote his Epistle to 'the saints' there, may not yet have been completely organized into a local Church. That was, as it is now, a work of time. But a Christian, as such, is a member of the *Christian society*, and, unless in exceptional circumstances, of an organized local Church.
[5] 1 Cor. xi. 2 "the traditions"; 1 Cor. xv. 3; 2 Thess. iii. 6; 1 Cor. vii. 17 "So ordain I in all the Churches"; Gal. i. 7, 8 "Though we, or an angel from heaven, should preach unto you any other gospel . . . let him be anathema."
[6] 1 Cor. xii. 28, xv. 9; Gal. i. 13.

derives from Christ by the communication of the Spirit, and of the one truth which 'apostles and prophets' delivered from Christ, and of the love which binds, or ought to bind, its members in one[1] —he is indeed describing the Christian society "from an ideal point of view;" that is to say, he is describing all that the Church potentially is, as when we too proclaim the Church 'one, holy, and catholic.'[2] Nevertheless it is the visible, actual Church of which he is speaking,[3] the Church to which Christ gave visible officers—"some apostles, some prophets, some evangelists, some pastors and teachers," for the building up of the body of Christ into an ever more perfect unity. This visible organization or hierarchy belongs plainly to a visible society, —exactly that same society which St. Paul similarly describes in his Epistle to the Corinthians as "the body of Christ," even as part of Christ,[4] the Church in which "God set first apostles, secondly prophets, thirdly teachers,"[5] that is the general community which is

[1] Eph. iv. 3-16: It is 'one body' in virtue of the 'one Spirit' whose indwelling is Christ's indwelling; it holds 'one faith' (the 'one faith' mentioned in between the 'one Lord' and the 'one baptism,' both objective, must be objective too). It *ought to live*, therefore, in the unity of love (ver. 3), but the 'bond of love' is a duty which may be neglected. The inward unity of life, though dependent on outward facts (e.g. 'one baptism'), is a reality, whether recognised in practice or not.

[2] The Church has never yet so developed all the fulness within her as to exhibit herself in her full catholic glory and holiness as the 'bride of Christ.' She is potentially more than she is actually. Potentially catholic, for example, she still leaves outside her fold the mass of Oriental peoples.

[3] See Pfleiderer's account of the Epistle to the Ephesians (*Paulinism.* ii. pp. 190-193).

[4] 'The Christ' consists of the head and the members (1 Cor. xii. 12).

[5] 1 Cor. xii. 27-28. This passage (vv. 12-28) about the body of Christ, taken with such passages as Gal. iii. 27 ("baptized into Christ") and 1 Cor. x. 16, 17 (about the Eucharist), seems to me to contain all the truth that

The Foundation of the Church.

locally represented in the Churches of Corinth and Ephesus.[1] St. Paul then means by the Church "a visible society or aggregation of societies."

It is sometimes argued that St. Paul could not have believed in salvation through the Church, because this contradicts his doctrine of the justifying effect of individual faith.[2] But in fact there is no such contradiction. The Christian life is a correspondence between the grace communicated from without and the inward faith which, justifying us before God, opens out the avenues of communication between man and God, and enables man to appropriate and to use the grace which he receives in Christ. There is thus no *antagonism*, though there is a *distinction*, between grace and faith. Now grace comes to Christians through *social* sacraments, as members of one 'spirit-bearing body.' "By one Spirit are we all baptized into one body"; "we being many are one bread

Church doctrine not inconsistent with justification by faith;

---

is developed in the Epistle to the Ephesians; nor can I see that there is anything in the expression—"the Church, the pillar and ground of the truth" (1 Tim. iii. 15), which might not have occurred in the Epistles to the Ephesians or to the Corinthians.

[1] Dr. Hatch calls it an unproved assumption that "the Church of which St. Paul speaks as the body of Christ, 'the fulness of Him which filleth all in all,' be really, as the Augustinian theory assumes it to be, a visible society, or aggregation of societies" (*B. L.* pref. sec. ed. p. xii). His view appears to coincide with that of Bishop Hoadley, who was Law's opponent. The Bishop held "as the only true account of the Church of Christ," in general, that it was "the number of men, whether small or great," who were sincere Christians—i.e. the invisible society of the elect. This, he held, is what St. Paul calls *the Church*. "It cannot be supposed," he pleads, "that a man's being of the invisible Church of Christ is inconsistent with his joining himself with any visible Church;" but the first is essential, the second is voluntary. Law deals with trenchant power with this utterly unscriptural distinction between the 'universal invisible' and 'particular visible' Churches (*Letter* iii. p. 6 f.).

[2] Pfleiderer *Hibbert Lectures* lect. vi.

and one body, for we are all partakers of that one bread." Thus the doctrine of the Church as the household of grace is the complement, not the contradiction, of the doctrine of faith. Faith is no faith if it isolates a man from the fellowship of the one body, and the one body has no salvation except for the sons of faith. Ignatius then with his strenuous insistence on churchmanship can rightly, so far, "claim to be a good Paulinist."[1] In fact St. Paul's teaching about the Church is given nowhere with more practical force than in the Epistles to the Corinthians, which belong to that very group of Epistles in which he fights the battle of faith. And both principles are brought into play by him to vindicate against Judaism the catholicity of the Gospel. Christianity is a catholic religion, he argues in his earlier Epistles, because it appeals to a faculty as universal as human nature —the faculty of faith: men are justified by nothing of national or local observance like the Law; "it is one God Who will justify the circumcision by faith and the uncircumcision through faith." Christianity is catholic, he argues again in effect, in the Epistles of the first captivity, because the Person of Christ is a catholic, a universal Personality; "by Him were all things created—by Him and for Him—and in Him all things have their consistence." Therefore also His redemptive power transcends all local, national distinctions; "He hath made both (Jews and Gentiles) one . . . in one body." For the unity of that body, in which on the basis of faith the Gospel offers sancti-

---

[1] Pfleiderer *l.c.* p. 262; Ignatius *ad Phil.* 8.

I.]   *The Foundation of the Church.*   51

fication to mankind, is by its very essence as the body of Christ universal in its capacity. But these two grounds of catholicity are correlative, not antagonistic.

Once again, if there be such a thing as liberty in law or a "law of liberty,"[1] the obligations of church membership and the authority of a common rule of truth are not in any way antagonistic to the freedom of the spirit. The good citizen, whether of the earthly or heavenly city, is free *in* the law by being at one with the spirit of the law. Here again the same St. Paul held to both sides of the antithesis, which is represented by authority and freedom, by fellowship and individuality. <small>nor with the 'freedom of the spirit';</small>

The doctrine of the Church is indeed only one expression of a principle as broad as human society —the principle that man realizes his true self only by relation to a community, that "he is what he is only as a member of society." Aristotle said of old that "the society (the city) is prior to the individual" —prior, that is, in idea, because it is essential to his being really man, because man is by his very essence "a social animal."[2] By isolating himself he hinders, he narrows himself, he perishes: by merging himself in the larger whole, he realizes his true individuality and his true freedom. So when God sent redemption upon the earth, He sent it in a community or kingdom. Fellowship with God is to be won through fellowship with His Son, but that not otherwise than through <small>but agreeable to the principle of all human society.</small>

[1] St. James i. 25.
[2] On the Greek idea of the πόλις see Newman *Politics of Aristotle* i. p. 560: "a strongly individualized unity, which impresses its dominant ideas upon its members; etc."

fellowship with His Church. "That ye may have fellowship *with us*"—that is why St. John writes his Epistle [1]—"and truly our fellowship is with the Father, and with His Son Jesus Christ." Nor are we to suppose that this association is only a temporary and painful expedient—that we are to submit to be one body for a while in order to live a more separate and isolated life hereafter. No, as the life of perfected humanity [2] is presented to us in the vision of the Apocalypse, it is the life of a city indissolubly one. It is the life of the one bride of Christ, the one humanity, whose white robes are the distinctive, yet coincident, "righteousnesses of the saints." [3]

Two misconceptions of the growth of the Church.

Now that we have brought this investigation to a conclusion, we are in a position to repudiate two ways of conceiving the development of Christianity.

1. That it developed out of previous individualism,

1. It has been represented [4] as if at the first stage we must conceive of Christians rather as individual believers who were led to unite in local associations. This is accounted for by the "tendency to association," characteristic of the Roman empire of that date. But association was not at first "a fixed habit;" it was not "universally recognised as a primary duty;" it did not "invariably follow belief."

---

[1] 1 St. John i. 3. " Manifeste ostendit B. Iohannes quia quicunque societatem cum Deo habere desiderant primo ecclesiae societati debent adunari ' (Bede, quoted by Westcott *in loc.*).

[2] I am not wishing to deny that St. John is representing the Church as she now is. Cf. Milligan *The Revelation of St. John* p. 228. But it is certainly a picture of what she will not only be, but *be wholly and manifestly*, hereafter.

[3] Rev. xix. 8.

[4] By Dr. Hatch (*B. L.* p. 29 f.), if I can understand him rightly. Dr. Sanday interprets him otherwise (*Expositor*, Jan. 1887, p. 10 n[1]).

I.]   *The Foundation of the Church.*   53

Afterwards the local associations succeed in so asserting themselves over individual Christians that adhesion to a community ceases to be voluntary; a man is no Christian unless he belongs to one. This is the state of things which the Ignatian letters were intended to promote. Still, however, Christians might be supposed to unite in Churches how and where they pleased. But later "this free right of association" vanishes;[1] each Church with its bishop and presbytery asserts itself as the exclusive local "ark of the covenant." All who would be within the pale must belong to this one and none other. This is the successful contention of Cyprian. Still later these authoritative local Churches grow into closer and closer combination. The idea of the Catholic and Apostolic Faith, due to St. Irenæus,[2] had already formed a bond of union under a common authoritative Creed. Now, the Churches become one great confederation of societies in a unity which found expression in ecumenical councils with their common authority.[3] Gradually, meanwhile, the hierarchical gradations amongst the various bishops develop on the lines of the imperial system.

Now this mode of conceiving the progress of Christianity is in direct violation of the evidence. The only evidence produced for the supposed first stage which preceded obligatory association consists in the fact that the earliest church teachers found it neces-

—a theory contrary to the evidence.

---

[1] Hatch *B. L.* pp. 103-106.
[2] *Ib.* p. 96: "Its first elaboration and setting forth was due to one man's genius."
[3] *Ib.* pp. 97, 175-189.

sary to preach the duty of association, "if not as an article of the Christian faith, at least as an element of Christian practice."[1] This is evidenced by the warning in the Epistle to the Hebrews against forsaking the Christian assemblies;[2] by St. Jude's denunciation of those who "separate themselves";[3] by the passages in the Shepherd of Hermas[4] about those who "have separated themselves" and so "lose their own souls." What do such utterances really go to prove? A separatist tendency on the part of *those who had been Christians*[5]—a sin of schism, denounced like any other sin. But the idea is nowhere discernible that every Christian was not, as such, a member of the Church, bound to the obligations of membership.[6] Schism is a sin in Scripture[7] as really as in Ignatius' letters. Next, the supposed right of free association into Churches never existed. No doubt the tendency to association in the Roman empire made (as has been said) for the spread of the Christian Church. It made the idea of a Church easier to men's minds. But more than this the facts of the case will not allow us to grant. Christ Himself constituted the Church and gave it its authority, so that it came upon men as a divine gift, with a divine claim, through the apostolic preaching. "Jesus," says Mr. Stanton, "never speaks

---

[1] Hatch *B. L.* p. 29.   [2] Hebrews x. 25.
[3] St. Jude 19.   [4] See above, p. 22.
[5] That they *had been members of the Church* is quite plain in the passages quoted from Hermas.
[6] Of course he might find himself in an isolated position away from church privileges, as may happen to-day.
[7] The 'heretic' is the man of self-willed, separatist tendencies (Tit. iii. 10). Cf. St. Jude 19; St. Matt. xviii. 17.

of the kingdom as something which men could constitute for themselves; it must come to them."[1] From the beginning of Christianity it came to men and took them up, one by one, out of their isolation and alienation from God into its holy and blessed fellowship. It was never a creation of their own by free association. The idea is a figment. From the first each local Church with its organization represented the Divine will for man's salvation in one body. Those who would share what Christ came to give must be added to it. Once added to it, they must remain in it, obedient children of the divine mother, loyal citizens of the city of the saints. Thus Cyprian's vigorous condemnation of schismatics who broke off from the Church at Carthage or in Rome involved no new principle at all,[2] nothing that was not implied in Ignatius' cry—"one altar, one Eucharist, one bishop"[3]—or in Clement of Rome's remonstrance with the schismatical party at Corinth. Nor was the Catholic Apostolic Faith an idea originated or substantially developed by Irenaeus, though he gave it a new and powerful application. Irenaeus is anything rather than a genius who originates. This idea of the universal authoritative tradition of the Christian faith, as it made possible in a later epoch the general councils, as it inspired Clement in Alexandria quite as much as Irenaeus in the West, so in earlier days

---

[1] *Jewish and Christian Messiah* p. 218.

[2] The Eastern Churches which were at first inclined to accept Novatian would have accepted him as *the bishop of Rome*, not as one among a number. The question was simply who was the bishop. See further in chap. iii.

[3] *ad Phil.* 4.

it made possible the 'Catholic Epistles,'[1] and was present in the Church since men first rallied to the apostolic doctrine. Whatever development there was, then, from the day of Pentecost till the Council of Chalcedon did not touch the truth of the visible Church or aggregation of Churches, which it always presupposed, nor the corresponding obligation of membership in it: it presupposed the doctrine of the visible Church with its threefold unity in the life which it derived from its Head, Christ, in the truth of the apostolic tradition, and in the fellowship and intercourse of love.

2. That the church idea was a Roman development:

2. It remains to point out that this idea of the Church, known as Catholicism, was not the creation of western influences and cannot historically be identified (as is sometimes[2] done) with Romanism. Was there, then, nothing new in that western conception of the Church which was finally expressed in the mediæval papacy? Novelty there undoubtedly was, but it was not in any sense the doctrine of the visible Church. What then do the facts of history allow us to describe as Catholicism and what as Romanism?

but there is an original doctrine of the visible Church

Church unity in the New Testament is expressed primarily in such metaphors as those of the body

---

[1] Harnack *Texte u. Untersuch.* ii band. heft 2. p. 105.

[2] See for this idea, in a curiously unhistorical shape, Allen's *Continuity of Christian Thought* pp. 100-105. Cf. Harnack's *Dogmengesch.* i. pp. 362-371 (Katholisch u. Römisch); also Renan's *Hibbert Lectures.* The latter assumes in support of his theory that St. Luke's writings (p. 132), the 'Preaching of Peter'—the basis of the Clementine Homilies and Recognitions (p. 134)—and probably the Pastoral Epistles (p. 163) derive from the Roman Church and represent its ideas. At least the Pastoral Epistles, like the Ignatian (p. 170), exhibit what is characteristically the Roman temper!

of Christ or the Vine with its branches. What primarily constitutes the unity of the Church is the life of Christ derived to its members by His Spirit. The Church is one on account of the spiritual presence which makes her the temple of God or the 'Christ-bearer.' None the less the Church is an external reality, a visible society; for the principle of the Incarnation, which governs the Church, links the inward to the outward, the spiritual to the material —there is 'one body' as well as 'one Spirit.' Spiritual gifts are given by sacraments, and sacraments are visible and social ceremonies of incorporation, or benediction, or feeding. Thus the Christian's spiritual privileges depend on membership of a visible society; but the visible society exists not as an instrument of external secular authority, but as the divine home of spiritual edification, for the 'building up of the body of Christ,' for the perfecting of men into one—into the unity of the life of God.[1] Therefore the instrument of unity is the Spirit; the basis of the unity is Christ, the Mediator; the centre of the unity is in the heavens, where the Church's exalted Head lives in eternal majesty—human, yet glorified. If it be the case, as Ignatius taught (and of course that is still an open question in this discussion), that a

---

[1] St. John xvii. 23. It is characteristic of the scriptural and fundamental idea of church unity that it should be a progressive thing, progressing with a spiritual advance; not an external thing once for all imposed. See St. John as above, St. Paul's Epistle to the Ephesians iv. 13 εἰς ἄνδρα τέλειον. See also on the *Shepherd of Hermas*, above p. 21. The unity of the Church becomes constantly closer as the barriers which sin interposes between man and God, and so between man and his fellows, are removed. Sin, on the other hand, tends to mar the unity by 'schisms' which may be more or less pronounced.

bishop is an essential element of the organization of each visible Church, then he will be the centre and symbol of local unity; but, as the local Church exists only in order to bring men into relation to Christ and to the redeemed humanity which Christ is gathering to Himself in the unseen world, so the catholic Church, the society which each local Church represents, has its centre of unity in Christ.[1] Only (so to speak) the lower limbs of the body of Christ are on earth. The Church is a society in the world, but not *wholly* in the world, nor existing for the world's ends. Thus the primary importance of its organization is *local*. Each local Church exists to keep open (so to speak) the connection of earth and heaven; to keep the streams of the water of life flowing; to maintain and teach and protect the creed which moulds the Christian character. Of course the Christian Churches have a necessary relation to one another. They constitute together one body; they maintain one tradition, and the test of it is found in their consent; they exhibited, they ought still to exhibit, an unbroken fellowship. At the same time each has a relative independence,[2] for the authority over all is that of a common tradition, of which the witness lies in the general consent (as expressed most fully in a general council), coupled with the canon of Scripture.[3] Such is the conception of the Church as existing for the

---

[1] See the passage from Ignatius quoted before (p. 24) with the Bishop of Durham's comment.

[2] As St. Cyprian emphasized. See in chap. iii.

[3] So the rule of faith is formulated by Irenaeus, i. 10. 1, 2, and iii. 1-5, Tertull. *de Praescr.* 27-36, Vincent. *Commonit.* 2, 9, 20, 23, 29.

ends of 'grace and truth,' which can be justly described as Catholic.[1]

Enough has been said to enable us to indicate by contrast what may historically be called its *Roman* development. distinct from the Roman modification of it. The scriptural and catholic conception admitted of development—in this sense, that, saving the original principle, the relations between the different Churches admitted of elaboration as facilities for communication increased under imperial recognition, or as the authority of the common tradition was forced into prominence by the disintegrating effects of Gnosticism and other heresies. But the Roman development gave a new colour to the idea of the Church, not indeed by the introduction of any wholly novel element, but by distorting the idea of its function and unity. It has been already noticed how the Roman Church inherited the imperial conceptions of empire and government. The injunction—

" Tu regere imperio populos, Romane, memento,
Parcere subiectis et debellare superbos "—

might have been spoken to the popes as well as to the emperors. At Rome, then, to a slight extent

[1] On this conception of the Church see a typical passage in St. Augustin *Enarr. in Psalm.* Ps. lvi. 1 : " Quoniam totus Christus caput est et corpus . . . caput est ipse salvator noster, passus sub Pontio Pilato, qui nunc postea quam resurrexit a mortuis, sedet ad dexteram Patris : corpus autem eius est ecclesia ; non ista aut illa, sed toto orbe diffusa ; nec ea quae nunc est in hominibus qui praesentem vitam agunt, sed ad eam pertinentibus etiam his qui fuerunt ante nos et his qui futuri sunt post nos usque in finem saeculi. Tota enim ecclesia constans ex omnibus fidelibus, quia fideles omnes membra sunt Christi, habet illud caput positum in caelis quod gubernat corpus suum ; etsi separatum est visione, sed annectitur caritate." Cf. the excellent account of the Church in Mr. Mason's *The Faith of the Gospel* ch. vii. §§ 9, 10 and ch. viii.

perhaps even from Victor's days—to a more palpable extent from the fifth century, the idea of the Church becomes in a measure secularized. The Church becomes a great world-empire for purposes of spiritual government and administration. The primary conception of her unity becomes that of *unity of government*, the sort of unity which most readily submits itself to secular tests and most naturally postulates a visible centre and head: the dominant idea becomes that of authority. All the needs of the early mediæval period tended to add strength to this tendency, for what the world wanted was above all things order, discipline, rule. Thus the conception of government tends to overshadow earlier conceptions of the Church's function even in relation to the truth. Compare the Roman Leo's view of the truth with that of the Alexandrian Didymus or Athanasius, and the contrast is marked. Both the western and eastern writers insist equally on the truth of the Church dogma; but to the eastern it is the guide to the knowledge of God, to the western it is the instrument of authority and of discipline. Once again, the over-authoritativeness of tone which becomes characteristic of the Roman Church makes her impatient of the more slow and laborious and complex methods of arriving at the truth on disputed questions which belonged to the earlier idea of the 'rule of faith.' The comparison of traditions, the elaborate appeal to Scripture, these methods are too slow and sometimes (as the revelation in this world is *incomplete*[1]) yield no

---

[1] Cf. 1 Cor. xiii. 9-12.

decisive result: something is wanted more rapid, more imperious. It is no longer enough to conceive of the Church as the catholic witness to the faith once for all delivered. She must be the living voice of God, the oracle of the Divine will. Now, as the strength and security of witness lies in the consent of independent testimonies, so the strength of authoritative, oracular utterance lies in unimpeded, unqualified centrality, and Christendom needs a central shrine where divine authority speaks.

Thus an essentially different idea of the Church's function finds expression in the general councils and in the papacy. At least a differently balanced idea of the function of the episcopate finds expression in the catholic conception of the bishop as securing the channels of grace and truth and representing the divine presence, and in the Roman conception of an external hierarchy of government centering in the papacy. The conflict between the two conceptions begins perhaps even in the days of Victor or Stephen; it bears fruit in the Great Schism and in the further schisms of the Reformation.[1] Of course the Roman doctrine of church unity does not *annihilate* the other and older conception. The bishop remains still in the Roman Church what he was from the beginning, but another idea has been superadded, and it is this superadded idea which differentiates the Romanized from the primitive and undivided Church. With this superadded conception we shall not be further

---

[1] It is not suggested that the Roman claims were more than one among several causes of these schisms.

concerned in this argument. We have only to do with the fundamental doctrine of the visible Church as the body of Christ, which is inseparably associated with the doctrine of the faith and the sacraments, and which we are now in a position to assume was a conception held from the first, and which runs up for its primary authority to the will of Christ the King.

CHAPTER II.

APOSTOLIC SUCCESSION.

JESUS CHRIST, we are now in a position to assume, founded a visible society, which, as embodying God's new covenant with men and representing His goodwill towards them, was intended to embrace all mankind. As that society has existed in history, it has exhibited a more or less broad and marked distinction between clergy and laity, priests and people, pastors and their flocks. Such a distinction would, it may be argued, inevitably grow up on the same principles which regulate the division of labour in other departments of human life. The question then arises: Is the Christian ministry simply, like a police force, a body which it has been found advantageous to organize and may be found advantageous to reorganize? Did Christ in instituting His society leave it to itself to find out its need of a differentiation of functions and develop a ministry, or did He, on the other hand, when He constituted His society, constitute its ministry also in the germ? Did He establish not only a body, but an organized body, with a differentiation of functions impressed upon it from the beginning?

It may be urged that the former alternative is

Did Christ institute a ministry?

The idea not improbable;

more in accordance with what we should expect,[1] for it will exhibit the Christian ministry as of a piece with the ordinary products of social evolution. Such a presumption might be met in a measure, antecedently to the question of historical evidence, by the consideration that founders of great institutions, where they successfully observe and correspond to the conditions of their time, are able, to a certain degree at least, to anticipate the results of evolution and impress upon their foundations from the first an abiding form.[2] But it is a more satisfactory consideration that the Church is naturally of a piece with the Incarnation, the fruits of which it perpetuates, and that, as was pointed out in the last chapter, has a finality which belongs to its very essence. It is not that the religion of Christ, as final and supernatural, has no progress or development in it; it is not a code of rules covering all possible occasions of the future. But it is a religion which in its principles and essence is final,—which contains in itself all the forces which the future will need; so that there is nothing to be looked for *in the department of religion* beyond or outside it, while there is everything to be looked for from within. This essential finality is expressed in the once for all delivered faith, in the fulness of

---

[1] As by Hatch *B. L.* pp. 17-20.

[2] This is conspicuously the case with Islam. Mahommed incorporated pre-existing elements of Arab and Jewish belief—of the Christian faith also in a debased form; it may be said with truth that there was no originality in the theology of Islam. But its founder incorporated the elements that came to hand into a book, and on the basis of his book founded a religion which with its motives, its institutions, its obligations was a new thing in the world and yet had a remarkable completeness *ab ovo*. That is to say, it was as complete as its fundamental idea would allow of its being.

Apostolic Succession.

the once for all given grace, in the visible society once for all instituted; and it is at least therefore a 'tenable proposition'[1] that it should have been expressed in a once for all empowered and commissioned ministry.

That it is much more than a 'tenable proposition'—that it is a proposition which states a fact of history—it will be the business of succeeding chapters to show. What it is proposed to do now is to clear up the *idea* of the Christian ministry—to explain what is meant by it, and why it is a reasonable idea,—before we go on to test, with as rigorous a criticism as can be applied, its basis in history. *but the principle of the ministry must be first explained,*

Why adopt such a method? it will be said. Why explain first what you are going to look for, and then proceed to look for it? Why not let the principle, whatever it may be, emerge simply from the facts? The answer is perhaps a twofold one. First, that the method here proposed corresponds to the method by which we actually in most cases arrive at convictions. We do not start afresh; we take the traditional belief, the traditional position, and test it. This is the normal method of human progress. If the traditional belief will not bear the light of facts, it has to be modified, or even reversed; we have to go through the process which a modern writer calls 'the correction of our premises.' But we give, and rightly give, a prerogative to an accepted position, so far at least as to start from it. Secondly, it may

---

[1] See Hatch *B. L.* [sec. ed.] pref. p. xii, where the coherence of ideas is recognised.

be answered that the method of hypothesis is one of the most normal methods of scientific inquiry. The scientific investigator is not asked to approach the facts without antecedent ideas, without anticipations, without desires; to ask this of him in the field of nature or of history is, in most cases, to ask an impossibility. What we have a right to expect is that the facts shall be looked at with severe impartiality and be allowed their legitimate weight to support, or contravene, or modify the original hypothesis. And further, the scientific investigator, when he makes public demonstration of the results of his investigations, is not expected to re-enact all the process he has himself gone through. He asks the right question at once; he propounds at once the right hypothesis, and proceeds to verify it. That is what it is proposed to do here. There have been several theories—or, to speak more accurately, modifications of one theory—of the Christian ministry, which, as having more or less authority in tradition, have some prerogative claims to be examined, but which will not, as they are, stand the verifying test of facts. Underlying them there is a theory that will. There is, that is to say, a number of more or less perverted conceptions of what the Christian ministry has always essentially meant, as well as a true one. In what follows an attempt will be made to distinguish the true idea from its perversions.

Any one who undertakes to vindicate for any Christian truth or institution its claim to permanence or authority—its claim, that is, to be an integral part of the Christian revelation—is confronted on the threshold of his undertaking with a difficulty. The idea or institution has been abused, or overlaid with what exaggerates or disfigures it. He has to attempt what makes a considerable claim on mental patience, to draw distinctions between the abuse of a thing and its use, between the permanence of a thing in its fundamental principle and its permanence with the particular set of associations which in this or that epoch have clustered round it. This is remarkably true of the institution of the Christian ministry and the associated idea of the apostolic succession. It is maintained, though not perhaps with very much truth, that superseded elements of Judaism survived and discoloured more or less the conception of the ministry in the Church: it is much more certain that in the early Middle Ages this, with every other Christian institution, ran a great risk of becoming incrusted with associations left by the dying forms of paganism. Again, the ambition of the clergy and the spiritual apathy and ignorance of the mass of the laity have led to its assuming false claims and a false prominence. Feudal and other passing forms of political society have adopted it and more or less perverted it to their own ends, so that, when their day was over or their support withdrawn, it has been left with its hold on human life weakened, because its true nature was overlaid and forgotten. Once again, it has lived in the security of uncritical epochs and based its claims on careless statements, and the steady rise of an exacter examination of facts has seemed to shake its foundations.

because its perversions have caused misunderstanding.

Thus the conception of the ministry needs purging before it can be vindicated.¹ "There is a short way," says St. Cyprian, "for religious and simple minds to lay aside error, or to find and elicit the truth. For, if we go back to the head and origin of the divine tradition, human error ceases: the real nature of the

¹ The learned Oratorian Morinus, in his work *de Sacris Ordinationibus* (A.D. 1686), offers a good example of a Christian student purging an idea in order to vindicate it. At the time when he wrote there were several false conceptions current on his subject. Notably, it was held that the essential 'matter' (or rite) of ordination lay in the 'tradition of the instruments,' i.e. the giving to the ordinand the characteristic vessels of his ministry. This scholastic doctrine had gained expression in a formal papal decree, though Morinus does not mention this. Eugenius IV. had written thus in his *Decretum de Unione Armeniorum* (the decree which affirmed the doctrinal basis of union with the see of Rome for the benefit of the Armenians, who were seeking reunion at the time of the Council of Florence A.D. 1439): "Sextum sacramentum est ordinis, cuius materia est illud per cuius traditionem confertur ordo, sicut presbyteratus traditur per calicis cum vino et patenae cum pane porrectionem. Diaconatus vero per libri evangeliorum dationem.... Forma sacerdotii talis est: Accipe potestatem offerendi sacrificium in ecclesia pro vivis et mortuis, in nomine Patris et Filii et Spiritus sancti: et sic de aliorum ordinum formis prout in pontificali Romano late continetur" (Labbe *Collect. Concil.* xviii. p. 550). Here, it will be seen, there is no mention at all of the laying-on of hands, and this represented for some centuries the authoritative doctrine. The absence of the porrectio instrumentorum, with the accompanying words, from our ordination of priests had been made the standing objection against the validity of our orders (cf. Estcourt *Question of Angl. Ord.* pp. 260-1). This was due, as Morinus remarks (p. iii. ex. i. 1. 1), to the fact that the "doctores scholastici" were "Graecarum ordinationum ignari et antiquae Latinorum traditionis incuriosi." He was at pains to make an appeal to antiquity. He investigated and reproduced in his work types of early Oriental ordinations from ancient Greek and other Eastern MSS, and demonstrated the absence of the ceremony in question from these rites. Yet Oriental ordinations were confessedly valid. He then reproduced the earliest types of Western ordinations from Latin MSS, and demonstrated that in the West the ceremony with its accompanying words was a later addition unknown in the first thousand years of the Church's history. He then asserted the principle that only that could be essential which had been the practice both in East and West and the constant practice from the first, i.e. the laying-on of hands with accompanying prayer. Thus he purged the tradition. It is the frank inquiry which characterizes his work, and his genuine belief in historical evidence and its value as a corrective of current teaching, which has given his work the high place among works on ecclesiastical subjects which it deservedly holds.

heavenly mysteries is seen, and whatever was hid in darkness and under a cloud is opened out into the light of truth. If a canal which used to give a copious supply of water suddenly fails, men go to the fount to find the reason of the failure—whether the water has dried up at the spring, or has been intercepted in mid-course; so that, if this happened through a defect in the canal preventing the flow of the water, it may be repaired and the water gathered for the supply of the city's wants may reach them in the abundance and purity with which it left the fount. This is what, on the present occasion, the priests of God should do, keeping the divine precepts, so that, if the truth in any matter has been weakened or impaired, we may go back to the original of our Lord and His Gospel or to the apostolic tradition, and let the principles of our action take their rise there, where our order has its origin."[1]

Whether the idea now to be expounded represents 'the original of our Lord' and the 'apostolic tradition,' will be the question afterwards. We take it now only as an hypothesis, and it is this. Let it be supposed that Christ, in founding His Church, founded also a ministry in the Church in the persons of His Apostles.[2] These Apostles must be supposed to have

The idea of the apostolic succession of the ministry.

---

[1] *Ep.* lxxiv. 10.
[2] "By the Church on earth," says Möhler (*Symbolism* pt. i. ch. 5 § 36), "Catholics understand the visible community of believers, founded by Christ, in which, *by means of an enduring apostleship, established by Him and appointed to conduct all nations, in the course of ages, back to God*, the works wrought by Him during His earthly life for the redemption and sanctification of mankind are, under the guidance of His Spirit, continued unto the end of the world."

had a temporary function in their capacity as founders under Christ. In this capacity they held an office by its very nature not perpetual—the office of bearing the original witness to Christ's resurrection and making the original proclamation of the Gospel.[1] But underlying this was another—a pastorate of souls, a stewardship of divine mysteries. This office instituted in their persons was intended to become perpetual, and that by being transmitted from its first depositaries. It was thus intended that there should be in every Church, in each generation, an authoritative stewardship of the grace and truth which came by Jesus Christ and a recognised power to transmit it, derived from above by apostolic descent. The men,

[1] See Pearson *Determinatio Theol.* i (in his *Minor Theol. Works* i. pp. 283, 284, and quoted by Dr. Liddon in *A Father in Christ* [sec. ed.] pref. pp. x-xii): "Ordinem episcopalem fuisse in ipsis apostolis institutum ac per successionem ab ipsis propagatum. Ad hanc assertionem explicandam sciendum est, concessam fuisse apostolis duplicem potestatem, temporariam unam et extraordinariam, ordinariam alteram diuque permansuram. Prior potestas duplicem respectum habuit, ad Christum et ad ecclesiam. Respectu Christi facti sunt apostoli peculiares testes resurrectionis eius: respectu domus Dei facti sunt lapides in fundamento, h.e. ad praedicandam fidem haud prius revelatam, ad fundandas ecclesias, ad colligendum populum Deo instituti et instructi. Posterior potestas erat regendi ecclesias iam fundatas, praedicandi verbum fidelibus collectis, administrandi sacramenta populo Dei, ordinandi ministros ad ecclesiastica munia, peragendi omnia ad salutem Christianorum necessaria. Quod erat in iis temporarium, id erat pure et peculiariter apostolicum; quod autem erat ordinarium et perpetuum, idem erat in eisdem proprie episcopale. Acceperunt totam potestatem a Christo: quicquid erat in eis personale, cum ipsis mortuum est; quicquid erat omnibus ecclesiae temporibus necessarium, ipsorum, dum viverent, manibus transmissum est. Dixit Christus apostolis 'Sicut misit me Pater, ita et ego mitto vos.' Sicut ipse habuit a Patre mandatum docendi populum et ministros ad hoc necessarios necessaria auctoritate instructos deputandi, ita et apostoli habuerunt idem officium et mandatum cum eadem potestate ministros eligendi et ita successive usque ad consummationem saeculi continuata successione. Est itaque apostolus episcopus extraordinarius, est episcopus apostolus ordinarius; atque ita episcopatus fuit in apostolis a Christo institutus, in successoribus apostolorum ab apostolis derivatus."

who from time to time were to hold the various offices involved in the ministry and the transmitting power necessary for its continuance, might, indeed, fitly be elected by those to whom they were to minister. In this way the ministry would express the representative principle.[1] But their authority to minister in whatever capacity, their qualifying consecration, was to come from above, in such sense that no ministerial act could be regarded as *valid*—that is, as having the security of the divine covenant about it—unless it was performed under the shelter of a commission, received by the transmission of the original pastoral authority which had been delegated by Christ Himself to His Apostles.

This is what is understood by the apostolic succession of the ministry. It will be seen how, thus conceived, the ministry corresponds in principle to the Incarnation and the sacraments, and, indeed, to the original creation of man. In all these cases the material comes from below. Christ's humanity is of real physical origin of the stock of Adam. The material of the sacraments is common water, "bread of the earth," common wine. "Of the dust of the ground the Lord God formed man." But this material, which is of the earth, is in each case assumed (though not in each case in the same sense) by the Spirit from above. The Divine Son assumes the humanity, and makes it redemptive. A consecration from above comes upon the sacrament; "the bread which is of

It corresponds to the Incarnation, etc.

---

[1] Proper election was requisite, "not for the authority itself but for the success of the exercise of it:" cf. Denton's *Grace of the Ministry* p. 183.

the earth," which man offers for the divine acceptance, "receiving the invocation of God, is no longer common bread, but Eucharist made up of two things, an earthly and a heavenly."¹ "God breathed into man's nostrils the breath of life." In each of these cases we have the material offered from below and the empowering consecration from above. It is just these two elements, then, that are present to constitute the ministry. Those who are to be ordained are, like the Levites, *the offering of the people*; but they receive, like Aaron and his sons, their consecration from above.²

The principle of succession more important than the form of the ministry.
It is a matter of very great importance—as will appear further on—to exalt the principle of the apostolic succession above the question of the exact

---

¹ Iren. iv. 18. 5.

² In the *Dissertation on the Christian Ministry*, appended to his commentary on the Philippians, (on which see Appended Note A,) Dr. Lightfoot maintains that the priests of the Old Testament were only the "delegates of the people"—"the nation thus deputes to a single tribe the priestly functions which belong to itself as a whole" (*Dissert.* pp. 182, 183). Surely 'dormitat Homerus.' His reference is to the laying-on of hands *by the people upon the Levites* (Numb. viii. 10). But whatever significance this act had, it had surely nothing to do with the ordination of the priests, the sons of Aaron. These had been consecrated to their office "before this laying-on of hands upon the Levites took place, and with far different ceremonies, by Moses himself, without any intervention of the people whatever" (Willis *Worship of the Old Covenant* p. 112). Thus, if the Levites represent the self-consecration of the people, the 'lay-priesthood,' (Numb. viii. 10-20,) Aaron, who is to "offer the Levites before the Lord" (ver. 11)—Aaron, *to whom, with his sons*, God is said to have "given the Levites as a gift to do the service of the children of Israel" (ver. 19)—Aaron, and his sons the priests, represent the ministers of the covenant instituted by God Himself, whose prerogative was so jealously guarded, even against the sons of Levi, 'in the matter of Korah' (Numb. xvi). "Moses himself, as the representative of the unseen King, is the consecrator" (*Dict. Bible*, s.v. PRIEST, ii. p. 917). [I am speaking of the whole Old Testament, as the writers of the New Testament knew it, without discussing the question of the date of different portions of the Law.]

form of the ministry, in which the principle has expressed itself, even though it be by apostolic ordering. What is meant is this: the apostolic succession has taken shape—how uniformly the next chapter will show—in a threefold ministry, consisting of a single bishop in each community or diocese with presbyters and deacons, the bishop alone having the power of ordaining or conferring ministerial authority on others, the presbyters constituting a 'co-operative order' which shares with him a common priesthood, and the deacons holding a subordinate and supplementary position. But this is rather the outcome of a principle than itself a principle, at any rate a primary or essential principle.[1] No one, of whatever part of the Church, can maintain that the existence of what may be called, for lack of a distinctive term, *monepiscopacy* is essential to the continuity of the Church. Such monepiscopacy may be the best mode of government, it may most aptly symbolize the divine monarchy, it may have all spiritual expediency and historical precedent on its side—nay, more, it may be of apostolic institution: but nobody could maintain that the continuity of the Church would be broken if in any given diocese all the presbyters were consecrated to the episcopal office, and governed as a co-ordinate college of bishops without presbyters or presbyter-bishops.[2] A state of things quite as abnor-

---

[1] See *Church Principles*, by W. E. Gladstone, pp. 244, 245, 252, 253.

[2] "The things proper to bishops," says Bishop Bilson (*Perpet. Govt. of Christ's Church* ch. xiii), "which might not be common to presbyters, were singularity in succeeding and superiority in ordaining." But of these two things *the latter* is really that which forms the vital distinction between the orders.

mal as this existed for many centuries in the Celtic Church of Ireland. Something equivalent to this very arrangement has been commonly believed in the West to have existed in the early Church.

Why was the violation of the ordinary arrangement of the ministry regarded in these cases as a matter of only secondary importance? Because the principle of the apostolic succession was not violated. There have always (it is here supposed) existed in the Church ministers, who, besides the ordinary exercise of their ministry, possess the power of transmitting it; they may, so far, be one or many in each community; but, when they ordain men to the holy offices of the Church, they are only fulfilling the function intrusted to them out of the apostolic fount of authority. There are other ministers, again, who have certain clearly understood functions committed to them, but not that of transmitting their office. Should these ever attempt to transmit it, their act would be considered invalid. For this is the church principle: that no ministry is valid which is assumed, which a man takes upon himself, or which is merely delegated to him from below. That ministerial act alone is valid which is covered by a ministerial commission received from above by succession from the Apostles. This is part of the great principle of tradition. "Hold the traditions," reiterates the Apostle. The whole of what constitutes Christianity is a transmitted trust—a *tradition* which may need purging, but never admits of innovation, for 'nihil innovandum nisi quod traditum' is a fundamental Christian principle. For instance, the truth revealed in Christ is adequate to all time. It is fruitful of innumerable applications and adaptations to the new wants of each age. It may need setting free and purifying from accretions from time to time, but not more. What breaks the tradition is heresy—the intrusion, that is, of a new and alien element into the deposit, having its origin in personal self-assertion. This conception of heresy is involved in the very idea of a revelation once for all made. Now, what heresy is in the sphere of truth, a violation of the apostolic succession is in the tradition of the ministry. Here too there is a deposit handed down, an ecclesiastical trust transmitted; and its continuity is violated, whenever a man 'takes any honour to himself' and assumes a function not committed to him. Judged in the light of the Church's mind as to the relation of the individual to the whole body, such an act takes a moral discolouring. The individual, of course, who is guilty of the act may not incur the responsibility in any particular case through the absence of right knowledge, or from other causes which exempt from responsibility in whole or in part; but judged by an objective standard, the act has the moral discolouring of self-assertion. The Church's doctrine of succession is thus of a piece with the whole idea of the Gospel revelation, as being the communication of a divine gift which must be received and cannot be originated,—received, moreover, through the channels of a visible and organic society; and the principle (this is what is here emphasized) lies at the last resort in the idea of succession rather than in the continuous existence of episcopal government—even though it should appear that this too is of apostolic origin, and that the Church, since the Apostles, has never conceived of itself as having any power to originate or interpolate a new office.[1]

<small>Its importance</small>

It will be easy to see that the existence of an apostolic succession serves several important ends.

<small>(i) as a bond of union in a spiritual society;</small>

(i) It forms a link of historical continuity in a society intended to be universal and permanent. Nations have many bonds of union. There is the unity of blood and language and common customs: there is the unity of a common government over men inhabiting a common territory. Such bonds of union are lacking to a universal spiritual society such as the Church claims to be. Embracing all peoples and languages, admitting and consecrating the greatest varieties of local custom and taste, inhabiting no common territory but spread over all the earth,[2] how should the Church preserve or exhibit its identity and continuity as a visible society without some such

---

[1] The words of the Anglican Art. XXIII. are: "Non licet cuiquam sumere sibi munus publice praedicandi aut administrandi sacramenta in ecclesia, nisi prius fuerit ad haec obeunda legitime vocatus et missus. Atque illos legitime vocatos et missos existimare debemus, qui per homines, quibus potestas vocandi ministros atque mittendi in vineam Domini publice concessa est, in ecclesia cooptati fuerint et asciti in hoc opus."

[2] We know how familiar a boast this is with early Christian writers. Cf. e.g. *Ep. ad Diognet.* 5: "Christians (of the 'new race' which has just come into the world, c. 1) are distinguished from the rest of mankind neither by land, nor by language, nor by customs. They have neither cities of their own, nor exceptional language, nor remarkable mode of life. But inhabiting Greek or barbarian cities as the lot of each determined, and obeying the local customs in dress and food and general conduct of life, the character of their own polity which they exhibit is everywhere wonderful and confessedly strange." Cf. Iren. i. 10. 2.

Apostolic Succession.

instrument and evidence of succession as is afforded by the ministry as traditionally conceived? No doubt it may be urged, and with partial truth, that the real unity of the Church lies in the Spirit, which lives in her, and the truth she holds and teaches; but that truth was committed to a society, as what Irenaeus calls "its rich depository,"[1] and that Spirit has a body—and how can the outward organization, which enshrines and perpetuates the inner life, maintain or exhibit its identity without some such bond as the apostolic succession of the ministry affords?[2]

(ii) The ministerial succession serves the end of impressing upon Christians that their new life is a *communicated gift*, and from this point of view it is naturally associated with the sacraments. A Christian of apostolic days was taught by St. Paul to look back to the day of baptism as the moment of his incorporation into the life of Christ.[3] He had received the gift of the Spirit by the laying on of apostolic hands.[4] He was fed with the Body and Blood of Christ through the 'effectual signs' of bread and wine.[5] This sacramental method went to

(ii) as declaring men's dependence on the gifts of Christ;

---

[1] Iren. iii. 4. 1: "quasi in depositorium dives."
[2] For an interesting statement of the function of the episcopal succession from this point of view, see F. D. Maurice's *Kingdom of Christ* pt. ii. ch. iv. § 5; also Gladstone *Church Principles* ch. v. esp. pp. 193, 194: "If it were attempted to insist on succession in doctrine as the sole condition of the essence of a Church, any such proposition would be self-contradictory, inasmuch as that which would be thus perpetuated would not be a society at all, but a creed or body of tenets." What is required is "succession of persons," as well as "continuous identity of doctrine."
[3] Gal. iii. 27; Rom. vi. 3; 1 Cor. xii. 13.
[4] Acts viii. 17-20, xix. 6; cf. Rom. i. 11.
[5] 1 Cor. x. 16, 17. I do not see how it is possible to deny that the New Testament does attach inward gifts to external channels, i.e. is sacramental.

impress upon his mind the idea of his dependence upon grace given from without. True, this grace given from without could only be appropriated, incorporated, used, by the inward faculty of faith. This is the Christian principle of correspondence. As, when Christ was on earth healing men's sickness, the 'virtue which went out of Him' could only be liberated to act in effective power on those who had 'faith to be healed,' and thus men's faith made them whole, though the means of their healing was the virtue of Christ's body which came from without; so is it with His permanent spiritual agency. He saves in virtue of an inward faith but by the instrumentality of a gift given from outside. This outward bestowal of grace was no peculiarity of the apostolic age, though the symbolic miracles which at first called attention to it passed away. It is impossible to deny that the early Christians, in East and West, believed in the sacraments as the covenanted channels of grace.[1] It is, indeed, part of God's condescending

---

[1] I may refer, in confirmation of what is said above, to the way in which the Fathers, at the end of the second century, emphasize the sacramental principle as of a piece with the principle of the Incarnation against the Gnostic depreciation of what is material. See a vigorous passage of Tertullian (*de Resurr. Carn.* 8), emphasizing how, at each stage of the spiritual life, the inward gift is mediated through the material body—and that, of course, implies through a material sacrament. "As the soul is attached to God, it is the flesh which enables it to be united. The flesh is washed that the soul may be cleansed: the flesh is anointed that the soul may be consecrated: the flesh is marked with the Cross that the soul may be protected: the flesh is shadowed with the imposition of hands that the soul may be illuminated by the Spirit: the flesh is fed with the Body and Blood of Christ that the soul may feed upon the fatness of God." Cf. *de Bapt.* 2, quoted on p. 179. This is no advance upon the principle of Irenaeus. To Irenaeus the bread and wine are consecrated to become the Body and Blood of Christ, and so to impart eternal life even to man's body (iv. 18. 5): "the mixed cup and the bread which has been made receives the word of God,

compassion that He should thus embody in visible form His divine gift. So is it made most easily intelligible and accessible to the ignorant.[1] So was it most easily and forcibly impressed on men that Christ had come, not merely to show them what in any case they are if they will be true to themselves, but to make them what apart from Him they cannot be.

and the Eucharist becomes the Body [and Blood] of Christ, and the substance of our flesh grows and gains consistence from these. How, then, can they say that our flesh is not susceptible of the gift of God, which is eternal life —our flesh, which is nourished by the Body and Blood of the Lord, and which is His member" (v. 2. 3). Irenaeus' contemporary at Alexandria, Clement (as there can, I think, be no doubt, though his exact view of the Eucharist is hard to grasp or state) certainly believed that the sacraments, convey to us the life and being of Christ; cf. *Paed.* i. 6. This would appear in Dr. Bigg's references *B. L.* pp. 105, 106. But we may go back earlier. The simple account, which, earlier in the second century, Justin Martyr gives of the meaning of the Christian sacraments (*Apol.* i. 61, 65-67), carries conviction that Irenaeus and Tertullian are stating no new doctrine. We go back to the beginning of the century, to Ignatius, and we find the same stress on the sacraments in the earliest stage of controversy with Gnosticism. "The heretics," he writes (*ad Smyrn.* 7), "abstain from the Eucharist and prayer, because they confess not that the Eucharist is the Flesh of our Saviour Jesus Christ, which suffered for our sins, which by His goodness the Father raised up. They, therefore, who speak against the gift of God die by their disputing." [Dr. Lightfoot would interpret this in the light of Tertullian's "Hoc est corpus meum: id est figura mei corporis." But Tertullian's language about the Eucharist as a whole makes it quite certain that he believed it to be a *real* gift of the Flesh and Blood of Christ, and not *merely* a figure. The sacraments are 'figures,' 'symbols,' 'types,' 'signs,' but they are 'effectual signs,' they effect what they symbolize.] The earliest language about baptism also is very emphatic in making it the instrument of the new birth and its accompanying purification. See Hermas *Vis.* iii. 3, *Sim.* ix. 16, and Barnabas *Ep.* 11. The only early Christian writings which seem to take a low view of the sacraments are very Judaic, e.g. the (Ebionite) Clementines and the *Didache*, which, though not Ebionite, has no hold on the doctrine of the Incarnation and of the grace which flows from it.

[1] It is instructive to contrast in this respect Christianity with Neo-Platonism. Communion with God—oneness with God—was regarded by the philosophers as attainable only through intellectual self-abstraction from the things of sense and an ecstatic rapture possible but to a very few 'select' natures. In the Church it was believed to depend upon a simple act, possible to the most ignorant. "Take, eat; this is My Body." "He that eateth My Flesh dwelleth in Me, and I in him."

"Except ye eat the Flesh of the Son of Man, and drink His Blood, ye have no life in you."[1]

Aristotle represented man as 'self-sufficient'—not indeed as an individual, but as a member of an organized society, the city of Greek civilization. If he needed to come into contact with God, that was rather at the circumference of his life and as the remote goal of its highest efforts. Christianity, on the contrary, represents man as fundamentally and from the first dependent upon God. It proclaims that man's initial step of true progress is to know his utter, his complete dependence,—that the essence and secret of all sin is his claim to be independent, to be sufficient for himself. Thus Christ, when He came to restore men to their true selves and to God, did all that was necessary to emphasize that their restoration must be by the communication of a gift from outside, which they had not and could not have of themselves. This is the essential message of Christianity, and is what differentiates its whole moral scheme from its very foundations. But in the second part of the Aristotelian position Christianity recognises a divine truth, of which man had never lost his hold: man still must realize his true being in a society, the city of God. Only in the divine household of the Church can he be fed with his necessary portion, the bread of life.

---

[1] F. W. Robertson (*Sermons*, 2d series, pp. 55, 56) attempts to make baptism merely an *announcement of what is*, instead of a creative or re-creative act: but this is to do violence to the whole body of Scriptural and ecclesiastical language. The Church is the 'new creation,' and the sacraments are 'practica' or 'efficacia signa.'

Yet if it be important to impress upon men's minds, permanently and persistently, as a part of a catholic system, their dependence upon gifts bestowed from outside, it must be admitted that there is no way of making the impression more effective than by the institution in the Christian household of a stewardship, which should represent God, the giver, distributing to the members of the divine family their portion of meat in due season; and it is quite essential that such stewards should receive their authorization by a commission which makes them the representatives of God the giver, and not of men the receivers. "It is the doctrine of the ministerial succession by commission from the Apostles, which makes, and which alone makes, this required provision for representing to us, along with the matter of the revelation, and as needful to its due reception, this lively idea of its origin."[1]

(iii) The apostolic succession seems to correspond, as nothing else does, to the moral needs of the ministers of Christ's Church.[2] "How shall they preach," said St. Paul, "except they be sent?" He himself had been sent by an immediate mission from Christ as direct, as *visible* (so he believed) as that which empowered the other Apostles. When he exhorts Timothy to make "full proof of his ministry," it is by recalling his mind to an actual external commission received, with its actual and accompanying gift. "There is not in the world," says Bishop Taylor,

(iii) as meeting the moral needs of those who minister.

---

[1] Gladstone *Church Principles* p. 208.
[2] See Dr. Liddon's sermon *The Moral Value of a Mission from Christ.*

F

"a greater presumption than that any should think to convey a gift of God, unless by God he be appointed to do it."[1] Such appointment or commission, to be valid, must be of an authority—not unquestioned, indeed, for St. Paul's was questioned, but not justly open to question, as representative of Christ. Men are needed for Christ's ministry who have ready wills and clear convictions, men, that is, with a sense of vocation; but they must be also men of humility, distrustful of their own impulses and powers, like the prophets of old. The very thing that such men need is the open and external commission to support the internal sense of vocation through all the fiery trials of failure and disappointment, of weariness and weakness, to which it will be subjected—nay, to be its substitute when God's inward voice seems even withdrawn—maintaining in the man the simple conviction that, as a matter of fact, 'a dispensation has been committed to him.'

The idea of the apostolic succession is, then, we may claim, in natural harmony both with the moral needs of men and with the idea of the Church. Such a succession of ministers would serve, as nothing else could serve, both as a link of continuity in the society, and as an institution calculated to represent to men's imaginations the dependence of the Christian life upon God's gifts, and as a means for supplying a satisfying commission to those called to share the ministry.

But it is objected to on the following grounds: On the other hand, objections are raised against it which may best be considered before we approach

[1] *Ductor Dubitant.* in his *Works* [ed. 1822] xiv. p. 26.

the discussion of the historical evidence, especially as the consideration of them will serve to put more clearly before our minds what the exact conception is which is to be subjected to the test of history.

The most important of them may be summarized under five heads :—

  (1) the doctrine of the apostolic succession is sacerdotal:

  (2) it postulates—what is so incredible—that bad or unspiritual men can impart spiritual gifts to others:

  (3) it is incompatible with the true ideal of liberty:

  (4) the chances against its having been actually preserved are overwhelming:

  (5) it is exclusive in such a sense as to be fatal to its claim.

(1) 'The doctrine of the apostolic succession is sacerdotal.' This we admit in one sense and deny in another. It is necessary for us in fact to draw a distinction between what we regard as legitimate and what as illegitimate sacerdotalism.[1] For the term is associated historically with much that is worst, as well as much that is best, in human character. Priesthood has been greatly abused. But must not the same be said of liberty or of State authority? Must not it be said of religion itself, in common with all the greatest and most ennobling truths? What would become of us if we should agree to abandon every idea and

(i) 'It is sacerdotal.

---

[1] Dr. Liddon *University Sermons*, 2nd series, p. 191: "A formidable word, harmless in itself, but surrounded with very invidious associations." See the whole passage.

institution which has become corrupt, or been exaggerated, or made to minister to ambition and worldliness? Life would be a barren thing indeed! There is surely no better task for the wise man than to set himself to vindicate the truths which lie behind persistent and popular errors and abuses—to the reality and power of which, indeed, the very popularity and persistence of the abuses bear witness.

<small>The ministerial priesthood, however, is not vicarious</small>

The chief of the ideas commonly associated with sacerdotalism, which it is important to repudiate, is that of a *vicarious* priesthood.[1] It is contrary to the true spirit of the Christian religion to introduce the notion of a class inside the Church who are in a closer spiritual relationship to God than their fellows. " If a monk falls," says St. Jerome, " a priest shall pray for him; but who shall pray for a priest who has fallen?" Such an expression, construed literally, would imply a closer relation to God in the priest than in the consecrated layman, and such a conception is beyond a doubt alien to the spirit of Christianity. There is "no sacrificial tribe or class between God and man." " Each individual member [of the Christian body] holds personal communion with the Divine Head."[2] The difference between clergy and laity " is not a difference in kind"[3] but in function. Thus the completest freedom of access to God in prayer and intercession, the closest personal relation to Him, belongs to all. So far as there is gradation in the

---

[1] See Maurice *Kingdom of Christ* ii. p. 216.
[2] Dr. Lightfoot *Dissert. on the Christian Ministry* p. 181.
[3] Liddon *l.c.* p. 198.

efficacy of prayers, it is the result not of official position but of growing sanctity and strengthening faith. It is an abuse of the sacerdotal conception, if it is supposed that the priesthood exists to celebrate sacrifices or acts of worship in the place of the body of the people or as their substitute. This conception had, no doubt, attached itself to the 'massing priests' of the Middle Ages. The priest had come to be regarded as an individual who held, in virtue of his ordination, the prerogative of offering sacrifices which could win God's gifts. Thus spiritual advantages could be secured for the living and the dead by paying him to say a mass, and greater advantages by a greater number of masses. Now this distorted sort of conception is one which the religious indolence of most men, in co-operation with the ambition for power in 'spiritual' persons, is always tending to make possible. It is not only possible to believe in a vicarious priesthood of sacrifice, but also in a vicarious office of preaching, which releases the laity from the obligation to make efforts of spiritual apprehension on their own account. But in either case the conception is an unchristian one. The ministry is no more one of vicarious action than it is one of exclusive knowledge or exclusive spiritual relation to God. What is the truth then? It is that *but representative;* the Church is one body: the free approach to God in the Sonship and Priesthood of Christ belongs to men as members of 'one body,' and this one body has different organs through which the functions of its life find expression, as it was differentiated by the act and appointment of Him who created it. The reception, for instance, of Eucharistic grace, the approach to God in Eucharistic sacrifice, are functions of the whole body. "*We* bless the cup of blessing," "*we* break the bread," says St. Paul, speaking for the community: "*we* offer," "*we* present," is the language of the liturgies.[1] But the ministry is the organ—the necessary organ—of these functions. It is the hand which offers and distributes; it is the voice which consecrates and pleads. And the whole body can no more dispense with its services than the natural body can grasp or speak without the instrumentality of hand and tongue. Thus the ministry is the instrument as well as the symbol of the Church's unity, and no man can share her fellowship except in acceptance of its offices.

[1] 1 Cor. x. 16. It is remarkable that Hugh of St. Victor (*Summ. Sentent.* tract. vi. c. 9, quoted by Morinus *de Sacr. Ord.* p. iii. ex. v. 1. 4) gives as the current reason for denying that heretics or schismatics could consecrate the Eucharist the fact that in the Eucharist the *priest speaks for the whole Church*: "Aliis videtur quod nec excommunicati nec manifeste haeretici conficiunt [corpus Christi]. Nullus enim in ipsa consecratione dicit offero, sed offerimus, ex persona totius ecclesiae. Cum autem alia sacramenta extra ecclesiam possint fieri, haec nunquam extra, et istis magis videtur assentiendum." The idea of the representative character of the priesthood in the ministry of the eucharistic sacrifice finds beautiful expression in the prayers (ascribed traditionally to St. Ambrose) which are used in the West as a *Preparatio ad Missam*: "Profero etiam," the celebrant prays, "(si digneris propitius intueri) tribulationes plebium, pericula populorum, captivorum gemitus, miserias orphanorum, necessitates peregrinorum, inopiam debilium, desperationes languentium, defectus senum, suspiria iuvenum, vota virginum, lamenta viduarum." He is the mouthpiece of the needs of 'all sorts and conditions of men.' As the necessary mouthpiece for the expression of these needs in the eucharistic celebration, the representative priest is in a certain sense a go-between, a mediator. Thus this same prayer has earlier these words: "quoniam me peccatorem inter te et eundem populum tuum medium esse voluisti, licet in me aliquod boni operis testimonium non agnoscas, officium saltem dispensationis creditae non recuses, nec per me indignum eorum salutis pereat pretium, pro quibus victima salutaris dignatus es esse et redemptio."

II.] *Apostolic Succession.* 87

Why is this conception unreasonable? The people of Israel of old were "a kingdom of priests, and an holy nation" (Exod. xix. 6). But that priestliness which inhered in the race had its expression in the divinely ordained ministry of the Aaronic priesthood.[1] The Christian Church is in an infinitely higher sense "a royal priesthood, a holy nation."[2] But why should that priesthood exclude, and not rather involve, a ministry through which it finds official and formal expression—and that not by mere expediential arrangement, but by divine ordering?[3] Take the notion of the general priesthood of all Christians as it finds expression, for example, in Justin Martyr in the earlier part of the second century.[4]

On the analogy of the old covenant,

it is not inconsistent with the general priesthood,

as taught by Justin,

"Just," he says, "as that Joshua, who is called by the prophet (Zech. iii. 1) a priest, was seen wearing filthy garments ... and was called a brand plucked out of the burning because he received remission of sins, the devil also, his adversary, receiving rebuke, so we, who through the name of Jesus have believed as one man

---

[1] It is maintained without any adequate ground (*Dict. Bible* s. v. PRIESTHOOD) that the Levitical priesthood was *the substitute* in a sense for the general priesthood, instead of its expression—that the special priesthood was appointed because the people refused to realize the priesthood which belonged to them all—so that it was in this sense a *pis aller*, a δεύτερος πλοῦς. There is no evidence for this. The same chapter which recognises the general, recognises also a special priesthood (? of the first-born), Exod. xix. 22-24.

[2] βασίλειον ἱεράτευμα, 1 Pet. ii. 9. βασιλεία, ἱερεῖς τῷ θεῷ, Rev. i. 6. St. Peter is quoting and St. John referring to the words in Exodus.

[3] I do not wish to press the argument too far. Single Christians are often spoken of as 'priests,' and not merely as belonging to a priestly race. This is natural enough. For undoubtedly all Christians have an individual union with God and freedom of approach to God, which (so to speak) individualizes that in them which can be rightly called priesthood. I only use the argument to prove this—that a ministerial priesthood is in no contradictory relation to a general priesthood.

[4] *Dial. c. Tryph.* 116, 117.

in God, the Maker of all, have been stripped through the name of His First-begotten Son of the 'filthy garments' of our sins; and being set on fire by the word of his calling are the genuine high-priestly race of God, as God beareth witness Himself, saying that 'in every place amongst the Gentiles men are offering sacrifices acceptable to Him and pure,' and God receives from no man sacrifices, except through His priests. So, then, of all the sacrifices through this name, which Jesus the Christ delivered to be made, that is (the sacrifices) at the Eucharist of the bread and of the cup, which in every place of the earth are made by the Christians, God by anticipation beareth witness that they are acceptable to Him."

Here is indeed a vivid consciousness of the priesthood, which belongs to the Church as a whole[1] but finds expression in a great ceremonial action—the Eucharist—an action which belongs not to the individual but to the whole body, and is celebrated by the "president of the brethren."[2] How, then, is this priesthood interfered with, if we should find reason to believe that Christ Himself ordained ministers of this mystical action—such as did actually exist in Justin

---

[1] It should be noticed that the idea of priesthood always seems to involve that of 'approach to God *on behalf of others.*' The Christians are high priests on behalf of the world. They are the "soul of the world" (*Ep. ad Diognet.* 6). They can plead effectually, so the apologists urged, for the empire and mankind (Tertull. *Apol.* 30). This function of the Church St. Paul presses on St. Timothy. The Church is not to confine her intercessions to her own body—"I exhort that prayer, etc. be made *for all men,*" "for God will have *all men* to be saved;" "He is the Saviour of all men," though "specially of them that believe" (1 Tim. ii. 1-4; iv. 10).

[2] προσφέρεται τῷ προεστῶτι τῶν ἀδελφῶν ἄρτος καὶ ποτήριον (*Apol.* i. 65). He offers the prayer and Eucharist, and the people say Amen. This 'president' is no doubt the bishop. So Harnack (*Expositor*, May 1887, p. 336).

Martyr's days—to be the mouthpieces of the Church in its celebration?

No one, again, is more identified than Irenaeus with the principle of the apostolic succession. He regards it undoubtedly as of the essence of the Church. Her mark, her character, is "according to the successions of the bishops."[1] Yet he does not hesitate to say that in some sense "every just man is of the priestly order," and "all the disciples of the Lord are priests and Levites"—that is, they have the freedom of the old priesthood, not its ministry.[2] If it be said that Irenaeus is admittedly 'unsacerdotal,' that is, that he does not apply the term priesthood to the Christian ministry,[3] it may be pointed out, further, that writers, who confessedly are sacerdotal in their conception of the ministry, still continue down into the Middle Ages to speak also without hesitation of the general priesthood.[4] For the official hierarchy

Irenaeus, and later writers.

---

[1] iv. 33. 8: "character corporis Christi secundum successiones episcoporum."

[2] iv. 8. 5 and v. 34. 3; see Lightfoot *Dissert.* p. 252. The point in both passages is that our Lord in justifying the conduct of His disciples when they broke the Sabbath (St. Matt. xii. 1-5) claimed for them and for David in virtue of their righteousness the freedom of priests, 'who profane the Sabbath and are blameless.' Again, inasmuch as, like the Levites, our Lord's disciples had 'no inheritance,' they could, like the Levites, claim support. Thus "they were allowed when hungry to take food of the grains." In both cases the priesthood which belongs to good men or disciples lies in a certain *freedom*, not in any power of ministry.

[3] See further in chap. iii. I have endeavoured there to point out that the idea of a gradual growth in sacerdotalism in the early Church hardly corresponds to the facts. There is a change rather in language than in principle.

[4] Thus Origen (for whose admittedly sacerdotal view of the ministry see further in chap. iii.) in some passages "takes spiritual enlightenment and not sacerdotal office to be the Christian counterpart to the Aaronic priesthood" (Lightfoot *Dissert.* p. 255); cf. *in Ioann.* i. 3: "Those who are devoted to the divine word, and are dedicated sincerely to the sole worship of God, may not unreasonably be called priests and Levites according to the differ-

offered no bar to its recognition, provided that the general priesthood was not supposed by those church-

ence in this respect of their impulses tending thereto. . . . Those that excel the men of their own generation perchance will be high-priests" (Lightfoot's trans.); see also *in Lev.* iv. 6, vi. 5, ix. 1, 8, xiii. 5. He uses such language, however, with qualifications "secundum moralem locum," "secundum spiritalem intelligentiam," (*in Lev.* i. 5, ii. 4, ix. 6, xv. 3) i.e. he draws a distinction between the *moral* and *ministerial* sense of priesthood; see Dr. Bigg's note, *B. L.* p. 215 note [1]. He adds that "*in Num.* ii. 1 . . . priests, virgins, ascetics are said to be in professione religionis. *in Iesu Nave* xvii. 2 shows that there was a strong tendency in Origen's mind to restrict the language concerning the priesthood of the Christian to those 'religious.'" So also among the scholia on the Apocalypse ascribed to Victorinus of Petau (but not by him in their present form) occurs the following on c. xx: "Qui enim virginitatis integrum servaverit propositum et decalogi fideliter praecepta impleverit . . . iste vere sacerdos est Christi et millenarium numerum perficiens integre creditur regnare cum Christo et apud eum recte ligatus est diabolus."

For a recognition of the general priesthood among later sacerdotal writers, cf. Leo the Great *Serm.* iii. 1: "ut in populo adoptionis Dei, cuius universitas sacerdotalis atque regalis est, non praerogativa terrenae originis obtineat unctionem, sed dignatio caelestis gratiae gignat antistitem." *Serm.* iv. 1: "In unitate igitur fidei atque baptismatis indiscreta nobis societas et generalis est dignitas, secundum illud beatissimi Petri. . . . Vos autem genus electum, regale sacerdotium." August. *de Civ. Dei* xvii. 5. 5: "Sacerdotium quippe hic ipsam plebem dicit, cuius plebis ille sacerdos est mediator Dei et hominum homo Christus Iesus." *Quaest. Evang.* ii. 40. 3: "Sacerdotium vero Iudaeorum nemo fere fidelium dubitat figuram fuisse futuri sacerdotii regalis, quod est in ecclesia, quo consecrantur omnes pertinentes ad corpus Christi summi et veri principis sacerdotum. Nam nunc et omnes unguuntur quod tunc regibus tantum et sacerdotibus fiebat, . . . ipsi nondum accepto baptismatis sacramento nondum spiritaliter ad sacerdotes pervenerant." See the same idea in a collect of the Gelasian Sacramentary (Bright *Ancient Collects* p. 99). Hence we get a priesthood ascribed, as by St. Irenaeus, to *each Christian* (though of course as a member of the one body) in virtue of baptism and unction. St. Jerome (*adv. Lucifer.* 4) writes: "sacerdotium laici id est baptisma." So Isidore of Seville (*de Eccl. Off.* ii. 25) writes: "Postquam Dominus noster verus rex et sacerdos aeternus, a Deo Patre caelesti mystico unguento est delibutus, iam non soli pontifices et reges sed omnis ecclesia unctione chrismatis consecratur, pro eo quod membrum est aeterni sacerdotis et regis. Ergo quia genus regale et sacerdotale sumus, ideo post lavacrum ungimur, ut Christi nomine censeamur." Cf. Alcuin [Albinus Flaccus] *Ep. ad Oduinum*, ap. Hittorp. *de Div. Cath. Eccl. Offic.* [Colon. 1568] p. 100: "Sacro chrismate caput pungitur . . . ut intelligat se diadema regni et sacerdotii dignitatem portaturum." Rabanus Maurus *de Inst. Cler.* i. 29, ap. Hittorp. p. 322; Walafrid Strabo *de Reb. Eccl.* 16, ap. Hittorp. p. 401—of the common priesthood of all in the Eucharist, the generale sacerdotium;

men who recognised it (as in fact it was not) to carry with it the power of ministry. It may be worth while to quote a passage which seems to push to its extremest point the right of the priesthood, which is common to all in virtue of their baptism and confirmation.

"From that day and that hour in which thou camest out of the font thou art become to thyself a continual fountain, a daily remission. Thou hast no need of a doctor, or of the priest's right hand. As soon as thou descendedst from the sacred font thou wast clothed in a white robe and anointed with the mystic ointment; the invocation was made over thee, and the threefold power came upon thee, which filled the new vessel (that thou wert) with this new doctrine. Thenceforth it made thee a judge and arbiter to thyself; it gave thee knowledge to be able of thyself to learn good and evil—to discern, that is, between merit and sin. And because thou couldest not, whilst thou art in the body, remain free from sin, it placed thy remedy after baptism in thyself, it placed remission in thine own judgment, that thou shouldest not, if necessity was urgent, seek a priest; but thyself,

Ivo Carnot. ap. Hittorp. p. 469. St. Thomas Aquinas *Sum.* iii. q. 82. art. 1: "laicus iustus unitus est Christo unione spiritali per fidem et charitatem non autem per sacramentalem potestatem: et ideo habet spiritale sacerdotium ad offerendum spiritales hostias."

The consideration of such passages as these will serve to show that sacerdotalism is not incompatible with an even zealous recognition of a lay priesthood. The only form of expression which seems to have passed away was that by which all Christians were called in some sense *priests and Levites*, and even "high-priests" (Origen). But they were not so called, either by Origen or Irenaeus, in any sense which suggests *ministerial* powers. The point of comparison lies in nearness to God and constant service (Origen), or in a certain sort of freedom and privilege (Irenaeus).

as a cunning and clear-sighted master, mightest correct thine error within thee and wash away thy sin in penitence, and so hardness might cease, despair be over, apathy at an end. The fountain never fails; the water is within, the washing is in thine own judgment, sanctification is in activity, remission in the dew of tears."[1]

Such language sounds unsacerdotal, but it comes out of the sacerdotal Church of the West in the sixth century, as it would seem. It could have been used in any age previous to the time when confession was made compulsory. But the writer of these words would not have dreamt of admitting that this freedom of the Gospel belonged to a man, except as a member of the Church, baptized and anointed and a communicant, and therefore dependent on the ministry of her clergy.

Thus the principle of the ministry must not be assailed either on the ground that it "interposes a sacerdotal caste between the soul and God," or on the ground that it connives at the spiritual indolence of men, by offering them official substitutes to do their religion at second hand.[2]

---

[1] S. Laurentii *Hom.* i *de Poenit.* in *Bibl. Max. Vet. Patr.* ix. p. 466 h. This and the following sermon of Laurentius (probably of Novera, c. A.D. 507; see *Dict. Chr. Biog.*, s. v. LAURENTIUS (15) surnamed Mellifluus) are full of the thought of various activities of the will as opening the way of restoration from sin and making despair foolish : "Homo, noli diffidere : res in promptu est, vita in manu est: virtus in voluntate est: victoria in arbitrio est: si voluisti, vicisti" (*l.c.* pp. 468-9). The activity emphasized is sometimes penitence and tears; sometimes almsgiving, "aqua et ablutio et remissio in eleemosyna largientis est" (ib.); sometimes fasting (p. 474 g). These avail against any abundance of sins.

[2] A word must be said to vindicate the true sacerdotalism from interfering with the unique Priesthood or High-Priesthood of Christ. Surely the representatives of a king do not interfere with his monarchy, and a Christian

The ministerial principle, then,—the sacerdotalism *The true sacerdotalism.* which cannot be disparaged or repudiated—means just this: that Christianity is the life of an organized society in which a graduated body of ordained ministers is made the instrument of unity. The religious life, so far as it concerns the relations of man to God, has two aspects. It is first an approach of man to God. And in this relation each Christian has in his own personal life a perfect freedom of access. But he has this because he belongs to the one body, and this one body has its central act of approach to God in the great memorial oblation of the Death of Christ. Here it approaches in due and consecrated order; all are offerers, but they offer through one who is empowered to this high charge, to 'offer the gifts' for God's acceptance and the consecration of His Spirit. In the second place, religion is a gift of God to man—a gift of Himself. What man receives in Christ is the very life of God. Here again, each Christian receives the gift as an endowment of his own personal life; his

---

minister is in a relation to Christ infinitely more dependent than that of any representative of an absent king to him who sends him. If we were consistent, such a notion of the 'jealousy' of Christ as militates against a ministerial priesthood would make us 'fifth-monarchy men,' because kings as much interfere with His unique Kingship as ministers do with His Ministry. Nor is it very consistent to accuse the ministerial priesthood at once of interfering with the incommunicable Priesthood of Christ and also with the priesthood which He has communicated to all His members. The Church indeed must have a priesthood, not although Christ has one, but because He has. What He is, the Church is in Him. All He is in His Human Nature, the Church is; in Him the Church has a priesthood therefore, because Christ is High Priest. The only question is as to the distribution of functions in the Church, and whether Christ has willed to delegate a special sort of authority to a special class of men to be exercised in His name for the good of the whole body—and this is a question of evidence, with which we are not here dealing.

whole life may become a life of grace, a life of drinking in the Divine Spirit, of eating the Flesh of Christ, and drinking His Blood. But the individual life can receive this fellowship with God only through membership in the one body and by dependence upon social sacraments of regeneration, of confirmation, of communion, of absolution,—of which ordained ministers are the appointed instruments. A fundamental principle of Christianity is that of social dependence.

In all departments of life we are dependent one on another. There is a priesthood of science ministering the mysteries of nature, exercising a very real authority and claiming, very justly, a large measure of deference. There is a priesthood of art, ministering and interpreting to men that beauty which is one of the modes of God's revelation of Himself in material forms. There is a priesthood of political influence, and that not exercised at will, but organized and made authoritative in offices of state.[1] There is a natural priesthood of spiritual influence belonging (whether they will it or not) to men of spiritual power. It is to this natural priesthood that God offers the support of a visible authoritative commission in sacred things—'to feed His sheep.' The Christian ministry is at once, under normal circumstances, God's provi-

---

[1] "If it be granted, as it well may be, that proper qualifications are a hundredfold more requisite for the Christian ministry than for any other office, this would not remove nor lessen the obligation not to dispense with a divine commission, supposing it to have been granted and still attainable, any more than the highest legal knowledge or perfect integrity of character would dispense with the necessity of a commission from the source of temporal power to render the decisions of a magistrate of state binding and effectual" (Denton *Grace of the Ministry* p. 23).

sion to strengthen the hands of the spiritual men, the natural guides of souls, by giving them the support which comes of the consciousness of an irreversible and authoritative commission: and it is also God's provision for days when prophets are few or wanting, that even then there may be the bread of life ministered to hungering souls, and at least the simple proclamation of the revealed truth, so that even then 'men's eyes may see their teachers.'

(2) But it will be said: Such a doctrine would be credible enough if the priests of the Gospel had been, or were at present, in the main men of spiritual power, or even universally good men. But how is it conceivable that men of evil or utterly unspiritual lives, such as too many of the clergy have been, can be God's instruments to impart His spiritual gifts to others? Surely spiritual gifts must come from spiritual persons. *(2) 'Unspiritual men cannot impart spiritual gifts.'*

Church history records how strongly this objection has often appealed to men, but it is one which rather admits of being strongly felt than consistently argued. It would have of course much more force if it were possible reasonably to deny that, on the whole, in Christian history spiritual office and spiritual character have tended to converge; that, on the whole, the ministry has been a spiritualizing force in society. As it is, it may be briefly met with a threefold answer. First, we reply, with Pope Stephen and St. Augustin of old,[1] that 'the unworthiness of the *But we are forced to distinguish between character and office*

---

[1] See *Dict. Chr. Biog.* s.v. CYPRIAN i. p. 752. Of course the force of this argument depends on the recognition that there are such things as sacra-

ministers hinders not the grace of the sacrament,' because the Holy Spirit, and not they, is the giver of the grace; they neither 'give it being nor add force to it.' Secondly—and so far as the argument relates to the intention of Christ in founding His Church—we reply that He clearly recognised that moral unworthiness does not interfere with official authority. The Scribes and Pharisees who sat in Moses' seat—who held, that is, the succession from Moses—were to be obeyed, even where they were least to be imitated; and all 'the twelve' had equally the authority and powers of the apostolate, though 'one of them was a devil.' Thirdly, we reply that the possibility of ministers unworthy of their office is involved in the very idea of a visible society in which good and bad are to be mixed together. There is really no more difficulty in believing that bad men can share the functions of the ministerial priesthood than that bad men share the priesthood which belongs to all Christians and which differs from the other, as has been said, not in kind but in application and degree. Yet the whole method of appeal used by the apostolic writers to unworthy Christians, is to address them not as men who lack the prerogatives and spiritual powers of the Christian life, but as men who do not 'walk worthily of the vocation with which they were called.' There is really again no more difficulty in recognising in a bad priest a steward of

mental channels of grace. The personal defects of the minister gain a wholly new importance in religious bodies where sacraments, creeds, and liturgies are unrecognised, i.e. where all his usefulness depends on his personal character and capacities.

Apostolic Succession.

divine mysteries than in a bad magistrate a steward of the divine justice, a 'minister of God for good.'[1] "There is this difference," says an old writer,[2] "betwixt the ecclesiastical ministers or magistrates and ministers or magistrates of state; if these offend, the whole world can distinguish between their persons and their functions; no disparagement falleth upon any but the offenders. But if ecclesiastical persons become obnoxious, then they confound their persons and their functions, and transfer the shame of the faults of some even upon all, yea upon the whole order itself."

(3) Now we approach another objection: The apostolical succession is associated with bygone ideas of authority, with the divine right of kings, and a state of society which is gone for ever; it is incompatible with the true ideal of liberty. *(3) 'It is inconsistent with the modern ideal of liberty.'*

It is astonishing how frequently, and from what opposite quarters, we meet with the identification of Christianity with that phase of Christianity which is characteristic of the Middle Ages. At that period we become witnesses of a process which is at least of absorbing interest. The untamed, undisciplined races which formed the material of modern nations are subjected to the yoke of the Church (mostly at the will of kings or chiefs), as to an external law which is to train, mould, restrain them. The one need of such an age is authority, discipline, rule. The Church becomes largely a 'schoolmaster to bring men to *But the Church is not to be identified with mediaeval absolutism,*

---

[1] Rom. xiii. 3-6.
[2] Isidore of Pelusium *Epist.* ii. 52 (paraphrased by Hickes *Dignity of Episc. Order* in his *Treatises* [Oxon. 1847] ii. p. 288).

G

Christ'—a law preparing for a Gospel. She has, under these circumstances, to do with children in mind. The one faculty which is in full exercise is faith, in the form of a great readiness to accept revelations of the supernatural world and to respect their ministers—the sort of faith which wants nothing but dogmatic clearness and a sufficiently firm voice of authority.[1] Christianity thus becomes, by a one-sided development, a great imperial and hierarchical system.

Such a state of things is not permanent. Men's faculties develop into free exercise, and constitute their separate departments according to an inevitable law, as knowledge grows and life becomes more complex. Other natural 'priesthoods' arise—in art, in science, in medicine, in politics, in trade, in law—and become the successful rivals, in their own spheres, of the spiritual hierarchy. The Church, to all appearance, suffers loss, though in regions which were not properly her own at all, at least in such sense as to justify her in dictating terms to the pioneers in each on their own subject-matter. Thus the area in which religious authority speaks and faith accepts becomes limited. More than this: authority itself tends to change its character; it ceases to be absolute in religion no less than in politics; and this change affects the Church, not only as a dogmatic authority, but as a government. It affects her hierarchical

[1] The saintly writers, like St. Bernard, who lived in these vaunted 'ages of faith,' do not suggest a too favourable view of them. They help us to see that an unspiritual credulity, such as characterized those times, is no nearer Christian faith, in its full sense, than a good deal of modern scepticism.

system. Mere imperialism will no longer suffice, at least for the most vigorous or intelligent races, in the Church, any more than in the State. Democracy, the representative system, is in the air as much as free inquiry and has to be reckoned with.

But in politics this transition does not mean a repudiation of the principle of authority. "What the world thirsts for at present," said Joseph Mazzini, who was surely no friend to despotism, "is authority."[1] What has come about is a change in the conditions of authority, in the character which it must assume. This holds true in the Church also; there, too, authority must cease to be absolutism and faith mere acceptance. Authority, however, is not less real because it is limited, or faith less zealous because it is rational and inquiring.[2] But then it is said: 'You are really abandoning the principle; you are only trying to cloak your surrender by keeping a name, emptied of its power. The authority of a Church or hierarchy really ceases when it cannot dictate its own terms, when it has to submit to criticism.' To this objection there seems to be a complete answer, and one which

[margin: and true liberty is opposed to absolutism not to authority.]

---

[1] See his *Thoughts upon Democracy in Europe*, cf. "On the Duties of Man," chap. viii : "Liberty is not the negation of all authority : it is the negation of every authority which fails to represent the *Collective Aim* of the nation."

[2] "Is a limited, conditional government in the State such a wise, excellent, and glorious constitution? And is the same authority in the Church such absurdity, nonsense, and nothing at all, as to any actual power? If there be such a thing as obedience upon rational motives, there must be such a thing as authority that is not absolute, or that does not require a blind, implicit obedience. Indeed, rational creatures can obey no other authority; they must have reasons for what they do. And yet because the Church claims only this rational obedience, your Lordship explodes such authority as none at all" (Law's *First Letter to the Bishop of Bangor* in his *Works* [ed. 1762] i. pp. 30, 31).

needs to be forced on the consideration of men. Christianity did not come into existence in the West or just in time for the Middle Ages. Christianity spread in a Greek world—in a society of the most developed sort, containing all the elements of intellectual development in free activity. If we want to know the original character of Christian authority and Christian faith, we should study Greek church life from St. Paul to the fifth century, or, at any rate, early church life before Western Christianity took the peculiar colour of Romanism.

<small>Government in the early Church was representative.</small>

We are concerned here, however, not with Christianity as a dogma, but with the social life and government of the Church. In this department then, when we look back to the life of the early Christian communities, what a beautiful picture of freedom, of representative institutions, of the correlation of rights and duties, we find for our contemplation. The sacred ministry receives indeed its authority from above, and acts in God's name, as God's representative; but the man who is to minister is the elect of the people, and is their representative also. Thus the Apostles ordained the first deacons, but the Church elected them. "Look ye out, brethren, from among you seven men of good report, whom we may appoint over this business." So spoke the Apostles to the first Christians. "And the saying pleased the whole multitude: and they chose seven men: whom they set before the Apostles: and when they had prayed, they laid their hands upon them." So in the subapostolic age Clement speaks of the presbyter-bishops as ordained from above,[1] but with *the consent of the whole Church,* and in such a way as to suggest that, under certain circumstances, they were not exempt from the judgment of the Church. Other documents of the first age speak in the same way of the election of bishops by the community.[2] Nor does this method of popular election, or control over election, appear only in the dim shadow of the subapostolic age: counteracted at all times by other influences,[3] it yet lasted on as the ideal of the Church for centuries. The emperor Alexander Severus " was fond of praising the careful way in which the Church posted the names of all whom she destined for the priesthood, so that any, who knew evil of them, might object."[4] He would have it made a model in the appointment of provincial governors. We know, again, that the bishop to be elected over any Church was to be thoroughly known in the Church—one who had passed through the inferior grades of the ministry. "That custom is to be diligently observed," says Cyprian, "as of divine tradition and apostolic observance, which is maintained amongst us also and almost over all provinces, that,

---

[1] Clem. *ad Cor.* 40 and 44. More will be said on this.

[2] *Didache* xv. 1: χειροτονήσατε οὖν ἑαυτοῖς ἐπισκόπους καὶ διακόνους. Cf. also the curious and very ancient *Apost. Ch. Ordinances* 16: "If there be a paucity of men, and in any place there be a number less than twelve of those who can vote for a bishop."

[3] As in the first period by prophetic nomination; see Clem. Alex. *Quis Dives* 42: "St. John would go about here to appoint bishops, . . . there to ordain to the clergy *some one of those pointed out by the Spirit.*"

[4] Mason *Diocletian Persecution* pp. 84, and 85n.[1] "dicebatque grave esse, cum id Christiani et Iudaei facerent in praedicandis sacerdotibus qui ordinandi sunt, non fieri in provinciarum rectoribus quibus et fortunae hominum committerentur et capita " (Ael. Lampr. *Alex.* xlv. 7).

with a view to the due celebration of ordinations, the neighbouring bishops of the same province should come together to the community for which a ruler is to be ordained, and the bishop should be chosen in the presence of the people who have complete knowledge of each man's life and conduct by his conversation among them."[1] This popular check on ordinations he requires no less for the presbyterate and the diaconate. So, again, it is regarded by Pope Julius as monstrous that "Gregory, a stranger to the city, who had not been baptized there and was not known to the community in general and had not been asked for by presbyters or bishops or people," should be obtruded on the Church of Alexandria, "whereas the ordination of a bishop ought not to have taken place thus lawlessly and contrary to the ecclesiastical canon, but he should have been ordained in the Church itself (over which he is to rule), out of the priesthood, out of the actual body of the clergy, and not, as now, in violation of the canons which come from the Apostles."[2] Again Leo the Great, 'the founder of the papacy,' writes: "He who is to preside over all must be elected by all." "Before a consecration must go the suffrages of the citizens, the approbation of the people, the judgment of persons of distinction, the choice of the clergy—that the rule of apostolic authority may be in all respects observed, which enjoins that a priest to govern the Church should be supported not only by the approval of the

---

[1] *Ep.* lxvii. 5; see Bingham *Ant.* ii. 10. 2.
[2] ap. Athan. *Apol. c. Ar.* 30.

faithful, but also by the testimony of those without." "No metropolitan should we allow to ordain a priest (bishop) on his own judgment without the consent of clergy and people: the consent of the whole community must elect the president of the Church:" only where division makes unanimity impossible the metropolitan may decide the election in favour of the man who has the best support. "No reason can tolerate that persons should be held to be bishops" (so he says on another occasion to the African clergy) "who were neither chosen by the clergy, nor demanded by the laity, nor ordained by the provincial bishops with the consent of the metropolitan."[1] Quotations to this effect might be greatly multiplied, and from later sources. The Latin rites of ordination are framed in recognition of this representative system.[2] This then was undoubtedly *the ideal* of the bishop's election in the early Church.[3] The bishop was to be really the *persona* of the Church he ruled.

This, moreover, he was enabled to be in some real sense in virtue of the very small community over which he presided. Through the greater part at least of the Roman empire each town community had its bishop, and the country-bishop supplemented his authority in the surrounding district, first in the East and later in the West. The bishop of Rome

[1] Leo *Epp.* x. 4-6; xiii. 3; xiv. 5; clxvii. 1.
[2] See App. Note C. Cf. also Bp. Woodford *The Great Commission*, pp. 126-132.
[3] On the extent and limits of its observance see Bingham *Ant.* ii. 10. 3-7; also *Dict. Chr. Ant.* s.v. BISHOP. Mr. Haddan, the author, remarks how vaguely the words suffragium testimonium iudicium consensus are used (i. p. 214). Vague unformulated rights are more easily overridden.

was in an extraordinary position in the middle of the third century, because he had under him as many as forty-six presbyters, seven deacons, and seven sub-deacons, besides those of minor orders.¹ Ordinarily the numbers would have been very much smaller. Thus the bishop, according to the early ideal, was by no means the great prelate; he was the pastor of a flock, like the vicar of a modern town, in intimate relations with all his people.²

and not absolute. Nor was he in theory absolute even within the limits of his 'parish' or diocese. For, in the first place, he was himself subject to the laws which he administered. When St. Chrysostom is referring to the custom of holding the Gospel over the head of the bishop who is being ordained, he says that it is to remind him that "if he is the head of all, yet he acts under these laws (of the Gospel), ruling all and ruled by the law, ordering all and himself ordered:" it is a symbol of the fact that he is "under authority."³ At first indeed this authority had no visible sanction; St. Cyprian claims repeatedly for the bishop that he is "responsible to none but God." Later it came to be embodied in provincial and ecumenical councils. Secondly, within his own diocese he shared his rule with others. No doubt his power was not subject to *formal* limitations; but round him there was the council of his presbyters, "the Church's senate;"⁴ and St. Cyprian tells us that he made it a fixed rule

---

[1] Euseb. *H.E.* vi. 43.
[2] The facts are well known: see Bingham *Ant.* ii. 12, Hatch *B.L.* lect. viii. The principle is exemplified in the *Apost. Ch. Ordinances* 16.
[3] Bingham *Ant.* ii. 11. 8.   [4] Bingham *Ant.* ii. 19. 7.

from his consecration "to do nothing on his own private judgment, but everything with the counsel of his clergy and the consent of his laity."¹ The whole conception indeed of the diocesan synod was the basis of a great representative system which culminated at last in the ecumenical council.² Thus the ideal of church government in early days was not at all absolute. If the guilds of the Roman empire represented, as they did, the elements of free life and spontaneous movement through all the classes of non-Christian society down to the lowest, the principle of liberty and spontaneity was at least as prominent and real in the supernatural society of the Church. It was by no means necessarily an imperialist institution, though its officers were of divine authority and apostolic descent.

But the effect of 'establishment' in the East was to tend to assimilate the Church to the empire in ideas and methods no less than in gradation of dignities. In the West the essentially imperialist temper of Rome moulded the institutions of Christendom, and gave them a new direction and new characteristics. Thus in the fifth century Socrates remarks that "the episcopate of the Romans, like that of the Alexandrians, had already for some time advanced beyond the limits proper to the priesthood to the point of despotism."³ So it was that episcopacy passed into *The change to imperialism.*

---

¹ *Ep.* xiv. 4. See other references in Bingham *Ant.* ii. 19. 7, 8.

² Cf. art. CYPRIAN in *Dict. Chr. Biog.* i. p. 753: "the assembly representative: each bishop the elect of his flock."

³ πέρα τῆς ἱερωσύνης ἐπὶ δυναστείαν ἤδη πάλαι προελθούσης (*H.E.* vii. 11). He is speaking of Celestine suppressing the Novatian body in Rome. Cf. vii. 7.

a new phase. The authority of kings and popes overwhelmed the democratic elements in the Christian polity. If they survived, they survived rather as names and forms than as realities. But names and forms still bear witness beyond their present power to a principle which is not dead.

Thus the mediaeval and modern prelate, Anglican or Roman, is not the only, or the original, type of bishop. He differs a good deal from the bishop of the earliest period—not indeed in fundamental, spiritual principle, but in outward appearance and rank.[1] We need not necessarily deplore the change. The age of barbarism and the age of feudalism had each its own needs, and the Church adapted herself to them. But there is a protest, based on the facts of church history, which it is essential to make:— it is against all language such as would imply that Christianity had no history before it became dominated by imperialism and embedded in feudalism. The catholic principle is not Romanism merely or Byzantinism, nor is it identified with the Anglican episcopate of monarchical and aristocratic days. It has its roots deeper down in human nature than any of these. If, then, the imperialism which coloured church theology and church organization is becoming a thing of the past, there is nothing in church principles to prevent our saying: Let it die. 'The powers that be'—the actually existing authorities of the new age—'are ordained of God.' Meanwhile

not necessarily permanent.

---

[1] Dr. Hatch describes the change in *B.L.* lect. viii and *Growth of Ch. Instit.* See also Rosmini *Five Wounds of the Holy Church* ch. v.

let us disentangle the essential and permanent creed, the essential and permanent organization, from the passing phase of civilization in which it has become embedded; let us make clear what church principles essentially are. We shall not be afraid of the 'democratic' temper within the Church, so far as it is a return upon the Church's earliest spirit or an application of it. There is however one essential principle of all politics, secular and spiritual, which must be kept steadily in view: 'political rights are only the correlative of political duties done.' This is always the church principle. Whatever rights the Christian layman should have, it must be as a Christian layman, i.e. as subject himself to the divine authority of the Gospel and to the Church, the common mother of clergy and of laity. For it is only as subject to discipline that we can take any part in the exercise of it, and the lesson which Chrysostom finds in the ceremony of episcopal consecration applies to the layman in his degree, at least as much as to the bishop in his: 'the layman is bound by the layman's ordinances.'

(4) It has been contended by Lord Macaulay—and the contention was not a new one—that, however much the Church may have insisted on apostolic succession, as a matter of fact the chances are overwhelming against its having been preserved. "Whether a given clergyman be really a successor of the Apostles depends on an immense number of such contingencies as these; whether, under King Ethelwolf, a stupid priest might not, while baptizing

^{(4) 'It cannot have been maintained unbroken.'}

several scores of Danish prisoners who had just made their option between the font and the gallows, inadvertently omit to perform the rite on one of these graceless proselytes; whether, in the seventh century, an impostor, who had never received consecration, might not have passed himself off as a bishop on a rude tribe of Scots; whether a lad of twelve did really, by a ceremony huddled over when he was too drunk to know what he was about, convey the episcopal character to a lad of ten."[1]

<small>This objection does not hold;</small> Such an argument has nothing to recommend it except the vigour of Lord Macaulay's style. Indeed, if we take it on its own level, its force is gone when once it is borne in mind that failures of baptism do not enter into the question of the permanent succession, except where the person whose baptism was omitted or irregular subsequently became a bishop; and that invalidating irregularities in episcopal ordinations, when they exist, would not have the effect which the objection supposes, because succession comes of interlacing lines, each bishop having as a rule been consecrated by three of his order.[2] In fact it has

---

[1] Essay on *Gladstone on Church and State*. Chillingworth cannot be quoted in this sense, because in his argument (*Relig. of Prot.* ch. ii. 67) he is taking into account that "very dungeon of uncertainty," the Romanist doctrine of intention.

[2] The three consecrators were required originally not to secure validity (in case one of the bishops was, by some accidental omission of a necessary rite, no real bishop at all), but as a guarantee of general provincial recognition. The other consideration is perhaps too materialistic to have entered into the mind of the early Church. When things were duly done according to Christ's ordinance, they were regarded as certainly having His certificate. But when validity came to be conceived under more materialistic conditions at a later period of theology, it was natural to suppose that each bishop who joined in the act of consecration gave additional security that it was valid. They were cooperatores and not merely testes. The point is, however,

II.] *Apostolic Succession.* 109

been mathematically argued that, even if we make the absurd supposition of one consecrator in twenty at any particular moment in history having been, through some accident, himself not validly consecrated, the chances will be 8000 : 1 against all three consecrators in any given case being in a like position, and the chances against a bishop consecrated under such circumstances, who would thus be no bishop, being combined with coadjutors similarly incapacitated to continue the succession, are "as 512,000,000,000 to unity."[1]

But a much better answer to such a suggested difficulty lies in the consideration that, if we have reason to believe that Christ intended to institute a self-perpetuating ministry in His Church, He makes Himself responsible for its possibility, and His power is not limited by such material conditions. "Leaving, then, all hidden things to Him to whose sole cognizance they belong, we may securely depend on His goodness and justice, that so long as His sacred appointments are maintained, as far as lies in our power, we shall never suffer through any secret blemish or incapacity of His ministers."[2] *and we are responsible for no more than obedience.*

(5) 'But,' it will be exclaimed, 'however reasonable the idea of a ministerial succession may be—however adaptable in principle to new conditions of society and thought—*in fact* it has become so unreasonable and so stereotyped, so fatally conservative of what was *(5) 'It would unchurch non-episcopal bodies.'*

discussed: see Estcourt *Question of Angl. Ord.* pp. 110-114. I do not pursue the question, because I do not lay stress on the argument in the text.

[1] Gladstone *Ch. Princ.* pp. 235, 236.
[2] Archbp. Potter: quoted by Denton *Grace of the Ministry* p. 258.

shown to be false and corrupt, at epochs of past history that great Christian nations, or great bodies of Christian men, have broken away from its organization. Are these, then, which have no succession, or a succession which you declare invalid, to be " unchurched "—to be declared outside the pale of the covenant and left in unrecognised isolation?' This question is always being asked in tones of passionate appeal or indignant remonstrance. As we shall have occasion to recur to Preliminary answer. the problem the less need be said here. Suppose, however, an impartial investigation to convince us that a ministerial succession was really part of Christ's intention and belongs only to the episcopal Churches in a legitimate sense, it will surely be our duty to maintain it and be faithful to it. Nor, if we are at all familiar with the disappointing side of church history, shall we be greatly surprised that its corruptions have bred revolt. These corruptions are, no doubt, so many apologies for the revolters. It is conceivable that they may reach the point of excusing revolt in particular cases and throwing the blame of it on the representatives of authority. If that were so, or so far as it was so, we shall abstain from condemning individuals or races, but we shall not abandon principles. Men are dealt with according to their opportunities; and as God's love is not limited by His covenant, so He *can* work through ministrations which are not 'valid'—that is, ministrations which have not the security of the covenant. But though God can do this, we have no right to claim it of Him. If He is not bound to His sacraments, we men, up to the limits of our knowledge,[1] certainly are. However excusable many may be in ignorance of divine institutions, we shall not be excusable if we are faithless to them for fear of hurting other men's feelings or disturbing existing arrangements. Such conduct would be most false charity, most real treachery. Bishop Butler[2] reminds us "how great presumption it is to make light of any institutions of divine appointment;" and he emphasizes to us "the moral obligation, in the strictest and most proper sense," which attaches to any command "merely positive, admitted to be from God." And if anything could increase this obligation, it would be the sense that we are living through an age of change. It is when there is a general 'shaking' of existing establishments—of all that has been merely recognised and customary—that religiously-minded men are likely to be driven back upon those institutions which can give the completest guarantee of security and permanence.

With this much preface, giving (it may be hoped) a clearer idea of what the principle of the ministry and of the apostolic succession may really be said to mean, we turn to the witness of history.

[1] When we speak of 'essentials' in religion, it is of course important to recall that God is a father and equitable, and that His action is not tied to His covenanted channels. There is a useful distinction drawn by Roman Catholic theologians between things necessary to salvation necessitate medii, i.e. absolutely and in all cases, and things necessary necessitate praecepti, i.e. obligatory upon all who are within the hearing of a divine ordinance. Only the right disposition of will is (we may say) essential in the first sense. This may exist under all conditions of ignorance. All else is necessary in proportion as we come under the responsibilities of nearness to God's revelation of Himself (cf. Newman's *Parochial Sermons* vol. vi. pp. 170, 171— 'Faith the Title for Justification').

[2] *Analogy* part II. ch. i.

CHAPTER III.

THE WITNESS OF CHURCH HISTORY.

The ministry in church history

THE conception of the Christian ministry described in the last chapter is confessedly no mere ideal. It represents what has been, beyond a doubt, a fact of primary importance in the Christianity of history.

In many respects, indeed, if we were to trace back the genealogy of the ministry in the Church, we should find that it has passed through strange vicissitudes, and from time to time has wonderfully changed its appearance. It may be well to call attention to this at once, so that variations of aspect, which are even startling, may serve to make more emphatic the principles and facts which have been throughout permanent and unchanging.[1]

in spite of variable features

For example, the episcopate of the first period, when, speaking generally, every town Church had its independent episcopal organization and country bishops arose to superintend the scattered flocks of the rural districts, was a very different thing from the episcopate of the mediaeval epoch, when the great dioceses of Teutonic Europe were formed, when bishops became great feudal lords, and the feudal character at times almost superseded the spiritual.

---

[1] Cf. Dr. Liddon *A Father in Christ* p. 26 f.

Very different again was the organization of the Celtic Church of Ireland (and thence of Scotland), where the presbyter-abbots were the real ecclesiastical rulers and the succession of abbots the important succession, while the episcopate, indefinitely multiplied, had its place only as the necessary 'instrument of spiritual generation,' or the appropriate decoration of sanctity, in entire subordination to the monastic authority.

Again, there have been vast changes in the relation of the bishops to secular society, and in their relation to one another. There has been the slow development of the metropolitan system on the lines of the imperial organization; the upgrowth of the papacy; the rise of national Churches; the schisms of the eleventh and sixteenth centuries. There have been 'Erastian' epochs, whether under the Byzantine and Frankish emperors or under English kings, and epochs, on the other hand, when a king[1] could complain that "absolutely the only persons who reign are the bishops," or when a pope could claim, as in the famous bull *Unam Sanctam*, to have the sword of secular authority committed to him as well as that of ecclesiastical government.

Again, there have been days when bishops administered, and submitted to, a rigorous discipline, such as finds expression in the early Spanish council of Elvira, and days of the collapse of discipline, such as gives the tone of something like despair to the lamentations of Basil and Gregory of Nyssa in the Arian

---

[1] Chilperic (Greg. Tur. *H. F.* vi. 46); but the context, as well as the circumstances, take away from the force of this.

period in the East, or such as Isidore and Gregory of Tours describe in the West.

There have been, once again, great changes in the idea of episcopal election, as it passes out of the primitive method—which made the bishop the real representative of the community in the midst of which he had grown up, 'behaving himself well in the inferior offices,'—to become the prerogative in fact, if not in name, of metropolitans, or popes, or kings.

<small>has been governed throughout by fixed principles.</small>
These have been immense changes. In part they have been inevitable and beneficial; in part the recognition of them should be a stimulus to the Church to recover in idea, and so at last in fact, a primitive standard which ought never to have been abandoned. But all through these changes there have been certain fixed principles[1] of supreme importance, which have been uniformly maintained, and which all the changes in outward circumstance only serve to throw into stronger relief, and it is with these alone that we are here concerned. These fixed principles represent what the Church has continuously believed with reference to the ministry, and consistently acted upon (let us say to start with) since the middle of the second century down to the period of the Reformation. They may be expressed thus:

[1] A sermon of Dean Stanley's—"The Burning Bush" (quoted in *Remarks on Dr. Lightfoot's Essay on the Christian Ministry*, by C. Wordsworth, Bishop of St. Andrews, pp. 2-6)—illustrates how these fixed principles can be ignored. He describes, for instance, the mediaeval abbeys and the great universities as "fragments of presbyterianism imbedded in the midst of the episcopate" (p. 4). Their relation to the papacy is quite forgotten.

(1) that Christ instituted in His Church, by succession from the Apostles, a permanent Ministry of truth and grace, 'of the word and sacraments,' as an indispensable part of her organization and continuous corporate life: such as the requirement of apostolic succession, etc.

(2) that while there are different offices in this ministry, especially an episcopate, a presbyterate, and a diaconate—with functions and mutual relations fundamentally fixed, though containing also variable elements,—there belongs to the order of Bishops,[1] and to them alone, the power to perpetuate the ministry in its several grades, by the transmission of the authority received from the Apostles, its original depositaries; so that, as a consequence, no ministry except such as has been received by episcopal ordination can be legitimately or validly exercised in the Church:

(3) that the transmission of ministerial authority, or Ordination, is an outward act, of a sacramental

---

[1] I reckon the bishops as a distinct *order*, discussing, however, such a position as that of Ambrosiaster or Jerome on the subject and such considerations as are involved in the supposed peculiarities of the early Alexandrian ministry. The later tendency to reckon the episcopate as constituting with the presbyterate only one ordo sacerdotum (*Catech. Conc. Trident.* ii. 7. 25) was due partly to the desire to emphasize the pre-eminent dignity of the sacerdotium; partly to the desire to reduce church orders to the mystical number of seven; partly to the wide influence of Jerome in the West. It has its parallel in early days when the bishop was sometimes reckoned with the presbytery. But so long as bishops are regarded as having special functions of their own, which presbyters cannot validly perform, and are ordained with a special ordination (*Catech. Conc. Trident.* l.c.) the exact ordering of grades is rather a matter of nomenclature. See on the variations *Dict. Chr. Ant.* ii. pp. 1474-5 s.v. ORDERS, HOLY. Morinus, however, among more recent Roman theologians (A.D. 1686) says of those who reckon eight orders of the ministry, major and minor, by counting the episcopate as a distinct order: "huic sententiae plurimum favent rituales omnes tam Graeci quam Latini et universa prope ecclesiae traditio" (*de S. Ord.* p. iii. ex. i. 2. 26), and his authority is deservedly very high.

character, in which the laying-on of hands, with prayer, is 'the visible sign.' It will appear also

(4) that the Church, without change of principle, and merely by the clearing-up of ideas, came to reckon the effect of ordination as indelible, and to recognise as a Priesthood the ministry of bishops and presbyters, which it conferred.

The general recognition of these principles during the period specified will hardly be matter of dispute. "In the latter part of the second century of the Christian era, the subject [of the apostolic succession] came into distinct and formal view; and from that time forward it seems to have been considered by the great writers of the catholic body a fact too palpable to be doubted, and too simple to be misunderstood."[1] The agreement, however, as to what has historically been accepted in the Church on the subject of the ministry is not nearly complete enough to render argument unnecessary. We proceed then, first of all, to review the evidence for the existence of the threefold ministry, after the middle of the second century,[2] with the accompanying principle of the apostolic succession, and the limitation to bishops of the right of ordination.

Evidence produced I. Of the episcopal successions from A.D. 150,

as appealed to by Irenaeus.

I. The basis shall be laid in the testimony of Irenaeus. Irenaeus had been born in Asia Minor not later than A.D. 130.[3] He tells us that in early youth he had sat at the feet of Polycarp, "who had been appointed by

---

[1] Gladstone *Church Principles* p. 189.
[2] The reason for not at first going back behind about A.D. 150 will appear afterwards.
[3] For this and other details of St. Irenaeus' life see *Dict. Chr. Biog.* iii. p. 253 f.

Apostles a bishop for Asia in the Church of Smyrna "—a venerable old man, whose appearance and ways of life were, he assures us, indelibly imprinted on his memory —and that he had listened to his discourses in public and private,[1] and that he had also had opportunities of instruction by Asiatic "elders," amongst whom some at least had been disciples of Apostles. Thus imbued with the traditions of the Asiatic Church, in which especially St. John's influence was a living reality, he passed as a young man, probably before Polycarp's martyrdom (c. A.D. 155), from Asia to Rome. How long he remained there we do not know; but at the latest in the year 177, when the persecution fell upon the Churches of South Gaul and the aged bishop Pothinus was one of many victims, Irenaeus was a presbyter of Lyons, and he succeeded the martyr in his episcopal see. Previously, however, he had visited Rome, in order "to promote the peace of the Church" by bearing communications from the Gallican confessors to Eleutherus, the bishop, on the subject of the Montanist controversy.[2] True to his name of 'peaceful,' he again intervened, as has been already mentioned, in the dispute between Victor of Rome and the Asiatic Churches in the matter of keeping Easter, to rebuke Victor for his hasty breach of ecclesiastical unity on the ground of an indifferent matter of custom, not of the faith.

---

[1] See his epistle to Florinus in Euseb. *H. E.* v. 20.
[2] Euseb. *H. E.* v. 3, 4: *Dict. Chr. Biog.* iii. p. 937 s.v. MONTANUS. It is *possible* that there was at this time no other episcopal see in Gaul than that of Lyons and that Irenaeus was consecrated at Rome. Eusebius speaks of the παροικιαι κατὰ Γαλλίαν ἆs Εἰρηναῖος ἐπεσκόπει.

The value of his witness.

Thus much account of the man has been given in order to emphasize his remarkable connection alike with the apostolic traditions which lingered in that last home of the apostolic band, the Churches of Asia, and with the sentiments of the contemporary Churches both of East and West. Irenaeus was fitted by circumstances, as well as by character, to be what he preeminently claims to be, the staunch maintainer of apostolic tradition. Of course the "tradition of the elders"[1] to which he so frequently refers is not infallible.[2] Elders may have made mistakes, or Irenaeus' memory may have been treacherous as to this or that point of their record, in spite of his assertion that he recalled the scenes of his youth when he was in the company of Polycarp in all their details with more precision than recent events. The value of tradition depends very much on the exact point for which it is alleged. But a mistake or failure of memory, not hard to account for in details of tradition, cannot invalidate his testimony on matters of such primary importance as the character and traditional reputation of the church ministry, or, to take another example, the authority of the four Gospels during the period covered by his own eastern and western experience. On such matters a mistake is hardly possible.

---

[1] ap. Euseb. *H. E.* v. 20 (the epistle to Florinus).

[2] He gives us, on the authority not only of Papias but also of other "elders" who remembered St. John to have related it among our Lord's discourses, the fabulous prophecy ascribed to Him of the Millennium Vines (v. 33. 3, 4). He bases also on the authority of these same elders,—"all the elders who had intercourse with John, the disciple of the Lord, in Asia"—as recording St. John's teaching, the statement that our Lord was over forty years old (ii. 22. 5).

III.]   *The Witness of Church History.*   119

We take Irenaeus, then, for our primary witness as to the apostolic succession. He is combating Gnosticism in his great work *Against the Heresies*, written probably during his episcopate; and in view of the imaginative idealism of the Gnostic teachers, he rests his case in the main on the historical revelation. He is therefore not so much occupied in developing a Christian 'science' over against the 'science falsely so called' of his opponents—this was rather the work of the Alexandrians—as in emphasizing what the rule of faith has been in the Churches as derived from the apostolic preaching.[1] In the consent of all the Churches he finds the security of the tradition. The case was put by his more epigrammatic disciple Tertullian in the question: "Is it probable that so many Churches of such importance should have hit by an accident of error on an identical creed?"[2] There is, then, ever before Irenaeus' eye, the picture of the universal Church, spread over all the world, handing down in unbroken succession the apostolic truth: and the bond of unity, the link to connect the generations in the Church, is the episcopal succession. Irenaeus' use of language, indeed, about the bishop is not quite determinate;[3] the venerable title of 'presbyter,' the 'ancient' or 'elder,' is still used in

His appeal to the episcopal successions,

---

[1] Γνῶσις ἀληθὴς ἡ τῶν ἀποστόλων διδαχὴ καὶ τὸ ἀρχαῖον τῆς ἐκκλησίας σύστημα κατὰ παντὸς τοῦ κόσμου (iv. 33. 8).

[2] "Ecquid verisimile est, ut tot ac tantae [ecclesiae] in unam fidem erraverint?" (*de Praescr.* 28.)

[3] That is, he calls the bishops also *presbyters*. See iii. 3. 2 (compared with iii. 2. 2); iv. 26. 2, 4, 5; Ep. ad Vict. ap. Euseb. *H.E.* v. 24. So the Anonymous Presbyter who writes against Montanism (ap. Euseb. *H. E.* v. 16) speaks of the church authorities at Ancyra, bishop no doubt included, as "the presbyters." So (as will appear) Clem. Alex., Origen, Firmilian.

an inclusive sense for the Church's rulers. But the idea is quite determinate. He regards the bishops in every Church as succeeding in an especial sense to the Apostles. They represent in every place by apostolic succession the catholic faith; they have the "gift of the truth" and the apostolic authority of government;[1] they are the guardians also no doubt of the grace by which Christians live, of which as much as of the truth the Church is the "rich treasury."[2] But it is mainly as preserving the catholic traditions that Irenaeus regards the apostolic succession. From this point of view he makes it without hesitation one of the

[1] "Charisma veritatis certum" (iv. 26. 2); "quos et successores [apostoli] relinquebant suum ipsorum locum magisterii tradentes" (iii. 3. 1).

[2] "Depositorium dives" (iii. 4. 1). Cf. iii. 24. 1, where he speaks of the Church as possessing "eam quae secundum salutem hominum est solitam operationem, quae est in fide nostra; quam perceptam ab ecclesia custodimus et quae semper a Spiritu Dei, quasi in vase bono eximium quoddam depositum iuvenescens et iuvenescere faciens ipsum vas in quo est. Hoc enim ecclesiae creditum est Dei munus, quemadmodum ad inspirationem plasmationi, ad hoc ut omnia membra percipientia vivificentur: et in eo disposita [? deposita] est communicatio Christi, id est Spiritus sanctus, arrha incorruptelae et confirmatio fidei nostrae et scala ascensionis ad Deum. In ecclesia enim, inquit, posuit Deus apostolos, prophetas, doctores et universam reliquam operationem Spiritus, cuius non sunt participes omnes qui non currunt ad ecclesiam. . . . Ubi enim ecclesia, ibi et Spiritus Dei, et ubi Spiritus Dei, illic ecclesia et omnis gratia; Spiritus autem veritas. Quapropter qui non participant eum, neque a mammillis matris nutriuntur in vitam, neque percipiunt de corpore Christi procedentem nitidissimum fontem." We observe here in what close and inseparable connection he puts the gifts of grace and truth. The gifts of grace he connects specially with the sacraments, regeneration with baptism (v. 15. 3), incorruption with the Eucharistic gifts (iv. 18. 5: ὡς γὰρ ἀπὸ γῆς ἄρτος, προσλαμβανόμενος τὴν ἔκκλησιν τοῦ θεοῦ, οὐκέτι κοινὸς ἄρτος ἐστίν, ἀλλ' εὐχαριστία, ἐκ δύο πραγμάτων συνεστηκυῖα, ἐπιγείου τε καὶ οὐρανίου· οὕτως καὶ τὰ σώματα ἡμῶν μεταλαμβάνοντα τῆς εὐχαριστίας μηκέτι εἶναι φθαρτά). It cannot, I think, be reasonably doubted that Irenaeus would have regarded the episcopate as entrusted with the ministry of the sacraments, no less than of the truth, though it was not his present business to lay stress on this; cf. his words to Victor (ap. Euseb. *H. E.* v. 24): "Anicetus allowed Polycarp to celebrate the Eucharist in the Church at Rome" (παρεχώρησεν τὴν εὐχαριστίαν). Already in Clement's epistle (c. 44) the "offering of the gifts" is the characteristic function of the bishop

primary essentials of Christianity. "The true knowledge" (so he calls the Christian religion) "is the doctrine of the Apostles, and the ancient system of the Church in all the world: and the character of the body of Christ, according to the successions of the bishops, to whom they [the Apostles] delivered the Church in each separate place: the complete use (moreover) of the Scriptures which has come down to our time, preserved without corruption, receiving neither addition nor loss; its public reading without falsification; legitimate and careful exposition according to the Scriptures, without peril and without blasphemy: and the pre-eminent gift of love."[1] Again, "The way of those who belong to the Church is encompassing the whole world, because it holds the tradition firm from the Apostles, and enables us to see that the faith of all is one and the same, while all teach one and the same God the Father, and believe the same dispensation of the Incarnation of the Son of God, and acknowledge the same gift of the Spirit, and meditate the same precepts, and preserve the same form of that ordination which belongs to the Church, and expect the same coming of the Lord, and await the same salvation of the whole man, both soul and body."[2]

[1] iv. 33. 8: "Γνῶσις ἀληθὴς ἡ τῶν ἀποστόλων διδαχή, καὶ τὸ ἀρχαῖον τῆς ἐκκλησίας σύστημα κατὰ παντὸς τοῦ κόσμου: et character corporis Christi secundum successiones episcoporum, quibus illi eam, quae in unoquoque loco est, ecclesiam tradiderunt: quae pervenit usque ad nos custoditione sine fictione scripturarum tractatio plenissima, neque additamentum neque ablationem recipiens; et lectio sine falsatione et secundum scripturas expositio legitima et diligens et sine periculo et sine blasphemia: et praecipuum dilectionis munus." Cf. i. 11. 1 (ἴδιος χαρακτήρ); 24. 7; 28. 1.

[2] v. 20. 1: "Eorum autem, qui ab ecclesia sunt, semita circumiens mundum universum, quippe firmam habens ab apostolis traditionem, et videre nobis donans omnium unam et eandem esse fidem, omnibus unum et eundem

These summary statements of what constitutes Christianity are valuable as showing that to Irenaeus Christianity is not an idea but an institution, a catholic Church, and in the Church the essential link of continuity is the apostolic succession. To it therefore he makes his great appeal against the Gnostics.[1]

Deum Patrem praecipientibus, et eandem d'spositionem incaιnationis Filii Dei credentibus, et eandem donationem Spiritus scientibus, et eadem meditantibus praecepta, et eandem figuram eius quae est erga ecclesiam ordinationis custodientibus et eundem exspectantibus adventum domini, et eandem salutem totius hominis, id est animae et corporis, sustinentibus." ('Ordinatio' translates τάξις, i.e. ecclesiastical order, in iii. 3. 3.)

[1] iii. 3. 1-3 : "Traditionem itaque apostolorum in toto mundo manifestatam in omni ecclesia adest respicere omnibus qui vera velint videre ; et habemus annumerare eos qui ab apostolis instituti sunt episcopi in ecclesiis et successores eorum usque ad nos, qui nihil tale docuerunt neque cognoverunt, quale ab his deliratur. Etenim si recondita mysteria scissent apostoli, quae seorsim et latenter ab reliquis perfectos docebant, his vel maxime traderent ea quibus etiam ipsas ecclesias committebant. Valde enim perfectos et irreprehensibiles in omnibus eos volebant esse, quos et successores relinquebant, suum ipsorum locum magisterii tradentes ; quibus emendate agentibus fieret magna utilitas, lapsis autem summa calamitas. Sed quoniam valde longum est in hoc tali volumine omnium ecclesiarum enumerare successiones, maximae et antiquissimae et omnibus cognitae, a gloriosissimis duobus apostolis Petro et Paulo Romae fundatae et constitutae ecclesiae eam, quam habet ab apostolis traditionem et annuntiatam hominibus fidem, per successiones episcoporum pervenientem usque ad nos, indicantes confundimus omnes eos, qui quoquo modo vel per sibiplacentiam vel vanam gloriam vel per caecitatem et malam sententiam praeterquam oportet colligunt. Ad hanc enim ecclesiam propter potentiorem [? potiorem] principalitatem necesse est omnem convenire ecclesiam, hoc est eos qui sunt undique fideles, in qua semper ab his, qui sunt undique, conservata est ea quae est ab apostolis traditio. θεμελιώσαντες οὖν καὶ οἰκοδομήσαντες οἱ μακάριοι ἀπόστολοι τὴν ἐκκλησίαν, Λίνῳ τὴν τῆς ἐπισκοπῆς λειτουργίαν ἐνεχείρισαν· τούτου τοῦ Λίνου Παῦλος ἐν ταῖς πρὸς Τιμόθεον ἐπιστολαῖς μέμνηται. διαδέχεται δὲ αὐτὸν Ἀνέγκλητος. μετὰ τοῦτον δὲ τρίτῳ τόπῳ ἀπὸ τῶν ἀποστόλων τὴν ἐπισκοπὴν κληροῦται Κλήμης, ὁ καὶ ἑωρακὼς τοὺς μακαρίους ἀποστόλους καὶ συμβεβληκὼς αὐτοῖς καὶ ἔτι ἔναυλον τὸ κήρυγμα τῶν ἀποστόλων καὶ τὴν παράδοσιν πρὸ ὀφθαλμῶν ἔχων, οὐ μόνος· ἔτι γὰρ πολλοὶ ὑπελείποντο τότε ἀπὸ τῶν ἀποστόλων δεδιδαγμένοι . . . τὸν δὲ Κλήμεντα τοῦτον διαδέχεται Εὐάρεστος· καὶ τὸν Εὐάρεστον Ἀλέξανδρος· εἶθ' οὕτως ἕκτος ἀπὸ τῶν ἀποστόλων καθίσταται Ξύστος. μετὰ δὲ τοῦτον Τελεσφόρος, ὃς καὶ ἐνδόξως ἐμαρτύρησεν· ἔπειτα Ὑγῖνος, εἶτα Πίος, μεθ' ὃν Ἀνίκητος. διαδεξαμένου τὸν Ἀνίκητον Σωτῆρος, νῦν δωδεκάτῳ τόπῳ τὸν τῆς ἐπισκοπῆς ἀπὸ τῶν ἀποστόλων κατέχει κλῆρον Ἐλεύθερος. τῇ αὐτῇ τάξει καὶ τῇ αὐτῇ διαδοχῇ [Euseb. διδαχῇ, Lat. successione] ἥ τε ἀπὸ τῶν ἀποστόλων ἐν τῇ ἐκκλησίᾳ παράδοσις καὶ τὸ τῆς ἀληθείας κήρυγμα κατήντηκεν εἰς ἡμᾶς."

"All who wish to see the truth have it in their power both in West and East, to fix their eyes on the tradition of the Apostles, which is manifested in all the world; and we can recount the number of those, who were appointed by the Apostles as bishops in the Churches, and their successors down to our own time, who neither taught nor had any knowledge of the wild notions of these men. For had the Apostles known any mysteries which they taught to the perfect in private and unknown to the rest, they would have delivered them to those surely before all others to whom they intrusted the very Churches themselves. For they desired them to be eminently perfect and utterly without reproach, whom they left behind as their actual successors, handing on to them their own position of presidency." Thus he appeals to the successors of the Apostles. Then, "because it would be tedious in a volume like this to enumerate the successions of all the Churches," he gives that of the greatest of all, the Church of Rome—a Church to which he attributes a specially representative character[1]—and records how Peter and Paul intrusted the ministry of the episcopate there to Linus, and how he in turn was succeeded by Anencletus, Clement, Evarestus, Alexander, Xystus, Telesphorus the martyr, Hyginus, Pius, Anicetus, Soter, and finally in his own day Eleutherus. Thus "there has come down to us with the same order and the same

---

[1] It seems most probable that the words of disputed meaning should be translated "for to this Church, on account of its special pre-eminence all Churches must needs come together, that is the faithful from all sides, and in her the apostolic tradition has been always preserved by those who are *from all parts.*" I think Langen (*Gesch. der Römischen Kirche* i. pp. 170-174) has made this interpretation good. But it does not concern us here.

succession the tradition from the Apostles in the Church and the preaching of the truth." With this tradition of truth "coming down to us through the succession of the bishops," Irenaeus proceeds to "confound" his opponents, corroborating, however, the tradition of the West, according to his essential principle, with the apostolic tradition of the Church of Smyrna and "all the Churches of Asia."[1]

What we have quoted will be enough to illustrate his method of appeal. The results of it he constantly presses on the men of his time. "We must obey those who are the elders in the Church, those who, as we have shown, have the succession from the Apostles; who, with the succession of the episcopate, have received also the sure gift of truth according to the will of the Father: but as for the rest, who leave the original succession and come together wherever it may be, them we must hold in suspicion, whether as heretics of a wrong opinion, or as men who make division through pride and self-pleasing, or again as hypocrites."[2] "Where one is to find [the true elders], Paul teaches, when he says, 'God set in the Church first apostles, secondly prophets, thirdly teachers.'

---

[1] iii. 3. 4: καὶ Πολύκαρπος ... ὑπὸ ἀποστόλων κατασταθεὶς εἰς τὴν Ἀσίαν ἐν τῇ ἐν Σμύρνῃ ἐκκλησίᾳ ἐπίσκοπος ... ταῦτα διδάξας ἀεί, ἃ καὶ παρὰ τῶν ἀποστόλων ἔμαθεν, ἃ καὶ ἡ ἐκκλησία παραδίδωσιν, ἃ καὶ μόνα ἐστὶν ἀληθῆ. μαρτυροῦσι τούτοις αἱ κατὰ τὴν Ἀσίαν ἐκκλήσιαι πᾶσαι.

[2] iv. 26. 2: "Quapropter eis qui in ecclesia sunt presbyteris oboedire oportet, his qui successionem habent ab apostolis, sicut ostendimus; qui cum episcopatus successione charisma veritatis certum secundum placitum Patris acceperunt; reliquos vero, qui absistunt a principali successione et quocunque loco colligunt, suspectos habere vel quasi haereticos et malae sententiae, vel quasi scindentes et elatos et sibi placentes, aut rursus ut hypocritas quaestus gratia et vanae gloriae hoc operantes."

Where, then, the gifts of God are placed, there he should learn the truth, with those who have the Church's succession from the Apostles and maintain a sound and irreproachable mode of life and uncorruptness of speech."[1]

The position of Irenaeus is thus very clear and definite. It is accepted by his more brilliant but less stable disciple, Tertullian, who reproduces his argument with striking vigour in his work, called *Praescriptiones* (or 'Preliminary Pleas') against the Gnostic teachers. In it he has a double question to ask these pretenders to represent Christianity. First—do they hold the rule of faith? Secondly—have they an apostolic succession? "Let them produce the account of the origins of their Churches; let them unroll the line of their bishops, running down in such a way from the beginning that their first bishop shall have had for his authorizer and predecessor one of the Apostles, or of the apostolic men who continued to the end in their fellowship. This is the way in which the apostolic Churches hand in their registers: as the Church of the Smyrnaeans relates that Polycarp was installed by John, as the Church of the Romans relates that Clement was ordained by Peter. So in like manner the rest of the Churches exhibit the names of men appointed to the episcopate by Apostles, whom they possess as transmitters of the apostolic

accepted by Tertullian, c. A.D. 200;

---

[1] *ib.* § 5 : " Ubi igitur tales inveniat aliquis, Paulus docens ait : Posuit Deus in ecclesia primo apostolos, secundo prophetas, tertio doctores. Ubi igitur charismata domini posita sunt, ibi discere oportet veritatem, apud quos est ea quae est ab apostolis ecclesiae successio et id quod est sanum et irreprobabile conversationis et inadulteratum et incorruptibile sermonis constat."

seed."[1] "So now," we resume after a few chapters, "you who wish to exercise your curiosity to better profit in the matter of your salvation, run through the apostolic Churches, where the very chairs of the Apostles still preside in their own places"—Corinth, Philippi, Thessalonica, Ephesus, Rome. Make it your business to inquire what they have learnt and taught! This is his challenge.[2] The unchanging tradition goes hand in hand with the steadfast ministerial succession, just as on the contrary the novelties of heresy are associated with carelessness about order. "Their ordinations are heedless, capricious, changeable. At one time they appoint neophytes; at another, men bound to secular employment; at another, apostates from us—so that official distinction may act as a bond to hold them where truth cannot. Nowhere is promotion so easy

[1] *de Praescr.* 32: "Ceterum si quae [haereses] audent interserere se aetati apostolicae, ut ideo videantur ab apostolis traditae, quia sub apostolis fuerunt, possumus dicere: Edant ergo origines ecclesiarum suarum, evolvant ordinem episcoporum suorum, ita per successiones ab initio decurrentem, ut primus ille episcopus aliquem ex apostolis vel apostolicis viris, qui tamen cum apostolis perseveraverit, habuerit auctorem et antecessorem. Hoc enim modo ecclesiae apostolicae census suos deferunt, sicut Smyrnaeorum ecclesia Polycarpum ab Ioanne collocatum refert, sicut Romanorum Clementem a Petro ordinatum. Itidem proinde utique et ceterae exhibent, quos ab apostolis in episcopatum constitutos apostolici seminis traduces habeant. Confingant tale aliquid haeretici. Quid enim illis post blasphemias illicitum est?"

[2] *ib.* 36: "Age iam, qui voles curiositatem melius exercere in negotio salutis tuae, percurre ecclesias apostolicas, apud quas ipsae adhuc cathedrae apostolorum suis locis praesidentur, apud quas ipsae authenticae literae eorum recitantur, sonantes vocem et repraesentantes faciem uniuscuiusque. Proxima est tibi Achaia? habes Corinthum. Si non longe es a Macedonia, habes Philippos, habes Thessalonicenses. Si potes in Asiam tendere, habes Ephesum. Si autem Italiae adiaces, habes Romam, unde nobis quoque auctoritas praesto est . . . Videamus quid didicerit [ecclesia Romana], quid docuerit, quid cum Africanis quoque ecclesiis contesserarit." *ib.* 37: "Si haec ita se habent, ut veritas nobis adiudicetur, quicunque in ea regula incedimus, quam ecclesia ab apostolis, apostoli a Christo, Christus a Deo tradidit, constat ratio propositi nostri."

as in the camp of rebels, where even one's presence is in itself a claim. And so one is a bishop to-day, another to-morrow; the reader of to-morrow is a deacon to-day; the layman of to-morrow a presbyter to-day. For they impose even on laymen the functions of the priesthood."[1]

The age of Irenaeus is to be for the present our starting-point; but it is important to emphasize that there is no originality about his ecclesiastical conceptions. Not only does his own language exclude such a supposition, but we have external testimony to the same effect. Eusebius[2] has preserved for us some words of Hegesippus, 'the father of church history,' in which he is speaking of his journey to the West, made not later than A.D. 167: "The Church of the Corinthians," he says, "remained in the right word down to Primus' bishopric in Corinth. I had intercourse with them when I was sailing to Rome, and I passed some days with the Corinthians, in which we took comfort together in the right word. And when I was in Rome I made a succession [i.e., a list of the succession] down to Anicetus, whose deacon was Eleutherus.

anticipated by Hegesippus, c. A.D. 165.

---

[1] *ib.* 41: "Ordinationes eorum temerariae, leves, inconstantes. Nunc neophytos collocant, nunc saeculo obstrictos, nunc apostatas nostros, ut gloria eos obliget, quia veritate non possunt. Nusquam facilius proficitur quam in castris rebellium, ubi ipsum esse illic promereri est. Itaque alius hodie episcopus, cras alius; hodie diaconus, qui cras lector; hodie presbyter, qui cras laicus; nam et laicis sacerdotalia munera iniungunt."

[2] Hegesipp. ap. Euseb. *H. E.* iv. 22: Καὶ ἐπέμενεν ἡ ἐκκλησία ἡ Κορινθίων ἐν τῷ ὀρθῷ λόγῳ μέχρι Πρίμου ἐπισκοπεύοντος ἐν Κορίνθῳ· οἷς συνέμιξα πλέων εἰς Ῥώμην, καὶ συνδιέτριψα τοῖς Κορινθίοις ἡμέρας ἱκανάς, ἐν αἷς συνανεπάημεν τῷ ὀρθῷ λόγῳ. γενόμενος δὲ ἐν Ῥώμῃ διαδοχὴν ἐποιησάμην μέχρις Ἀνικήτου, οὗ διάκονος ἦν Ἐλεύθερος· καὶ παρὰ Ἀνικήτου διαδέχεται Σωτήρ, μεθ' ὃν Ἐλεύθερος. ἐν ἑκάστῃ δὲ διαδοχῇ καὶ ἐν ἑκάστῃ πόλει οὕτως ἔχει, ὡς ὁ νόμος κηρύσσει καὶ οἱ προφῆται καὶ ὁ κύριος.

And from Anicetus, Soter succeeds, and after him Eleutherus. Now in each succession and in each city it is as the law proclaims and the prophets and the Lord." Hegesippus then had found a succession in each city. He made a list for the purpose of his history at Rome; but there, as elsewhere, he had found the thing existing. Let Hegesippus' testimony then reinforce that of Irenaeus.

<small>Further evidence in detail.</small>

Starting thus from about the middle of the second century the episcopal succession is an undoubted fact in all known Christian Churches. It is, however, desirable to review the evidence not only of the fact, but also of the importance attached to it.

<small>A. The East. Palestine.</small>

A. We begin with the East, and in the East with the 'cradle of our religion'—Palestine. "As early as the middle of the second century all parties concur in representing James [the Lord's brother] as a bishop in the strict sense of the term."[1] The episcopate, that is to say, was at that date an institution certainly believed to derive in Jerusalem from St. James. Eusebius has preserved to us a complete list of the successors of Symeon, who was chosen in his place—first, thirteen Jewish bishops, and then, after the annihilation of Jerusalem and the foundation upon its site of Aelia Capitolina, thirteen Gentile bishops,[2] down to the accession of the venerable Narcissus, who was engaged in the Paschal contro-

---

[1] Lightfoot *Dissert.* p. 208. See Hegesipp. ap. Euseb. *H.E.* iv. 22; the Clementine *Ep. Petri*, *Ep. Clem.* init., *Hom.* xi. 35; and Clem. Alex. ap. Euseb. *H.E.* ii. 1. In this review of second century episcopacy I am mainly following Dr. Lightfoot.

[2] Euseb. *H.E.* iv. 5, v. 12.

versy.¹ There can be at least no doubt of the existence in Jerusalem of an episcopal succession of immemorial antiquity at the date which is our starting-point for the present. In the Paschal controversy we find the bishop of Jerusalem associated with three A.D. 198. other Palestinian bishops² (of Caesarea, Tyre, Ptolemais), in writing an encyclical letter in favour of the western view. The testimony of the Clementines,³ which may be taken to represent Ebionite ideas at the end of the second century, goes to assure us that at that date the episcopate at Caesarea, Tyre, Sidon, Berytus, Tripolis, and Laodicea could plausibly be represented as having been instituted by St. Peter.⁴ It must be noticed that there is the same insistence upon the episcopal succession in the Ebionite Clementines as in the fragments of Hege-

---

¹ Euseb. *H.E.* v. 23.   ² Euseb. *H.E.* v. 25.
³ The Clementine *Homilies* and *Recognitions* contain substantially the same narrative. They purport to contain an account given by Clement of his connection with St. Peter and of St. Peter's journeyings, discourses, etc., including his institution of bishops, presbyters, and deacons at various places in Syria. Both are Ebionite, though the *Recognitions* present Ebionite ideas in a very modified form. Both are based apparently on an earlier document, and are of Syrian origin. Dr. Salmon (*Dict. Chr. Biog.* CLEMENTINE LIT.) dates the *Recogn.* about A.D. 200 and the *Homilies* about A.D. 218. [Origen quotes the former about A.D. 230.] He thinks the document on which they are based may go back to A.D. 160. Dr. Lightfoot says: "the *Homilies* cannot well be placed later than the end, and should perhaps be placed before the middle of the second century" (*Dissert.* p. 211). There are also two letters to James from Peter and Clement, both now prefixed to the *Homilies*, but the latter probably served originally as preface to the *Recognitions* (*Dict. Chr. Biog.* i. p. 570). It describes St. Peter's ordination of Clement as bishop of Rome.
⁴ See *Recogn.* vi. 15 : "[Peter] appointed as bishop over them [at Tripolis] Maro ... and with him he ordained twelve presbyters and deacons at the same time." Cf. iii. 66 (Caesarea,—bishop, twelve presbyters, and four deacons), x. 68 (Laodicea); *Hom.* iii. 72 (Caesarea), vii. 5 (Tyre), 8 (Sidon), 12 (Berytus), xi. 36 (Tripolis,—bishop, twelve presbyters, and deacons), xx. 23 (Laodicea). See also *Ep. Clem. ad Iac.*

I

sippus and in the writings of Irenaeus; episcopacy, and episcopacy derived from the Apostles, was not, we perceive, a matter of dispute.[1]

Syria.
c. A.D. 110.

The episcopal succession at Antioch is historical at least from Ignatius. If we cannot fully rely upon the list of bishops given us by Eusebius,[2] at least bishop Theophilus, the apologist, and bishop Serapion come out into the light during the second century.

---

[1] It is worth while collecting the conception of the ministry given in the Clementine documents.

(1) There is the idea of succession to the Apostles. Clement succeeds St. Peter (*Ep. Clem.* 2, 19). St. Peter, in his letter to James, emphasizes the idea of succession on the analogy of the seventy elders who succeeded to "the chair of Moses." Here the successors seem to be the whole presbyterate, but subordination to the bishop is strongly marked (*Ep. Petr.* 4. § 2). The bishop's chair is also called "the chair of Christ" (*Ep. Clem.* 17, and *Hom.* iii. 70).

(2) The idea of the episcopal succession is mainly that of succession to the teaching office, in order to keep the tradition (cf. Irenaeus): see *Ep. Petr.* init. and *Ep. Clem.* 2, 6: ἡ τῶν λόγων καθέδρα, ὁ τῆς ἀληθείας προκαθεζόμενος, ὁ τῆς ἀληθείας πρεσβύτης. But the bishop has intrusted to him "the authority to bind and loose" with divine sanction (*ib.* 2: αὐτῷ μεταδίδωμι τὴν ἐξουσίαν τοῦ δεσμεύειν καὶ λύειν, ἵνα περὶ παντὸς οὗ ἂν χειροτονήσῃ ἐπὶ τῆς γῆς ἔσται δεδογματισμένον ἐν οὐρανοῖς: cf. *ib.* 6, *Hom.* iii. 72); he is the προεστώς (*Ep. Clem.* 6); he has the general administration of the Church (διοίκησις, *ib.* 3, etc.); and all is to be done by the presbyters with his knowledge (*Ep. Petr.* 4. § 2). He is to be kept clear from secular cares (*Ep. Clem.* 5, 6). St. Peter is represented as baptizing and breaking bread; also the elders at Jerusalem as baptizing (*Ep. Petr.* 4. § 1).

(3) Presbyters are to exercise moral discipline; to administer charitable relief; to reconcile disputants (*Ep. Clem.* 7-10; *Hom.* iii. 67, 68). The deacons are "the eyes of the bishop," to assist his pastoral care in the distribution of alms, with considerable independence in the latter department (*Ep. Clem.* 12; *Hom.* iii. 67). There is also mention of catechists, but the bishop is represented in one place as the catechist (*Ep. Clem.* 13, 14). The Ship of the Church is described elaborately with her full equipment of officers, etc. (*ib.* 14, 15).

(4) Ordination is by laying on of hands (*Ep. Clem.* 19; *Hom.* iii. 72; *Recogn.* iii. 66), with accompanying prayer (*Hom.* iii. 72).

In all this there is nothing specially Ebionite; but James is called "bishop of bishops," and has a universal authority ascribed to him (*Ep. Clem.* init.). Even Peter, though he is called "first of apostles" (*ib.* 1), has to give an annual account to him of his doings (*Recogn.* I. 17), and is subject to him (*ib.* 72). This is Ebionite. [2] Euseb. *H.E.* iv. 20, 24; v. 22.

So much for the Church of Palestine and the Greek Church of Syria. Of the early "Syrian Church, strictly so called"—the Syriac-speaking Church—we have no authentic history. It is, however, worth while noticing that the early traditions of that Church represent the "ordination to the priesthood" as the means of the propagation of the Gospel, venerate the threefold ministry as of apostolic institution, and lay great stress on the episcopal succession deriving in each Church from an apostle through the laying on of hands.[1]

We pass from Syria to 'Asia' to find the epis- Asia Minor. copal succession a very old established institution. It is enough to say that Ignatius had impressed A.D. 110. upon the Churches of Ephesus, Magnesia, Tralles, Philadelphia, and Smyrna, that the bishop, with the

[1] See *The Teaching of Addaeus the Apostle* and *The Teaching of the Apostles*—ancient Syriac documents, trans. in Clark's Ante-Nicene Library, vol. xx—esp. pp. 32, 48. See Tixeront *Origines de l'église d'Édesse* pp. 114 ff. The former is a retouched version, dating apparently from about 400 A.D., of the document quoted by Eusebius (*H.E.* i. 13), which existed in "the archives of Edessa, at that time a royal city." The latter document uses an old pre-Peshitto Syriac reading. As to their ecclesiastical ideas, it may be noted that the bishop is called by a word translated "guide and ruler." Addaeus, the apostle, ordains Aggaeus, and he "made priests and guides in the whole country of Mesopotamia." The authority of the guide is limited: "it is not lawful for him to transact the affairs of the Church apart from those who minister with him" (*Teaching of the Apostles* p. 41). Cf. Lightfoot *Dissert.* p. 211 n.[6] It should be noticed that the apostles who originate "ordination to the priesthood" (*Teaching of the Apostles* p. 48) are reckoned at *seventy-two*, and amongst them are Luke and Addaeus, whom Eusebius calls Thaddaeus and describes as "one of the seventy disciples of Christ" (*H. E.* i. 13). The number seventy-two represents the older Curetonian Syriac reading of St. Luke x. 1; the Peshitto has "seventy." (On the relations of the Cur. Syr. to the Pesh. see Westcott and Hort *Introd. to N. T.* pp. 84, 85.) The Arab, El Makrizi (who wrote a history of the Coptic Church in the fourteenth century, but drew upon earlier authors, such as Eutychius) speaks likewise of "seventy apostles" (in Malan *Orig. Doc. of the Copt. Ch.* iii. p. 23); this *may* represent some old Alexandrian statement, directly or indirectly.

presbyters and deacons, represents the authority of God, and we are not allowed to doubt that at least they learned the lesson. Besides Polycarp of Smyrna, Onesimus of Ephesus, Damas of Magnesia, and Polybius of Tralles, whom Ignatius mentions, we hear during the second century of Papias, a contemporary of Polycarp, and Claudius Apollinaris, bishops of Hierapolis,[1] of Sagaris, bishop of Laodicea, and Melito, bishop of Sardis.[2] Polycrates, bishop of Ephesus at the end of the second century, speaks of himself as having had seven of his own family before him in the episcopate, whose traditions he followed.[3] If we pass from the proconsular province to Asia Minor, in the wider sense of the term, we have not much evidence bearing on the subject; but we hear of bishops in the second century at Sinope[4] and at Eumenia,[5] at Amastris, at Comana, at Apamea[6]; and there is no indication such as would lead us to doubt the universal extension of the episcopate in the Churches of that country. Towards the end of the century episcopal synods become common; at the time of

---

[1] The episcopate of Claudius, c. A.D. 171, rests on the authority of his contemporary, Serapion (ap. Euseb. *H.E.* v. 19); Papias' on that of Eusebius representing the common account (*H. E.* ii. 15).

[2] c. A.D. 150-170, on the authority of Polycrates in Euseb. *H. E.* v. 24.

[3] Euseb. *H. E.* v. 24.

[4] Marcion of Sinope is described as "episcopi filius" in [*adv. Omn. Haer.* appended to] Tertull. *de Praescr.* 51. Marcion propagated his system before the middle of the second century. He was himself recognised as bishop by his sect and organized it on the Church's model; "faciunt favos et vespae, et faciunt ecclesias Marcionitae" (Tertull. *adv. Marc.* 5).

[5] Polycrates ap. Euseb. *H. E.* v. 24.

[6] Palmas of Amastris is mentioned by Dionysius of Corinth writing to the Churches of Pontus (Euseb. *H. E.* iv. 23). Zoticos of Comana and Julianus of Apamea are mentioned by the anonymous contemporary adversary of the Montanists (ap. Euseb. *H. E.* v. 16).

the Paschal controversy there were a number of bishops in Pontus; and Polycrates[1] speaks of "great crowds" of bishops whom he had summoned to conference on that subject.

If there is less evidence of the diffusion of episcopacy in Greece in the latter half of the second century, this probably does not mean more than that the Church there was less prominent than the Church in Asia.[2] Where we hear of church government it is episcopal. At Corinth, when Hegesippus visited it, there was not only a bishop, Primus, but a succession;[3] after him we hear of Dionysius, and at the time of the Paschal controversy of Bacchyllus.[4] In the mention which Eusebius makes of one of Dionysius' letters "to the Athenians" (about A.D. 170), we hear of at least two bishops in the succession of Athens prior to that date— Publius, who was martyred, and Quadratus, who had recalled their Church from something like "apostacy from the word," into which they had fallen.[5] If this bishop is that Quadratus who presented his Apology to Hadrian at Athens, this record carries back the Athenian succession at least very early in the century. The tradition of the earlier episcopate of Dionysius the Areopagite is not here in question.

<small>Greece.</small>

<small>c. A.D. 165.</small>

We have the names of no bishops on contemporary evidence during the second century in Macedonia, but when Tertullian is rhetorically bidding the

<small>Macedonia.</small>

---

[1] Euseb. *H. E.* v. 24.
[2] The problems presented by the Epistles of Clement and Polycarp will be considered below. They do not fall within this period.
[3] Euseb. *H. E.* iv. 22.
[4] Euseb. *H. E.* iv. 23; v. 22, 23.
[5] Euseb. *H. E.* iv. 23. Publius is called ὁ προεστὼς αὐτῶν.

heretical teachers to take counsel of "the apostolic Churches, where the very chairs of the Apostles still preside," he goes on, "Is Achaia nearest to you? you have Corinth; if you are not far from Macedonia, you have Philippi, you have Thessalonica,"—showing that at the end of the century Macedonia had episcopal successions which were believed to derive from apostolic ordination.[1]

Thrace. If we pass from Macedonia to Thrace we pass to a district almost without Christian record, but towards the end of the century we find a bishop of Debeltum signing an encyclical letter, directed against the Montanists,[2] "and the existence of a see at a place so unimportant implies the wide spread of episcopacy in these regions."[3]

Crete. On our passage from Greece to Egypt we may take Crete by the way. There we know that at least two episcopal sees existed about A.D. 170, for Dionysius of Corinth wrote a letter "to the Cnossians," with words of advice to Pinytus their bishop, and another "to the Church at Gortyna, with the other parishes [i. e. dioceses] in Crete," specially commending Philip, the bishop of Gortyna, who is also known as the author of a work against Marcion.[4]

Alexandria. On arriving at Alexandria we shall undoubtedly find ourselves in a Church of the three orders. It is true that we cannot trace to its source or verify the

---

[1] Tertull. *de Praescr.* 36. Cf. Origen on Rom. xvi. 23: "fertur sane traditione maiorum quod hic Gaius [St. Paul's host] primus episcopus fuerit Thessalonicensis ecclesiae."
[2] Euseb. *H.E.* v. 19.
[3] Lightfoot *Dissert.* p. 217. [4] Euseb. *H.E.* iv. 23, 25.

complete and dated list of Alexandrian bishops, which Eusebius gives us, reaching back to St. Mark as founder of the Church. We do not in fact know the *name* of any Alexandrian bishop on indisputable evidence till we get to Demetrius, Origen's contemporary; for "the Alexandrian succession, in which history is hitherto most interested, is not the succession of the bishops, but of the heads of the catechetical school."[1] But Clement's evidence gives us all that we want. He was born about the middle of the second century, and not only had the Church which he knew bishops, presbyters, and deacons,[2] but it had even passed out of

The existence of bishops at Alexandria indisputable;

---

[1] Lightfoot *Dissert.* p. 226.

[2] "The grades in the Church here of bishops, presbyters, deacons, I believe to be imitations of the angelic glory" (*Strom.* vi. 13. 107: αἱ ἐνταῦθα κατὰ τὴν ἐκκλησίαν προκοπαὶ ἐπισκόπων, πρεσβυτέρων, διακόνων, μιμήματα οἶμαι ἀγγελικῆς δόξης). The whole chapter runs thus :—The perfect Christian gnostic is even here equal to the angels : he may be made equal to the Apostles : "not that they became apostles because they were chosen for some special peculiarity of nature, for Judas was chosen with them; but they were capable of becoming apostles on being chosen by Him Who foresaw even how they would end. For Matthias, who was not chosen with them, on showing himself fit (ἄξιος) to become an apostle, is substituted for Judas. So now too, those who have exercised themselves in the Lord's commandments and have lived perfectly and with knowledge (γνωστικῶς), according to the Gospel, may be enrolled (ἐγγραφῆναι) in the chosen body of the Apostles. Such an one is in reality a presbyter of the Church and a true deacon of the will of God, if he do and teach the things of the Lord, not being ordained (χειροτονούμενος) by man, nor reckoned just because he is a presbyter, but counted (καταλεγόμενος) in the presbyterate because he is just. And even if here upon earth he be not honoured with the chief seat (πρωτοκαθεδρία), he will sit on the four and twenty thrones judging the people, as John says in the Apocalypse." The four and twenty elders, he continues, are the chosen of the chosen, equally from Jews or Greeks. "Since I think the grades in the Church here of bishops, presbyters, deacons are imitations of the angelic glory and of that dispensation (οἰκονομίας) which the Scriptures say await those who, following the footsteps of the Apostles, have lived in perfection of righteousness according to the Gospel. For these, the Apostle writes, 'lifted up in the clouds' will serve their diaconate first (διακονήσειν), then be reckoned with the presbyterate in a higher grade of glory, for glory differeth from glory, until they grow up into a perfect man." Clement's meaning is apparently that moral excellence and gnostic enlightenment were qualifications for the apostolate of

memory that 'bishop' and 'presbyter' were interchangeable titles in St. Paul's days.¹ We have additional

old and make a man a true priest now (cf. the exclamation of the people in demanding Athanasius' election 'ἀληθῶς ἐπίσκοπος,' Athan. *Apol. c. Ar.* 6); not, however, in the sense that they can enable a man to dispense with ordination or justify him in assuming ministerial functions without it, but only in the sense that, if he be not admitted to the clergy here, he will be hereafter raised to those grades of glory which the present distinctive offices in the Church adumbrate here below; they are titles for a place in the hierarchy *in heaven, if not here.* It will be noticed that though Clement divides the hierarchy into three orders, he can still (like Origen and many others) speak of the presbyterate as the "chief seat" (§ 106 above). The *main* distinction with him, as with Irenaeus and many after them, is between presbyters and deacons. Thus in another passage (*Strom.* vii. 1. 3), contrasting the two sorts of ministry to men—the more menial service (ὑπηρετική) and the higher ministry of improvement (βελτιωτικὴ θεραπεία)—he finds the former exemplified in the Church's diaconate, the latter in the presbyterate, thus dividing the church ministry into *two* sorts (ὁμοίως κατὰ τὴν ἐκκλησίαν τὴν μὲν βελτιωτικὴν οἱ πρεσβύτεροι σώζουσιν εἰκόνα, τὴν ὑπηρετικὴν δὲ οἱ διάκονοι); here the presbyterate must include the bishop.

Clement's position on many points is somewhat hard to define. His line of thought is not one which, like that of Irenaeus, leads him to speak much about the ministry. At the same time there is an intellectualism in his whole conception of religion, a recognition of a 'priesthood of knowledge' (for reffs. see Bigg *B.L.* p. 101), which represents an opposite tendency to the 'priesthood of enthusiasm' among the Montanists. This, we must acknowledge,—whatever fascination Clement's gentle, pious, generous spirit has for us—had in it dangerous elements of Gnosticism, and led him even to shrink from attributing to our Lord real human feelings, a real flesh and blood like ours (Bigg *B.L.* pp. 93, 71 n.⁵); it makes him in a measure depreciate mere faith and desire to create 'a Church within a Church,' a Church of the spiritually enlightened (Bigg p. 85 f.). Thus it *may* have tended to make him depreciate the ministry which comes of ordination by comparison with the priesthood of knowledge, but there is no evidence of this. His point of view is not at all *unecclesiastical*. Christianity is not by any means to him a mere idea or philosophy; it is embodied in a visible society. Nor in the passage quoted is there anything to lead us to suppose that he shrank from recognising the necessity for orders in the Church, or their exclusive rights, any more than he shrank from recognising the exclusive prerogative of the Church. Dr. Bigg says no more than is true when he says: "It is important to add . . . that Clement lays great stress upon the observance of the existing church discipline, the regular use of all the ordinary means of grace" (pp. 96, 97). He very likely, however, did not recognise fully that 'the unworthiness of the minister hinders not the grace of the sacraments,' and he speaks of baptism administered by heretics as οὐκ οἰκεῖον καὶ γνήσιον ὕδωρ (*Strom.* i. 19. 96). On this, and on his not using sacerdotal language of the ministry, see below, p. 196 f.

¹ *Paed.* iii. 12. 97: "there are an infinite number of suggestions in the

III.] *The Witness of Church History.* 137

reason to believe that the episcopal office was recognised at Alexandria as distinct from the presbyterate very early in the century. The emperor Hadrian visited Alexandria in A.D. 130, and he gave an account of his visit in a letter to Servianus which is preserved. Amidst the motley crowd of the devotees of all sorts of religions and superstitions, whose fickle inconsistency, as it appeared in his eyes, half amused and half disgusted him, he recognised the "bishops of Christ" as distinct figures from the Christian presbyters.[1]

There is thus no ground for doubting the existence of an episcopal succession at Alexandria long before the middle of the second century. But we have it on Jerome's evidence that this succession had some peculiarity. He is writing[2] in a state of great indignation with the arrogance of deacons in the Church of Rome. He (like other patristic writers) wishes to emphasize, as a corrective to their self-assertion, the especial dignity of that priesthood, which, with some differences of function, presbyter and bishop share in common. His view will be considered later, but he illustrates it by a practice which he attributes to the Church of Alexandria in earlier days, and with this illustration we are now concerned.

but Jerome reports

---

sacred books directed to select persons, some to presbyters, some to bishops, some to deacons, others to widows."

[1] See his letter to Servianus (ap. Vopisc., quoted by Lightfoot *Ignatius* i. 464; cf. *Dissert.* p. 225): "Illic qui Serapem colunt Christiani sunt, et devoti sunt Serapi qui Christi se episcopos dicunt. Nemo illic archisynagogus Iudaeorum, nemo Samarites, nemo Christianorum presbyter, non mathematicus, non haruspex, non aliptes. Ipse ille patriarcha, cum Aegyptum venerit, ab aliis Serapidem adorare, ab aliis cogitur Christum.' The "patriarcha" is (no doubt) the Jewish patriarch.

[2] *Ep.* cxlvi *ad Evangelum.*

that, down to A.D. 233-249 and A.D. 249-265, the bishops were constituted by mere election.

Jerome then asserts that "from the days of St. Mark the Evangelist down to the episcopates of Heraclas and Dionysius the presbyters at Alexandria used always to appoint as bishop one chosen out of their number and placed upon the higher grade, just as if an army were making a general, or deacons were choosing one of themselves whose diligence they knew and calling him arch-deacon. For what" (he asks) "except ordination does a bishop do which a presbyter does not?"[1] The language of this statement is ambiguous, but Jerome seems to mean, as he was certainly understood to mean by later Latin writers, that there was no fresh consecration or ordination required in earlier days at Alexandria to make a presbyter bishop, but that he became bishop simply in virtue of his election by the other presbyters. There would have been thus a substantial identity between the two orders. Jerome had of course resided at Alexandria, and had had opportunities of making himself acquainted with Alexandrian traditions; but, if this is his meaning, his statement is wholly without independent support in Latin or Greek literature.[2] Epiphanius, for example, Jerome's older contemporary and bishop of Salamis in Cyprus,—though he knew Egypt

His statement (a) lacks support;

---

[1] The Latin is quoted in Appended Note B, where there is some further discussion of the matter.

[2] His statement is copied by later Latin writers, and an Arab patriarch of the tenth cent., Eutychius, is quoted in support; on whom see App. Note B. Surely Dr. Lightfoot is mistaken (*Dissert.* p. 231 n.²) when he quotes Ambrosiaster (*in Eph.* iv. 12) in support of Jerome: "denique," says Ambrosiaster, "apud Aegyptum presbyteri consignant si praesens non sit episcopus." The reference here is to confirmation, not ordination. Moreover Didymus, who lived and taught at Alexandria and was Jerome's teacher, says absolutely: ἐπίσκοπος μόνος τῇ ἄνωθεν χάριτι τελεῖ τὸ χρῖσμα (*de Trin.* ii. 15).

better than Jerome and was acquainted with the peculiar position of the Alexandrian presbyters, which anticipated that of the parish priests of later days— was seemingly ignorant of any such fact as Jerome mentions.[1] There is no trace of it in any Alexandrian writer of the third or fourth centuries. Thus Athanasius records how a council at Alexandria, in A.D. 324, had declared null and void a pretended ordination by a schismatical presbyter, Colluthus. It has been recently suggested that the mere fact of such an ordination having occurred is a sign that the older traditions of the substantial identity of the bishop and the presbyter still survived in the byways of the Alexandrian Church. But Athanasius' language, or rather the language he quotes from the letter of a synod of Egyptian bishops held in A.D. 340, does not countenance this. "How then," they ask, "is Ischyras a presbyter? Who appointed him? Colluthus, was it not? This is the only plea left. But that Colluthus died a presbyter, and that his every ordination is invalid and all who were appointed by him in his schism have come out laymen and are so treated, *is plain, and nobody doubts it.*"[2] This is not the lan-

[1] *Haer.* lxix. 1. Had he been acquainted with the supposed fact, it probably would have appeared in his language against Aerius, which is referred to later. It would have needed explanation.

[2] Athan. *Apol. c. Ar.* 11, 12 (quoting from a synodical letter of Egyptian bishops): οὗτος δέ ἐστιν ὁ πολυθρύλλητος ᾿Ισχύρας, ὁ μήτε ὑπὸ τῆς ἐκκλησίας χειροτονηθεὶς καί, ὅτε τοὺς ὑπὸ Μελετίου καταστανθέντας πρεσβυτέρους ᾿Αλέξανδρος ἐδέχετο, μηδὲ ἐκείνοις συναριθμηθείς· οὕτως οὐδὲ ἐκεῖθεν κατεστάθη. πόθεν οὖν πρεσβύτερος ᾿Ισχύρας; τίνος καταστήσαντος; ἆρα Κολλούθου; τοῦτο γὰρ λοιπόν. ἀλλ' ὅτι Κόλλουθος πρεσβύτερος ὢν ἐτελεύτησε, καὶ πᾶσα χεὶρ αὐτοῦ γέγονεν ἄκυρος καὶ πάντες οἱ παρ' αὐτοῦ καταστανθέντες ἐν τῷ σχίσματι λαικοὶ γεγόνασι καὶ οὕτω συνάγονται, δῆλον, καὶ οὐδενὶ καθέστηκεν ἀμφίβολον. Cf. 74 (and 76): οὐδέποτε λειτουργὸς τῆς ἐκκλησίας γέγονεν ... ἐκπεσὼν καὶ τῆς ψευδοῦς ὑπονοίας τοῦ πρεσβυτερίου.

guage which could have been used if there had been an appeal in the matter to any ancient tradition of the Church.

(b) is not easily harmonized with Origen's witness;

The language and silence of Origen are also significant. Origen was thirty-eight years old when Heraclas became bishop, in whose time the gradual exaltation of the episcopate is supposed to have begun. Origen, besides giving us to understand that the method of ordaining bishops was by laying-on of hands,[1] also speaks of them frequently as occupying a quite different grade to presbyters, and he uses language which implies that the position of bishops was one of immemorial antiquity.[2] It must also be remembered

---

[1] When Origen (*in Num.* xxii. 4) is rebuking the "principes ecclesiae" (i.e. bishops) for appointing their own relations or even their sons to succeed them in their sees, he quotes Num. xxvii. 18-20 (where Moses is directed to choose Joshua and lay hands upon him, etc.) and continues: "audis evidenter ordinationem principis populi tam manifeste descriptam, ut paene expositione non egeat." Just above he had distinguished the "princeps populi" from the "presbyteri" of Num. xi. 16. Cf. also *in Exod.* xi. 6.

[2] Origen's language about church offices is of this nature:—

(1) Bishops and presbyters are classed together as ἐν ἐκκλησιαστικῇ δοκοῦντες εἶναι ὑπεροχῇ (*in Ioann.* xxxii. 7); cf. *in Matt.* xvi. 22: οἱ δὲ τὰς πρωτοκαθεδρίας πεπιστευμένοι τοῦ λαοῦ ἐπίσκοποι καὶ πρεσβύτεροι.

(2) Much more frequently they are spoken of as constituting *distinct* classes; cf. *in Luc.* xx: "Si Iesus subiicitur Ioseph et Mariae, ego non subiiciar episcopo qui mihi a Deo ordinatus est pater? non subiiciar presbytero qui mihi Domini dignatione praepositus est?" Again, in the beautiful contrast which he draws (*c. Cels.* iii. 30) between the Christian and the pagan ἐκκλησία, he distinguishes the ἄρχων of the Christian community from the βουλευταί—the bishop from the presbyters—in several typical Churches, of which Alexandria is one. Again, speaking (*de Orat.* 28) of the different "debts" which different classes of the community have to pay, he specifies the distinct debt of widow, deacon, presbyter, and continues: καὶ ἐπισκόπου δὲ ὀφειλὴ βαρυτάτη ἀπαιτουμένη ὑπὸ τοῦ τῆς ὅλης ἐκκλησίας σωτῆρος καὶ ἐκδικουμένη εἰ μὴ ἀποδιδῷτο. And in a similar strain *in Ierem.* xi. 3: οὐ πάντως ὁ κλῆρος σώζει ... πλεῖον ἐγὼ ἀπαιτοῦμαι παρὰ τὸν διάκονον (this was after he was ordained priest), πλεῖον ὁ διάκονος παρὰ τὸν λαικόν· ὁ δὲ τὴν πάντων ἡμῶν ἐγκεχειρισμένος ἀρχὴν αὐτὴν τὴν ἐκκλησιαστικὴν ἐπὶ πλεῖον ἀπαιτεῖται. Cf. *in Ezech.* v; *in Luc.* xvii.

(3) He puts the bishops alone in a remarkable way, as the Church's rulers:

that Origen had suffered severely from specially episcopal authority at Alexandria. He had been ordained presbyter, as is well known, at Caesarea, without the consent of Demetrius, the bishop of Alexandria. Now, while a mixed synod of Egyptian bishops and presbyters had consented only to banish him for this breach of canonical discipline, a synod of *bishops alone* had gone further and deposed him from his presbyterate, as he and his friends thought, unjustly.[1] This severer treatment would make him quick, like Jerome, to notice the arrogance of bishops.[2] If then Heraclas, Demetrius' successor, had deprived the presbyters of an ancient right, it would not have escaped his attention; yet, writing at the end of Heraclas' episcopate, he characterizes the Alexandrian Church among others as "a mild and stable" society, and speaks of want of zeal, not of rivalry, as the fault likely to be found in

"per singulas ecclesias bini sunt episcopi, alius visibilis, alius invisibilis; ille visui carnis, hic sensui patens" (*in Luc.* xiii). He is alluding to the Angel of the Apocalypse, whom he conceives of as the spiritual guardian of the Church and counterpart of the earthly bishop. This leads to the remark that—

(4) He conceives the bishop of his day to be the bishop of whose qualifications St. Paul instructs us (*in Matt.* xi. 15; *c. Cels.* iii. 48). Also he speaks of bishops as the immemorial tradition in the Church; he speaks of people who have to boast of fathers and ancestors προεδρίας ἠξιωμένοις ἐν τῇ ἐκκλησίᾳ ἐπισκοπικοῦ θρόνου ἢ πρεσβυτερίου τιμῆς ἢ διακονίας εἰς τὸν λαόν (*in Matt.* xv. 26). And as he singles out "stability" as a note of the Church, when he is contrasting it with the pagan societies (*c. Cels.* iii. 30: πραεῖά τις καὶ εὐσταθής)— and this when Alexandria is specially mentioned among other Churches—he is clearly not conscious of any change in the Church's constitution which is going on. Nor does his language at all suggest that the episcopate at Alexandria was in a peculiar position.

[1] *Dict. Chr. Biog.* s.v. ORIGEN iv. p. 100.

[2] He does, as a fact, rebuke the bishops, especially those of great cities, for secularity and pride, but not as if their order was exalting itself at the expense of the presbyters; cf. *in Matt.* xvi. 8, *in Exod.* xi. 6, and *Dict. Chr. Biog.* s.v. ORIGEN iv. p. 127.

bishops and clergy.¹ So far then as Jerome's theory postulates at Alexandria an original lack of clear distinction between the orders of bishop and presbyter, followed by a gradual exaltation of the episcopate, during the period of Origen's life, it has all the testimony of his language against it.²

(c) if true, is not inconsistent with the principle of succession.

It requires, then, a great effort of confidence to trust Jerome's witness, especially when we consider that it is the witness of Jerome in a temper,³ and that under such circumstances he is not too careful with his facts; but it has been so generally accepted by western writers from the fourth to the twelfth century and by modern critics, that it will be the better course, as our object is not merely archæological, to face what is at any rate the possibility of its being true. It should then be noticed that, when western church writers of the Middle Ages quote and accept Jerome's statement, it causes them no disquietude in view of the existing distinction of bishops and priests. They would maintain that no one can validly

---

¹ c. Cels. iii. 30.

² So far again as Jerome's words postulate that the elective authority for the episcopate lay simply with the presbytery, it has against it the evidence that the ancient mode of episcopal election at Alexandria gave great power to the vote of the whole people. It is not likely that the presbytery should have lost power and the people gained it. See Athan. Apol. c. Ar. 6 πᾶν τὸ πλῆθος καὶ πᾶς ὁ λαός; Greg. Naz. Orat. xxi. 8.

There were remarkable features about Alexandrian episcopal elections in later days. They were made rapidly to avoid disturbance (Epiphan. Haer. lxix. 11), and Liberatus speaks thus of the episcopal consecration (Breviar. 20): "Consuetudo quidem est Alexandriae illum qui defuncto succedit excubias super defuncti corpus agere, manumque dexteram eius capiti suo imponere et, sepulto manibus suis, accipere collo suo beati Marci pallium et tunc legitime sedere."

³ Dr. Bigg, in another case, makes short work of Jerome's "unsupported testimony" (B. L. p. 214 n.¹).

execute any ecclesiastical function which does not belong to him by the proper devolution of ecclesiastical authority. But this no one accuses the Alexandrian presbyters of having done. They were ordained, *ex hypothesi*, on the understanding that under certain circumstances they might be called, by simple election, to execute the bishop's office. They were not only presbyters with the ordinary commission of the presbyter, but also bishops *in posse*.[1] Elsewhere there were two distinct ordinations, one making a man a bishop and another a presbyter; at Alexandria there was only one ordination, which made a man a presbyter and potential bishop. When this arrangement ceased and Alexandria was assimilated to other Churches, the presbyters began to be ordained as mere presbyters; and henceforward any assumption by one of them of episcopal powers, such as Colluthus was guilty of, was treated as a mere assumption, the results of which were simply invalid. It is unnecessary to do more than recall, in view of such an hypothetical situation, the contention of the last chapter, namely that the church principle of succession would never be violated by the existence in any Church of episcopal powers, whether free or conditional, in all the presbyters, supposing that those powers were not assumed by the individual for himself, but were understood to be conveyed to him by the ordination of the Church.

---

[1] Their position would not have been very unlike that of the chorepiscopi, who could only ordain validly (in the mind of the early Church) where they had the sanction of the town bishop.

The state of things, then, which is assumed to have existed at Alexandria violates the complete *uniformity* of the church ministry in the period we are considering—it requires us to introduce qualifications into our generalization of results—but it does not affect the principle.[1]

<small>Further evidence as to how the ministry was conceived from</small>

So far we have been going through the evidence supplied by the history of Eastern Christianity on the existence of episcopal successions in every Church. It remains to seek additional light on the *conception entertained of the ministry;* and that from three sources—

    (1) writings which are concerned with worship and church order :

    (2) the canons of councils :

    (3) some representative Fathers.

<small>(1) Liturgies, etc.</small>

(1) Besides the oriental offices of ordination, of ancient though uncertain date,[2] and some mediaeval commentaries on the ancient rites, such as that of Symeon of Thessalonica, we have older sources of evidence. There is the work of the (Syrian) pseudo-Dionysius, *On the Ecclesiastical Hierarchy,* a work probably of the end of the fifth century, elaborating the mystical significance of the Church's orders; and, more ancient, the work which by gradual accretions took shape in the *Apostolical Constitutions.* We have reason to know that this book existed substantially as we have it about the middle of the fourth century,[3]

---

[1] See Simcox *Early Church History* p. 359 n.[1]

[2] Given in Morinus *de S. Ord.* p. ii.

[3] Dr. Lightfoot has shown (*Ignatius* i. p. 253)—shown is not too strong a word even in face of Harnack—that the interpolator of the Ignatian letters

and it undoubtedly embodies a great deal of a much earlier date. Now, all this body of writings puts before us the ministry of bishops, presbyters, and deacons as constituting without any possibility of doubt the Church's hierarchy. There are minor orders, but they are on a different level.[1] Nor is there any tendency, as in some similar western works, to minimize the original distinction of bishops and presbyters. There is a difference indeed between one document and another in respect of the dignity of the presbyterate. The earlier work makes the bishop the typical priest, and, while it acknowledges the priestly character of the presbyter, tends to make him simply the bishop's assistant. In the later writings a more independent priesthood is recognised as belonging to the presbyter. This corresponds to the historical fact; for, while at first the bishop was the officiating priest in each community and the presbyters were his assistants, the process of decentralizing which went on in the East as in the West, though not to the same

plagiarized from the *Apostolical Constitutions*. "Moreover," he adds, "the plagiarisms are taken from the work as we have it now . . . The obligations to the two last books are hardly less considerable in comparison with their length than to the earlier and larger part of the work." But the date of the interpolated letters is fixed with great certainty by their doctrinal tone; they were composed in the latter half of the fourth century—perhaps soon after 350. "There is nothing," says Dr. Lightfoot, "in the Apostolic Constitutions, even in their present form, inconsistent with an earlier date than this, while their silence on questions which interested the Church in the middle and latter half of the fourth century is in itself a strong presumption that they were written before that date." This would still leave room for minor alterations—such as must have occurred in v. 17 (on the keeping of Easter), since it was quoted by Epiphanius.

[1] Cf. Symeon ap. Morinus *de S. O.* p. ii. p. 129. The orders treated of by Dionysius are three; he lays great stress on their separate dignity (ap. Morinus *de S. O.* p. ii. p. 53 f.). Cf. *Apost. Const.* viii. 46: bishops, priests, and deacons were ordained by the Apostles.

extent, resulted in the presbyter gaining a more independent ministry. So far as a change took place, it was in this direction rather than in the other. But it did not touch the distinction of orders; the bishop has from the first, and retains, the exclusive power to consecrate the chrism for confirmation and to ordain to the several orders of the clergy.[1] Nor is it unimportant to notice that there is no growth in the sacerdotal conception. On the contrary, while the mediaeval rites of ordination are moderate[2] in their expression of it, there is an overstrained tone sometimes apparent in the sacerdotalism of the earliest of these writings, the *Apostolical Constitutions*. The general conception of the priesthood is, however, practically identical through all the literature now under discussion.[3] The earliest description of the modes of ordaining a bishop and a presbyter will give us a clear impression of the way in which the ministry is regarded.

The 'apostolical constitutions.

Mode of ordaining a bishop.

At the ordination of a bishop,[4] there is first to be the gathering on the Sunday of the bishops, pres-

---

[1] See *Apost. Const.* vii. 42, viii. 28; cf. Dionysius (ap. Morinus *de S. O.* p. ii. p. 55): ἡ θεία θεσμοθεσία τὴν τῶν ἱεραρχικῶν τάξεων ἁγιαστείαν καὶ τὴν τοῦ θείου μύρου τελείωσιν καὶ τὴν ἱερὰν τοῦ θυσιαστηρίου τελετουργίαν ταῖς τῶν ἐνθέων ἱεραρχῶν [i.e. the bishops] τελεσιουργοῖς δυνάμεσιν ἐνιαίως ἀπεκλήρωσεν. So much later Symeon (*ib.* p. 129) reckons μύρον ἐνεργεῖν among episcopal powers; the presbyter has not the μεταδοτικὴ χάρις, nor is he able to do anything τελεστικὸν ἢ φωτιστικόν, but he can consecrate the mysteries and baptize.

[2] It is noticeable how the phrase occurs in the ordination of a deacon (ap. Morinus *de S. O.* p. ii. pp. 69, 79, 86): "Not through the laying-on of my hands, but by the visitation (ἐν ἐπισκοπῇ) of Thy rich mercies is grace given, that he may stand purged from all sin in the dreadful day of judgment." The distinction is thus emphasized between *order* and *sanctity*.

[3] The correlation of the high priest, priests, and Levites of the Old Testament with the bishops, presbyters, and deacons of the New appears in the *Apost. Const.*, only mingled with other comparisons.

[4] *Apost. Const.* viii. 4, 5. Dr. Hatch calls this ceremony of the ordina-

byters, and people. Then the presiding bishop is solemnly to question the presbyters and laity as to their choice of the candidate, as to his worthiness and character. This is to be done thrice, and they are to reply as at the tribunal of God and of Christ, and in the presence of the Holy Spirit and of the angels. "Then, silence having been made, one of the first bishops, standing with two others near the altar —the rest of the bishops and presbyters silently praying, and the deacons holding the Gospels open upon the head of him who is being ordained (χειροτονουμένου)—shall address God." He invokes Him under His attributes of supremacy and as the governor of the Church,[1] "who through the coming of Thy Christ in the flesh didst give laws to Thy Church, with the testimony of the Paraclete through Thine Apostles and us Thy bishops here present by Thy grace: who didst foreordain priests from the beginning for the government of Thy people, first Abel, Seth, Enos, Enoch, Noah, Melchizedek, and Job: who didst appoint Abraham and the rest of the patriarchs, with Thy faithful servants Moses and Aaron, Eleazar and Phinehas: who of them didst ordain rulers and priests in the tabernacle of witness: who didst choose Samuel for priest and prophet: who hast never left Thy sanctuary without a ministry: who wast pleased to be glorified in those whom Thou didst choose:" he then goes on to pray "now also do Thou by the intercession of Thy Christ, pour down by

tion of a bishop "the earliest eastern form of what in later times would have been called the ritual of 'ordination' or 'consecration'" (*B.L.* pp. 131, 132).

[1] For the two forms of the prayer, see Pitra *Iur. Eccl. Gr.* i. p. 50.

means of us the power of Thy ruling Spirit, who is ministered by Thy well-beloved Son Jesus Christ,[1] whom He gave by Thy will, who art the eternal God. Grant in Thy name, O God, who knowest the heart, to this Thy servant whom Thou hast chosen to be bishop, that he may rule (shepherd) Thy holy flock and exercise his high priesthood to Thee, blamelessly ministering day and night, and, propitiating Thy face, gather together the number of those who are being saved and offer to Thee the gifts of Thy holy Church: give him, O Lord almighty, through Thy Christ the participation of the Holy Ghost, that he may have authority to remit sins according to Thy commandment, to ordain clergy (διδόναι κλήρους) according to Thy ordinance, to loose every bond according to the authority which Thou hast given unto the Apostles,[2] and to please Thee in meekness and a pure heart unchangeably, unblamably, unimpeachably, offering to Thee [a pure and unbloody sacrifice, which through Christ Thou didst institute as the mystery of the new covenant, for] a savour of sweetness through Thy holy Servant Jesus Christ, our God and Saviour, through whom to Thee, be glory, honour, and reverence in the Holy Ghost, now and ever and for the ages of ages." "And when the bishop has thus prayed, the rest of the priests with the people shall respond 'Amen.' And after the prayer one of the bishops shall lift up (ἀναφερέτω)

---

[1] Αὐτὸς καὶ νῦν μεσιτείᾳ τοῦ χριστοῦ σου δι' ἡμῶν ἐπίχεε τὴν δύναμιν τοῦ ἡγεμονικοῦ σου πνεύματος, ὅπερ διακονεῖται τῷ ἠγαπημένῳ σου παιδί.

[2] Neither the power of ordination nor the power of binding and loosing is specified in the later rites. See App. Note C.

the sacrifice upon the hands of him who is ordained (χειροτονηθείς). And in the morning he shall be enthroned."

In the ordination of a priest,[1] the injunction is that the bishop lay his hand upon his head, with the presbytery and deacons standing by, and offer a prayer, in which God is invoked as providing "for things immortal by mere preservation, but for mortal things by a succession." He is implored "to look upon and increase the Church and multiply her rulers, ... to look upon this His servant raised to the presbytery by the vote and judgment of all the clergy, and to fill him with the Spirit of grace and counsel, that he may help and govern His people with a pure heart." As God did order Moses to elect elders and filled them with the Spirit, so now He is entreated "to supply and keep unfailing in us the Spirit of His grace, that he (the presbyter), filled with powers of healing[2] and the word of teaching, in meekness may instruct God's people and serve Him sincerely and accomplish unblamably the priestly ministries on behalf of His people."

Mode of ordaining a priest.

It is not necessary to quote the office for the ordination of a deacon. But it must be pointed out that what has been quoted above could easily be illustrated from different parts of this work. There is an intense insistence on the necessity for ordination to qualify a man for any ministerial work[3]: there

General doctrine of the priesthood.

---

[1] *Apost. Const.* viii. 16.

[2] This expression seems to derive from very early days; but similar expressions are found in the western prayers of ordination. See App. Note C.

[3] E.g. ii. 27: Πῶς οἷόν τε ἄνθρωπον ἑαυτὸν εἰς ἱερωσύνην ἐπιρρίπτειν, μὴ λαβόντα

150   *Christian Ministry.*   [CHAP.

is a reiterated magnifying of the office of bishops, whether as priests ministering the oblations of the new covenant, especially the eucharistic sacrifice,[1] or as prophets and kings ("he is your king and ruler," nay more, "he is your earthly god after God"[2]), or as mediators between God and His people,[3] as, "after God, their fathers, begetting them to adoption through water and the Holy Ghost": there is an emphatic distinction drawn between the powers of a bishop and those of a presbyter [4] ("the distinction of names

τὸ ἀξίωμα παρὰ κρείττονος, καὶ ποιεῖν ἐκεῖνα ἃ μόνοις τοῖς ἱερεῦσιν ἔξεστιν. Cf. ii. 28, iii. 10: οὔτε λαικοῖς ἐπιτρέπομεν ποιεῖν τι τῶν ἱερατικῶν ἔργων. It seems admitted (viii. 46) that God's supernatural or miraculous call, as in the case of Ananias (Acts ix), dispenses with the necessity for human ordination. But cf. viii. 26: an exorcist with the gift of healing would require to be ordained to the regular ministry.

[1] E.g. ii. 25: 'Ὑμεῖς οὖν σήμερον, ὦ ἐπίσκοποι, ἐστὲ τῷ λαῷ ὑμῶν ἱερεῖς, λευῖται, οἱ λειτουργοῦντες τῇ ἱερᾷ σκηνῇ, τῇ ἁγίᾳ καὶ καθολικῇ ἐκκλησίᾳ, καὶ παρεστῶτες τῷ θυσιαστηρίῳ κυρίου τοῦ θεοῦ ἡμῶν καὶ προσάγοντες αὐτῷ τὰς λογικὰς καὶ ἀναιμάκτους θυσίας διὰ Ἰησοῦ τοῦ μεγάλου ἀρχιερέως· ὑμεῖς τοῖς ἐν ὑμῖν λαικοῖς ἐστε π ρ ο φ ῆ τ α ι, ἄρχοντες καὶ ἡγούμενοι καὶ βασιλεῖς, οἱ μεσῖται θεοῦ καὶ τῶν πιστῶν αὐτοῦ, οἱ δοχεῖς τοῦ λόγου καὶ ἀγγελτῆρες, οἱ γνῶσται τῶν γραφῶν καὶ φθόγγοι τοῦ θεοῦ καὶ μάρτυρες τοῦ θελήματος αὐτοῦ, οἱ πάντων τὰς ἁμαρτίας βαστάζοντες καὶ περὶ πάντων ἀπολογούμενοι. Cf. ii. 27, 28.

[2] ii. 26: Οὗτος ἄρχων καὶ ἡγούμενος ὑμῶν. οὗτος ὑμῶν βασιλεὺς καὶ δυνάστης· οὗτος ὑμῶν ἐπίγειος θεὸς μετὰ θεόν· ὃς ὀφείλει τῆς παρ' ὑμῶν τιμῆς ἀπολαύειν. περὶ γὰρ τούτου καὶ τῶν ὁμοίων αὐτὸς ὁ θεὸς ἔλεγεν· Ἐγὼ εἶπα Θεοί ἐστε καὶ υἱοὶ ὑψίστου πάντες, καὶ Θεοὺς οὐ κακολογήσεις. ὁ γὰρ ἐπίσκοπος προκαθεζέσθω ὑμῶν ὡς θεοῦ ἀξίᾳ τετιμημένος, ᾗ κρατεῖ τοῦ κλήρου καὶ τοῦ λαοῦ παντὸς ἄρχει. Cf. ii. 33. This is surely rather overstrained language.

[3] ii. 25, 26: The bishop is μεσίτης θεοῦ καὶ ὑμῶν ἐν ταῖς πρὸς αὐτὸν λατρείαις . . . οὗτος μετὰ θεὸν πατὴρ ὑμῶν, δι' ὕδατος καὶ πνεύματος ἀναγεννήσας ὑμᾶς εἰς υἱοθεσίαν. ii. 32: δι' οὗ [sc. ἐπισκόπου] τὸ ἅγιον πνεῦμα ὁ κύριος ἐν ὑμῖν ἔδωκεν ἐν τῇ χειροθεσίᾳ, δι' οὗ ἅγια δόγματα μεμαθήκατε καὶ θεὸν ἐγνώκατε καὶ εἰς Χριστὸν πεπιστεύκατε, δι' οὗ ἐγνώσθητε ὑπὸ θεοῦ, δι' οὗ ἐσφραγίσθητε ἐλαίῳ ἀγαλλιάσεως καὶ μύρῳ συνέσεως, δι' οὗ υἱοὶ φωτὸς ἀνεδείχθητε, δι' οὗ κύριος ἐν τῷ φωτισμῷ ὑμῶν, τῇ τοῦ ἐπισκόπου χειροθεσίᾳ μαρτυρῶν, ἐφ' ἕκαστον ὑμῶν τὴν ἱερὰν ἐξέτεινε φωνὴν λέγων· Υἱός μου εἶ σύ, ἐγὼ σήμερον γεγέννηκά σε.

[4] viii. 46: Ἴστε γὰρ πάντως ἐπισκόπους παρ' ἡμῶν ὀνομασθέντας καὶ πρεσβυτέρους καὶ διακόνους εὐχῇ καὶ χειρῶν ἐπιθέσει, τῇ διαφορᾷ τῶν ὀνομάτων καὶ τὴν διαφορὰν τῶν πραγμάτων δεικνύοντας· οὐ γὰρ ὁ βουλόμενος παρ' ἡμῖν ἐπλήρου τὴν χεῖρα, ὥσπερ ἐπὶ τῆς κιβδήλου τῶν δαμάλεων ἐπὶ τοῦ Ἱεροβοὰμ παρακεκομμένης ἱερωσύνης, ἀλλ' ὁ καλούμενος ὑπὸ τοῦ θεοῦ. iii. 10: Οὐκ ἐπιτρέπομεν πρεσβυτέροις

III.] *The Witness of Church History.* 151

is a distinction of realities"—specially, only a bishop can ordain): there is a strong and powerful assertion of the principle of order: finally, there is a striking passage on the apostolical succession, with special reference to the perpetuating of the eucharistic sacrifice. "Christ, the only-begotten, was the first high priest by His Nature, not having snatched the honour for Himself, but being appointed by the Father; who became man for us, and, when offering His spiritual sacrifice to His God and Father before His passion, appointed us [1] only to do this, though there were with us others too who had believed on Him; but a believer did not, as such, become a priest or obtain the high priestly honour; but after His assumption, we, having offered according to His commandment a pure and bloodless sacrifice, appointed bishops and presbyters and deacons, seven in number."[2]

The later writings to which we have alluded are without the exaggerated tone which sometimes appears in the *Constitutions,* and the thoughts connected with the various ordinations are often of great moral beauty and interest. It is tempting to dwell upon them.[3] But, in spite of certain differences, the whole literature

χειροτονεῖν. viii. 46: 'Εκεῖνο κοινῇ πάντες παραγγέλλομεν, ἕκαστον ἐμμένειν τάξει τῇ δοθείσῃ αὐτῷ καὶ μὴ ὑπερβαίνειν τοὺς ὅρους.

[1] The Apostles are supposed to be the speakers.

[2] viii. 46: Πρῶτος τοίνυν τῇ φύσει ἀρχιερεὺς ὁ μονογενὴς Χριστός, οὐχ ἑαυτῷ τὴν τιμὴν ἁρπάσας, ἀλλὰ παρὰ τοῦ Πατρὸς κατασταθείς· ὃς γενόμενος ἄνθρωπος δι' ἡμᾶς καὶ τὴν πνευματικὴν θυσίαν προσφέρων τῷ θεῷ αὐτοῦ καὶ πατρὶ πρὸ τοῦ πάθους, ἡμῖν διετάξατο μόνοις τοῦτο ποιεῖν, καίτοι ὄντων σὺν ἡμῖν καὶ ἑτέρων τῶν εἰς αὐτὸν πεπιστευκότων· ἀλλ' οὐ πάντως ὁ πιστεύσας ἤδη καὶ ἱερεὺς κατέστη ἢ ἀρχιερατικῆς ἀξίας ἔτυχε· μετὰ δὲ τὴν ἀνάληψιν αὐτοῦ ἡμεῖς, προσενέγκοντες κατὰ τὴν διάταξιν αὐτοῦ θυσίαν καθαρὰν καὶ ἀναίμακτον, προεχειρισάμεθα ἐπισκόπους καὶ πρεσβυτέρους καὶ διακόνους ἑπτὰ τὸν ἀριθμόν.

[3] Some of the chief passages are quoted in App. Note C.

is pervaded by the same principles and it has been better for our purpose to exhibit them as they appear in the earliest documents.

(2) Canons of councils.

(2) What is the witness of oriental councils? It is very slight. For, as the principle of the ministry was little opposed, it was as little contended for; and it is not till the fourth century that we begin to have the canons of councils. The canonical literature is occupied a good deal with clerical discipline, and the distinctive powers of bishops, priests, and deacons are throughout assumed and guarded. The earliest recorded canons are those of Ancyra. The council held here was of the nature of a "general council" of the Churches of Asia Minor and Syria, "to heal the wounds inflicted on the Church by the persecution under Maximin."[1] The language of its twenty-five canons implies throughout the threefold ministry: there is the general government of the bishop,[2] the priestly ministration of the presbyters,[3] and the assistant ministry of the deacons.[4] The thirteenth canon has been much quoted as (implicitly) giving not only country bishops but also *town presbyters* a power to ordain, with the leave of the bishop of each diocese; but the reading which would give this meaning is not supported by the manuscripts. The true meaning seems to be represented in the Syriac

A.D. 314.

---

[1] Hefele *Conciliengesch.* § 16.

[2] Cc. 2, 5, 10, 15. The clergy in general (c. 3) constitute a τάξις.

[3] C. 1: presbyters τῆς τιμῆς τῆς κατὰ τὴν καθέδραν μετέχουσιν; their functions are προσφέρειν, ὁμιλεῖν, λειτουργεῖν τὰς ἱερατικὰς λειτουργίας.

[4] C. 2: ἡ ἱερὰ λειτουργία, ἢ τοῦ ἄρτον ἢ ποτήριον ἀναφέρειν—i.e. either the *presenting* the oblation to the presbyter who 'offers' (προσφέρει, c. 1; cf. the use of ἀναφέρειν in the account of the ordination of a bishop, *Apost. Const.* viii. 5): or the communicating the people (see below, Can. Nicaen. 18).

version: "It is not lawful for country bishops to create presbyters or deacons in the country, but also not in the city, without the permission of the bishop, which is everywhere granted by letters."[1] It has been mentioned already that a council at Alexandria (A.D. 324) declared the man who had been ordained by a presbyter to be a mere layman. The great Council [A.D. 325.] of Nicaea, among other canons,[2] prohibits deacons "who have no power to offer" from "giving the body of Christ to the presbyters" who have the sacrificial authority;[3] it also sternly rebukes a practice, which had come to the ears of the Fathers, of deacons communicating even before bishops. "Let all these things, then," the canon concludes, "be done away,

---

[1] On this see App. Note D. There were 'country priests' as well as 'country bishops.' Each class, having in some sense the same powers as the corresponding class of the town, had limited rights in the exercise of them. Thus only on an emergency could country priests celebrate in the town church (Can. Neo-Caes. 13); on the other hand country bishops could 'offer' in the town freely (Can. Neo-Caes. 14), but not ordain without special permission. The council of Neo-Caesarea was almost contemporary with that of Ancyra. It may be mentioned that the canons of Neo-Caesarea mention a current idea that the imposition of hands in ordination carried with it the absolution from all sins except carnal ones.

[2] The legislation about the metropolitan sees, i.e. the distinction of rank amongst bishops, does not here concern us. Notice will hereafter be taken of the absence of clear distinction between a *valid* and a *canonical* ordination.

[3] C. 18 (προσφέρειν, διδόναι τὸ σῶμα τοῦ χριστοῦ); cf. Can. Laodic. 19. The practice here rebuked, of deacons communicating presbyters, may have some analogy with the western custom, which gave the deacons an independent authority to minister the consecrated elements. "As the consecration belongs to the priest, so the dispensation of the sacrament belongs to the minister (deacon) . . . the former sanctifies the oblations, the latter dispenses them when they are sanctified. Moreover, the priests themselves are not allowed for fear of presumption to take the chalice from the Lord's table, unless it have been given them by the deacon." Thus "without deacons a priest has his name but not his office." This comes from Isidore of Spain *de Eccl. Off.* ii. 8 (ap. Hittorp. p. 23); it is repeated by Rabanus Maurus *de Inst. Cler.* i. 7 (ap. Hittorp. p. 316), and Ivo, bishop of Carnot (ap. Hittorp. p. 472). At the same time the deacon's 'ministerium' is carefully distinguished from the priesthood. Cf. Can. Ancyr. 2.

and let the deacons remain within their proper limits, knowing that they are the servants of the bishop and inferior to the presbyters: and let them take the Eucharist according to their rank after the presbyters, when it is given them either by the bishop or the presbyter. And deacons must not even sit down in the midst of the presbyters, for this is contrary to rule [canon] and order. And if any one will not obey, even after these regulations, let him be deposed from his diaconate." At Nicaea, and in the synods which followed, we have a great multitude of canons bearing on clerical discipline—insisting on clergy passing gradually through the various grades of the hierarchy, prohibiting their passing from one diocese to another, limiting their respective rights, regulating the gradations of rank—but nothing more that concerns our present purpose.

(3) Greek Fathers. 2d century.

(3) What is the witness of the Greek Fathers? The powerful testimony of Ignatius to the divine and exclusive authority of the bishop, as in each community the sole source of government and ministry, falls outside the period now under consideration and will be taken account of later. In the Clementines we have found a theory of the functions of the threefold ministry, in which the bishop has the supreme administration and the authority to bind and loose, but in which his *teaching* authority, as the successor to the "chair of the apostle," or "the chair of Christ," the great Prophet, is mainly emphasized.[1] Clement of Alex-

---

[1] See p. 130, n.[1] It must be remembered that the Clementines are Ebionite, and that their view of the Eucharist is a very low one.

III.] *The Witness of Church History.* 155

andria says but little of the ministry, as we have seen, but speaks of its three orders as representing ascending grades of spiritual dignity.

In the third century almost all that we get on the 3d century. theory of the ministry[1] in the East consists of scattered references in the writings of Origen. To him the ministry not only represents the divine authority of government, but is a priesthood, after the analogy of the Mosaic, and in application of the one priesthood of Christ.[2]

---

[1] It should, however, be said that Firmilian of Caesarea, one of the most distinguished bishops of the third century, in his letter in reply to Cyprian, A.D. 256 (ap. Cypr. *Ep.* lxxv), reproduces all Cyprian's language about the episcopate. See § 16: "Potestas ergo peccatorum remittendorum apostolis data est et ecclesiis quas illi a Christo missi constituerunt et episcopis qui eis ordinatione vicaria successerunt." § 17: "Stephanus se successionem Petri tenere contendit." It may be noticed that he speaks of bishops as *presbyters:* "quando omnis potestas et gratia in ecclesia constituta sit, ubi praesident maiores natu [i.e. οἱ πρεσβύτεροι] qui et baptizandi et manum imponendi et ordinandi possident potestatem" (§ 7); yet he also (§ 8) specifies bishops as claiming to give the Holy Ghost by laying on of hands: "ut hi quidem [i.e. episcopi qui nunc] possint per solam manus impositionem venientibus haereticis dare Spiritum sanctum." Cf. § 4: "seniores et praepositi." The word 'presbyter' could still be used in such a sense as to cover the bishops. This letter must have been translated by Cyprian. The traces of a Greek original, however, are plain; see *Dict. Chr. Biog.* s.v. CYPRIAN i.˙p. 751 n.[x] We can hardly be wrong so far in concluding that Firmilian accepted and repeated Cyprian's language about the episcopate, though he uses presbyter in a sense which leads to Cyprian translating it into maior natu.

[2] See *in Levit.* v. 3: Christ is the only sacrifice and the only priest; but He has given His priesthood to His Church; "consequens est ut secundum imaginem eius qui sacerdotium ecclesiae dedit, etiam ministri et sacerdotes ecclesiae peccata populi accipiant, et ipsi imitantes magistrum, remissionem peccatorum populo tribuant." The priests who preside in the Church are said repropitiare delicta (§ 4), but this is explained of the moral process by which they bring men back to God. There are strong exhortations to confession, which is to be private or public at the confessor's discretion, *in Psalm.* xxxvii. 6, hom. ii.; *in Levit.* ii. 4.

It should be mentioned at the same time that Origen seems to say that the unworthiness of the minister *does* affect the spiritual validity of his ministrations; cf. *in Levit.* v. 12: the unworthy priest "non est sacerdos nec potest sacerdos nominari." See Bigg *B.L.* p. 215 f.

We have quoted from Origen above (p. 140 n.[2]) on the threefold ministry.

156 *Christian Ministry.* [CHAP

4th century.

Athanasius.

In the fourth century the body of testimony grows with the mass of writings. There is, to quote some examples, the beautiful letter of Athanasius to Dracontius. Dracontius was a monk, who had been elected to a bishopric close to Alexandria and had received the "grace of the episcopate," but afterwards, moved by various fears, fled into concealment and left his high charge. Athanasius endeavours to recall him to his duty, in part by reminding him of monks who have made good bishops, but principally by recalling to his mind the dignity of the episcopate—as instituted by Christ through His Apostles and having, therefore, not merely the authority of the Church but the authority of Christ Himself, and as being the essential condition of the continuous life of the Church and the handing down of grace; by reminding him also that he has received an actual grace in his ordination as real as the grace of baptism, for which he will be in any case responsible.[1]

There is a temptation to dwell on the spiritual beauty and power which is put into the patristic conception of the ministry. When is Gregory of

[1] *Ep. ad Dracont.* 3, 4: Εἰ δὲ τῶν ἐκκλησιῶν ἡ διάταξις οὐκ ἀρέσκει σοι, οὐδὲ νομίζεις τὸ τῆς ἐπισκοπῆς λειτούργημα μισθὸν ἔχειν, ἀλλὰ καταφρονεῖν τοῦ ταῦτα διαταξαμένου σωτῆρος πεποίηκας σαυτόν· παρακαλῶ, μὴ τοιαῦτα λογίζου μηδὲ ἀνέχου τῶν ταῦτα συμβουλευόντων· οὐ γὰρ ἄξια Δρακοντίου ταῦτα· ἃ γὰρ ὁ κύριος διὰ τῶν ἀποστόλων τετύπωκε, ταῦτα καλὰ καὶ βέβαια μένει· ἡ δὲ τῶν ἀδελφῶν δειλία παύσεται. εἰ γὰρ τὸν αὐτὸν νοῦν εἶχον πάντες, οἷον νῦν ἔχουσιν οἱ συμβουλεύοντές σοι, πῶς ἂν ἐγένου σὺ χριστιανός, ἐπισκόπων μὴ ὄντων; ἐὰν δὲ καὶ οἱ μεθ᾽ ἡμᾶς ἀναλάβωσι τὸν τοιοῦτον νοῦν, πῶς ἂν συστῆναι δυνήσωνται αἱ ἐκκλησίαι; ἢ νομίζουσιν οἱ συμβουλεύοντές σοι μηδὲν εἰληφέναι σε, ὅτι καταφρονοῦσιν; ἀλλὰ καὶ τοῦτο ψευδῶς. ὥρα γὰρ αὐτοὺς νομίζειν μηδὲν εἶναι μηδὲ τὴν τοῦ λουτροῦ χάριν, ἐάν τινες τουτοῦ καταφρονῶσιν· ἀλλ᾽ εἴληφας, ὦ ἀγαπητὲ Δρακόντιε· μὴ ἀνέχου τῶν συμβουλευόντων σοι, μηδὲ ἀπάτα σαυτόν· ἀπαιτηθήσεται γὰρ τοῦτο παρὰ τοῦ δεδωκότος θεοῦ. ἢ οὐκ ἤκουσας τοῦ ἀποστόλου λέγοντος Μὴ ἀμέλει τοῦ ἐν σοὶ χαρίσματος. The expression ἡ τῆς ἐπισκοπῆς χάρις occurs in § 2.

Nazianzus' eloquence so high as in speaking of the priesthood? There is the intense sense of the dignity of the priesthood, of the surpassing moral claim which it makes on those who share it;[1] there is the clear and powerful realization of its connection with the whole purpose of the Incarnation; of the dependence of the priesthood of the Christian ministry upon the unique priesthood of Christ, and of its relation to the Mosaic priesthood as being its spiritual counterpart and fulfilment[2]; there is the unfailing spirituality of idea —the outward sacrifice which it is the priest's high vocation to offer, always being kept in close connec-

---

[1] See especially *Orat.* ii. 94, 95 (on the occasion of his ordination as presbyter, A.D. 361): Οἶδα δ' ἔγωγε μηδὲ τοὺς ἐν τοῖς σώμασι τῶν ἱερέων ἢ τῶν θυμάτων ἀνεξετάστους μένοντας ἀλλὰ τελείους τέλεια προσάγειν νενομισμένον, σύμβολον, οἶμαι, τοῦτο τῆς κατὰ ψυχὴν ἀρτιότητος· μηδὲ στολῆς τῆς ἱερατικῆς ἢ σκεύους τινὸς τῶν ἁγίων ψαύειν παντὶ θεμιτὸν ὄν· μηδὲ τὰς θυσίας αὐτὰς ὑφ' ὧν καὶ ὅτε καὶ οὗ μὴ καθῆκον ἦν ἀναλίσκεσθαι· μηδὲ τὸ ἔλαιον ἀπομμεῖσθαι τῆς χρίσεως μηδὲ τὸ θυμίαμα τῆς συνθέσεως· μηδὲ εἰς τὸ ἱερὸν εἰσιέναι, ὅστις ἢ ψυχὴν ἢ σῶμα οὐ καθαρός, μέχρι καὶ τῶν μικροτάτων· τοσούτου δεῖ εἰς τὰ ἅγια τῶν ἁγίων προσφοιτᾶν θαρροῦντα, ὧν ἑνὶ καὶ ἅπαξ τοῦ ἐνιαυτοῦ μόνον ἐπιβατὸν ἦν· τοσούτου δεῖ τὸ καταπέτασμα ἢ τὸ ἱλαστήριον ἢ τὴν κιβωτὸν ἢ τὰ Χερουβὶμ ἢ προσβλέπειν εἶναι παντὸς ἢ προσάπτεσθαι. ταῦτα οὖν εἰδὼς ἐγώ, καὶ ὅτι μηδεὶς ἄξιος τοῦ μεγάλου καὶ θεοῦ, καὶ θύματος καὶ ἀρχιερέως, ὅστις μὴ πρότερον ἑαυτὸν παρέστησε τῷ θεῷ θυσίαν ζῶσαν, ἁγίαν, μηδὲ τὴν λογικὴν λατρείαν εὐάρεστον ἐπεδείξατο, μηδὲ ἔθυσε τῷ θεῷ θυσίαν αἰνέσεως καὶ πνεῦμα συντετριμμένον, ἣν μόνην ὁ πάντα δοὺς ἀπαιτεῖ παρ' ἡμῶν θυσίαν, πῶς ἔμελλον θαρρῆσαι προσφέρειν αὐτῷ τὴν ἔξωθεν, τὴν τῶν μεγάλων μυστηρίων ἀντίτυπον, ἢ πῶς ἱερέως σχῆμα καὶ ὄνομα ὑποδύεσθαι, πρὶν ὁσίοις ἔργοις τελειῶσαι τὰς χεῖρας.

[2] *Orat.* x. 4: Διὰ τοῦτο εἰς μέσον ἄγεις καὶ ὑποχωροῦντος λαμβάνῃ καὶ παρὰ σεαυτὸν καθίζεις· τοῦτο τὸ ἐμὸν ἀδίκημα, φαίης ἄν; καὶ κοινωνὸν ποιῇ τῶν φροντίδων καὶ τῶν στεφάνων· διὰ τοῦτο χρίεις ἀρχιερέα καὶ περιβάλλεις τὸν ποδήρη καὶ περιτίθης τὴν κίδαριν καὶ προσάγεις τῷ θυσιαστηρίῳ τῆς πνευματικῆς ὁλοκαυτώσεως καὶ θύεις τὸν μόσχον τῆς τελειώσεως καὶ τελειοῖς τὰς χεῖρας τῷ πνεύματι καὶ εἰσάγεις εἰς τὰ ἅγια τῶν ἁγίων ἐποπτεύσοντα καὶ ποιεῖς λειτουργὸν τῆς σκηνῆς τῆς ἀληθινῆς ἣν ἔπηξεν ὁ κύριος καὶ οὐκ ἄνθρωπος· εἰ δὲ καὶ ἄξιον ὑμῶν τε τῶν χριόντων καὶ ὑπὲρ οὗ καὶ εἰς ὃν ἡ χρίσις, οἶδε τοῦτο ὁ πατὴρ τοῦ ἀληθινοῦ καὶ ὄντως χριστοῦ, ὃν ἔχρισεν ἔλαιον ἀγαλλιάσεως παρὰ τοὺς μετόχους αὐτοῦ, χρίσας τὴν ἀνθρωπότητα τῇ θεότητι, ὥστε ποιῆσαι τὰ ἀμφότερα ἕν, καὶ αὐτὸς ὁ θεὸς καὶ κύριος ἡμῶν Ἰησοῦς Χριστός, δι' οὗ τὴν καταλλαγὴν ἐσχήκαμεν, καὶ τὸ πνεῦμα τὸ ἅγιον, ὃ ἔθετο ἡμᾶς εἰς τὴν διακονίαν ταύτην ἐν ᾗ καὶ ἐστήκαμεν καὶ καυχώμεθα ἐπ' ἐλπίδι τῆς δόξης τοῦ κυρίου ἡμῶν Ἰησοῦ Χριστοῦ, ᾧ ἡ δόξα εἰς τοὺς αἰῶνας τῶν αἰώνων. ἀμήν.

tion with its inward and spiritual correlative, "the sacrifice of praise and of a contrite heart, which is the only sacrifice which God asks of us;"[1] there is the anxious sense of the difficulty of the pastoral cure, in view of all the perplexing varieties in men's dispositions and necessities, capacities and states of life, all of which the pastor must have in constant and instinctive view;[2] there is, lastly, the strong belief in the reality of ordination grace conveyed through the laying on of hands.[3]

Chrysostom. A great deal which can be said of Gregory in this connection can be said of John Chrysostom also. Two points are specially worthy of notice. First, that alive as Chrysostom is to the spiritual dignity of the priesthood, in virtue alike of its sacrificial and of its judicial powers,[4] he is equally alive to its responsibility for individual souls—laying immense stress on the necessity for considerateness, for gentle and patient self-adaptation to the different characters and needs and weaknesses of men, whether of high or low estate.[5] He

---

[1] See the quotation above from *Orat.* ii. On the true succession to the episcopate—moral as well as actual—see *Orat.* xxi on St. Athanasius.

[2] *Orat.* ii.

[3] Cf. the account of St. Basil on his death-bed (*Orat.* xliii. 78): θαυματουργεῖ τῶν προειρημένων οὐκ ἔλαττον—waking his faculties of speech and action on the verge of death to ordain some of his disciples, τὴν χεῖρα δίδωσι καὶ τὸ πνεῦμα.

[4] See especially his famous work *de Sacerdotio* iii. 4-7 ; vi. 4.

[5] Cf. *de Sacerdot.* ii. 3, 4; iii. 16 (on the case of the widows); iv. (latter part); vi. 8. This is a remarkable feature of the patristic conception of the ministry: for great orators, like Gregory and Chrysostom, are apt to be more alive to the common sensibilities of man than sympathetic with the differences of individual temperament. This insistence on the need of discerning men's different needs and characters appears equally in the western writers on the ministry. If it is not so prominent in St. Ambrose's *de Officiis*, it appears sometimes remarkably in St. Leo's conception of government where we should not expect it, and it is very prominent in St. Gregory

is as impressive on the function of the pastor as on that of the priest. Secondly, while he, like Gregory, speaks of the common priesthood which belongs to bishops and presbyters and emphasizes (like some westerns) the closeness of the two orders to one another in dignity, he never fails to distinguish the unique privilege and power of ordaining which belongs to the bishop.[1]

This special power of the episcopate was empha- *Epiphanius.* sized in the famous saying of Chrysostom's younger contemporary, Epiphanius, that while presbyters could beget children to the Church, i.e. by baptism, only bishops could beget fathers to the Church, i.e. by ordination. This passage in Epiphanius [2] is important (like the action of the Alexandrian council in the case of Colluthus), because it gives us an expression

(*de Cura Pastorali* ii init. and iii. This work had immense recognition and authority in the West and even in the East; see pref. to Mr. Bramley's translation). The same characteristic appears in the instructions to the penitentiary priest in the ancient *Ordo Romanus* (ap. Hittorp. p. 25 f.).

[1] Cf. *Hom. in* 1 *Tim.* xi. 1: Οὐ πολὺ μέσον αὐτῶν [πρεσβυτέρων] καὶ ἐπισκόπων· καὶ γὰρ καὶ αὐτοὶ διδασκαλίαν εἰσὶν ἀναδεδεγμένοι καὶ προστασίαν τῆς ἐκκλησίας. καὶ ἃ περὶ ἐπισκόπων εἶπε, ταῦτα καὶ πρεσβυτέροις ἁρμόττει· τῇ γὰρ χειροτονίᾳ μόνῃ ὑπερβεβήκασι, καὶ τούτῳ μόνον δοκοῦσι πλεονεκτεῖν τοὺς πρεσβυτέρους. *Hom. in Phil.* i. 1: οὐκ ἂν δὲ πρεσβύτεροι ἐπίσκοπον ἐχειροτόνησαν. *Hom. in* 1 *Tim.* xiii. 1: οὐ γὰρ δὴ πρεσβύτεροι τὸν ἐπίσκοπον ἐχειροτόνουν. Chrysostom (on Phil. i. 1) admits that St. Paul uses the terms bishop and presbyter interchangeably. But so also, he adds, is the word διακονία applied to the bishop's office. The language was not fixed, but the three offices were distinct: ὅπερ οὖν ἔφην, καὶ οἱ πρεσβύτεροι τὸ παλαιὸν ἐκαλοῦντο ἐπίσκοποι καὶ διάκονοι τοῦ Χριστοῦ, καὶ οἱ ἐπίσκοποι πρεσβύτεροι· ὅθεν καὶ νῦν πόλλοι συμπρεσβυτέρῳ ἐπίσκοποι γράφουσι καὶ συνδιακόνῳ· λοιπὸν δὲ τὸ ἰδιάζον ἑκάστῳ ἀπονενέμηται ὄνομα, ὁ ἐπίσκοπος καὶ ὁ πρεσβύτερος.

[2] *adv. Haer.* lxxv. 4: Ὅτι μὲν ἀφροσύνης ἐστὶ τὸ πᾶν ἔμπλεων [sc. Aerius], τοῖς σύνεσιν κεκτημένοις τοῦτο δῆλον· τὸ λέγειν αὐτὸν ἐπίσκοπον καὶ πρεσβύτερον ἴσον εἶναι. καὶ πῶς ἔσται τοῦτο δυνατόν; ἡ μὲν γάρ ἐστι πατέρων γεννητικὴ τάξις· πατέρας γὰρ γεννᾷ τῇ ἐκκλησίᾳ· ἡ δὲ πατέρας μὴ δυναμένη γεννᾶν διὰ τῆς τοῦ λουτροῦ παλιγγενεσίας τέκνα γεννᾷ τῇ ἐκκλησίᾳ, οὐ μὴν πατέρας ἢ διδασκάλους. καὶ πῶς οἷόν τε ἦν τὸν πρεσβύτερον καθιστᾶν μὴ ἔχοντα χειροθεσίαν τοῦ χειροτονεῖν, ἢ εἰπεῖν αὐτὸν εἶναι ἴσον τῷ ἐπισκόπῳ;

of the Church's mind in clear view of the antagonistic position. Aerius[1] had definitely held that there was no difference of order[2] between a bishop and a presbyter. "The bishop lays on hands," he said, "but so does the presbyter:[3] the bishop baptizes, so does the presbyter likewise: the bishop is the minister of worship, so is the presbyter: the bishop sits upon the raised seat (throne), and the presbyter too." There is then no difference. Aerius does not seem to have appealed to any church tradition, but simply to facts in the Church's present constitution and to the common use of the words 'presbyter' and 'episcopus' in the New Testament. Epiphanius meets his argument from the New Testament with a mixture of truth and error with which we are not at present concerned.[4] He meets him, however, first of all with an appeal to the mind of the Church

---

[1] Aerius was still alive (§ 1) when Epiphanius wrote. His original motive in formulating his anti-ecclesiastical views was not apparently a noble one, though Epiphanius does not make the best of those against whom he writes. He was in opposition not only to the right of bishops but to other church customs, and he was also of Arian antecedents.

[2] μία τάξις, μία τιμή, ἐν ἀξίωμα (§ 3).

[3] I.e. in certain benedictions of penitents the priest used prayer with laying-on of hands—'the prayer of imposition of hands.' This at least the Church would have admitted; πρεσβύτερος χειροθετεῖ, οὐ χειροτονεῖ (*Apost. Const.* viii. 28). See note (22) on *Apost. Const.* viii in Migne *Patrol. Graec.* i. p. 1083.

[4] He denies (unlike Chrysostom) that St. Paul uses πρεσβύτερος and ἐπίσκοπος of the same person. So far he has a bad case. On the other hand he argues that the Church in the apostolic days was incomplete; in some places there were bishops and deacons, in others presbyters, according to the degree of completeness of each Church or the fitness of individuals: οὐ γὰρ πάντα εὐθὺς ἠδυνήθησαν οἱ ἀπόστολοι καταστῆσαι . . . οὔπω [οὕτω MSS] τῆς ἐκκλησίας λαβούσης τὰ πληρώματα τῆς οἰκονομίας. οὕτω κατ' ἐκεῖνο καιροῦ ἦσαν οἱ τόποι. καὶ γὰρ ἕκαστον πρᾶγμα οὐκ ἀπ' ἀρχῆς τὰ πάντα ἔσχεν· ἀλλὰ προβαίνοντος τοῦ χρόνου τὰ πρὸς τελείωσιν τῶν χρειῶν κατηρτίζετο (§ 5). He also calls attention to the fact that the presbyters have at least some one over them in the Pastoral Epistles. Cf. Theodore Mops. on 1 Tim. iii. 8.

III.]   *The Witness of Church History.*   161

on the matter. His customary abusiveness of tone must not blind us to the fact that he speaks clearly, with the consciousness that he is on quite sure ground, when he says that, whatever the presbyter may do, he cannot lay on hands in ordination—that in this sense bishops alone constitute the "generative order" of the Church.[1]

Now the evidence of the Eastern Church has been passed in review. What is the result? Leaving out of account for the moment some elements in the estimate formed of the ministry which will come into consideration later, it is enough to say at present that everywhere, where there is any evidence forthcoming, we have found the threefold ministry existing and regarded as alone authoritative in virtue of succession from the Apostles. In all cases the authority to ordain the clergy has been found, wherever the question can be raised, to belong to the bishops, nor can fair evidence be produced of any single instance in which ordination by a presbyter (or in view of the exceptional arrangement supposed to have existed at Alexandria, we must say, by a presbyter with the ordinary commission) was either allowed[2] or even contemplated as under any circumstances allowable or valid.

Summary for the East.

B. We pass from the witness of Greek to that of Latin Christianity. Here we may deal very briefly with the evidence for the existence of the successions

B. The West. Episcopal successions not doubted.

---

[1] There is a passage about the apostolic succession, which may be referred to, in Ephraem Syrus *adv. Haer.* serm. xxii, ap. *Opp. Syr.* [ed. Rom. 1740] ii. p. 488.

[2] See on the case of Paphnutius App. Note E.

L

of bishops in the period under consideration, for it is not disputed. The episcopal succession was clearly of immemorial antiquity at Rome when Irenaeus wrote. There is no trace of a pre-episcopal age in any other part of Italy, or in Africa, Gaul, or Spain. The beautiful letter of the Churches of Lyons and Vienne, giving an account of the persecution which fell upon them in the time of Marcus Aurelius confirms the testimony of Irenaeus for Gaul.[1] The language of Tertullian is evidence enough for Africa, where indeed episcopacy developed into an exuberance of sees rivalled only in Asia. It is true that in later centuries episcopacy took some remarkable forms, especially, as has been noticed, in the Irish Church.[2]

[1] Euseb. *H.E.* v. 1. There is the aged bishop—Pothinus, ὁ τὴν διακονίαν τῆς ἐπισκοπῆς ἐν Λουγδούνῳ πεπιστευμένος; there is the deacon—Sanctus; there is the presbyter—Irenaeus (c. 4).

[2] A satisfactory account of the episcopate in the Scotic Church of Ireland may be found in Todd's *St. Patrick, Apostle of Ireland*, and Reeves' *Eccl. Antiquities of Down, Connor, and Dromore*. Its three notable features were (1) its indefinite multiplication; (2) its undiocesan character; (3) its subordination to the abbot-chiefs. The Church outside the empire, as inside it, was organized on the lines of the existing society. Thus in Ireland it became *tribal*, and small chieftaincies would have resulted in small episcopates (Reeves p. 303: "the spiritual jurisdiction of the bishop was coextensive with the temporal sway of the chieftain"). But what introduced its unique features into church organization here was its predominantly monastic character. The abbot was the real church ruler, and he was not always or generally a bishop. Hence the subordination of the episcopate. The bishops even lost control over the ordinations which they administered (cf. Bede *H. E.* iii. 4; Todd pp. 7-25). The episcopate, having thus lost its characteristic functions of government, was given as a mark of spiritual distinction (Todd p. 5). Thus it became indefinitely multiplied; seven bishops are often found together in one spot (Todd pp. 33-35). Also it lost its diocesan character (Reeves p. 135 f. on "the ambulatory nature of episcopacy"). When the Danish invasions (c. A.D. 795 and onward) drove the Irish clergy and monks in great numbers on to the continent of Europe, the bishops seem to have behaved themselves as if they were in their own country, in entire neglect of diocesan restrictions. Hence conciliar enactments against these "Scoti qui se dicunt episcopos esse" (Reeves p. 135). And up to the twelfth century, when the Irish Church was organized on diocesan lines under papal influence, the

There Christianity was monastic in a unique sense. The abbot took his place as spiritual head side by side with the chieftain of the clan. Often, indeed, the same person was both abbot and chieftain, and the old clan government continued with a new monastic character. Under these circumstances the bishop lost the governing authority which properly belonged to his office and became a mere instrument kept to perform those spiritual functions which he only could fulfil. But for such purposes he was kept: "the bishops were always applied to, to consecrate churches, to ordain to the ecclesiastical degrees or Holy Orders, including the consecration of other bishops; to give Confirmation, and the more solemn benedictions; and to administer the Holy Communion with peculiar rites."[1] No accession of power to abbot or king ever militated against the principle of ministerial succession. Through all the different forms which the church ministry assumed, and they have been very various, this has been the constant principle. Never has it been supposed that the accident of ecclesiastical

---

looseness of Irish episcopacy was a standing scandal to 'canonical' Europe; see the protests of Anselm and Bernard, quoted by Todd pp. 2, 4 : "dicitur," writes Anselm to a titular king of Ireland, "episcopos in terra vestra passim eligi et sine certo episcopatus loco constitui, atque ab uno episcopo episcopum sicut quemlibet presbyterum ordinari." [This latter irregularity was characteristic of the Celtic Church, but the canonical rule seems to have been observed at Iona; cf. Bede *H.E.* iii. 17-22.] So St. Bernard (*de vita S. Mal.* 10): "nam, quod inauditum est ab ipso Christianitatis initio, sine ordine, sine ratione mutabantur et multiplicabantur episcopi pro libitu metropolitani ita ut unus episcopatus uno non esset contentus, sed singulae paene ecclesiae singulos haberent episcopos." He clearly does not understand the situation.

[1] Todd *St. Patrick* p. 5. Cf. *Vita S. Brigidae*, ed. Colgan in the *Triadis Thaumaturgae Acta*, p. 523; Adamnan *Vita S. Columbae* i. 36, ed. Reeves [Dublin, 1857], pp. 66-69.

authority, apart from episcopal order, gave a man the power to ordain.¹

The conception of the ministry in

It remains then to seek the light thrown upon this conception of the ministry in the West—

(1) by typical theologians after A.D. 150 :²
(2) by writers on worship and by the church offices:
(3) by the canons of councils.

(1) Western Fathers.

Cyprian, c. A.D. 250.

(1) St. Cyprian, the great bishop of Carthage, stands out prominently among western writers who vindicated the claim of the apostolic ministry. It cannot be rightly maintained that he added anything new to the belief of his predecessors, western or eastern, in the visible unity of the Church or the authority of the episcopate. Nor did he bring these two doctrines into any new connection; Ignatius and Irenaeus had already put the bishop in a very clear position in relation to church unity. Nor again is it true to say that Cyprian in any way created the doctrine of schism or destroyed an existing "freedom of association" in the Church.³ He did not in fact

---

¹ See App. Note E on some supposed cases of presbyterian ordination.

² Clement of Rome is therefore not yet in discussion. The conception of the ministry held by Irenaeus and Tertullian has been already exhibited. A passage from Hippolytus is noticed in another connection, App. Note G.

³ Dr. Hatch (*B.L.* p. 103) has maintained that "the rule [that 'there should be only one bishop in a community'] was not firmly established until the third century. Its general recognition was the outcome of the dispute between Cyprian and Novatian." "For this assertion," says Dr. Salmon truly, "he offers no proof whatever. Cyprian certainly treats it as a monstrous and impious thing, that when one bishop had been duly elected another should be ordained; but there is no evidence that this view was then either novel or singular. Novatian no doubt had a respectable following, but there is no evidence that he claimed to be anything less than *the* bishop of Rome, or that either he or any of those who acknowledged him as bishop of Rome acknowledged Cornelius also as bishop" (*Expositor*, July 1887, p. 8 n.¹). The opposite is in fact quite plain : cf. the letters of Cornelius to

create or innovate, but he gave emphatic expression to an existing church principle in view of the particular circumstances of his episcopate.

The Church is one, then,—this is his position—with a visible external unity. The essence of that unity lies indeed in a spiritual fact—the life of Christ which is communicated to the Church; but this life is communicated to a visible society, bound together by visible bonds of external association.[1] To this visible society he that would be Christ's must belong; "he cannot have God for his father who has not

Fabian and of Dionysius to Novatian, ap. Euseb. *H. E.* vi. 43, 45. The Novatianist confessors clearly imply that there was no question of acknowledging both: see their profession ap. Cyprian *Ep.* xlix. To go back a long way before Cyprian, it is surely of the essence of Ignatius' conception that there should be but 'one bishop' in each community. Of course difficulties may have arisen in particular cases in determining what constituted a community. Ordinarily, no doubt, the civil 'civitas' became the ecclesiastical 'parish'; but we should like to hear something more definite about the position of Hippolytus at Rome, and how he was regarded by his contemporaries. He regarded himself, we can hardly doubt, as the bishop of Rome. He was in that capacity in antagonism to the regular bishop Callistus, who represented the laxer policy of the Church. But was he ordained bishop in antagonism to Callistus on the ground that he had lapsed into heresy and betrayed the church discipline? or is some other suggestion, such as Dr. Salmon makes (*Dict. Chr. Biog.* s.v. HIPPOLYTUS iii. pp. 90, 91), possible?

Harnack appends to his translation of Hatch's work (*die Gesellschaftsverfassung etc.* p. 252) a note in disagreement, in the above sense: "Ich kenne überhaupt keinen Grund, der gegen die Annahme spricht, dass sich die Regel, in jeder Stadt sei stets nur *ein* katholischer Bischof zu dulden, bereits am Ende des zweiten Jahrhunderts festgestellt hat." Dr. Hatch has more recently quoted in support of his view (*Growth of Ch. Instit.* p. 17) some words of Epiphanius: οὐ γάρ ποτε ἡ ᾿Αλεξάνδρεια δύο ἐπισκόπους ἔσχεν ὡς αἱ ἄλλαι πόλεις (*adv. Hær.* lxviii. 7). But the second bishop here spoken of as existing in other Churches of Egypt but not at Alexandria is the schismatic Meletian bishop. The Meletian schism is the subject of the whole section, and the context leaves no doubt as to the meaning. On the subject of this note see *Ch. Quart. Rev.*, July 1888, "Ancient and Modern Ch. Organization."

[1] Cf. *de Unit. Eccles.* 5: "Ecclesia Domini luce perfusa per orbem totum radios suos porrigit: unum tamen lumen est quod ubique diffunditur, nec unitas corporis separatur: ramos suos in universam terram copia ubertatis extendit, profluentes largiter rivos latius pandit: unum tamen caput est et origo una et una mater fecunditatis successibus copiosa."

the Church for his mother."¹ The sin of schism separates from Christ in such completeness that not even martyrdom can expiate it.² Of this unity the bishop is in each community at once the symbol,³ the guardian,⁴ and the instrument. He is the instrument of it because "the bishops, who succeed to the Apostles by an ordination which makes them their representatives," are the possessors of that sacerdotal authority and grace with which Christ endowed His Church, and which is necessary for her existence.⁵

---

¹ *Ep.* lxxiv. 7 (quoted above, p. 16, with other passages).

² *de Unit. Eccles.* 14. Great light is thrown on Cyprian's conception of the sin of schism, so far as concerns the relations of different Churches, by his subsequent attitude towards Stephen of Rome. He would no doubt have said that the sin of schism in the case of any division lies with the Church from which the unjust claim proceeds which causes the division. Stephen made such a claim, i.e. a claim affecting the independence of the Churches of Africa in an open question, and endeavoured to enforce it by an excommunication which Cyprian and the Africans ignored. "Make no mistake," wrote St. Firmilian of Caesarea, speaking of Stephen, "you have excommunicated yourself" (ap. Cypr. *Ep.* lxxv. 24). It is to be remarked that St. Augustin makes St. Cyprian in this matter the type of the unschismatical temper, because, while he maintained the independent judgment of the African Churches, he did not break off communion with those who differed from them; but, as far as in him lay, remained at unity with them in spite of differences (*de Bapt.* v. 25. 36). Augustin is following Jerome in this, who commends Cyprian on the same grounds (*adv. Lucifer.* 25: "non cum anathemate eorum qui se sequi noluerant").

³ *Ep.* xliii. 5: "Deus unus est et Christus unus et una ecclesia et cathedra una super Petrum Domini voce fundata. Aliud altare constitui aut sacerdotium novum fieri praeter unum altare et unum sacerdotium non potest."

⁴ *de Unit. Eccles.* 5: "Quam unitatem firmiter tenere et vindicare debemus, maxime episcopi qui in ecclesia praesidemus, ut episcopatum quoque ipsum unum atque indivisum probemus."

⁵ *Ep.* lxvi. 8: "Unde scire debes episcopum in ecclesia esse et ecclesiam in episcopo et si qui cum episcopo non sit in ecclesia non esse." *ib.* 4, 5: "[Christus] dicit ad apostolos ac per hoc ad omnes praepositos qui apostolis vicaria ordinatione succedunt: Qui audit vos, me audit . . . qui reiicit vos, me reiicit. . . . Unde enim schismata et haereses obortae sunt et oriuntur? dum episcopus qui unus est et ecclesiae praeest superba quorundam praesumptione contemnitur et homo dignatione Dei honoratus indignus hominibus iudicatur." *Ep.* xxxiii. 1: "Dominus noster, cuius praecepta metuere et servare debemus, episcopi honorem et ecclesiae suae rationem disponens in

This plenitude of the priesthood[1] is in every bishop, and in every bishop equally, just as every one of the Apostles was "endowed with an equal fellowship of honour and power." But the apostolate, which was finally given to all equally, was given first to St. Peter, that by its being given first to one man, there might be emphasized for ever the unity which Christ willed to exist among the distinct branches or portions of His Church.[2] The episcopate which belongs to each bishop belongs to him as one of a great brotherhood linked by manifold ties into a corporate unity.[3]

evangelio loquitur et dicit Petro: Ego tibi dico quia tu es Petrus, et super istam petram aedificabo ecclesiam meam, et portae inferorum non vincent eam, et tibi dabo claves regni caelorum, et quae ligaveris etc. . . . Inde per temporum et successionum vices episcoporum ordinatio et ecclesiae ratio decurrit ut ecclesia super episcopos constituatur et omnis actus ecclesiae per eosdem praepositos gubernetur. Cum hoc ita divina lege fundatum sit, miror quosdam audaci temeritate sic mihi scribere voluisse ut ecclesiae nomine litteras facerent, quando ecclesia in episcopo et clero et in omnibus stantibus sit constituta."

[1] As having this plenitude of the priesthood, the word sacerdos is generally used of the bishop; but the presbyter also has sacerdotal powers. Cyprian speaks of our Lord as "adorning the body of the presbyterate with glorious priests," i.e. at the ordination of a presbyter (*Ep.* xl). Cyprian did not draw out the usual analogy of bishop, priest, and deacon to high-priest, priest, and Levite of the Old Testament (*Dict. Chr. Biog.* s.v. CYPRIAN i. p. 741).

[2] *de Unit. Eccles.* 4: "Loquitur Dominus ad Petrum: Ego tibi dico, inquit, quia tu es Petrus etc. . . . Super unum aedificat ecclesiam, et quamvis apostolis omnibus post resurrectionem suam parem potestatem tribuat et dicat: Sicut misit me Pater et ego mitto vos: accipite etc. . . . tamen ut unitatem manifestaret, unitatis eiusdem originem ab uno incipientem sua auctoritate disposuit. Hoc erant utique et ceteri apostoli quod fuit Petrus, pari consortio praediti et honoris et potestatis, sed exordium ab unitate proficiscitur, ut ecclesia Christi una monstretur. Quam unam ecclesiam etiam in cantico canticorum Spiritus sanctus ex persona Domini designat et dicit: Una est columba mea." *ib.* 5: "Episcopatus unus est, cuius a singulis in solidum pars tenetur," i.e. in such a way that each has the responsibility of the whole; the whole is in each.

[3] *Ep.* lv. 24: "Cum sit a Christo una ecclesia per totum mundum in multa membra divisa, item episcopatus unus episcoporum multorum concordi numerositate diffusus."

A bishop stands, then, in various relations to the Church. In virtue of his election he represents his flock:[1] he is a part of the Church and in a sense responsible to it and stands in a certain constitutional, though not clearly defined, relation to his presbyterate and the clergy generally. They are his recognised council, advisers, co-operators; he does nothing without them.[2] But over and above this he represents divine authority. He is divinely appointed; he has not taken his honour upon himself.[3] Moreover, in the exercise of his authority, he is responsible to no man outside his Church but to God only. Cyprian does not explain, in connection with this position, the meaning of the provincial council of which he made so much use. Presumably the provincial council has a certain authority over the individual bishop,[4] but none the less the independence of each bishop is asserted by Cyprian with unrestricted completeness.[5] His respect

---

[1] "Ecclesia in episcopo est." Cf. *Ep.* lv. 5, and *Dict. Chr. Biog.* i. p. 741.

[2] See above, p. 105, and also Cyprian's letters to his presbyters, when in retirement, explaining the grounds on which he had ordained to the clergy without consultation; *Ep.* xxxviii. 1 : "In ordinationibus clericis, fratres carissimi, solemus vos ante consulere et mores ac merita singulorum communi consilio ponderare." *Ep.* xxx. 5 : "collatione consiliorum cum episcopis, presbyteris, diaconis, confessoribus, pariter ac stantibus laicis." See *Epp.* xxix; lxvii. 5.

[3] *Ep.* lxx. 3 : "Secundum [Domini] dignationem sacerdotium eius in ecclesia administramus." *Ep.* lix. 5 : "Existimat aliquis summa et magna aut non sciente aut non permittente Deo in ecclesia Dei fieri, et sacerdotes, id est dispensatores eius, erunt non de eius sententia ordinati ?" On the contrary: "plane episcopi non de voluntate Dei fiunt, sed qui extra ecclesiam fiunt."

[4] St. Augustin expresses the gradations in the authority of bishop and of church councils (*de Bapt.* v. 22. 30).

[5] *Ep.* lxii. 3 : "Qua in re nec nos vim cuiquam facimus aut legem damus, quando habeat in ecclesiae administratione voluntatis suae arbitrium liberum unusquisque praepositus, rationem actus sui Domino redditurus." *Ep.* lxxiii. 26 : "nemini praescribentes aut praeiudicantes, quo minus unusquisque episcoporum quod putat faciat, habens arbitrii sui liberam potestatem."

III.]   *The Witness of Church History.*   169

for the see of Rome, as being in a special historical sense—what every episcopate is essentially, as possessing the same authority—the see of Peter, will not go to the length of allowing it any jurisdiction over other Churches. It may be in a special way the symbol of unity, as Peter was among the Apostles, but it is nothing more.[1]

This is the theory of the episcopate into which St. Cyprian poured all the force of his great character, all the dignity of his strong holiness, to make it a living reality. He stands out in church history as the typical bishop, and with his weighty sentences he impressed on the episcopal theory an abiding form.

Next to Cyprian, it will be well to quote a vivid expression of the principle of the succession from a bishop of Cagliari in Sardinia—that Lucifer who was

<small>Lucifer, c. A.D. 360.</small>

---

[1] It is "locus Petri," "Petri cathedra, ecclesia principalis, unde unitas sacerdotalis exorta est" (*Epp.* lv. 8, lix. 14). These last words mean, I suppose, simply that Peter's priesthood was the first given: he goes on to assert the independent jurisdiction of each episcopate. Cf. Jerome *Ep.* cxlvi *ad Evangelum*: "Ubicunque fuerit episcopus sive Romae, sive Eugubii, sive Constantinopoli, sive Rhegii, sive Alexandriae, sive Tanis, eiusdem meriti, eiusdem est etiam sacerdotii. Potentia divitiarum et paupertatis humilitas vel sublimiorem vel inferiorem episcopum non facit. Ceterum omnes successores apostolorum sunt." It is not the place here to discuss whether the conception of the see of Peter, as in a special way the symbol and centre of unity, had any effect on the development of Petrine claims. The conception reappears in St. Optatus of Milevis (*de Schism. Don.* ii. 2, vii. 3—with a more 'papal' tone, but cf. vi. 3) and in St. Augustin; see *ABCDarium* l. 232: "Numerate sacerdotes vel ab ipsa Petri sede;" *c. Ep. Man.* 4: "Multa sunt alia quae in [ecclesiae catholicae] gremio me iustissime teneant . . . tenet ab ipsa sede Petri apostoli, cui pascendas oves suas post resurrectionem Dominus commendavit, usque ad praesentem episcopatum successio sacerdotum." Elsewhere he speaks of all the Apostles as the source of the succession: "ecclesia ab ipso Christo inchoata et per apostolos provecta certa successionum serie usque ad haec tempora, toto terrarum orbe dilatata. . . . ecclesia, quae ab ipso per apostolos succedentibus sibimet episcopis usque ad haec tempora propagata dilatatur" (*c. Faust.* xxviii. 2, 4).

Athanasius' friend, but whose impatience and violence led him at last into being the founder of a schismatical body. He is addressing Constantius the emperor out of his place of exile in Palestine and speaking of his nobler friend Athanasius.[1]

"You persecute the man," he says, "whom you ought to listen to. While he is still alive, you send to succeed him that George who is your partner in heresy, when, even if Athanasius had been set free from the body, it was not lawful for you to send any one, but it was and is in God's hand to appoint whom He thought proper as bishop of His people, and that through His servants the catholic bishops. For no man can be filled with the power of the Holy Ghost to govern God's people, save he whom God has chosen, and on whom hands have been laid by the catholic bishops, just as, when Moses was dead, we find his successor Joshua, the son of Nun, filled with the Holy Ghost; because, says Scripture, Moses had laid his hands upon him."[2]

---

[1] Whether he was himself ever actually separated from the Church is doubtful; see *Dict. Chr. Biog.* s.v. LUCIFER. His writings date from his exile.

[2] *de S. Athan.* I. 9: "Persequeris eum per quem te audire praeceperit Dominus; agente eo in rebus humanis cohaereticum tuum Georgium mittis successorem, cum, tametsi fuisset liberatus iam Athanasius ex corpore, tibi non licuerit mittere, sed fuerit ac sit in Dei manu quem fuisset dignatus populo suo antistitem instituere per servos videlicet suos, hoc est catholicos episcopos. Neque enim posset impleri virtute Spiritus sancti ad Dei gubernandum populum nisi is quem Deus allegisset cuique manus per catholicos episcopos fuisset imposita, sicut defuncto Moyse impletum Spiritu sancto invenimus successorem eius Iesum Naue. Loquitur scriptura sancta dicens: Et Iesus filius Naue impletus est spiritu intelligentiae; imposuerat enim Moyses manum super eum: et audierunt eum filii Israel et fecerunt secundum quod mandavit Dominus Moysi. Conspicis ordinationi Dei te obviam isse contra Dei faciendo voluntatem, temet mucrone gladii tui iugulatum, siquidem non licuerit ordinari, nisi fuisset defunctus Athanasius, et defuncto Athanasio catholicus debuerit per catholicos ordinari episcopos."

III.]   *The Witness of Church History.*   171

Now we approach an interesting class of writers who represent a tendency in the western Church to minimize the position of the episcopate. There is, first, the author of the Commentaries on St. Paul's Epistles who is commonly called Ambrosiaster and wrote in Damasus' episcopate at Rome.¹ Whoever he was, he was a man of considerable mental power and spiritual insight—" brief in words, but weighty in matter." Secondly, we have the author of some Questions on the Old and New Testament, once ascribed to Augustin,—probably a presbyter at Rome of the same epoch as the last writer, but so far later that he uses his commentaries.² Thirdly, there is Jerome, who expresses the same sentiments as the other two writers, but at a later date, apparently

<small>Ambrosiaster, Jerome, etc., c. A.D. 360-400.</small>

---

¹ "Cuius [ecclesiae] hodie rector est Damasus" (in 1 Tim. iii. 14). We may assume that St. Augustin is right in calling him Hilary (see for evidence *Dict. Chr. Biog.* s.v. AMBROSIASTER). It is however hardly possible that he can be Hilary, the Sardinian deacon, associated with Lucifer in his embassage to Constantius in A.D. 354, and subsequently a 'Luciferian.' Not so much (a) because St. Augustin calls him "sanctus," for Jerome calls Lucifer "beatus" and "bonus pastor" even when he is deploring his grave mistake (*adv. Lucifer.* 20—though, be it remembered, St. Augustin borrows considerably from this little treatise in his argument against the Donatists and in it Hilary is pilloried with all the power of Jerome's sarcasm)—not so much, however, on this account as (b) because the commentary on 1 Cor. i. 12-16 is not the work of one who followed Lucifer, a rigorous anabaptist (*adv. Lucifer.* 26), and (c) because he acknowledges Damasus as bishop. But we have not the means of saying how much the Commentaries may have been interpolated, or when.

² He wrote at Rome (*Qu.* cxv; cf. his polemic against Roman deacons in *Qu.* ci; the "we" who are opposed to the Romans in *Qu.* lxxxiv are probably the Christians—see Langen *Gesch. der Röm. Kirche* i. p. 600) about 300 years after the destruction of Jerusalem under Vespasian (*Qu.* xliv) i.e. A.D. 370-380. He was seemingly a priest—"sacerdos Dei et praepositus plebis" (*Qu.* cxx); and we gather that he was a presbyter from his polemics against deacons and depreciation of bishops (*Qu.* ci). This, however, does not give us any ground for saying that he belonged to the Luciferian party. The same tone meets us in Jerome. He uses the Commentaries of Ambrosiaster, but his style seems to imply that he is a different man.

when he had become thoroughly disgusted with the Church at Rome, and had changed his earlier tone towards it and its clergy.[1] It must be added that Jerome's sentiments passed into the writings of some later western authors.[2]

<small>These last writers (a) are sacerdotal;</small>

What then is it that these writers teach about the ministry? First, it must be said that they in no way minimize the sacerdotal character of the ministry. Jerome is indeed something of an extreme sacerdotalist; and if the unknown Commentator is not that, at least he gives us a substantial view of the priestly function. "Layings-on of hands [i.e. ordinations]," he says, "are mystical words, by which the selected man is confirmed for his work, receiving authority, so that he should venture in the Lord's place to offer sacrifice to God." "That," says St. Jerome, "can be no Church which has no priest."[3]

<small>(b) do not dispute the exclusive powers of bishops in their day,</small>

Next, none of these writers disputes the present authority of the threefold ministry or the limitation to bishops of the power of ordination. They do not maintain that, even in the extremest circumstances,

---

[1] In Jerome's earlier years his tone is papal, e.g. in his letters to Damasus from the East A.D. 375-380 (*Epp.* xv, xvi). Afterwards, disgusted with Roman manners and disappointed of the Roman episcopate, he broke with the Church there A.D. 385, and his abusive tone about the Roman clergy is subsequent to this date, e.g. *Ep.* lii *ad Nepotian.* is after A.D. 393. His Commentaries on the New Testament, which contain the passages minimizing the episcopal office by comparison with the presbyterate, date A.D. 386-392. His letter to Evangelus (*Ep.* cxlvi) is marked by its hostile tone towards Rome to belong to the period subsequent at any rate to A.D. 385, and *Ep.* lxix *ad Oceanum* is about A.D. 400.

[2] See App. Note F. "S. Hieronymi sententia," says Morinus (*de S. Ord.* p. iii. ex. iii. 2. 19), "universae ecclesiae Latinae acceptissima fuit et immerito a multis theologis cum gravi censura repudiata: imprudentes enim cum S. Hieronymo universam prope ecclesiam Latinam condemnarunt."

[3] For all quotations from these writers see App. Note F.

a presbyter—a presbyter of the existing Church—could validly ordain. Thus the Commentator is emphatic "that none of the clergy, who has not been ordained to it, should take to himself any office which he knows not to have been intrusted or granted to him" (in spite, that is, of what may have been the primitive practice). "It never was lawful or permitted," he says again, "that an inferior should ordain a superior, for nobody gives what he has not received." "All orders are in the bishop;" "the dignity of all ordinations is in the bishop." "What does a bishop do," says St. Jerome, even when he is minimizing the episcopate, "that a presbyter does not do, *except ordination?*" The bishop and the presbyter are to one another as the high priest and priest of the old covenant.

Once more, they do not regard the present threefold arrangement of the ministry as an innovation of the postapostolic Church, so that it should lack the authority of the Apostles. The present constitution represents *their* ordering. Nay, according to the Commentator, it represents more: "because all things are from one God the Father, He hath decreed that each Church should be presided over by one bishop." or since the Apostles:

Jerome, however, seems to hold that, while Christ instituted only one priestly office, it was the exigencies of church life which led to its being subdivided under apostolic sanction into the presbyterate and the episcopate. At any rate, whether the distinction was 'ordained by Christ Himself' or of apostolic only they maintain that presbyters were at first also bishops,

authority, these writers were agreed that (as the names 'bishop' and 'presbyter' are used in the New Testament of the same officers) the presbyters originally were also bishops, and it was because of the dangers of rivalry and division which threatened this arrangement from the first that it was determined that in future only one person should have the authority and name of the episcopate, the rest receiving only the commission of presbyters.[1] How much truth there is in this view is not now in question. They thought also that this original identity of the presbyterate and episcopate had left its mark on the subsequent constitution of the Church in such sense that presbyters and bishops still share a common priesthood, and that (waiving the question of confirmation[2]) there is nothing which is reserved to a bishop except the function of ordination. Jerome used this view with powerful effect to exalt the priesthood of the presbyter, as against the arrogance of Roman deacons on the one hand, and on the other against the overweening self-assertion of bishops. It was a bad custom, he thought, which prevailed in some Churches, that presbyters should not be allowed to preach in the presence

and somewhat minimize the subsequent difference.

---

[1] Jerome affirmed, as has been said, that the old constitution had in a measure been maintained at Alexandria down to the third century.

[2] The western councils strictly limit to bishops the consecration of the chrism. St. Jerome makes no remark on the subject where he is speaking controversially on the subject of bishops, but he assumes (*adv. Lucifer.* 9) the limitation of confirmation to bishops in a sense which implies that under no circumstances, not even of imminent death, could a presbyter confirm. At Alexandria, say the Commentator and the author of the *Quaestiones*, a presbyter confirms (consignat or consecrat) if the bishop be absent, but they are contradicted by the contemporary Alexandrian Didymus. See p. 138 n.[2]

of bishops.¹ Their exalted dignity is a thorn in Jerome's side; "as if they were placed in some lofty watch-tower, they scarcely deign to look at us mortals or to speak to their fellow-servants."² A priest should indeed " be subject to his bishop [pontifex] as to his spiritual father, but bishops should know that they are priests, not lords, and if they wish their clergy to treat them as bishops, they must give them their proper honour."³ This is the animus in Jerome's theory.⁴

Now when we have clearly considered this view, we shall see surely that it is not what it is sometimes represented as being. It is not a 'presbyterian' view. It does indeed carry with it the conception of the great church order being the priesthood; it emphasizes that the distinction of presbyter and bishop is nothing compared to the distinction of deacon and priest. Moreover, it involves a certain tentativeness in the process by which the Apostles are held to have established the church ministry; it admits a survival of an older constitution into the later life of the Church. But it does not carry with it the idea that the presbyter, pure and simple, the presbyter of the settled church constitution, has the power under any circumstances to assume episcopal functions. It teaches something quite different, viz. that the earliest presbyters were ordained with episcopal functions—were, *This view not unacceptable.*

---

¹ *Ep.* lii *ad Nepot.* 7 : "Pessimae consuetudinis est in quibusdam ecclesiis tacere presbyteros et praesentibus episcopis non loqui."
² in Gal. iv. 13. ³ *Ep.* lii. 7.
⁴ "S. Hieronymus in aestu contentionis indulgere solet exaggerationibus rhetoricis" (Morinus).

in fact, bishops as well as presbyters—till the subsequent ordination of presbyters without episcopal functions put an end to the old arrangement and brought about—not episcopacy—but what we have called monepiscopacy.¹ St. Paul, says the Commentator, passes from the ordination of bishops to that of deacons, because the ordination of a bishop and a presbyter is the same. But this 'is' must be an 'historical present.' The ordinations of a bishop and a presbyter were wholly distinct in his day. "In our day," he says, a few lines further on, "there should be in a city seven deacons and a certain number of presbyters and one bishop." Church authority had in fact restrained to one the functions which at first were more widely extended, and no one can at all enter into the feelings of the early Church about ordination who does not perceive how much stress they laid on church authority, as conditioning a man's spiritual status.²

(2) Canons of councils.

(2) We need not dwell long on the western councils. After the Carthaginian council in 256 A.D., which simply echoes the mind of Cyprian on the rebaptism of heretics and only gives us evidence we hardly need that Cyprian's view of the bishop's office was also the view of his colleagues, the record of western councils opens with that of Elvira

---

¹ See Thomassin *Vetus et Nova Ecclesiae Disciplina* p. 1. lib. i. c. 1. § 6.

² Morinus sees the more modern representation of Jerome's view in the scholastic opinion that the episcopate does not differ from the presbyterate in *sacerdotal character*, but is an *extension* of the same character by the addition of a new authority. The consecration of a bishop does not impose a new *character*, but only superadds a new authority. See *de S. Ord.* p. iii. ex. iii. c. 1.

(Illiberis) in Andalusia, which occurred in the early years of the fourth century, and that of Arles—a representative western council—in A.D. 314.[1] Both these councils assume as a matter of course the sacerdotal ministry of the Church and the three orders of bishops, presbyters, and deacons.[2] So far as they are concerned with the ministry, they are occupied only with the maintenance of discipline and the regulation of inter-episcopal relations.[3]

(3) When we turn to the Latin rites of ordination, we find a constant implication of the doctrine of

(3) Latin liturgies indicate

---

[1] Augustin even calls it a "plenarium ecclesiae universae concilium."

[2] Episcopi, presbyteres et diaconos (Elvira, cc. 18, 19; cf. 27, 75 and Arles, cc. 20, 21): clerical office a status (Elvira, c. 53): the bishops sacerdotes (Elvira, c. 48): the sacerdotal function sacrificare (Arles, c. 19).

[3] E.g. there is the restraining of deacons in Arles, c. 18, whose arrogance we hear of first in Cyprian's letters (*Ep.* iii. 3: the deacon must "honorem sacerdotis agnoscere"). In days of persecution deacons had been known even to offer the Eucharist in many places, and this is curtly reprimanded: cf. Arles, c. 15 "De diaconibus quos cognovimus multis locis offerre, placuit minime fieri debere." [There is no reason whatever for thinking that this represents any remains of an earlier discipline. How in days of persecution such an abuse should have sprung up is intelligible enough. It must be remembered that the fourth century is full of lament over the decay of discipline, as e.g. in Basil the Great, *Ep.* xc.] In Spain there is no trace of such a license, but we hear of deacons in charge of congregations, as in later ages, and Elvira c. 77 enacts thus: "Si quis diaconus regens plebem sine episcopo vel presbytero aliquos baptizaverit, episcopus eos per benedictionem perficere debebit [i.e. confirm]: quod si ante de saeculo recesserint, sub fide qua quis credidit poterit esse iustus."

Elvira c. 32 restrains to bishops the function of dealing with penitents; only in cases of necessity may a presbyter admit to communion, or even a deacon, if the priest order him. Cf. Carthage, A.D. 390, cc. 3, 4; Hippo Regius, A.D. 393, c. 30. Other canons concern clerical discipline (Elvira, c. 33, Arles, c. 2); the mutual relation of bishops (Elvira, cc. 53, 58, Arles, c. 17); the requirement of at least three bishops to consecrate another (Arles, c. 20); the permission, in necessity, of lay baptism, to be followed by episcopal confirmation (Elvira, c. 38).

We notice specially in later councils (e.g. Carthage, A.D. 390, cc. 3, 4; Hippo, A.D. 393, c. 34; Toledo, A.D. 400, c. 20) the limitation to bishops of the consecration of the chrism. There was clearly a tendency in the presbyters to assume this function.

the priesthood and of the orders in the ministry of bishops, priests, and deacons.[1] The distinction between these and the minor orders is marked in the West by the subdeacon not receiving the laying-on of hands.[2] It should be noticed in this connection that the uniformity of idea which pervades the various rites of ordination (and in this respect we may include the Greek with the Latin) makes a great impression upon the mind. It is not indeed the case that there is no change of ideas, but it is not in any way fundamental. The conception of the Christian pastorate and priesthood in succession to the apostles is the constant element.

(a) increase in ritual, not in doctrine; Such change as appears is mainly of two sorts. There is, first, the elaboration of ritual. It is important indeed to remind ourselves that a more elaborate ritual of ordination does not necessarily mean a deepening of the conception of what ordination brings with it. The earliest writing devoted to the consideration of a Christian sacrament—Tertullian's treatise *On Baptism*—is as full of belief in the spiritual effect of the laver of regeneration as any treatise of a mediaeval schoolman could be; but he makes it his special point that it is on account of the real spiritual efficacy of Christian sacraments that they

---

[1] This statement is justified in App. Note C. The episcopate is called an ordo (episcopatus ordo) in the Gregorian Sacram. ap. Muratori *Lit. Rom. Vet.* ii. p 358.

[2] So the so-called canons of the fourth council of Carthage ordained (c. 5 quoted by Morinus *de S. Ord.* p. ii. p. 260). Cf. Isidore *de Eccl. Off.* ii. 10 ap. Hittorp. p. 23: "hi [sc. subdiacones] igitur cum ordinantur, sicut sacerdotes et Levitae, manus impositionem non suscipiunt." So Rabanus Maurus *de Inst. Cler.* i. 8 ap. Hittorp. p. 316.

do not need to be made impressive by outward pomp. They can be simple, because they have so real an inward grace attached to them. It is pagan rites which need decking out with pomp and circumstance, just because they have nothing else to trust to for impressing men's minds.[1] The belief in baptismal grace, then, did not grow with the elaboration of baptismal ceremony. Just in the same way it does not follow that, because ordination rites became more complicated, the Christian Church was growing to rate more highly the consecration which they conveyed. To the last there remains in the western office a reminder that, while outward pomp was of the essence of the old priesthood, for the very reason that that was essentially external and symbolical, the essence of the new priesthood lies in inward and spiritual reality. The prayer for the consecration of a bishop calls to mind the glory of the vestments of the Aaronic priesthood, and prays that whatever those vestments signified by the brilliancy of gold, by the splendour of gems, by the variety of manifold workmanship, may shine forth now in the characters of Christian bishops, and that the precious ointment upon the head which runs down unto the beard and goes down to the skirts of the clothing may be to

---

[1] The passage is well worth quoting. *de Bapt.* 2 : "Nihil adeo est, quod tam obduret mentes hominum, quam simplicitas divinorum operum quae in actu videtur et magnificentia quae in effectu repromittitur: ut hic quoque quoniam tanta simplicitate sine pompa, sine apparatu novo aliquo, denique sine sumptu homo in aqua demissus et inter pauca verba tinctus non multo vel nihilo mundior resurgit, eo incredibilis existimetur consecutio aeternitatis. Mentior, si non e contrario idolorum sollemnia vel arcana de suggestu et apparatu deque sumptu fidem et auctoritatem sibi exstruunt. Pro misera incredulitas, quae denegas Deo proprietates suas, simplicitatem et potestatem!"

them the unction within, aye and without, of spiritual grace and spiritual power.¹

(b) a growing independence in the priesthood of the presbyter.

Secondly, beside ritual adjuncts there is a certain change in idea noticeable in the rites of ordination. It consists chiefly in emphasizing the special sacerdotal functions of the *presbyter*. Thus in the later forms we have the commissions to the priest: 'Receive power to offer sacrifice;' 'Receive the Holy Ghost: whose sins thou dost remit, they are remitted, etc.' Now these later forms are significant. There is indeed nothing new in the conception of sacrifice or of the power of absolution as belonging to the priesthood, nor is any new idea involved in the imperative form of commission; what is new is the specification of them and especially of the latter in the case of the presbyter. It belongs to a stage of church organization in which the presbyter is regarded as having a more independent priesthood, attaching to him as an individual. In earlier days the priesthood is kept more closely in connection with the Church or community. In the Church or community the high priest or bishop exercises the sacerdotal and pastoral functions, and the presbyters are attached to him as 'co-operators of his order.' This idea of co-operation is what is remarkably emphasized in the early prayers for their ordination. Later—owing to the more independent position which the circumstances of large dioceses gave to the presbyter—his substantive priesthood, inhering in him as an individual, comes more to the front.

¹ See App. Note C.

III.]   *The Witness of Church History.*   181

A presbyter is not so much a man who occupies a certain position and grade in the hierarchy of the community; he is an individual with special powers. His priesthood has become detached.[1]

[1] It will be useful at this point to quote some summary statements from western writers of what belongs to the presbyter's office. Thus from St. Isidore, c. A.D. 620, *de Eccl. Off.* ii. 7 ap. Hittorp. p. 22 : "[Presbyteris] sicut episcopis dispensatio mysteriorum Dei commissa est. Praesunt enim ecclesiis Christi et in confectione divina corporis et sanguinis consortes cum episcopis sunt, similiter et in doctrina populorum et in officio praedicandi." He follows Jerome, and quotes him in saying that only ordination is reserved to the bishop. But later (c. 25) he adds confirmation (quoting Pope Innocent), "nam presbyteri, licet sint sacerdotes, pontificatus tamen apicem non habent. Hoc autem solis pontificibus deberi, ut vel consignent vel paracletum Spiritum tradant, quod non solum ecclesiastica consuetudo demonstrat, verum et superior illa lectio apostolorum, etc. . . . Nam presbyteris, sive extra episcopum, sive praesente episcopo baptizant, chrismate baptizatos ungere licet, sed quod ab episcopo fuerit consecratum : non tamen frontem ex eodem oleo signare, quod solis debetur episcopis, cum tradunt Spiritum paracletum." When speaking of penitence, he specifies "sacerdotes" as the ministers of it —"astante coram Deo sollemniter sacerdote"—without mentioning whether bishop or presbyter (ii. 16). The *Ordo Romanus* (ap. Hittorp. p. 93) specifies offerre, benedicere, praeesse, praedicare, baptizare, as the functions of the presbyter. Pseudo-Albinus Flaccus (ap. Hittorp. p. 50) while repeating the older canon which allows a deacon to receive confessions where there is no priest, makes the bishops *or* presbyters—"quibus claves regni caelorum traditae sunt"—the proper ministers of the penitential discipline. Rabanus Maurus (*de Inst. Cler.* ii. 30), while making bishop *or* presbyter the minister of *private* confession, makes the bishop the minister of public penance, and the bishop or presbyter *at his desire* (iussu tamen episcopi) the minister of public absolution.

All this is summed up in canon 7 of the second council of Seville presided over by Isidore A.D. 619 : "Nam quamvis cum episcopis plurima [presbyteris] ministeriorum communis sit dispensatio, quaedam tamen auctoritate veteris legis, quaedam novellis ecclesiasticis regulis sibi prohibita noverint : sicut presbyterorum et diaconorum ac virginum consecratio ; sicut constitutio altaris, benedictio vel unctio : siquidem nec licere iis ecclesiam vel altarium consecrare ; nec per impositionem manus fidelibus baptizatis vel conversis ex haeresibus paracletum Spiritum tradere ; nec chrisma conficere, nec chrismate baptizatorum frontem signare ; sed nec publice quidem in missa quemquam poenitentium reconciliare ; nec formatas cuilibet epistolas mittere. Haec enim omnia illicita esse presbyteris, quia pontificatus apicem non habent, quod solis debere episcopis auctoritate canonum praecipitur, ut per hoc et discretio graduum et dignitatis fastigium summi pontificis demonstretur. Sed neque coram episcopo licere presbyteris in baptisterium introire, neque praesente antistite infantem tingere aut signare, nec poenitentes sine praecepto episcopi sui reconciliare, nec eo praesente sacramentum

Conclusion for the history from A.D. 150:
(i) the principle of apostolic succession accepted:
(ii) an episcopate, with exclusive powers of ordination, universal.

Now the evidence which early Christian history affords for the position of the ministry has been passed in review. If reference is made to the four positions which were enunciated at the beginning of this chapter, it will be found that the two first—to go at present no further—have been thoroughly justified. Everywhere we have found a ministry, recognised as having authority by succession from the Apostles: everywhere the three distinct orders of bishop, presbyter, and deacon: everywhere the limitation to the episcopate of the power of ordination. The only qualification which has to be made lies in the recognition that a school of western writers held that *originally* there had been no substantial distinction between a bishop and presbyter; and one of these writers affirms, in effect, that this state of things continued in the Church of Alexandria into the third century. It has however been pointed out that in the view of these writers, so long as the presbyters were understood to have episcopal powers (either generally or under certain circumstances), there was no separate ordination to the episcopate.[1] They do not hold that episcopal functions could under any circumstances be assumed by the later presbyters of the settled church constitution, who have been ordained as presbyters and nothing more and

corporis et sanguinis Christi conficere, nec eo coram posito populum docere vel benedicere aut salutare nec plebem utique exhortari."

[1] St. Paul implies that normally a man will pass from one grade of the church ministry up to another. This was always the canonical method; see *Apost. Const.* viii. 17. But ordinations *per saltum*, even to the episcopate, were known and recognised in early days. See *Dict. Chr. Ant.* s.v. BISHOP i. p. 219.

would require a separate ordination to make them bishops.

Some further points have still to be made good in order to justify the remaining positions which we enunciated at starting.

Evidence produced.

II. The Church did from the first, we maintain, regard ordination as a 'sacramental'[1] rite, to which was attached a special authorization or grace, of which the laying-on of hands was the 'outward sign.' On the other hand it has been recently urged that the idea of 'ordination' in the earliest Church carried with it only the association of official appointment, such as belonged to contemporary secular society. The words by which it is described "were in use to express appointment to civil office. When other ideas than those of civil appointment came beyond question to attach themselves to ecclesiastical appointment other words were used."[2] This is a strange argument in view of the history of Christian terminology. 'Ecclesia'

II. That ordination was regarded sacramentally,

---

[1] I use this expression without exact definition of a sacrament. The conception of ordination, for example, given by Rabanus Maurus, *de Inst. Cler.* i. 4-7, is sacramental in the sense that the laying on of episcopal hands is regarded as an act conferring certain mystical powers. Yet when he comes to speak (c. 24) of the sacraments of the Church, he reckons three only: "Sunt sacramenta baptismum et chrisma, corpus et sanguis, quae ob id sacramenta dicuntur, quia sub tegumento corporalium rerum virtus divina secretius salutem eorundem sacramentorum operatur: unde et a secretis virtutibus vel sacris sacramenta dicuntur. Quae ideo fructuose penes ecclesiam fiunt, quia sanctus in ea manens Spiritus eundem sacramentorum latenter operatur effectum." Earlier, however, St. Augustin had in substantially this sense spoken freely of ordination as a sacrament. But I want to avoid, as much as possible, the history of terminology.

[2] Dr. Hatch *B.L.* p. 129. In notes 33 and 34 he says: "The words in use in the first three centuries are χειροτονεῖν, καθιστάνειν, κληροῦσθαι, constituere, ordinare. . . . After the first three centuries there were not only other words of the same kind, e.g. προελθεῖν, προάγεσθαι, *promoveri, praeferri*, but also χειροθετεῖσθαι, ἱερᾶσθαι, *consecrari, benedici*."

was a common term enough in the Greek language; but did it carry to St. Paul no special Christian associations? 'To break bread,' 'to give thanks,' were common terms; but "the bread which we break," St. Paul says, "is the communion of the body of Christ." 'Baptism' had common enough associations in connection with pots and cups, brazen vessels and tables; but we could not therefore argue that it was only when the sacrament of initiation came to be known as 'the enlightenment' or 'the salvation,' that associations of spiritual power began to be attached to it.¹ It is the earliest Christian writings that are most suggestive in this respect. It is the simplicity of the language in which Tertullian speaks of Christian baptism and Justin describes the Christian Eucharist, which throws into high relief the profound conception which they entertained of their spiritual efficacy.² So far as technical language is concerned, certainly Christianity poured new wine into old bottles. Accordingly, it will not at all surprise us that the author of the Acts should speak simply of Paul and Barnabas 'appointing' elders in every Church (χειροτονεῖν, Acts xiv. 23), or that St. Paul should leave Titus to 'appoint' elders (καθιστάνειν, Tit. i. 5); and that we should afterwards be, as it were, let into the secret of this 'appointment' by St. Paul attributing it to the Holy Ghost (Acts xx. 28), and speaking

¹ Bingham *Ant.* xi. 1. 4, 5.
² Tertullian is quoted above. Justin Martyr's account of the Eucharist is studiedly simple. There is no term which is not of common life, yet he concludes with the well-known passage: "We receive it not as common bread and common drink . . . but we have been taught that the food . . . is the flesh and blood of that Jesus who was made flesh" (*Apol.* i. 65, 66).

to Timothy of the gift or special endowment of the Spirit "which was in him by means of the laying-on of his hands."

We may recognise, further, that in the whole process of her ordinations the Church seems to have borrowed a good many elements from civil society round about her. The elements of appointment to civil offices "were nomination, election, approval, and the declaration of election by a competent officer"—the 'renunciatio.' Then there was the 'usurpatio iuris'; the consul or praetor designate, for example, formally exercised his office and by exercising it entered upon its legal tenure.[1] Now some of the steps of this process belong to human nature and would reproduce themselves in all appointments; but it is impossible to avoid tracing back to this civil process some of the features of the Church's later forms of ordination. If election, testimony, examination, approval must necessarily have been there, yet we need not have found, as in fact we do, the 'renunciatio' to be an element in the ordination ceremony of the West, and still more of the East, though in characteristic Christian language.[2] Further, the reading of the Gospel by the newly-ordained deacon; the 'concelebration' of the newly-ordained priest; the enthronization of the bishop; the giving to the persons ordained to the minor or (much later) to the higher orders the 'instruments' of their ministry—all these ceremonies are probably enough

and conferred by laying-on of hands.

---

[1] See Dr. Hatch *B.L.* p. 129; *Dict. Chr. Ant.* s.v. ORDINATION ii. pp. 1503-1507.
[2] *Dict. Chr. Ant.* ii. p. 1507; and below, App. Note C.

the Christian form of the 'usurpatio iuris.'[1] But all these features in the ordination ceremonies of East or West were additions of varying and uncertain date. As what stamped the Christian ministry from the first had been the idea of divine mission and authorization, so the rite which corresponds to this idea had been all

---

[1] Morinus saw this, and seems to draw the right conclusion. He notes:
(1) The fundamental identity of the method of ordaining bishops, presbyters, and deacons in East and West.
(2) The divergence with reference to the minor orders as they grew up: in the East they were ordained with laying-on of hands, but in the West by the 'tradition of the instruments' of their office, with some appropriate injunction. (See the canon of IV Carthage, quoted by Morinus p. ii. p. 260: after the description of the method of ordaining bishops, presbyters, and deacons by laying-on of hands and prayer, the canon continues, "subdiaconus cum ordinatur, quia manus impositionem non accipit, patenam de episcopi manu accipiat vacuum et calicem vacuum; de manu vero archidiaconi urceolum cum aqua et mantile et manutergium:" and so on for the other orders.) This he compares to the method of assuming civil or military office by adopting or receiving the 'insignia.' So e.g. Dio Cassius (*Hist. Rom.* lxviii. 16) speaks of the *giving of the sword* by the emperor as the method of appointing prefects of the praetorians: ὅτε πρῶτον τῷ μέλλοντι τῶν δορυφόρων ἐπάρξειν τὸ ξίφος, ὃ παραζώννυσθαι αὐτὸν ἐχρῆν, ὤρεξεν, ἐγύμνωσέ τε αὐτὸ καὶ ἀνατείνας ἔφη· Λάβε τοῦτο τὸ ξίφος, ἵνα, ἂν μὲν καλῶς ἄρχω, ὑπὲρ ἐμοῦ, ἂν δὲ κακῶς, κατ' ἐμοῦ αὐτῷ χρήσῃ. Reimar says in his note: "hinc periphrasis praefecti praetorio ἐφ' ᾧ τὸ ξίφος ἦν, ap. Philostratum;" and gives references, quoting also "cum insigne potestatis, uti mos est, pugionem daret" from Victor. *Caes.* xiii. 9.

Morinus concludes that, whereas the higher spiritual orders which were derived from the Apostles were always conferred in East and West by the apostolic method (even though much later the 'traditio instrumentorum' was added in their case too), the minor orders, which were a gradual and utilitarian development, were imparted differently in East and West, and in the West by ceremonies suggested by the method of secular appointment (*de S. Ord.* p. iii. ex. xi. c. 5). This would be borne out by the evidence recently adduced by Harnack connecting the development of the minor orders in Rome with the reorganization of civil offices (*Text. u. Untersuch.* ii. band, heft 5, pp. 97-103): "Die römische Gemeinde es verstanden hat ... brauchbare Elemente des Sacral- und Staatswesens zu adoptiren." He thinks the seven subdeacons were instituted, probably by Fabian, to equalize the diaconate—without losing the sacred number—with the fourteen newly-instituted curatores urbis. Certainly the church organization was developed closely on the lines of the imperial system, as convenience no doubt suggested. On the other hand, the emperor Alexander Severus was disposed to take a lesson from the Church's method " in praedicandis sacerdotibus."

along the central and characteristic rite. Derived from Jewish traditional practice but stamped by the Apostles with a new significance, it was the laying-on of hands—accompanied no doubt from the first with a prayer for the gift of the Holy Spirit—which consecrated and empowered the minister in the Christian Church for his pastoral charge.[1]

III. Now we approach the subject of the 'indelible character' impressed by ordination. So far as church officers are elected representatives and ministers of the congregation, they would naturally be regarded, and all down church history have been regarded, as holding their place on terms of their good behaviour. The disorderly cleric has been deposed. But this does not exhaust the matter. The church officer is also a representative of God: his ordination has given him a divine commission and gift of grace; and as 'the gifts and calling of God are without repentance,' so from this point of view it is necessary to regard him who is once a priest as always a priest, whether

III. That permanent character was believed to accompany it:

---

[1] The 'laying-on of hands' in the Old Testament appears with a double significance. (*a*) When the people laid their hands upon the Levites, when the priest or the sacrificer laid his hand on the victim, the ceremony meant that the subject of it was made a *representative*—a substitute (Numb. viii. 10; Levit. xvi. 21, iii. 2-15, iv. 4-29). The Levites were to represent the people; the victim was taken as a substitute for the offerer. (*b*) It expressed the idea of *benediction* (Gen. xlviii. 14), and so specially it is used of Moses consecrating Joshua (Numb. xxvii. 18; Deut. xxxiv. 9: "Joshua was full of the spirit of wisdom, for Moses had laid his hands upon him"). It also became, before our Lord's time, the Jewish mode of appointing magistrates and rabbis (Morinus *de S. Ord.* p. iii. ex. vii. c. 3), and they laid stress upon *a succession from Moses* (*ib.* § 8). The characteristic use of it in the New Testament is by the Apostles to convey the gift of the Holy Ghost (Acts viii. 17, xix. 6). Cf. the way in which the apostolic succession is connected with the Jewish in the Clementine *Ep. Petri*. See further, for the evidence and significance of the rite in the Christian Church, App. Note G.

he adorn his office or no.¹ The later doctrine of the 'indelible character' impressed by ordination, in common with baptism and confirmation, and the clearly drawn distinction between *valid* and *canonical* ordinations, were the final outcome in the West of the conflict between these two principles involved from the first in the position of the Christian ministry.

We see these opposite principles at work in St. Clement's Epistle. On the one hand, because the presbyterate has been appointed from above and has a divine authority, it is declared to be "no light sin to cast out of their episcopate those who have holily and blamelessly offered the gifts."² On the other hand, it is implied that had these holders of the sacred office been bad men, the Church, with whose consent they had been elected, might have deposed them from their charge. When Callistus, a bishop of Rome in the beginning of the third century, repudiates this idea,—issuing his edict that "if a bishop sin, though it be a sin unto death, he may not be removed"—he is stating the 'indelibility of ordination character'³ in a form against which the canonical depositions of bishops, all down church history, are a continuous protest.

[1] Harnack states the conditions of the problem well in modification of Dr. Hatch (*die Gesellschaftsverfassung etc.* p. 234 n. ¹³): "As far as concerns the bishops and deacons, their activity was almost without control and *ranked as charismatic*. This, without any doubt, carries with it the reason why the officers in the Christian communities occupied from the beginning a position so wholly different from that held by the officers in the θίασοι, or 'guilds.'"

[2] Clem. *ad Cor.* 44.

[3] Harnack *l.c.* p. 258. The words are (Hippolytus *Ref. Omn. Haer.* ix. 12): οὗτος ἐδογμάτισεν ὅπως εἰ ἐπίσκοπος ἁμάρτοι τι, εἰ καὶ πρὸς θάνατον, μὴ δεῖν κατατίθεσθαι.

In what sense then did the early Christian Church hold this doctrine? In such sense, first of all, that there is no record from the beginning of church history of the reordination of any one episcopally ordained in the Church. Once let a man be ordained to any office, and his ordination held good in every Church where he offered satisfactory evidence of his status.¹ This at least is the tendency of all the evidence we have. Thus, to take the earliest case in

[1] The 68th of the *Apostolic Canons* condemns to deposition any bishop, presbyter, or deacon, who receives a second ordination, both him and his ordainer, "unless it should appear that his (first) ordination was from heretics"; the synod of Capua, A.D. 391, forbade rebaptisms, reordinations, and translation of bishops, and the canon was incorporated into the African collection (Hefele *Conciliengesch.* § 108); so Theodoret tells us that a foolish monk, who was afraid he should be ordained over again (having been ordained once without knowing it), was assured that "it was not possible to give him twice the same ordination" (*Rel. Hist.* xiii ap. Migne *Patrol. Graec.* lxxxii. p. 1404); so the author of the *Quaestiones in Vet. et Nov. Test.* assures us (*Qu.* ci): "quamquam apud . . . Deum unicuique hic honor maneat, qui decretus est singulis ecclesiarum officiis, ut qui diaconus est diaconi honorem per omnes ecclesias habeat." When bishops are forbidden to ordain clerics who belong to other dioceses (Can. Nicaen. 16, cf. Can. Apost. 15 and later), this of course means to a higher grade than they already held. Dr. Hatch's statement (*Growth of Ch. Inst.* p. 36; cf. *Dict. Chr. Ant.* ii. p. 1479) that in early days "the transference of the officer of one Church to another . . . when allowed, involved reappointment, or, as it would now be called, reordination," is absolutely gratuitous and unsupported by facts.

Dr. Hatch has often quoted a Galatian sepulchral inscription of A.D. 461 (*Corp. Inscr. Graec.* No. 9259: δὶς γενόμενος πρεσβύτερος) as evidence of a double ordination; cf. his *B. L.* p. 137 n.[51] On this inscription I should like to make three remarks.

(1) That the whole inscription does not at all support the sense that Dr. Hatch puts on it (and Harnack accepts, *l.c.* p. 234 n.[13]). A certain Tarasis there buried is described as δὶς γενομενος (sic) πρεσβ˙ καὶ παραμονάριος παροικησας εν τω τοπω τουτω. A παραμονάριος (or προσμονάριος) is the Latin *mansionarius*. He is a 'residentiary' in charge of any institution belonging to the Church. This Tarasis was twice appointed "presbyter and residentiary"—of a particular Church or monastery. There is nothing here to suggest that he was twice ordained in the fifth century. A similar expression (referring, I think, to one man) occurs twice in the *Ordo Romanus* ap. Hittorp. pp. 1, 10: "presbytero et mansionario."

(2) If the words had stood alone, as Dr. Hatch quotes them, I think a suggestive parallel might have been found in the *Libell. Prec. Faustin.*

point, St. Peter is represented in the Clementines as travelling about with some attendant 'presbyters,' who are clearly conceived of as being more than local officers—as being presbyters wherever they are.¹ Nor, again, when we hear of the reinstatement of clergy who had been deposed, or who had lapsed into heresy or schism, do we ever hear of their re-ordination. It is not indeed till comparatively late that we hear of any such case: for the severe view which was taken of deadly sin in the clergy forbade that they should resume their office, just as it was forbidden to 'penitents' to be ordained at all.²

though deposed clergy were treated as laymen, Such lapsed or deposed clergy were treated as laymen, or, when their sin was grave, deprived even of lay communion.³ But after the middle of the fourth century we have plenty of instances in which clergy, who had become Arians, Nestorians, Pelagians,

et Marcellin. ap. *Bibl. Vet. Patr.* vol. v. p. 659 b: "egregius ille bis episcopus." This is referring ironically to the *reordinations* of the Arians.

(3) It surely is important to remember that tombstone inscriptions all over the world express a lax popular theology. This has been brought out lately by recent investigations in the Christian sepulchral inscriptions of Egypt, Syria, and Asia. Those of Phrygia, for example, perpetuate for a long time the pagan maledictions on those who lay hands on the tomb. See Mr. Ramsay in *Journal of Hellenic Studies*, Oct. 1883, p. 400; also a very interesting article by M. E. Revillout in the *Revue Egyptologique*, 4me ann. [1885], no. i.

¹ See *Clem. Hom.* vii. 12: ἀπὸ τῶν ἑπομένων αὐτῷ πρεσβυτέρων ἕνα ἐπίσκοπον αὐτοῖς καταστήσας (cf. 5, 8).

² "Nullum mihi occurrit exemplum spatio trecentorum et quinquaginta annorum clerici catholici ad haereticos transfugae post reversionem ad ecclesiam cum ordinum exercitio recepti" (Morinus *de S. Ord.* p. iii. ex. v. 10. 2). Cf. *Apost. Can.* 62: μετανοήσας ὡς λαϊκὸς δεχθήτω; and Cyprian *Ep.* lv. 11: "sic tamen admissus est Trofimus ut laicus communicet, non . . . quasi locum sacerdotii usurpet." Morinus, *l.c.*, deals with some instances advanced in the opposite sense.

³ E.g. Can. Sardic. 1: ἡγοῦμαι μηδὲ λαϊκῶν ἔχειν τοὺς τοιούτους χρῆναι κοινωνίαν. Cf. Cyprian *Ep.* lii. 1: "Evaristum de episcopo iam nec laicum remansisse."

or heretics of whatever sort, were readmitted to their 'order,' always without reordination;[1] and it is noticeable that St. Basil, though holding that clergy who fall away from the Church lose the power of administering valid sacraments, still speaks of the ordination gift as a permanent endowment.[2]

On the other hand, it is quite certain that the early Church did not draw the clear line which was drawn later between the reality of the priesthood and its regular exercise. The deposed priest was really regarded as a layman.[3] And in the same way ordinations, which later would have been regarded as uncanonical, were in early days regarded as invalid. Morinus expresses the matter admirably by saying, "moraliter magis et civiliter de istis philosophati sunt." They thought of ordination, that is, in connection with all its moral and social associations, as part of the whole life of the Church; thus very naturally, "they did not regard the validity of the ordination as lying *merely* in the character of the act, but they took into account also the authority of the Church and questions of moral expediency."[4] The

and uncanonical ordinations as invalid.

---

[1] They are "certainly not ordained again," St. Augustin says (*de Bapt.* i. 1. 2); cf. Hefele *Conciliengesch.* § 142 : "They [i.e. the Massalians] were admitted on condition of anathematizing their former errors." Morinus *l.c.* §§ 7, 8 f. collects other instances. The council of Toledo in A.D. 633 (c. 28) gives the form for the restoration to their order of some clergy who had been unjustly deposed. They are to receive their lost orders, "gradus amissos recipere," before the altar by a renewed *reception of the vestments or* (in the case of subdeacons) *instruments* proper to their office—" ea in reparationem sui recipiant, quae cum ordinarentur perceperant." This is not 'reordination' technically, as Dr. Hatch calls it (*Dict. Chr. Ant.* ii. p. 1520).

[2] *Ep.* clxxxviii : οἱ γὰρ πρῶτοι ἀναχωρήσαντες παρὰ τῶν πατέρων ἔσχον τὰς χειροτονίας καὶ διὰ τῆς ἐπιθέσεως τῶν χειρῶν αὐτῶν εἶχον τὸ χάρισμα τὸ πνευματικόν.

[3] πεπαύσθω τοῦ κλήρου is a common phrase. Cf. *Dict. Chr. Ant.* ii. p. 1520.

[4] Morinus *de S. Ord.* p. iii. ex. v. cc. 9. 8, 11. 2 ; cf. Bingham *Ant.* xvii. 2.

word 'valid' meant to them what, according to more elaborated definitions, is expressed by *both valid and canonical*. How could they believe an act done in violation of the will of God to carry with it His ratification and be valid? So they reasoned, and so reasoning they pronounced invalid (ἄκυρος, unratified) an ordination of which, in later days, it would only have been said: *fieri non debet: factum valet.*[1]

[1] ἄκυρος ἔστω ἡ χειροτονία, or καθαιρείσθω. This is very frequent: cf. e.g. Can. Apost. 36; Antioch. 13, 22; Sardic. 15; Constantin. 4; Chalcedon. 6. A person who had thus received an 'invalid' ordination became disqualified for the canonical ministry, and the question of his reordination did not therefore often occur. But the Church, as we shall see, accepted the Donatist ordinations. Before that the Church's action is more doubtful.

The Council of Nicaea (1) rejected the baptism of the disciples of Paul of Samosata (c. 19) on the ground, as Athanasius tells us, of their heresy—not owing to their use of a defective form (Bright *Notes on the Canons* p. 67). It therefore decreed also that those, who had been amongst the Paulianist clergy and were yet considered fit for church orders, should be first "baptized afresh and then ordained by the bishop of the catholic Church." The repudiation of their baptism carried with it a repudiation of their ordinations.

(2) With reference to the Novatian clergy (οἱ καθαροί) the Council decreed ὥστε χειροθετουμένους αὐτοὺς μένειν οὕτως ἐν τῷ κλήρῳ (c. 8). It has been disputed whether this means that they should be *reordained*, or receive the imposition of hands as a ceremony of reconciliation. The former interpretation seems perhaps *of the two* the more probable; see Bright *Notes* p. 25 f. But it is possible that the bishops of the council did not accurately distinguish between a fresh ordination and an act of reception by the Church which gave validity to an old one. They use the words μένειν ἐν τῷ κλήρῳ, and certainly the language does not suggest a new ordination, such as the Paulianists needed. So in the same way the clergy ordained by Meletius were allowed to retain their office (τιμὴν καὶ λειτουργίαν) when they had been "confirmed by a more sacred ordination" (μυστικωτέρᾳ χειροτονίᾳ βεβαιωθέντας, ap. Soc. *H. E.* i. 9); this certainly suggests the idea of an act giving validity to an old ordination, rather than a completely new ordination. Later western councils receive clergy ordained amongst the Gothic Arians by a similar laying-on of hands—"cum impositae manus benedictione" (1 Conc. Aurel. A.D. 511, c. 10), "accepta denuo benedictione presbyteratus" (Conc. Caesaraug. A.D. 592, c. 1). In the context of the passage quoted above from Socrates there is a clear recognition by the historian in the case of Meletius himself of the distinction between *being a bishop* and being allowed *to act as such*. The council allowed him (he says) to retain the ἀξία τῆς ἐπισκοπῆς, but took away the ἐξουσία τοῦ πράττειν αὐτόν τινα ὡς ἐπίσκοπον.

The Witness of Church History.

The great peril, however, of making the unworthiness of the minister hinder the grace of the sacrament soon became apparent, first in connection with baptism. Thus the council at Arles[1] decreed for the West the validity of heretical baptisms. But the rigorism, which was always ready to 'make a man an offender for a word' and then repudiate his ministry, was still felt in the case of the Luciferians and Donatists to be a real danger. Accordingly Jerome and Augustin lead the way in extending the principle of the decision at Arles, so as to admit of the recognition of ordinations made by Arians, where the person so ordained gave satisfactory evidence of his orthodoxy, or again by Donatists, if their clergy would communicate again with the Church on her terms.[2]

[margin: Distinction between 'canonical' and 'valid' slowly recognised in the West;]

---

[1] c. 8: "Si perviderint [haereticum] in Patre et Filio et Spiritu sancto esse baptizatum, manus ei tantum imponatur ut accipiat Spiritum sanctum." c. 13 decided that the ordinations of 'traditor' clergy were valid.

[2] This is the point of Jerome's argument against Lucifer. He has a beautiful passage on the rarity of perfect faith, and the necessity therefore of recognising that *imperfect faith* is no obstacle to God's Spirit being administered; "fides, quae etiam apud eos qui bene credunt difficile perfecta invenitur" (*adv. Lucifer.* 15). He also presses the principle involved in the recognition of heretical baptism: "eadem ratione episcopum ab Arianis recipio qua tu recipis baptizatum" (*ib.* 14). He does not, however, commit himself as Augustin does.

Augustin carries out the argument with great vigour, using in part and developing Jerome's material, in his anti-Donatist writings. The question (he contends) what a man believes who receives or administers the sacrament of baptism is of great importance for his own salvation, but is wholly immaterial for its effect on the sacrament—"ad quaestionem sacramenti" (*de Bapt.* iii. 14). Sacraments ministered by heretics are valid, but their benefits are suspended till those who receive them come over to church unity (*de Bapt.* vii. 54. 103; *c. Epist. Parmen.* ii. 13. 29). This is as true of ordination as of baptism; as ordained men, if they secede and return to the Church, "are certainly not ordained again, but either again exercise their former ministry, or if they do not exercise it at any rate *retain the sacrament of their ordination*," so also "we do not dare to repudiate God's sacraments even when administered in schism" (*de Bapt.* i. 1. 2). So, with great clearness, *c. Epist. Parmen.* ii. 13. 28: "nulla ostenditur causa cur ille,

And this was not a mere economical arrangement in view of particular cases. It was based by St. Augustin on general principles which would apply in many directions—the principle, namely, that "the sacrament of ordination remains in those who are ordained; and if from any fault a man be removed from his office, yet he will not be without the Lord's sacrament once imposed, though remaining now only to condemn him;"[1] and the associated principle transferred from baptism to ordination, that schism and heresy do indeed destroy the spiritual value of sacraments, but not their reality. This latter principle was not indeed generally admitted in the East,[2] nor was it quickly worked out to its results in the West. Still it took root. Leo the Great, for example, pronounces that some uncanonically consecrated bishops are *no bishops at all*,[3] but "pseudo-

<small>only partially in the East.</small>

qui ipsum baptismum amittere non potest, ius dandi potest amittere: utrumque enim sacramentum est: et quadam consecratione utrumque homini datur, illud cum baptizatur, istud cum ordinatur. Ideoque in catholica utrumque non licet iterari. Nam si quando ex ipsa parte venientes etiam praepositi, pro bono pacis correcto schismatis errore suscepti sunt et si visum est opus esse ut eadem officia gererent quae gerebant, non sunt rursum ordinati: sed sicut baptismus in eis, ita ordinatio mansit integra: quia in praecisione fuerat vitium quod unitatis pace correctum est, non in sacramentis, quae ubicunque sunt ipsa sunt."

[1] *de Bono Conjugali* 24. 32: "Quemadmodum si fiat ordinatio cleri ad plebem congregandam, etiamsi plebis congregatio non subsequatur, manet tamen in illis ordinatis sacramentum ordinationis: et si aliqua culpa quisquam ab officio removeatur, sacramento domini semel imposito non carebit, quamvis ad iudicium permanente."

[2] Not, e.g., by St. Basil. In *Ep.* clxxxviii he does not admit the principle of the validity of baptism by sects who are in fundamental heresy on the doctrine of God: nor quite thoroughly as regards the Novatians and Encratites, though some of their ordinations had been allowed. He seems to regard it as a matter *depending on the Church's judgment* in any case: so eastern writers subsequently.

[3] *Ep.* clxvii *ad Rusticum* inq. 1: "Nulla ratio sinit ut inter episcopos habeantur qui nec a clericis sunt electi nec a plebibus sunt expetiti nec a pro-

episcopi." But then he goes on to intimate that, where their ordinations—otherwise "vain"—were allowed by the canonical bishop, they could be accepted as "valid," showing clearly that, though he did not regard consecration with the proper form as absolutely valid by itself apart from canonical conditions, he yet did regard it as valid in such sense as that church recognition, subsequently given, might impart to it a retrospective validity.

In this uncertain and ambiguous position the matter long remained. "What is it," says Morinus, "to track the controversy [on the validity of heretical or schismatical or simoniacal ordinations] but to exhibit bishops against bishops, councils against councils, pontiffs against pontiffs, waging a Cadmeian war?"[1] The Eastern Church has, in fact, never got beyond the position that the Church has the power to ratify in any particular case, or set of cases, ordinations which in the West would be called *per se* valid but uncanonical.[2]

It can hardly be a subject for regret that the Church should have exhibited considerable unwilling-

vincialibus episcopis cum metropolitani iudicio consecrati. Unde, cum saepe quaestio de male accepto honore nascatur, quis ambigat nequaquam istis esse tribuendum, quod non docetur fuisse collatum? Si qui autem clerici ab istis pseudo-episcopis in eis ecclesiis ordinati sunt, qui ad proprios episcopos pertinebant, et ordinatio eorum consensu et iudicio praesidentium facta est, potest rata haberi, ita ut in ipsis ecclesiis perseverent: aliter autem vana habenda est creatio, quae nec loco fundata est nec auctore munita."

[1] *de S. Ord.* p. iii. ex. v. 8. 1.
[2] Morinus *l.c.* c. 11. 4: "His cum praecedentibus comparatis, colligitur ecclesiam orientalem varie pro variis temporibus haereticos admisisse. Constat enim quibusdam temporibus, praesertim nascente haeresi, ut via planior ad reditum iis sterneretur, certorum haereticorum ordinationes admisisse: aliis vero eas irritas declarasse et iterasse."

ness in isolating the consideration of the validity of ordination from its context in the whole question of what constitutes a right relation to the Church. It cannot, however, be denied that the analogy of all sacramental grace forced the Church to distinguish between the gift that is in the man by the laying-on of hands and its reverent or obedient exercise. It must also be borne in mind, especially from the point of view of our present argument, that whatever hesitation was felt in accepting and formulating this principle was due to the high regard in which the ordination gift was held—not to any disparagement of it: so that there was at no time any hesitation in recognising the indelibility of orders, when imparted and exercised in obedience to the Church.

IV. That use of sacerdotal terms implied no new idea of the ministry.

IV. It will be noticed that whereas the conception of the Christian ministry and pastorate of souls dates back behind our present period into the immemorial past, it is only at the beginning of our period that the title of the Priesthood begins to be applied to it. Irenaeus and Clement do not speak of the Christian ministers as priests, while Tertullian and Origen do, so that it is only towards the end of the second century that sacerdotal terms begin to be regularly[1] applied to the clergy.

The question arises: Does this change of language represent a change of ideas, or merely a readjustment

---

[1] Dr. Lightfoot thinks Polycrates' description of St. John as "a priest wearing the mitre—πέταλον" (ap. Euseb. *H.E.* v. 24) is perhaps the first instance of sacerdotal language being applied to the Christian ministry. But we have the expression in the *Didache* xiii. 3: "they are your high priests."

III.] *The Witness of Church History.* 197

of terms in view of changed circumstances? We cannot argue always or absolutely from a gradual change in language to a change in ideas. For instance, we have every reason for supposing that the first Christians believed in the Divine Sonship of Christ. A Christian of the first century, with the teaching of the Apostles in his mind, when he understood the controversy, would, we feel no doubt, have sided unambiguously with St. Athanasius and not with Arius; and that not because Athanasius would have persuaded him to give any new honour to Christ, but because he would have seen easily enough what his old faith implied: that it was indeed the teaching of St. John and St. Paul about Christ that He was 'God of God, very God of very God.' But, on the other hand, this faith of the Church could not be expressed so unreservedly in the first age as in later times. 'Jesus is very God' was not the first truth to put before a Jew, but 'Jesus is the Christ:' this is the substance of the first apostolic preaching as recorded in the Acts —the Messianic authority of Christ, not His divine nature. 'Jesus is the Son of God' was not the first truth to preach to the heathen with their polytheism and mythology, lest they should only too easily incorporate Him into their Pantheon: the basis of monotheism must be firmly laid before the Divine Sonship of Christ can be securely preached.[1] There is then a change of terminology which means a change of circumstances rather than of ideas. To take another

Reasons for earlier abstinence.

[1] See St. Paul's first preaching to heathen, Acts xiv. 14-18 and xvii. 22-31.

instance from the records of the language of the early Church. The early apologists believed in a Christian sacrifice in the Eucharist; if the sense in which they did so may be discussed, the fact is undoubted. But Justin Martyr, who expresses his appreciation of the eucharistic sacrifice to Trypho the Jew, denies to the heathen emperor that God needs material oblations.[1] Athenagoras makes the same denial, and then puts in parenthetically—as it were under his breath—"and yet we must offer a bloodless sacrifice and bring before God the spiritual service."[2] The Christian in fact had, or had not, a sacrifice according as the term was used in one sense or in another. The same seems to have been true of the priesthood. "It would only have caused confusion," Mr. Simcox justly says,[3] "when 'a great company of the priests was obedient to the faith,' to have said that St. Barnabas was a priest, when he was in fact a Levite." The term 'priest' indeed carried with it many associations, Jewish and pagan, which did not belong to Christianity. Outside the Epistle to the Hebrews Christ is not termed a priest, and even there it is said: "if He were on earth He would not be a priest at all, seeing there are those who offer the gifts according to the law."[4] So, too, it is conceivable that a Christian missionary of our own day might find it necessary, amidst the associations of a pagan priest-

---

[1] *Dial. c. Tryph.* 117 (cf. 22); *Apol.* i. 10.
[2] *Legat.* 13: καίτοι προσφέρειν δέον ἀναίμακτον θυσίαν καὶ τὴν λογικὴν προσάγειν λατρείαν.
[3] *Early Church History* p. 59.
[4] Hebr. viii. 4 (R. V.).

hood, to emphasize by the avoidance of the term the points of difference in the Christian ministry: just as it would have been wiser at times to have produced a monotheistic atmosphere as a preparation for preaching the divinity of Christ.

But when once the Christian atmosphere has been cleared,—when once the unique high-priesthood of Christ is realized and the communication of that priesthood to the Church,—it becomes natural to apply the term 'priest' to the divinely ordained ministers of this priestly congregation. As this special application has been shown in the last chapter to involve no loss of the general conception of the 'high-priestly race,' so also it carries with it no change of ideas about the ministry. The bishops whom Clement speaks of as "offering the gifts" in the spiritual temple of the Church under Christ, "the high-priest of our oblations," may as well as not be called priests. Hippolytus expresses by the term 'the high-priesthood' exactly the same idea of the episcopate as is expressed by Irenaeus without its use.[1] Ignatius, who does not call the Christian officers priests, em-

---

[1] See App. Note G. It is important to notice the triple derivation of sacerdotal language. There is (1) the idea of the high-priesthood of Truth. The term high priest is applied thus to the prophet (*Didache* xiii. 3), or to the bishop as sitting in the chair of the prophetic teacher (Hippolyt. *Ref. Omn. Haer.* prooem. and the Clementines). There is (2) the idea of the high-priesthood of Sacrifice realized in the Church through the mediation of Christ. This is the idea of priesthood in the Epistle to the Hebrews, in Clement of Rome, in Justin Martyr, in Irenaeus; and the term priest came to be applied in this sense to the bishop or presbyter as to him 'who offers the gifts.' It is noticeable that the unity of prophecy and priesthood underlies the use of the sacerdotal term λειτουργεῖν τῷ κυρίῳ of the prophets in Acts xiii. 2. There is (3) the idea of the Power of the Keys—the authority to bind and loose in the Christian society, belonging to the bishop with the presbyters, as it is emphasized in the Clementines.

phasizes their authority more than Origen, who uses the term freely, and not less than Cyprian. There is an overstrained expression of sacerdotal authority in the *Apostolical Constitutions*, but this comes from a slight hardening of Ignatius's teaching and is in no apparent connection with the change in terms. On the other hand, the Fathers are not, generally speaking, chargeable with a false conception of the priestly office; but (as these pages will have shown) in the old offices of ordination, in the writings on the pastoral charge and in the early canons the idea is kept in due proportion and harmony with the whole of church life and spiritual truth. If the Church is a high-priestly race, and if in the Church there is a ministry of divine authority both in the communication of God's gifts to man and in the offering of man's gifts to God, that ministry can quite legitimately be called a priesthood.[1]

V. The powers of the ministry 'exclusive.'

V. We may claim now to have fairly substantiated the four fundamental positions which were propounded at the opening of this chapter. It is still however necessary, in order to make our case complete, to

[1] It will be asked: Why do we not find in second century theology such passages about the dignity of the priesthood in connection with the Eucharist as are quoted, or referred to, on pp. 157-8? The answer to this seems to be that there is nothing in such passages which does not apply to the whole Christian life (cf. Hebr. xii. 22-24) and which should not be realized by every Christian, in his degree, in the eucharistic celebration; but a special necessity arises for emphasizing these thoughts in connection with the responsibilities of the ministry in days when the spirit of the world takes possession of the Church. It is in this way that the heart of the Church is kept sound. It is only when this sanctity is attributed to the ministry by contrast to the whole body that a new and false element is introduced into theology. Further than this, it is not, probably, more than 'an accident' that the divine authority of the clergy was emphasized first and the sanctity of their sacramental ministries later. See some further remarks in chap. vii.

refer to the *exclusive* character attributed to the powers of the ministry, and attributed to them, as far as the evidence goes, *from the first.*

A positive claim is in a certain sense necessarily also exclusive; the position involves a negation. 'I am empowered by ordination to minister' implies that 'you who have no such ordination have no such power.' The church ministry made, then, an exclusive claim. This, of course, needs qualification; however much the office of teaching or baptizing was kept under the bishop's control and practically confined to the clergy, still lay baptism was generally regarded as valid and allowable in circumstances of necessity,[1] while lay teaching also was from time to time permitted.[2] Ambrosiaster tells us, as has been noticed already, that there was at first greater freedom in this respect. But, though this be admitted, it is still true to say that certain functions have been regarded as confined to certain church officers, in such sense as that others cannot validly perform them. Thus St. Jerome writes:[3] "Since Hilary, a deacon, has withdrawn from the Church, a world in himself as he imagines, he can neither consecrate a Eucharist (for he has neither bishops nor presbyters) nor without a

---

[1] Cf. e.g. Tertull. *de Bapt.* 17; Council of Elvira, c. 38. Jerome (*adv. Lucifer.* 9) says: "Inde venit, ut sine chrismate et episcopi iussione neque presbyter neque diaconus ius habeant baptizandi. Quod frequenter, si tamen necessitas cogit, scimus etiam licere laicis."

[2] *Apost. Const.* viii. 32. 15 : ὁ διδάσκων, εἰ καὶ λαϊκὸς εἴη, ἔμπειρος δὲ τοῦ λόγου καὶ τὸν τρόπον σεμνός, διδασκέτω. See note (32) in Migne *Patrol. Graec.* i. p. 1132.

[3] Jerome *adv. Lucifer.* 21; the meaning of the clause about baptism is not plain, after the admission of lay baptism, quoted above. Cf. *Apost. Const.* viii. 28.

Eucharist hand on baptism; and when the individual is dead, his sect is gone with him; for, as a deacon, he could ordain no clergyman after him. And that is no Church which has no priests." Again, the eighteenth canon of Nicaea distinguishes between the deacons "who have not the authority to offer" and the presbyters who have. This of course represents the common doctrine; only a priest can offer or consecrate the Eucharist, as only a bishop can ordain. But it is sometimes urged that this is a later conception in the Church: earlier, as in Ignatius and Clement, you have the conception of the authority of the ministry strongly developed, but without this 'sacerdotal exclusiveness.' "Let that be esteemed a valid Eucharist," Ignatius says, "which is celebrated *under the bishop or his delegate*; . . . it is not lawful, apart from the bishop, to baptize or celebrate a love-feast:"[1] but here, it is urged, the idea is simply that a sacrament must be *duly authorized;* and this would be quite compatible with the validity of a lay Eucharist, if only the layman had authority given him to celebrate it. It was a question of order—not of exclusive grace.

The rights of the ministry a matter of order,

Now it is perfectly true that in the first age the dominant idea was that of church order.[2] The priesthood was not, as much as in later days, regarded as

---

[1] *ad Smyrn.* 8; see however further, in chap. vi, for Ignatius's whole conception.

[2] Cf. Tertull. *de Bapt.* 17: "Dandi quidem [baptismum] habet ius summus sacerdos, qui est episcopus: dehinc presbyteri et diaconi, non tamen sine episcopi auctoritate, propter ecclesiae honorem, quo salvo salva pax est." Cf. Jerome, in note above: and [Ambrose] *de Sacramentis* iii. 1. 4: "exordium ministerii a summo est sacerdote."

an endowment of the individual. There was not the same distinction drawn between what was valid and what was canonical. On this point enough has already been said. But it is obvious that the conception of church order is capable of embracing what is included in both the terms 'canonical' and 'valid.' Thus the language of Ignatius about the Eucharist is capable of covering the position that only a presbyter can have the bishop's license to consecrate, even if it also covers the position that a presbyter's celebration, *apart from episcopal authority*, would lack validity. And we certainly find that Clement assigns the 'offering of the gifts' to the episcopal (or presbyteral) office, and speaks of each order as having its own limited functions in the celebration of the Eucharist by divine appointment.[1] Again, when we go further back, we find in the Acts the idea of exclusive function: for, though nothing is said about the Eucharist in particular, only the apostle, or perhaps also the prophet, can lay on hands to give the gift of the Holy Ghost. And so, in special connection with ordination, St. Paul speaks of Timothy as empowered by a gift of grace given to him as an individual by the laying-on of hands, and presumably conveyed by him to those on whom he is directed to lay hands after the apostolic pattern.[2] It does not the least follow that, because Ignatius and Clement press the idea of divine order, they ignore the reality of ordination grace, which as positive is also exclusive. It is

but also of special 'charisma.'

[1] *ad Cor.* 40; see further, in chap. vi.
[2] The argument is the same, *for our present purpose*, if the Acts and Pastoral Epistles are relegated to the second century.

of course a fact that there is much more early evidence for the general position that no ministry was acknowledged in the Church which was not performed in accordance with church order and for the principle of special positive powers conveyed to individuals by ordination than for the particular limitation to presbyters of the celebration of the Eucharist: but it is a false supposition (considering the traditional character of the Church) that an institution or limitation only began to exist when we happen first to hear of it.[1]

Have we, then, any reason to believe that a layman would in any age have been allowed to celebrate the Eucharist even in case of necessity? Yes, it is at once answered: Tertullian says so.[2] It is in a Montanist treatise, where he is arguing, in the severe spirit of that body, against the lawfulness of second marriages. His opponent is supposed to urge that they are forbidden only to priests. "Vain," replies Tertullian, "shall we be if we think that what is not lawful for priests is lawful for laics. Are not even we laics priests? (Rev. i. 6 quoted.) It is the authority of the Church which makes a difference between the order and the people. . . . Thus, where there is no

Tertullian's view to the contrary

---

[1] It must have been a surprise to many people to find in the *Didache* the observance of the Wednesday and Friday fasts and of trine affusion. Cf. Harnack in *Expositor*, May 1887, p. 321.

[2] When Clement of Alexandria says of the Christian: ἑσπέρας δὲ ἀναπαύσασθαι καθήκει μετὰ τὴν ἑστίασιν καὶ μετὰ τὴν ἐπὶ ταῖς ἀπολαύσεσιν εὐχαριστίαν (*Paed.* ii. 10. 96), he is referring to the 'grace' for the supper. Εὐχαριστεῖν long continued to be used for 'saying grace' in the church of Alexandria; cf. pseudo-Athan. *de Virgin.* 12: ἔσθιε τὸν ἄρτον σου εὐχαριστήσασα τῷ θεῷ ἐπὶ τῆς τραπέζης σου (and so three times in c. 13). Dr. Bigg's suggestion of a domestic 'Eucharist' with only the head of the house to celebrate it (*B.L.* p. 103 n.²) seems, therefore, gratuitous and is not borne out by the words of Clement.

bench of clergy, you offer and baptize and are priest alone for yourself. Nay, where three are, there is a Church, although they be laics. . . . Therefore, if you have the rights of a priest in your person when it is necessary, it behoves you to have likewise the discipline of a priest when it is necessary to use his right. If you are a digamist, can you baptize? can you offer? How much more capital a crime is it for the digamist laic to act for the priest, when the priest himself, if he turn digamist, is deprived of the power of acting as priest?"[1] Tertullian is here confessedly speaking about abnormal cases, and in this same treatise he speaks of a man offering the Eucharist under usual circumstances for his wife or wives departed by the hands of the priest—*per sacerdotem*.[2] At the same time there is no doubt about his meaning; and if this passage could be fairly quoted as evidence of the mind of the Church at the time, it would go at least to show that while the right of the layman to baptize, in cases of necessity, was rather grudgingly conceded, there was no sharp line yet drawn in respect of his

---

[1] *de Exhort. Cast.* 7: "Vani erimus, si putaverimus quod sacerdotibus non liceat laicis licere. Nonne et laici sacerdotes sumus? Scriptum est: Regnum quoque nos et sacerdotes Deo et Patri suo fecit. Differentiam inter ordinem et plebem constituit ecclesiae auctoritas et honor per ordinis consessum sanctificatus. Adeo ubi ecclesiastici ordinis non est consessus, et offers et tinguis et sacerdos es tibi solus. Sed ubi tres, ecclesia est, licet laici. Unusquisque enim de sua fide vivit, nec est personarum acceptio apud Deum : quoniam non auditores legis iustificabuntur a Deo, sed factores, secundum quod et apostolus dixit. Igitur si habes ius sacerdotis in temetipso ubi necesse est, habeas oportet etiam disciplinam sacerdotis, ubi necesse est habere ius sacerdotis. Digamus tinguis? digamus offers? quanto magis laico digamo capitale erit agere pro sacerdote, cum ipsi sacerdoti digamo auferatur agere sacerdotem?"

[2] *ib.* 11: "Offeres pro duabus et commendabis illas duas *per sacerdotem* de monogamia ordinatum?"

powers between baptism and the Eucharist. But though we grant this, it is, on the other hand, certainly not the case that this passage can be fairly quoted as illustrating the mind of the Church at all. Tertullian, in fact, is writing as a Montanist;[1] that is as one of a body which was setting itself against the Church as in other respects, so also in reference to the authority of the episcopal ministry.[2] He had himself, before he became a Montanist, adopted a different tone. He had made carelessness about sacerdotal distinctions the very characteristic of heretical bodies. "Their ordinations are heedless, capricious, changeable. At one time they put novices in office; at another, men involved in secular employment; at another, men who have apostatized from us. . . . And so it comes about that one man is a bishop with them to-day, another to-morrow; to-day a man is a deacon, and to-morrow a reader; to-day a presbyter, and to-morrow a layman; for they *impose even on laymen the functions of the priesthood.*"[3] The *tone* here is undoubtedly different. Again, in another treatise, he makes it part of the unwritten but authoritative tradition of the Church, that only the "presidents"—that is, no doubt, the bishop

follows from his Montanist position.

---

[1] There is no doubt about this, for a prophecy of Prisca is quoted (*de Exh. Cast.* 10): "Item per sanctam prophetidem Priscam ita evangelizatur, quod sanctus minister sanctimoniam noverit ministrare. Purificantia enim concordat, ait, et visiones vident et ponentes faciem deorsum etiam voces audiunt manifestas, tam salutares quam et occultas." There can be little doubt that these words belong to the true text: (so Bonwetsch *Montanismus*, p. 198).

[2] Tertullian speaks of course as if his opponent would grant his position. But Tertullian though he is a very powerful is not a fair arguer, and it cannot be the least concluded that, when Tertullian uses or implies a 'Nonne, his opponent would have answered 'Yes.'

[3] *de Praescr.* 41. For the Latin, see p. 127 n.[1]

and presbyters—should administer the Eucharist.[1] The statement, then, that Tertullian makes as to the power of the layman 'to offer,' in cases of necessity, can no more be admitted as evidence of what the Church would have granted, than similar appeals made by Waldensians or Wesleyans of later days.

It is, however, necessary to explain a little more fully the position of the Montanists, and that especially in order to refute the notion that, in their claim to dispense with the church ministry, they represented in any way an older and fast vanishing "freedom of the spirit."[2]

<small>Characteristics of western Montanism:</small>

Montanism, then, as represented by Tertullian, had two chief characteristics.[3] First, it was a movement characterized by an intense ascetic rigorism. Tertul-

<small>(1) rigorism;</small>

---

[1] *de Corona* 3, 4: "Eucharistiae sacramentum et in tempore victus et omnibus mandatum a Domino, etiam antelucanis coetibus, nec de aliorum manu quam praesidentium sumimus." He then proceeds to argue on the authority of the church traditions, and on their claim to obedience: "harum et aliarum eiusmodi disciplinarum si legem expostules scripturarum, nullam invenies: traditio tibi praetendetur auctrix, consuetudo confirmatrix et fides observatrix. Rationem traditioni et consuetudini et fidei patrocinaturam aut ipse perspicies aut ab aliquo qui perspexerit disces: interim nonnullam esse credes, cui debeatur obsequium." Thus he makes this limitation of the distribution of the eucharistic sacrament to the clergy one of many immemorial traditions of the Church; and he speaks of the authoritativeness of church customs in a tone so different to what is to be quoted from the *de Virginibus Velandis* that, though the *de Corona* has some of the Montanist rigorism about it and dates not before the end of the century, it cannot belong to his latest and most Montanist period. In the *de Virg. Vel.* however, he still speaks of himself as "una ecclesia" with the apostolic Churches (c. 2).

[2] "The fact of the existence of Montanism," Dr. Hatch says (*B. L.* p. 125), "strongly confirms the general inferences which are drawn from other evidence, that church officers were originally regarded as existing for the good government of the community and for the general management of its affairs . . . that the functions which the officers performed were such as, apart from the question of order, might be performed by any member of the community."

[3] On the Montanist movement generally, see App. Note H.

lian, who had deplored [1]—but not corrected—his own impatience, was drawn into its ranks, as men of impatient, undisciplined zeal have been drawn in every age into puritan or Novatian parties. In this spirit, it was opposed to the laxer or more merciful tendencies of the authorities of the Roman Church of that day.[2] "I hear," says Tertullian with bitter scorn,[3] "that an edict has been issued, and that a peremptory one. That 'pontifex maximus,' that bishop of bishops,[4] decrees: I forgive the sins of adultery and fornication to those who have performed penance." This readiness to grant absolution for even the worst sins the Montanists intensely resented. Further, the Montanist discipline involved special fasts and special restrictions on marriage and other ascetic rules—for laity, no less than clergy—which find in Tertullian a vigorous advocate, and which enable him to heap contempt on the more ordinary standards of living, which were reckoned sufficient among churchmen or 'natural men,' as the Montanists called them.

(2) belief in the 'new prophets,'
The second characteristic of western Montanism, which it had derived from its Phrygian parentage, was a belief in the 'new prophets.' There had been in the persons of the first Montanist prophets a new outpouring of the prophetic spirit. They had been the subjects

---

[1] This is what gives such pathos to his treatise *de Patientia*.

[2] The view of the policy of the Roman Church which Mr. Pater gives in *Marius the Epicurean* is so far justified by the number of reactionary movements which history connects with the names of Tertullian, Hippolytus, and Novatian.

[3] *de Pudic.* 1.

[4] The first title no doubt implies the paganism of the proceedings, and the second its arbitrariness, in Tertullian's judgment.

of a new and absolute inspiration; and still (though they were gone) the Montanist society had brethren with 'the gift of revelations,' who saw visions and had access to divine truth denied to common men. Men who believe themselves inspired naturally tend to despise mere church officers who make no such claim. And, besides, the church officers in the East first, and later in the West, had judged and repudiated this claim to inspiration. The Church of the 'natural men' had, according to the Montanists, rejected the Spirit.[1] It will not therefore at all surprise us that the Montanists should have regarded their inspired prophets as organs of spiritual power, in the possession of whom they were enabled to despise the bishops with their official claims. The Church never expressed any opinion on the rights which could be recognised in genuine prophets, but she denied that these men were prophets of God at all. Hence the tone of antagonism. Tertullian is still speaking of the episcopal edict. "You say," he argues,[2] "that the Church has the power of forgiving sins. This I acknowledge more than you and determine—I, who have the Paraclete Himself in the person of the new prophets saying 'the Church can forgive the sin, but I will not do it lest they commit others withal.'" The claim to the power of absolution in the Church was based on our Lord's promise to St. Peter,

and consequent disparagement of the regular ministry.

---

[1] See Tertull. *adv. Prax.* 1 and App. Note H.
[2] *de Pudic.* 21: "Sed habet, inquis, potestatem ecclesia delicta donandi? Hoc ego magis et agnosco et dispono, qui ipsum Paracletum in prophetis novis habeo dicentem: Potest ecclesia donare delictum, sed non faciam, ne et alia delinquant."

and Tertullian proceeds to examine the promise and declares that it was given to St. Peter only as an individual. The promised power, therefore, of binding and loosing has nothing to do with those who claim to inherit it. "Now, then, what has this power to do with the Church, with your Church forsooth, mere natural man? For, in accordance with the person of Peter, it is to *spiritual* men that this power will belong,—either to an apostle, or else to a prophet. For the Church is properly and principally the Spirit Himself, in whom is the Trinity of the One Godhead—Father, Son, and Holy Spirit. The Spirit combines that Church which the Lord has made to consist in three persons. And thus, from that time forward, any number of persons, who may have combined together with this faith, is accounted 'a Church' from the author and consecrator of the Church. And, accordingly, the Church, it is true, will forgive sins; but it will be the Church of the Spirit by means of the spiritual man; not the Church which consists of a number of bishops."[1] It will now be seen that Tertullian's argument about three constituting a Church, in the passage which came first under discussion, is in direct connection with the argument of this last passage. The 'anti-sacerdotal' tone of it is quite

---

[1] *ib.* "Quid nunc et ad ecclesiam, et quidem tuam, psychice? Secundum enim Petri personam spiritalibus potestas illa conveniet aut apostolo aut prophetae. Nam et ecclesia proprie et principaliter ipse est Spiritus, in quo est trinitas unius divinitatis, Pater et Filius et Spiritus sanctus. Illam ecclesiam congregat, quam Dominus in tribus posuit. Atque ita exinde etiam numerus omnis, qui in hanc fidem conspiraverint, ecclesia ab auctore et consecratore censetur. Et ideo ecclesia quidem delicta donabit: sed ecclesia Spiritus per spiritalem hominem, non ecclesia numerus episcoporum."

manifest—or rather, what is manifest is that it substitutes a priesthood of supposed inspiration for the priesthood of an ordained and official ministry. It sets the Church of the Spirit against the Church of the bishops.

So far, then, Montanism gives us good evidence as to the temper of the Church when she rejected that movement in the second century. But is it, then, the case that Montanism represented the older mind of the Church—an older 'freedom of prophesying'?[1] Not in the least. The Church never in fact committed herself at all to any position with reference to the rights and powers which would be allowed to those whose real inspiration she could recognise. She did not admit Montanist inspiration and then deny that it had accompanying rights; she simply denied that it was inspiration. She was taking up no new line towards prophecy whatever. And the more closely we look at Montanism, whether in its origin or in its development, the less inclined shall we be to attribute to Montanism conservative or retrospective tendencies. "It was the element of conservatism in it," it has been recently said by one whose justice always commends his words, "the fact that it spoke the language and reaffirmed the idea of a bygone day, that gave Montanism its strength, and won over to it so powerful a champion as Tertullian."[2] Such language, however,

Montanism not conservative.

---

[1] We have not, it must be remembered, to deal in Montanism with a claim for 'liberty of prophesying' in any modern sense, but with a claim of supernatural inspiration. See Dr. Salmon's article in the *Dict. Chr. Biog.* on MONTANUS.

[2] Dr. Sanday in *Expositor*, Feb. 1887, p. 110. Bonwetsch, the best recent investigator of the matter, though he does not altogether accept this view

seems contrary to the evidence we have of the nature of Montanism. If we read Tertullian's *de Virginibus Velandis*, we shall be struck with its *un*conservative tone. Tertullian, the catholic, strikes the note of conservatism in the *Praescriptiones*. As a Montanist he still kept his hold on the ancient doctrine; but '*novitas*' is his watchword in matters of discipline. In this region he denounces custom: "custom, which, taking its origin from ignorance or simplicity, is *strengthened by succession into a practice*, and then makes its position good against the truth.... It is not the charge of novelty, but the truth, which refutes heresies. Whatever is against the truth, this is heresy, even though it be an old custom." The rule of faith indeed is immovable,[1] but "the other matters of discipline and life admit the novelty of correction, because the grace of God works and advances even till the end." There is a gradual development, then, in the Church as the Spirit—'the Lord's Vicar'— gradually works out His plan of discipline. This development has for its content "the direction of discipline, the revelation of Scriptures, the improvement of our understanding, the advance to a better state of things." It is like the natural development of

of Montanism as a conservative or reactionary movement, quotes some words from the acts of a bishop Achatius in the Decian persecution (§ 4 ap. Ruinart *Acta Martyr. Sincera*) as a sign that this view of them was held already in early days (*Zeitschr. f. k. Wissenschaft u. k. Leben*, 1884, heft ix. p. 473). The words are: "Cataphryges aspice homines religionis antiquae." But they are completely misunderstood. The words are put in the mouth of the *pagan* magistrate. He had first induced the Montanists to apostatize and sacrifice, and then held them up as examples of *return to the ancient religion, i.e. the old Roman religion;* "ad mea sacra conversos," he continues, "reliquisse quae fuerant, et nobiscum Diis vota persolvere."

[1] But is more fully unfolded to Montanists: see *ad Prax.* 2. 30: *de Res. Carn.* 63.

physical life. The infancy of mankind was under the Law and the Prophets; it came to its hot youth under the Gospel; now, through the Spirit (i.e. the Spirit which inspired the new prophets, the Montanist Spirit, in virtue of which they set the 'Church of the Spirit' against the 'Church of the bishops') it is realizing the strength of manhood.[1] This passage has no direct bearing on the claim to possess a substitute for ordained bishops in inspired prophets, but it disposes of the contention that Montanism represented conservative tendencies in matters of church discipline. As well, then, might one quote the contemporary humanitarians as illustrating what had hitherto been the Church's doctrine about Christ, as the Montanists to illustrate her doctrine of orders.[2]

Now we have come to the end of a long argument. Summary. Starting from the age of Irenaeus, we have traced downward the stream of church life, and everywhere we have found the Church recognising the authority of a ministry, derived by succession from the Apostles, and consisting of bishops, presbyters, and deacons;

[1] *de Virg. Vel.* 1: "Hac lege fidei manente, cetera iam disciplinae et conversationis admittunt novitatem correctionis, operante scilicet et proficiente usque in finem gratia Dei. . . . Cum propterea Paracletum miserit Dominus, ut quoniam humana mediocritas omnia semel capere non poterat, paulatim dirigeretur et ordinaretur et ad perfectum perduceretur disciplina ab illo vicario Domini Spiritu sancto. . . . Quae est ergo Paracleti administratio, nisi haec, quod disciplina dirigitur, quod scripturae revelantur, quod intellectus reformatur, quod ad meliora proficitur? Nihil sine aetate est, omnia tempus exspectant. . . . Sic et iustitia (nam idem Deus iustitiae et creaturae, primo fuit in rudimentis, natura Deum metuens; dehinc per legem et prophetas promovit in infantiam; dehinc per evangelium efferbuit in iuventutem: nunc per Paracletum componitur in maturitatem."

[2] These humanitarians really did make the claim to be the true conservatives; see Euseb. *H.E.* v. 28. The *Little Labyrinth* makes the suggestive rejoinder: "What they said might have been perhaps convincing, if, first of all, the Holy Scriptures had not contradicted them."

everywhere we have seen reason to believe that these ministers were qualified for their high functions by an ordination given after due election with the laying-on of the hands of the bishops who were before them, and only in virtue of such ordination held to possess the authority and the grace of God requisite for the ministry they were called to fulfil. It was of course only gradually that this ministerial principle gained complete and adequate expression. It was with this as with church doctrine. In both departments there is a development in explicitness of conception and in accuracy and fulness of language. But the principle held the ground from the first with thorough recognition; and the evidence of this is that, wherever the claim of the ministry was challenged, the spirit of the Church rose to maintain it and those who could not recognise the authority of their fathers in Christ found themselves aliens from the brotherhood. The challenge may have come from the side of Montanist enthusiasm or Novatian separatism; or it may have been due to the self-assertion of an individual against church order, as when Colluthus, who was no bishop, attempted to ordain a presbyter; or it may have had its origin in a collapse of discipline such as led to the attempt of some deacons, in days of persecution, to offer the Eucharist; or it may have been a challenge in theory rather than in practice, like Aerius' denial of the distinctive dignity of the episcopate. But, in whatever sense and from whatever quarter the authority of the ministry was challenged, the mind of the Church spoke out loud in its vindication. For the ministry was acknowledged, instinctively and universally, as the divinely given stewardship of truth and grace, as part of the new creation of God; and, "the things which the Lord instituted through His Apostles, these," in Athanasius' words, "remain honourable and valid." As an institution of Christ through His Apostles—divine, permanent, and necessary—the threefold ministry made its appearance on the horizon of our epoch and "the memory of man ran not to the contrary."

CHAPTER IV.

THE INSTITUTION OF THE APOSTOLATE.

The present position of the argument. HITHERTO we have been occupied in expounding a certain set of principles which are involved in the phrase 'the apostolic succession of the ministry,' and in adducing a great body of evidence calculated to show how completely, and (as far as appears) without exception, these principles obtained acceptance in the Church, and governed her action, from the middle of the second century onwards. It is, in fact, impossible to exaggerate the intimacy with which the episcopal succession is bound up with the fixed canon of Scripture and the permanent and stable creed to constitute what can rightly be called 'historical Christianity.' There was, indeed, the same tentativeness in the process by which the formulated nomenclature and (as some at least may think they have occasion to believe on reviewing the earlier period) the exact form of the ministry was arrived at, as appears in the corresponding formulation of the creed of the catholic Church, but in neither case did this development in language and form involve any change of principle or belief: and, if we compare the development of the ministry with the process by which the canon of Scripture was fixed, we are struck with the fact that the hesitation, which appears in the latter process as to what did and what did not fall within the canon, has no parallel in any hesitation as to what did or what did not constitute at any particular moment the ministry in the Church. On this subject there was no conflict or division of opinion inside the body of the Church which is brought under our notice. The discussion about Montanism was not (as we have seen) a discussion as to the rights of prophets, but as to whether certain people were or were not justified in claiming the prophetic inspiration.

Hitherto, however, we have not touched the period which lies behind the middle of the second century. The reason for this has been that we have such very fragmentary light on the pace which intervenes between this date and the point where the Acts of the Apostles comes to an end. "I have elsewhere," says Dr. Salmon, "described the paucity of documents dating from the age immediately succeeding the apostolic, by saying that church history passes through a tunnel. We have good light where we have the books of the New Testament to guide us, and good light again when we come down to the abundant literary remains of the latter part of the second century; but there is an intervening period, here and there faintly illumined by a few documents giving such scanty and interrupted light as may be afforded by the air-holes of a tunnel. If in our study of the dimly-lighted portion of the history we wish to distinguish what is certain from what is doubtful, we may expect to find the things certain in what can be seen from either of the two well-lighted ends. If the same thing is visible on looking from either end, we can have no doubt of its existence."[1]

<small>It remains to verify the postulates of church history,</small>

We proceed, then, to examine the beginnings of the ministry—in other words, *first*, to obtain an answer to the question whether the postulates of the later Church are verified by the intention of Jesus Christ as recorded in the Gospels: *secondly*, to interrogate the history of the apostolic Church as recorded in the Epistles and in the Acts of the Apostles, and draw out the witness which this record affords on the earliest development of the Christian ministry: *lastly*, to scrutinize the documents which shed a certain amount of light on the subapostolic period, and see whether they bear out the theory of the apostolic succession, and whether, further, they supply the links which enable us to form an adequate idea of the method by which the ministry of the apostolic days passed into the ministry of the better known period of church history.[2]

The first task before us is to investigate the inten-

---

[1] *Expositor*, July 1887, p. 3 f.

[2] Speaking of *The Church and the Ministry*, a pamphlet in review of his Bampton Lectures, Dr. Hatch says of the author: "He begins by asserting that he accepts the author's method, and that he wishes only to answer the question which the author proposed, viz. What does the existing evidence teach as to the early history of ecclesiastical organization? but he silently, and perhaps unconsciously, devotes the rest of his review to the consideration of a very different question, viz. How far can the existing evidence be interpreted on the Augustinian theory?" (*B.L.* pref. to 2nd ed. p. xiii). My contention is that the evidence at certain periods teaches positively, that is to say, the evidence collected in the last chapter and portions of the evidence now to be produced; but in the subapostolic period it is often necessary, on account of the deficiency of positive evidence, to be content with finding that what there is is consistent with the positive position, which the earlier and later evidence so strongly suggests as almost to force it upon us.

IV.]   *The Institution of the Apostolate.*   219

tion of Christ. It has been already pointed out that *first, in the light of Christ's intention.* the method of Christ was to withdraw from the many upon the few. While He healed widely and freely all who had 'faith to be healed,' He taught those only (except by the way) in whom He discerned the higher sort of faith which would make them disciples. These He trained to become a firm consolidated body, rooted and grounded in faith in Himself, that they might be the nucleus of His universal Church. Even within the body of these disciples there were inner and outer circles: there were the twelve and also 'they that were with them,'[1] the women who ministered to them and the seventy who shared at a certain stage the apostolic commission.[2] Confining our attention now to the inner circle, with whom Christ chiefly concerned *The Gospels suggest the institution of an official apostolate,* Himself, we ask ourselves: Was His training of the twelve the training merely of typical disciples? or was

---

[1] St. Luke xxiv. 33; cf. St. Mark iv. 10: οἱ περὶ αὐτὸν σὺν τοῖς δώδεκα.

[2] The seventy (or seventy-two according to another reading) of St. Luke x. 1 share the earliest apostolic commission: they are sent forth (St. Luke x. 3: ἰδοὺ ἀποστέλλω ὑμᾶς, cf. ix. 2), with authority over the powers of Satan (x. 17, 19, cf. ix. 1), as representatives of the kingdom, endowed with its peace and having power to communicate it (x. 9, cf. ix. 2, and observe x. 6: ἐπαναπαύσεται ἐπ' αὐτὸν ἡ εἰρήνη ὑμῶν· εἰ δὲ μήγε, ἐφ' ὑμᾶς ἀνακάμψει, and as representatives of Christ (x. 16: ὁ ἀκούων ὑμῶν ἐμοῦ ἀκούει, κ.τ.λ.). The number seventy or seventy-two is supposed to have reference to the seventy-two heads of the Sanhedrin; or to the seventy-two tribes of mankind (see Godet *in loc.* and *Clem. Recog.* ii. 42); or, much more naturally, to the seventy elders endued with the spirit of prophecy (Num. xi. 16-30). Thus the later Church saw here the institution of the presbyterate by our Lord; see *Clem. Ep. Petri* 1 and Jerome *Ep.* lxxviii *ad Fabiol.* mans. 6. (The seventy elders, however, were also regarded as the prototype of the chorepiscopi.) In some traditions these seventy are reckoned apostles. Thus the Syriac *Teaching of the Apostles* reckons seventy-two apostles as originating "the ordination to the priesthood," and a late Arab writer, historian of the Coptic Church, who may draw on an earlier tradition, speaks of the apostles as seventy, besides the twelve; see refs. p. 131, n.[1] This suggests the 'apostles' and 'prophets' of the *Didache*. It is important that those who accept the historical character of St. Luke's Gospel should recollect that there must have been in the apostolic

it, over and above this, the training of ministers, of officers in His kingdom? This latter seems undoubtedly the true answer. 'He called unto Him whom He Himself would, . . . and He appointed twelve that they might be with Him, and that He might send them forth to preach and to have authority to cast out devils.' 'He called His disciples and He chose from them twelve, whom also He named apostles.'[1] These, as appears from His instructions to them, are to be His authorized representatives in the ministry of mercy and judgment.[2] "Evidently," says Mr. Maurice, "He never separates the thought of training them in their office from that of performing His own. As evidently He is training them to an *office*; He is not teaching them to be great saints, to keep up a high tone of personal holiness as if that were the end of their lives." Thus, he adds, "if we called the four Gospels 'the Institution of a Christian Ministry,' we might not go very far wrong or lose sight of many of their essential qualities."[3] Further, this apostolic ministry which Christ is seen to be training, though at times it seems to constitute almost the whole of that definite body which is being prepared

as one element in the Church.

Church a number of these 'evangelists,' who had received our Lord's commission, and whom we certainly cannot identify with presbyters whose office was local.

[1] St. Mark iii. 13, 14; St. Luke vi. 13.

[2] The personal and official position of the twelve appears clearly in St. Matt. x, St. John vi. 67-70, St. Luke xxii. 29, 30; cf. St. Matt. iv. 19. They are called 'the disciples' *par excellence* (in e.g. St. Mark x. 23-46, St. John xviii. 1); so they mediated between Christ and the crowd in the feeding of the five thousand (St. Luke ix. 10-17), and at other times (St. Matt. xv. 32-39, St. John xii. 20-22); while for their position after the resurrection cf. St. Luke xxiv. 9, 33.

[3] *Kingdom of Christ* ii. p. 118 [3d ed.].

The Institution of the Apostolate.

to be the Church, is intended to be—what in history it became—not the whole Church, but only one element in it.[1] This is implied in a striking manner—and there is no doubt that what a teacher implies often produces as striking an effect upon the mind as what he explicitly teaches—in the parable in which Christ gives St. Peter a picture of the divine household which He is intending to establish. He had been uttering some warnings and encouragements to His disciples, partly in the form of parables, with reference to the spirit of detachment and its reward, and St. Peter questions Him whether He is speaking to them (the twelve) only or to all. Christ answers with another question: "Who is that faithful and wise steward whom his Lord shall set over his household of servants, to give them their portion of meat in due season? Blessed is that servant whom his Lord, when he cometh, shall find so doing."[2] Here is a picture of 'the household' of the Church which Christ is intending to organize, and it is represented with a permanent distinction, enduring till the Lord come again,—the distinction between

---

[1] Such a passage as St. Matt. xxiii. 8, referred to by Dr. Hatch *B. L.* p. 121, does not imply that our Lord condemned all grades and distinctions in His Church, any more than it implies a condemnation of all grades and distinctions in the State, or than St. Luke xiv. 26 implies a condemnation of all human affections, or St. Luke vi. 20, 24 of all wealth, or St. John x. 8 of all the O. T. prophets. In all these passages there is a mode of speech, which Christ often used, and of which we have to take account. He condemns all dignities which interfere with His unique mastership, not such as represent it, whether in Church or State; all wealth held as a possession or right instead of as a trust, not all wealth absolutely; all love which interferes with His divine jealousy, not domestic love in its right place; precursors who came with His claim, not those who came as His heralds.

[2] St. Luke xii. 41-43. The future καταστήσει is to be noticed; it is like the futures οἰκοδομήσω, δώσω, in St. Matt. xvi. 18, 19.

the ordinary servants and the steward who distributes the 'bread of life.' Thus the impression is left on us that in the Christian household there is to be, by distinction from the ordinary members, a stewardship, instituted by the Master and enduring till the end.[1]

This impression is confirmed by

This impression, derived from a general consideration of Christ's dealings with His Apostles, is deepened by the study of special commissions given to them.

(1) The commission to St. Peter,

(1) We have the commission promised to St. Peter.[2] Christ meets St. Peter's confession of His Messiahship or Divine Sonship with a special benediction. He pronounces him "Peter," the man of rock, and declares that on this rock He will build His Church. So far He is dealing with the human character of St. Peter. There is in His language, as it has been admirably explained,[3] a sense of relief,—the relief that comes of perceiving in St. Peter's deliberate acceptance of His divine claim a solid basis on which His spiritual fabric may be reared, or at least a basis capable of being solidified by discipline and experience till it

---

[1] M. Godet's comment on this parable is as follows (*S. Luc.* ii. p. 138): "This utterance seems to imply that the apostolate will perpetuate itself till Christ's return; and in fact it is an irresistible conclusion from the figure employed, that there will remain to the end, in the Church, a ministry of the word established by Christ. The Apostles perceived this so clearly that, when they left the world, they were at pains to establish a ministry of the word to take their place in the Church. This ministry was a continuation of their own, if not in its completeness, at any rate in one of its most indispensable functions—that of which Jesus speaks in this parable—the distribution of spiritual nourishment to the flock. . . . The theory which makes the pastorate emanate from the Church as its representative is not scriptural. This commission is rather an emanation from the apostolate, and therefore mediately an institution of Jesus Himself."

[2] St. Matt. xvi. 18, 19.
[3] Holland *Creed and Character* p. 49.

become a foundation stone on which the Church may rest. The rock then, of which Christ speaks, is the rock of a human character confessing the divine claim. It is as men, as human characters, that the twelve Apostles are the twelve foundation stones of the New Jerusalem. And, if the promise to St. Peter which follows must be interpreted of an official position which is to be given to him in the Church, we have here at starting an emphatic intimation that official dignity in the Church is meant to rest on a basis of moral fitness.[1] But does Christ pass in His promise to St. Peter from words which concern his moral character to words which imply his spiritual office? He certainly does. He promises that He will give him "the keys of the kingdom of heaven," or of the Church, and this is in other words promising to make him the official steward of the divine household. When Shebna was substituted for Eliakim in the treasurership or stewardship of the house of David, this was the word of the Lord:[2] "I will call my servant Eliakim the son of Hilkiah: and I will clothe him with thy robe, and strengthen him with thy girdle, and I will commit thy government into his hand. . . . And the key of the house of David will I lay upon his shoulder; so he shall open, and none shall shut; and he shall shut, and none shall open." It is

---

[1] Christ, however, in choosing Judas whom he 'knew from the first' among the twelve, showed that He distinguished between moral worth and spiritual authority, and this is also implied in His words about the Jewish authorities (St. Matt. xxiii. 2, 3): "the scribes and the Pharisees sit in Moses' seat: all therefore whatsoever they bid you observe, that observe and do, but do not ye after their works."

[2] Isai. xxii. 20 22, cf. Moberly *Great Forty Days* pp. 127-130.

promised, then, that St. Peter shall be made the steward of the divine household,[1] and this carries with it an authority to 'bind' or 'loose,' that is to prohibit or permit—in a word, to give legislative decisions—with that heavenly sanction and authority which is the proper endowment of the kingdom of heaven.[2]

as (a) the representative apostle, Two questions may be raised with reference to this promise. What, it may be asked *first*, is St. Peter's relation in respect of this official position to the other Apostles? The answer seems to be that the official position is here not given but promised, and that the commissions actually given after the resurrection, the commissions which are seen in action in the apostolic history, are given to the whole apostolic body, and acted upon by all alike with the same authority though St. Peter is their leader.[3] A

---

[1] Of course subordinately to Christ (Rev. iii. 7).

[2] See Edersheim *Life and Times of Jesus the Messiah* ii. pp. 81-85. Binding or loosing referred simply to the prohibition or else permission of things or acts. It was one of the powers claimed by the Rabbis. But in relation to persons it implies a judicial, administrative power.

[3] St. Cyprian's opinion in this sense has been already quoted. It coincides with Origen's in the East (*in loc.*) and represents in fact the general mind of the early Church. So Theophylact (*in loc.*): "They who have obtained the grace of the episcopate as Peter had (οἱ κατὰ Πέτρον τῆς ἐπισκοπικῆς ἀξιωθέντες χάριτος) have authority to remit and bind. For though the 'I will give thee' was spoken to Peter alone, yet the gift has been given to all the Apostles. When? When He said 'whosesoever sins ye remit, they are remitted.' For this 'I will give' indicates a future time—the time, that is, after the resurrection." Perhaps the strongest evidence of the truth of this view is the absence of any special claim made by, or for, St. Peter in the Acts or Epistles, especially in St. Peter's own first Epistle, where (v. 1, 2) his pastoral charge (St. John xxi. 15-17) is identified with that of the elders; and on the other hand St. Paul's strenuous claim to be, as an apostle, dependent on none but Christ and in no respect inferior to the others; see Gal. i. 11, 12, ii. 1-10. This of course admits of a primacy being assigned to St. Peter so that οἱ περὶ Πέτρον can be the name for all of them, as in the conclusion of St. Mark's Gospel in L (given in Alford, and Westcott and

question may be raised *secondly* as to St. Peter's relation to the whole Christian community: for on another occasion, when Jesus Christ was speaking of the duty, under which His disciples might lie from time to time, of bringing one of their brethren under the censure of the Church, He attributes to the Church as a whole that authority to bind and loose—which in its application to individuals is of course a judicial authority—to which He declares the heavenly or supernatural sanction to attach.[1] The answer to this question has already been indicated when the general subject of the relation of the ministry to the Church was under discussion. The supernatural

and (b) administrative officer of the Church.

Hort). I deal briefly with this matter because this book is meant to be simply a vindication of the catholic idea of the ministry and not to go into questions which arise within the area where this finds acceptance. Tertullian's view of the meaning of the passage now in question, referred to on p. 210, is essentially the view of a Montanist.

[1] St. Matt. xviii. 15-18. The declaration is still future, it is a promise. Afterwards follows the promise which attaches to the prayer of even two disciples (ver. 19), based on the fact that Christ's presence is with even so small a number as two or three if they are gathered together 'in His Name' (ver. 20: that is, in the knowledge of Him and in accordance with His will). This last declaration applies primarily to the promise which attaches to united prayer, for the 'two or three' refers back to the 'if two of you shall agree to ask.' It may however also refer to the promise of judicial authority, and would mean that this authority is not dependent on numbers, but can be enforced by even two or three in accordance with His will, so that they can speak with the voice of the Church and to disobey them would be to 'refuse to hear the Church': cf. among the *Pirqe Aboth* of Dr. Taylor p. 60 f. "When ten sit and are occupied in words of Thorah the Shekinah is among them, for it is said, God standeth in the *congregation* of the mighty. . . . And whence [is it proved of] even three? Because it is said . . . and hath founded his *troop* in the earth. And whence even two? Because it is said, Then they that feared the Lord spake often one to another." Cf. note [15]: "Every ten men that are assembled in the synagogue, the Shekinah is with them, for it is said, God standeth in the 'edah, etc. And whence even three that *judge*, because it is said, He judges among gods, etc.," i.e. the divine presence is amongst even three who constitute a *beth din*, or house of judgment, to administer justice. So Christ may have meant that His presence is with the smallest 'court of justice' which represents the Church. Cf. *Expositor*, March 1887, p. 229.

P

226   *Christian Ministry.*   [CHAP.

authority does inhere in the Church as a whole, but the Church has (not by her own but by Christ's authority) executive officers, and it is through them that her judicial power is put into effect. Christ makes two promises: He promises judicial authority to the Church, and He promises to make St. Peter a steward, an administrative officer in the Church, with special reference to this power, and these two promises are correlative, not contradictory.

(2) The commission to the whole apostolic body after the resurrection,

(2) Christ's dealings in the last days of His ministry are wholly concentrated upon the twelve. With them alone He celebrates the Last Supper and institutes the memorial of His death, which He commits to them to be perpetuated in the Church [1]; to them

---

[1] The Eucharist was certainly regarded from the first in the Church as a sacrifice. "The conception of the whole action of the Last Supper as a sacrificial action (Opferhandlung) is found clearly in the *Didache* (c. xiv), in Ignatius, and before all in Justin (*Apol.* i. 65 f.). But Clement of Rome also expresses it when he (cc. 40-44) draws a parallel between the bishops and deacons and the O. T. priests and Levites, and indicates the προσφέρειν τὰ δῶρα as their special function" (Harnack *Dogmengesch.* i. 152 n.[1]). See *Didache* xiv: Κατὰ κυριακὴν δὲ κυρίου συναχθέντες κλάσατε ἄρτον καὶ εὐχαριστήσατε προσεξομολογησάμενοι τὰ παραπτώματα ὑμῶν, ὅπως καθαρὰ ἡ θυσία ὑμῶν ᾖ... αὕτη γάρ ἐστιν ἡ ῥηθεῖσα ὑπὸ κυρίου· Ἐν παντὶ τόπῳ καὶ χρόνῳ προσφέρειν μοι θυσίαν καθαράν. Justin *Dial. c. Tryph.* 41: Καὶ ἡ τῆς σεμιδάλεως προσφορά, ὦ ἄνδρες, ἔλεγον, ἡ ὑπὲρ τῶν καθαριζομένων ἀπὸ τῆς λέπρας προσφέρεσθαι παραδοθεῖσα, τύπος ἦν τοῦ ἄρτου τῆς εὐχαριστίας, ὃν εἰς ἀνάμνησιν τοῦ πάθους, οὗ ἔπαθεν ὑπὲρ τῶν καθαιρομένων τὰς ψυχὰς ἀπὸ πάσης πονηρίας ἀνθρώπων, Ἰησοῦς Χριστὸς ὁ κύριος ἡμῶν παρέδωκε ποιεῖν· the offering, he explains, is to be made in thanksgiving for the blessings of creation and redemption through Christ's death; he then quotes the usual passage from Malachi i. 11 and continues: περὶ δὲ τῶν ἐν παντὶ τόπῳ ὑφ' ἡμῶν τῶν ἐθνῶν προσφερομένων αὐτῷ θυσιῶν, τουτέστι τοῦ ἄρτου τῆς εὐχαριστίας καὶ τοῦ ποτηρίου ὁμοίως τῆς εὐχαριστίας, προλέγει τότε εἰπὼν καὶ τὸ ὄνομα αὐτοῦ δοξάζειν ἡμᾶς ὑμᾶς δὲ βεβηλοῦν. Irenaeus iv. 17. 5: "Sed et suis discipulis dans consilium primitias Deo offerre ex suis creaturis ... eum qui ex creatura panis est, accepit et gratias egit, dicens: Hoc est meum corpus. Et calicem similiter, qui est ex ea creatura quae est secundum nos, suum sanguinem confessus est, et novi testamenti novam docuit oblationem quam ecclesia ab apostolis accipiens in universo mundo offert Deo."

He addresses the last discourses, which are calculated to prepare them in character and intelligence for the withdrawal of His visible presence and the substitution for it of that new and higher mode of inward presence by His Spirit, which He should give to His Church when He was glorified. In all this Christ is dealing with them no less as apostles than as

> It would not be in place here to discuss at length the sense in which the early Church believed the Eucharist to be a sacrifice. Briefly however it is in place to remark that
> (1) The whole language of the earliest Church seems most easily interpreted, if we suppose that the bread and wine, chosen out of the general offerings of the congregation and presented before God as a memorial of Christ's sacrifice with accompanying prayers, were regarded as constituting the thank-offering (Eucharist) or oblations (gifts) of the Church and as expressive of that relation of sonship and purity and freedom of approach to God, which belonged to the Church in virtue of her redemption, as being the 'high-priestly race.' These 'gifts' were then offered for the consecration of the Holy Spirit. They became "no longer common bread but Eucharist, made up of two substances, an earthly and an heavenly": they became to the Church 'the Body and Blood of Christ.' This response of God to the Church's invocation, this mingling of heavenly and earthly things, gave to the Church's sacrifice a new power and brought it into essential union with the One Sacrifice, with 'Jesus, the mediator of the new covenant,' and with 'the blood of sprinkling.' But for this, the Church's sacrifice would have been most Judaic in character.
> (2) The consent of the Church in regarding the Eucharist as a sacrifice appears to fix the meaning of Christ's words of institution. In this connection it requires to be observed (a) That Justin Martyr interprets ποιεῖν as = 'to offer' (*Dial. c. Tryph.* 41, just quoted, and 70), and this use of the word is common in the LXX without any qualification (Willis *Sacrificial Aspect of the Eucharist* p. 49 f.). It enables us in St. Luke xxii. 19, 20, 1 Cor. xi. 24, 25 to give, as is natural, the same meaning to τοῦτο in both corresponding clauses, τοῦτό ἐστιν . . . τοῦτο ποιεῖτε: and in 1 Cor. xi. 25 also to make τοῦτο the accusative, as the sentence requires, to both verbs, ποιεῖτε and πίνητε. (b) That there is an obvious reference to the words of Moses in Exod. xxiv. 8, ἰδοὺ τὸ αἷμα τῆς διαθήκης, and that agreeably with this reference the word ἐκχυννόμενον (Matt., Mark, Luke), expresses probably not the shedding of Christ's blood in death, but the sacrificial pouring out of it. See Rendall *Theol. of the Hebr. Chr.* p. 123 f., and cf. Exod. xxix. 12, Lev. iv. 7, 19, 25, 30, 34, viii. 15, ix. 9, etc., in LXX. (c) That ἀνάμνησις in the O. T. means a memorial before God, as is the case wherever it is used (Willis *l.c.* p. 17 f.); but see Heb. x. 3 and the reference in the liturgies: Μεμνημένοι οὖν ὧν δι' ἡμᾶς ὑπέμεινεν κ.τ.λ. (Hammond *Anc. Lit.* pp. 17, 42).

representative disciples. After His resurrection He does not cease to deal with them in the latter capacity, but it would appear that the commissions, which in the 'great forty days' were no longer promised but given, were addressed to them in their official character and to them alone. It would appear to be undeniable, if it had not been so often denied, that these commissions, taken together, are commissions given to an abiding *apostolate*, destined to be permanent till 'the end of the world.' The 'eleven disciples' are expressly mentioned as the subjects of the commission recorded by St. Matthew as given on the 'mountain where Jesus had appointed them,' which invested them with His royal power to go and make disciples of all the nations, baptizing them into the threefold Name and teaching them to observe all His precepts, and which was accompanied by the promise of His presence with them 'all the days till the completion of the age.'[1] The parallel account of the commission of Christ given in the verses which conclude St. Mark's Gospel describes it as given 'to the eleven.'[2] In St. Luke's narrative, where in connection with Christ's appearance on the evening of His resurrection mention is made of 'the disciples and those who were with them,' it is noticeable that, though there is a record of encouragement and enlightenment and pro-

as in St. Matthew.

St. Mark,

---

[1] St. Matt. xxviii. 16 f. It is urged that, as there were 'some who doubted,' so others must have been present beside the Apostles. I should have thought that, as a matter of Greek, οἱ δὲ ἐδίστασαν must express a subdivision of 'the eleven,' who are the subject of the whole sentence. See Meyer *in loc.* At any rate they are the only people mentioned in connection with the commission given.

[2] St. Mark xvi. 14-18.

IV.]   *The Institution of the Apostolate.*   229

mise, there is no record of a ministerial commission.[1] There was however such a commission, given appar- *and St. John* ently on this occasion, which is recorded by St. John.[2] It is there described as given to 'the disciples'; but this expression at the end of St. John's Gospel commonly refers to the twelve, who are the subjects of His typical training.[3] The words of the commission, moreover, and the analogy of that recorded in St. Matthew and St. Mark, seem to make it natural to conclude that, though others may have been present, it was addressed to the Apostles only.[4]   " As My Father

[1] St. Luke xxiv. 33 f. but cf. Acts i. 1-5.
[2] St. John xx. 19-23.
[3] So Dr. Westcott says that by 'the disciples' (in c. xxi. 1) is meant "in all probability the Apostles, the disciples in the narrower sense, though 'the twelve' were not all assembled on this occasion, but at most 'seven' only." This use of the word 'disciples' may be illustrated by a passage closely parallel to that under discussion. Our Lord's prayer in St. John xvii is spoken amongst 'the disciples' (xvi. 29, xviii. 1). Yet by this is meant 'the twelve' (St. Matt. xxvi. 20): thus He prays for them as those whom the Father 'has given Him' (xvii. 6, 9, 11) and whom 'He guarded,' so that 'not one of them perished but the son of perdition' (ver. 12), and whom He 'has sent into the world,' as the Father sent Him into the world (ver. 18). These are clearly the definite body, the twelve; and the expression 'As thou didst send me, so sent I them' (ver. 18) interprets that in xx. 21.

[4] I am of course aware that I have Dr. Westcott against me (*Revel. of the Risen Lord* pp. 81-83 and Comm. *in loc.*), as well as many others. On the other hand I am following M. Godet, one of the best recent commentators on St. John; and the arguments which seem to me of determining force in the matter are

(1) The parallel commissions to 'the eleven' in St. Matt. and St. Mark.

(2) The obvious reference to the apostolate in the words of St. John xx. 21; cf. xvii. 18. (The use of πέμπω in the former case hardly weakens the force of this.)

(3) The habitual reference of 'the disciples' at the end of St. John's Gospel to the Apostles.

(4) The implication of the Acts (as bearing on all the commissions taken together); if the Acts is accepted as historical, undoubtedly the Apostles must have received a commission distinct from the Church as a whole to account for their position.

On the other hand   (*a*) the presence of 'those with them' does not seem to be, in this case, more than in the case of any later ministerial commissions, an argument against the limitation to the Apostles; (*b*) the

hath sent Me," Christ said, "even so send I you," and when He had said this, He breathed on them and said: "Receive ye holy spirit:[1] whosesoever sins ye remit, they are remitted unto them; whosesoever sins ye retain, they are retained." Here the opening words contain a manifest reference to the apostolate, and the subsequent act of breathing, with the words accompanying, seems to be the actual bestowal in power and spirit of those 'keys of the kingdom' which Christ had formerly promised to the chief of the Apostles. What is bestowed is a judicial power with a supernatural sanction—the power, in pursuance of Christ's redemptive mission, to admit men into the new covenant of absolution and to exclude them from it according to considerations of their moral fitness.

(3) The commission restored to St. Peter.

(3) If the threefold pastoral commission to St. Peter[2] represents, as seems most probable, simply a personal restoration of St. Peter to the position of trust which his threefold denial might be supposed to have lost him, then we shall only be justified in concluding from our Lord's words on that occasion that the pastoral care, to govern and to feed, was supposed to be involved in the apostolic commission.[3]

Conclusion as to Christ's institution of the Apostles.

It may very well be maintained that it would be impossible to draw certain conclusions on the matter

absence of St. Thomas is no hindrance to the commission having been given to the Apostles, as such. The narratives are fragmentary, and we cannot say but that St. Thomas may have had his loss by absence made good to him. He was present among the eleven to receive the commission recorded in the other Gospels.

[1] Λάβετε πνεῦμα ἅγιον. Cf. 1 Cor. xiv. 12 where πνεύματα = χαρίσματα, and St. John vii. 39 where τὸ πνεῦμα = the Holy Ghost and πνεῦμα = His inspiration (Westcott *in loc.*).

[2] St. John xxi. 15-17. [3] St. John xxi. 15, 17 βόσκε, 16 ποίμαινε.

which has been under discussion from the four Gospels, if they existed as isolated documents with no history of the Church to interpret them; but from a mere examination of the narratives the conclusions arrived at above appear to be the most probable, and as a fact they are supported by all the evidence of church history from its beginning. It would appear, then, that Christ founded not only a Church but an apostolate in the Church, an apostolate moreover which was intended in some real sense to be permanent; this apostolic office included all that was necessary to perpetuate that mission on which the Father had sent the Son into the world: it involved the authority to teach in Christ's name, to govern, and to feed, and in this sense was described as a stewardship and pastorate: in order to its function of government, a supernatural sanction was attached to its legislative and judicial authority: and finally the two great sacraments of Baptism and the Eucharist were committed to its administration.[1]

Whether, then, it be true or no to say that the Church began *in* a ministry,[2] it appears certainly true

---

[1] Nothing is said to explain the sense in which baptism and the Eucharist respectively were committed to the apostolate. As a matter of fact St. Paul regarded the actual administration of baptism as not specially characteristic of the apostolic office. On the other hand it should be noticed that there is no mention in the Gospels of the institution of that which in the Acts appears as the complement of baptism and as specially administered by the Apostles, the rite of laying-on of hands.

[2] See Gladstone *Ch. Princ.* pp. 201-2: "In the Apostles, then, the Christian Church properly so called potentially lay, at the moment when our Saviour uttered those sacred and momentous words which St. Matthew has conveyed to us; but it had no other existence; and if we take that moment of time for our point of view, we see the heavenly gift arrested, as it were, on its passage from God to man, given from Him, but not yet arrived at its destination; not yet communicated to us; just as the loaves and the

to say that the Church began *with* a ministry. Those who had received the commission of the apostolate, and those who had not, awaited side by side—the same in discipleship but different in office and function—that Pentecostal gift which was to make all alike and for the first time, in the full sense, members of the Church of Christ.

<small>fishes were, after Jesus had given thanks and broken, and had given them to the twelve to distribute, but before they had actually served them to the multitude. . . . And so it was to remain until the day of Pentecost." Cf. *Gleanings* iii. p. 262: "No doubt (as I for one believe) the Church began with a clergy; nay, began in a clergy." I should have thought however that before the day of Pentecost there were others besides the apostolic clergy who were, in the same sense as they, themselves members of the Church. "The number of names together were about an hundred and twenty."</small>

CHAPTER V.

THE MINISTRY IN THE APOSTOLIC AGE.

THE task now before us is to investigate the witness of the apostolic Epistles and of the Acts of the Apostles as to the origin and nature of the Christian ministry and its development in the first period of the life of the Church. The most convenient method will be first to marshal the evidence and then to draw the conclusions which it seems to warrant. Accordingly we begin with the evidence of St. Paul's Epistles.

I. First of all then, St. Paul gives us in each group of his Epistles[1] a vivid impression of what he understood by the ministry of an apostle.[2] He is one who,

1. The evidences of St. Paul's Epistles.
(a) The apostle

---

[1] The two Epistles to the Thessalonians constitute the earliest group. Then come the two Epistles to the Corinthians, with those to the Romans and the Galatians—all bound together by close connections in subject and tone. Then follow 'the Epistles of the first captivity' to the Philippians, the Colossians, the Ephesians, and to Philemon. Last come the Pastoral Epistles. Of these Harnack recognises the first two groups as genuine, and the Epistle to the Philippians (*Contemp. Review*, August 1886, p. 224). I endeavour above to indicate how natural and harmonious a result is derived from the evidence of all of them, taken as genuine, on the subject of the ministry.

[2] I.e. in the narrower sense, so that a man could rank with 'the twelve.' We find the term used also in a wider sense in 2 Cor. viii. 23: Rom. xvi. 7, where Andronicus and Junias, St. Paul's kinsmen, are spoken of as 'of note among the apostles': Phil. ii. 25, where Epaphroditus is spoken of as St. Paul's fellow-labourer and 'the apostle' of the Philippian brethren, ὑμῶν δὲ ἀπόστολον καὶ λειτουργὸν τῆς χρείας μου. In the latter case the word probably means no more than the messenger sent by the Philippians to minister to St. Paul's need: see Lightfoot *in loc.*, but cf. Clem. *ad Cor.* 44

having seen Christ after His resurrection and so become qualified to witness to that fundamental fact,[1] has received by no mediating hands but personally from Christ a definite mission.[2] An authoritative mission is indeed essential for all evangelistic work, for 'how shall men preach, except they be sent?'[3]— how, that is, can any one take upon himself so responsible an office? But for an apostle it is essential that this mission should be direct from Him who said: "As my Father hath sent me, so send I you." Such a direct mission, actual and unmistakable, from Christ Himself, St. Paul believed himself to have received and was recognised as having received by his fellow-apostles, who had been appointed in the more normal way while Christ was still on earth.[4] The function of the apostle was primarily that of proclaiming the Gospel.[5] He had become a 'steward of

a teacher

οἱ ἀπόστολοι ἡμῶν. In the former cases however (and possibly in the latter) the term apostle is probably used much in the sense in which we find it in the *Didache*—perhaps as equivalent to 'evangelists.' For the idea that it included the seventy, see Salmasius *de Episcop.* p. 61. Theodoret on Phil. ii. 27 says: ἀπόστολον δὲ αὐτὸν κέκληκεν αὐτῶν ὡς τὴν ἐπιμέλειαν αὐτῶν ἐμπεπιστευμένον.

[1] 1 Cor. ix. 1, xv. 8.

[2] Gal. i. 1: οὐκ ἀπ' ἀνθρώπων οὐδὲ δι' ἀνθρώπου. Timothy's mission on the other hand, though not ἀπ' ἀνθρώπων, was δι' ἀνθρώπου (2 Tim. i. 6). St. Paul cannot have regarded the event recorded in Acts xiii. 1-3 as more than a recognition by the Church of a mission which he had already received from Christ.

[3] Rom. x. 15.

[4] St. Paul was an ἔκτρωμα (1 Cor. xv. 8); but he was recognised by his fellow-apostles. See Gal. ii. 7-9.

[5] 1 Cor. i. 17: "Christ sent me not to baptize, but to preach the Gospel" (for the reason of this see vv. 14, 15). 1 Cor. ix. 14. (Alford's comment here is quite beside the mark. 'Preaching the Gospel' is the primary function of the apostolate, or of the general ministry, as distinguished from the local ministry, whose primary function was administration. Cf. in Clement *Quis Dives* 42 how St. John does not himself baptize the young man but hands him over to the local ἐπίσκοπος.) 1 Thess. ii. 4-9; 1 Tim. ii. 7.

The Ministry in the Apostolic Age.

the mysteries of God'—an administrator, that is, of the divine revelations, which, having been kept in the secret counsels of God through ages and generations, had, now that the fulness of the time was come, been declared through the Incarnate Son.[1] This office at once involved absolute subordination and complete authority. For on the one hand the apostle was 'the slave of Jesus Christ.' As he had no personal, arbitrary lordship over the faith of the disciples, so he could proclaim nothing of his own: it was quite beyond his power to alter or innovate upon 'the tradition' which constituted his message.[2] On the other hand it involved a plenary authority to teach and to govern: for the message was not one to be cast loose as a disembodied truth among mankind, it was to be the basis on which organized societies were to be built. The apostle accordingly was a founder and ruler of Churches, with divine authority given him for their edification—ruling them all alike on the basis of a common tradition of doctrine and practice, and claiming from them the obedience of affectionate children to their spiritual father.[3] And inasmuch

and governor.

---

[1] 1 Cor. iv. 1 : οἰκονόμος μυστηρίων θεοῦ. Cf. Eph. iii. 1-13.

[2] He is personally a δοῦλος (Rom. 1. 1), officially a ὑπηρέτης (1 Cor. iv. 1) or διάκονος (1 Cor. iii. 5, 2 Cor. iii. 6, iv. 1). Cf. 2 Cor. 1. 24: οὐχ ὅτι κυριεύομεν ὑμῶν τῆς πίστεως, and 1 Pet. v. 3. Gal. 1. 8: ἐὰν ἡμεῖς ἢ ἄγγελος ἐξ οὐρανοῦ εὐαγγελίσηται [ὑμῖν] παρ' ὃ εὐηγγελισάμεθα ὑμῖν, ἀνάθεμα ἔστω. Thus again St. Paul distinguishes between his own judgment and the command of Christ (1 Cor. vii. 6, 10, 12, 25, 40). The primary requirement of his ministry is faithfulness to Christ (1 Cor. iv. 2). On the other hand for the authority of the apostle's teaching see 2 Cor. xiii. 3: τοῦ ἐν ἐμοὶ λαλοῦντος χριστοῦ, 2 Tim. i. 13: ὑποτύπωσιν ἔχε ὑγιαινόντων λόγων ὧν παρ' ἐμοῦ ἤκουσας.

[3] 2 Thess. iii. 14, ii. 15 ; 1 Cor. iv. 15-21, xi. 16, 34 ; 2 Cor. x. 8, xiii. 10: ἡ ἐξουσία ἡμῶν, ἧς ἔδωκεν ὁ κύριος εἰς οἰκοδομήν. (The word ἐξουσία expresses also the right to be supported which accompanied the apostolate, 2 Thess. iii. 9, 1 Cor. ix. 5 f.). Cf. 2 Cor. vi. 13, xii. 14. The 'word of God,' which the

as the whole purpose of Christ's coming is to reconcile man to God, so of course the authority of an apostle is that of an empowered ambassador and minister of the reconciliation with God which Christ has won: "God hath put in us," says St. Paul, "the word of reconciliation."[1] It was 'in him' moreover not merely in word as a message, but in power; so that he could pass sentence on the sins of individuals, to retain or forgive them, with a sanction which is not only supernatural in the spiritual sphere but miraculous also in the physical. An offender whose sins merit condign punishment can be "delivered to Satan," that he may be taught by physical penalties "not to blaspheme."[2] This plenary authority over individuals, which St. Paul describes himself in his pastoral Epistles as exercising in the case of Hymenæus and Alexander in his single person, we watch him in his Epistles to the Corinthians exercising in conjunction with the Corinthian congregation. He rebukes the Church there for not having "removed out of their midst," or, according to the later church phrase, 'excommunicated,' an incestuous man. Thus, where they had shown only too great a readiness to forgive, St. Paul proceeds, as controlling their action, to judge or to retain the sin. And, because this judgment of a sin has a miraculous physical sanction attached to it, it is

---

apostles minister, is declared in 1 Cor. xiv. 36 to be authoritative over all churches alike; cf. 1 Cor. iv. 17, xi. 16, xiv. 33.

[1] 2 Cor. v. 18, 19 : τὰ πάντα ἐκ τοῦ θεοῦ τοῦ . . . δόντος ἡμῖν τὴν διακονίαν τῆς καταλλαγῆς, ὡς ὅτι θεὸς ἦν . . . θέμενος ἐν ἡμῖν τὸν λόγον τῆς καταλλαγῆς. ὑπὲρ Χριστοῦ οὖν πρεσβεύομεν.

[2] 1 Tim. I. 20 παρέδωκα τῷ Σατανᾷ; 1 Cor. v. 5 παραδοῦναι τῷ Σατανᾷ. Cf. Job ii. 6 παραδίδωμί σοι αὐτόν, and Stanley's note *in loc.*

described as "delivering such an one unto Satan for the destruction of the flesh," in order that the physical penalty may startle him to repentance, and "his spirit may be saved in the day of the Lord."[1] And accordingly in the event, when presumably the isolation from the Christian community as well as the accompanying punishment had had its perfect work in the particular case, St. Paul exhorts the congregation to receive back their penitent brother; and again taking the initiative upon himself, speaks of himself as forgiving "in the person of Christ" the sin he had before 'retained.'[2]

An apostle can thus bring his authority to bear on the details of the life of a single congregation, but, speaking generally, his ministry is of the general or catholic order. He has 'the care of all the Churches.' He represents the general Church rather than the particular Churches. It is in this respect that the apostolate is primarily distinguished from the local ministry, of the origin of which we get no clear information in St. Paul's Epistles, but which yet appears as a recognised institution in that which is of earliest

His ministry catholic.

---

[1] 1 Cor. v. 3-5: κέκρικα τὸν τοῦτο κατεργασάμενον ἐν τῷ ὀνόματι τοῦ κυρίου Ἰησοῦ, συναχθέντων ὑμῶν καὶ τοῦ ἐμοῦ πνεύματος σὺν τῇ δυνάμει τοῦ κυρίου ἡμῶν Ἰησοῦ, κ.τ.λ. St. Paul seems to imply that the Corinthian Church, endowed as it was with the gift of 'government,' could have removed the evil-doer out of their midst by the disciplinary authority belonging to the community; cf. ver. 13. But probably only the apostle could inflict the physical punishment; see Alford *in loc.* It has been remarked above how clear cut is the distinction in this passage between 'those within,' whom the Church has a right to 'judge,' and 'those without,' over whom she has no such right (vv. 12, 13).

[2] 2 Cor. ii. 5-11 and 2 Thess. iii. 6, 14, 15. The punishment is spoken of as inflicted by the community in general (οἱ πλείονες) and the forgiveness also is assigned to them (ᾧ δέ τι χαρίζεσθε, κἀγώ), but St. Paul apparently has to take the initiative. For the expression ἐν προσώπῳ Χριστοῦ, cf. ἐν ὀνόματι Χριστοῦ (2 Thess. iii. 6).

238   *Christian Ministry.*   [CHAP.

(b) The local ministry: date. Over against the catholic authority of the apostle is the local authority of the 'presidents,' who 'labour amongst' the Thessalonian Christians and keep them in mind of their duties.¹ There were similar 'presidents' as well as 'ministers' and 'teachers' amongst the Roman Christians,² and corresponding officers of 'government' and 'assistance' amongst the Corinthians.³ But in the Epistles to Corinth

---

¹ 1 Thess. v. 12 : τοὺς κοπιῶντας ἐν ὑμῖν καὶ προϊσταμένους ὑμῶν ἐν κυρίῳ καὶ νουθετοῦντας ὑμᾶς. They are to be esteemed very highly for their work's sake. For κοπιᾶν cf. 1 Tim. v. 17 οἱ κοπιῶντες ἐν λόγῳ καὶ διδασκαλίᾳ, and, generally of labourers for Christ, apostolic or others, both male and female, Rom. xvi. 6, 12, 1 Cor. xv. 10, xvi. 16. It is to be noticed that St. Paul addresses to the whole Church (1 Thess. v. 14 f.) admonitions, the execution of which would fall to the presidents; see esp. v. 14 νουθετεῖτε τοὺς ἀτάκτους. Government was a function of the whole community exercised through certain official organs. It should be noticed that the Thessalonian Church needs to be admonished not to 'quench the spirit' or 'despise prophecy.' Its tendencies to disorder proceeded from a different cause to those which existed among the Corinthians.

² Rom. xii. 6. The different 'charismata' mentioned here are prophecy, ministry (διακονία), teaching, exhortation (παράκλησις), distribution, presidency, administration of mercy. This has a vaguer appearance than any of St. Paul's other lists of church gifts or officers. The prophet, the teacher, the president, the deacon, are well-known figures, and the ministration of mercy may refer to such a function as that of Phœbe, 'the deaconess' (xvi. 1. 2), unless indeed hers is the διακονία (cf. 1 Cor. xvi. 15) and the deacon is ὁ μεταδιδούς. But it still remains difficult to assign a distinct office to ὁ παρακαλῶν and ὁ ἐλεῶν. It has to be noticed that the Roman Christians had not yet been organized by any apostolic person into one Church; cf. xvi. 5, 10, 11, 15.

³ At Corinth the 'distinctions of gifts' (διαιρέσεις χαρισμάτων), each with its accompanying ministry (διακονία) and power (ἐνέργημα), are the word of wisdom, the word of knowledge, faith, gifts of healings, workings of miracles, prophecy, discernings of spirits, kinds of tongues, interpretation of tongues (1 Cor. xii. 4-11). These are strikingly different from those mentioned among the Roman Christians. They are much more miraculous and abnormal. The corresponding list of officers in the Church is (vv. 28-30): apostles, prophets, teachers, powers (i.e. workers of miracles), gifts of healings, helps (ἀντιλήμψεις, which may well correspond to the deacon's office), governments (κυβερνήσεις, which probably represents the 'presidents' of the Church), kinds of tongues. "Are all," St. Paul adds, "apostles? are all prophets? are all teachers? are all powers? have all gifts of healing? do all speak with tongues? do all interpret?" He is here clearly intent on

and to Rome these other 'ministries' are presented to us from a new point of view. The Church, as the Spirit-bearing body of Christ, is viewed as a richly diversified organism in which the life common to all is yet not given to all alike or to all for the same function. There is a great variety of 'gifts,' that is of special miraculous or spiritual endowments imparted to different individuals over and above the spiritual life necessary for the Christian profession as such, or as special determinations of it;[1] so that the Christian Church is presented to us as a great spiritual hierarchy of graduated orders or powers, with apostles, prophets, teachers, rulers, helpers, ministers of mercy and exhortation, workers of miracles, speakers with tongues, interpreters—each class being not self-constituted but instituted and empowered of God.[2]

among the spiritual endowments of the Church

A hint in the Epistle to the Romans would indicate—what is of course amply corroborated in the Acts of the Apostles and Pastoral Epistles—that these spiritual gifts, though they are specially described as the gifts of God's Spirit, were mediated

asserting the principle of unity in variety, not on enabling us to distinguish the variations.

[1] The word χάρισμα is used for an ordinary 'favour' or 'gift' of God, as in 2 Cor. i. 11. But it gets a technical sense in which it is distinguished from the fundamental spiritual qualifications of faith and love (1 Cor. xii. 4 and 31, cf. xii. 1, xiv. 1).

[2] The household of Stephanas is described in 1 Cor. xvi. 15 as having set themselves to minister to the saints: εἰς διακονίαν τοῖς ἁγίοις ἔταξαν ἑαυτούς. In consequence the Corinthians are exhorted to be subject to them, as to all workers for Christ. The reference is here probably to a ministry of mercy in general. These persons set themselves to supply the Church's needs, like good Christians in later days. There is probably no reference to any special office, and their authority is such as has been allotted to 'patrons' of the Church in later days; cf. προστάτις, used of Phœbe (Rom. xvi. 2).

through the apostolic agency.¹ Otherwise, though it is implied that the gifts were actual, recognisable endowments in all cases and were subject to the apostolic order in their exercise, we have no information as to how they were communicated, or (when they were non-miraculous, like the gift of 'government') how they were recognised. Some, however, of the gifts which caused the Corinthian Church to present such an appearance of wealth in spiritual endowment, were not destined to take a very important or permanent place in the equipment of the Church. The gift of tongues is heard of but for a little while, and the gifts of healing and miracles do not appear again, any more than some of the functions mentioned in the Epistle to the Romans as constituting distinct offices in the Church. In the Epistles of the next group the more permanent ministries of the Church are seen to emerge into clearer prominence. Christ, says St. Paul to the Ephesians, after His ascension, "gave some to be apostles, and some prophets, and some evangelists, and some pastors and teachers."² Here, with St. Chrysostom, we may recognise the apostles and prophets (who are elsewhere in this epistle classed together as the recipients of the divine secrets now revealed and as the foundation-stones of the Church³) as constituting, with the less clearly-

there emerge into prominence

---

[1] Rom. i. 11 : ἐπιποθῶ ἰδεῖν ὑμᾶς, ἵνα τι μεταδῶ χάρισμα ὑμῖν πνευματικὸν εἰς τὸ στηριχθῆναι ὑμᾶς, coupled with 1 Cor. xii. 4 ; cf. Acts viii. 14 f.

[2] Eph. iv. 11. The 'pastors and teachers,' under one τοὺς δέ, represent the same officers. The different orders are, as has been remarked, first gifted (ver. 7), and then themselves God's gifts to the Church (ver. 11).

[3] Eph. iii. 5, ii. 20. These prophets are, no doubt, the prophets of the new covenant. This seems to be generally admitted as to Eph. iv. 11 and iii. 5. But Chrysostom and others among the ancients, with Estius, etc., among

v.]   The Ministry in the Apostolic Age.   241

defined evangelists, the general or catholic ministry of the Church; while the pastors and teachers, as local officers,[1] are easily identified with the 'bishops' whom we hear of, coupled with 'deacons,' in the inscription of the Epistle to the Philippians.[2] There was, we should gather, a college or group of 'presidents' or 'bishops' in each community who discharged the office of government, and acted subordinately to the apostles and prophets, as pastors and teachers of the flock. To these was also attached the 'assistant' ministry of the 'deacons.' This is borne out in the Pastoral Epistles, where we learn further that these

local 'bishops' and deacons.

---

moderns, explain Eph. ii. 20 of the O. T. prophets. But it seems manifestly wrong to separate this passage from the other two. The intimations we get of the position of prophets in the earliest Church are somewhat perplexing. On the one hand they are assigned, in the Epistle to the Ephesians, as in Acts xiii. 1, 2 and in the *Didache*, a position of very great importance in the Church as a whole, closely allied to that of apostles. On the other hand, in the Epistle to the Corinthians, though prophets are ranked next to apostles, the gift of prophecy is regarded as a gift belonging to the local Church and exercised in it (1 Cor. xiv. 29-33, 39); cf. also Acts xix. 6. It would appear that at least certain persons with the gift of prophecy occupied a prominent place as prophets and were ranked in that capacity close to apostles as founders of the Churches. See esp. Eph. iii. 5, ii. 20, and Acts xiii. 1, 2, where Paul and Barnabas are ranked as 'prophets and teachers,' who are afterwards called 'apostles' (xiv. 4). All who were given an occasional power of prophecy were not 'prophets,' e.g. those in Acts xix. 6. Cf. App. Note I.

[1] Chrysostom says on Eph. iv. 11 : ποιμένας καὶ διδασκάλους τοὺς ὁλόκληρον ἐμπεπιστευμένους ἔθνος· τί οὖν ; οἱ ποιμένες καὶ οἱ διδάσκαλοι ἐλάττους ; καὶ πάνυ τῶν περϊόντων καὶ εὐαγγελιζομένων οἱ καθήμενοι καὶ περὶ ἕνα τόπον ἠσχολημένοι. He goes on however to cite Timothy and Titus as instances of the latter class.

Chrysostom here clearly does not (like Ambrose and Theophylact) identify evangelists with deacons. It is true that Philip, one of the seven (who, in Acts viii, clearly has not the apostolic function), is in Acts xxi. 8 called 'the evangelist';. but this was not in virtue of his 'diaconate,' but of his conversion of Samaria. There is also no reason why he should have remained in the lower office. The work of Timothy is described as that of an 'evangelist,' and such a relation to the apostolate suits better the rank assigned here to the evangelists.

[2] Phil. i. 1 : σὺν ἐπισκόποις καὶ διακόνοις. These are different officers.

Q

local 'presidents' or 'bishops' were also known as 'presbyters.'[1]

The importance of the Pastoral Epistles.

The Pastoral Epistles are the *locus classicus* in the New Testament on the subject of the Christian ministry. Elsewhere St. Paul writes to Churches or to a private Christian like Philemon, but here he writes to his own representatives, evangelists and ministers of Christ like himself, on the duties of their office. And these Epistles themselves supply the answer to the question what may have prompted the change of method. It was because the circumstances of St. Paul's last days led him to emphasize the necessity for government in the Church. In the department of doctrine he saw an unpractical profane spirit of speculation springing up, on a Jewish basis, but already displaying that sort of false spiritualism, that horror of what is material and actual, which has constantly characterized oriental thought, and which found such a conspicuous development, in a direction most opposed to Judaism, in the Gnostic movements of the second century.[2] This speculative tendency was

---

[1] Titus i. 5-7. More is said below on the identity of the 'bishop' and 'presbyter.' The προϊστάμενος among the Thessalonian and Roman Christians = the officer of 'government' among the Corinthians = the 'bishop' among the Philippians = the 'pastor and teacher' among the Ephesians = the 'presbyter' of the Pastoral Epistles. This is at least what St. Paul's Epistles suggest taken as a whole. The vague use of terms at first need not surprise. See Winterstein *Der Episcopat* p. 11. The apostolate is called a διακονία by St. Paul in 1 Cor. iii. 5; cf. 1 Tim. iv. 6, 2 Tim. iv. 5, and Acts i. 25; also (with reference to the Psalm) an ἐπισκοπή in Acts i. 20. The term presbyterate covers the episcopate long after this latter term had gained its later distinct sense. Again, Pothinus is spoken of in the Epistle of the Churches of South Gaul as "having been entrusted with the διακονία of the ἐπισκοπή" (Euseb. *H. E.* v. 1).

[2] 1 Tim. i. 4-7; iv. 1-5; vi. 20, 21; 2 Tim. ii. 16-18; Titus i. 10-16, iii. 8 9. The intellectual and moral phenomena in Ephesus and Crete are closely parallel. St. Paul's insistence on the duty of praying for secular

frequently joined to a self-seeking proselytism and a thinly-veiled covetousness;[1] and it allied itself with a terrible tendency to lawlessness, which clouded the whole moral atmosphere of the Christian Church, whether in the department of civil authority and secular occupations, or in the relations of master and servant, or in the inner sphere of church life.[2] There was a special need of government, then, in the circumstances of his last years, and this not only in face of the needs of the moment but even more in view of the future. In the earlier period of his life St. Paul seems to have expected the second coming of Christ during his own lifetime.[3] In these Epistles, on the other hand, he certainly contemplates his own death and, as in his speech to the Ephesian elders, views with apprehension the characteristics of lawlessness and disobedience, which he foresees will mark 'the last days' after he is gone, both in the department of doctrine and of life.[4] Both in view of present and of future needs, then, there is a profound need to stir up that gift of government which God has given to the Church. St. Paul in these Epistles is emphasizing no new thing. Just as in the Epistle to the Colossians he develops a doctrine of the person of Christ which had been implied in the expressions of his earlier Epistles, and in the Epistle to the

---

rulers and all men (1 Tim. ii. 1-5, obs. emphasis on πάντες, and iv. 10) seems aimed at a tendency which was anticipating the later Gnostic exclusiveness and depreciation of nature.

[1] Tit. i. 10, 11; 2 Tim. iii. 6, 7; 1 Tim. vi. 4, 5.
[2] 1 Tim. vi. 1, 2; Tit. ii. 9, iii. 1-3; 2 Tim. iii. 1-8.
[3] See 1 Thess. iv. 15; 1 Cor. xv. 51, 52.
[4] 2 Tim. iv. 6-8, cf. iii. 1-6, iv. 1-5; 1 Tim. iv. 1-5; cf. Acts xx. 17-35.

Ephesians works out the doctrine of the Church which had been more briefly suggested in his Epistles to the Corinthians, so now he emphasizes that idea of governmental and doctrinal authority in the Church which had been an element in his earlier teaching, especially in his Epistles to the Thessalonians and Corinthians, and consequently lets that gift of government, which in the Corinthian Church had been associated with other more exciting but less permanent and necessary endowments, emerge into greater isolation and distinctness.

<small>Their witness;</small>

We may class under three heads the lessons as to the ministry which are to be derived from these Epistles to Timothy and Titus.

<small>(i) On presbyter-bishops</small>

First, as to the local ministries of bishop and deacon, if we do not gain much new information, on the other hand we have a greater clearness and definiteness given to the picture we can form of their office. Thus the 'episcopus' is also called 'presbyter'; and, though the latter title would naturally suggest a dignity associated with the reverence due to age[1] and indicate rather a position than (like the first title) a definite office, yet this will not bear being pressed. A word is used for old men distinct from the title of

---

[1] Thus, though indicating a definite office with an assigned κλῆρος (1 Peter v. 3 and Huther *in loc.*), the title presbyter still retained its natural meaning and could be put into antithesis to 'young men' (1 Peter v. 5, Clem. *ad Cor.* 1. 3), on which more will be said. Later we have presbyter used, not only in its technical sense, but as a title of veneration for the Fathers of the Church by Papias ap. Euseb. *H. E.* iii. 39, and Irenaeus ap. Euseb. *H. E.* v. 20: "the elders before us and those associated with the Apostles." Cf. St. John's acceptance of the title for himself in 2 John 1 and 3 John 1. Thus the title presbyter, like that of deacon, retained a broader, side by side with a stricter, use. There is not I think sufficient reason to attach the idea of a definite office to the term 'young men' in Acts v. 6.

presbyter,[1] and the latter is markedly identified in the Epistle to Titus with the title of bishop.[2]

These 'bishops' constituted a college or group of 'presidents' in each Church,[3] and are spoken of as being really entrusted with the care of the Church.[4] They share the apostolic stewardship, and that not only in the sense of administration, but also in the sense of being entrusted really, though subordinately, with the function of teaching.[5] The proper discharge of their office is secured by their being carefully chosen, after due probation, in view not only of their moral fitness, but also of their capacities as rulers and teachers.[6] The lower ministry of the deacons is provided for in the older and more developed Church of Ephesus, not in the newer Churches of Crete, and it too is to be entrusted only after a due scrutiny of the moral fitness of the man who is to hold it.[7] We gain no

and deacons;

---

[1] πρεσβύτης, Tit. ii. 2.

[2] Tit. i. 5-7. This is quite unmistakable. There is nothing more in the singular ἐπίσκοπος (Tit. i. 7, 1 Tim. iii. 2) than in the singular πρεσβύτερος (1 Tim. iv. 1).

[3] 1 Tim. iv. 14 τὸ πρεσβυτέριον; cf. Tit. i. 5. Baur at first maintained that κατὰ πόλιν πρεσβυτέρους meant one presbyter in each city, but he abandoned the contention. See Holtzmann *Pastoralbriefe* pp. 208, 209.

[4] 1 Tim. v. 17 οἱ προεστῶτες πρεσβύτεροι; iii. 5 ἐκκλησίας θεοῦ ἐπιμελήσεται.

[5] Tit. i. 7 θεοῦ οἰκονόμον, cf. ver. 9 παρακαλεῖν ἐν τῇ διδασκαλίᾳ καὶ τοὺς ἀντιλέγοντας ἐλέγχειν: cf. 1 Tim. iii. 2 διδακτικός, v. 17 μάλιστα οἱ κοπιῶντες ἐν λόγῳ καὶ διδασκαλίᾳ (this need hardly imply that there were any presbyters who did not teach at all), 2 Tim. ii. 2 ἱκανοὶ ἑτέρους διδάξαι. ὁ κατηχῶν in Gal. vi. 6 seems in the context to be a local officer.

[6] 1 Tim. iii. 1-7; Tit. i. 6-9. μὴ νεόφυτον is omitted in reference to the newly-established Church of Crete, and τέκνα ἔχειν πιστά takes its place, see Kühl *Gemeindeordnung in den Pastoralbriefen* pp. 13-15.

[7] 1 Tim. iii. 8-13. The fact that the requirements for the diaconate are nearly the same as those for the presbyterate is to be accounted for by the fact that (with the exception of the exclusion of those twice married) the requirements are negative. St. Paul requires much of the Christian, as such. His requirements of the ministry are mainly such as are involved in the absence of any positive reproach—in what we should call 'a good character.'

light upon the functions of the diaconate, except so far as that the deacons would not be required, by contrast with the presbyters, to teach or to rule.¹

(ii) On the extension of apostolic office to legates,

Secondly, we gain important information as to the extension of the apostolic office. In Timothy and Titus we are presented with apostolic delegates,² exercising the apostolic supervision over the Church of Ephesus and the Churches of Crete respectively.³ They are not indeed what St. Paul and the other Apostles were, the original proclaimers of a revelation; they stand in this respect in the second rank, as entrusted only with the task of maintaining a tradition, of upholding a pattern of sound words.⁴ But in this task they exercise the supreme apostolic authority, and not in this respect only. To them belongs the function, in Titus' case of founding, in both cases of governing, the Churches committed to them.⁵ They ordain men to the church orders, after being duly satisfied of their fitness, and exercise

There are distinct offices in the Church, not different standards of living for clergy and laity.

[1] On the inferiority of the diaconate see Kühl *Gemeindeordnung* pp. 15, 16.

[2] Simcox *Early Ch. Hist.* p. 140 calls them "vicars apostolic." Lightfoot *Ignatius* i. p. 377 speaks of their exercising a "moveable episcopate." Winterstein *Der Episcopat* p. 18 calls them "apostolische Delegaten." Cf. Rom. xvi. 21 ὁ συνεργός μου.

[3] How many more of such 'viri apostolici' there may have been we cannot tell. The διακονία of Archippus at Colossæ (Col. iv. 17) may have been like that of Timothy at Ephesus. And there may be truth in such a tradition as that mentioned by Dionysius of Corinth as to the position of the Areopagite in the Church of Athens, or that mentioned by Origen as to the position of Gaius at Thessalonica.

[4] 2 Tim. i. 13; cf. 1 Tim. i. 3, iv. 11, 13, vi. 3: παραγγέλλειν, διδάσκειν, ἀνάγνωσις, παράκλησις. 2 Tim. iv. 2 ἔλεγξον, ἐπιτίμησον; Tit. i. 13 ἐλέγχειν ἀποτόμως, ii. 15 ἐλέγχειν μετὰ πάσης ἐπιταγῆς. The παραθήκη intrusted to Timothy is the truth he is to teach and hand on to others (1 Tim. vi. 20, 2 Tim. i. 14).

[5] As e.g. in matters of worship and female behaviour (1 Tim. ii. 1, 2, 8, 9, 11).

discipline even over the presbyters.¹ Again, as it is their function to maintain the truth, so in defence of it they are to oppose false teachers, and when these exhibit the temper of separatists and heretics and will not 'hear the Church,' they are to act in the spirit of Christ's directions and leave them to their wilful courses, having nothing further to say to them.² We do not, however, gather that they possessed the miraculous power to inflict physical penalties, which St. Paul describes in his phrase "delivering unto Satan for the destruction of the flesh." As apostolic legates, then, Timothy and Titus exercise what is essentially the later episcopal office, but it would not appear that their authority, though essentially *permanent*, is definitely localized like that of the diocesan bishop.³ Timothy indeed had been left at Ephesus

[margin: who act as later bishops, but are not diocesan;]

---

¹ Tit. i. 5, 1 Tim. v. 22. (There can be no doubt, I think, that St. Paul is in this latter place speaking of the laying-on of hands in ordination, not in the reception of a penitent. See, however, Pacian of Barcelona *Par. ad Poen.* 15 and Ellicott *in loc.*) 1 Tim. v. 19-21; these judicial powers apparently rest on Timothy's own judgment without appeal.

² Tit. iii. 10-11. This 'rejection' of a heretic seems to express the idea of St. Matt. xviii. 17. He is to be as one avoided—as 'the gentile or the publican.' He is among 'those without.' See for an interesting comment on the passage Origen *c. Cels.* v. 63, where he describes the true method of dealing with opponents of the faith.

³ Dr. Lightfoot calls the usual conception of Timothy by church writers as 'bishop of Ephesus' the "conception of a later age" (*Dissert.* p. 199), but he also describes it as not altogether without foundation. "With less permanence but perhaps greater authority, the position occupied by these apostolic delegates nevertheless fairly represents the function of the bishop early in the second century." Perhaps then the only question in dispute between Dr. Lightfoot and one who, like Prof. Shirley (*Apostolic Age* p. 116), represents the office of Timothy and Titus as "episcopal in the full range of its power" is as to the exact localization of the office. It can hardly be denied that Timothy and Titus possessed a permanent authority as apostolic delegates, with a permanent χάρισμα—in this sense a 'delegatio perpetua.' The only question is whether it was limited to one place, or still, like the apostolic office which it represented, general.

by St. Paul to represent himself in view of that Church's needs, and St. Paul *certainly* contemplates his continuing his ministry after his own death,[1] and presumably in the same Church of Ephesus, in which again it would appear that he had been solemnly ordained to his office.[2] Nor perhaps can we argue against his localization from the fact of St. Paul summoning him to Rome, or from the fact of his having gone there.[3] But there is a close analogy between the office of Timothy and that of Titus, and Titus certainly appears to have left Crete to join St. Paul, to have been his companion at Rome, and to have left again not for Crete but for Dalmatia.[4] Again we do not gather from these Epistles any clear intimation that Timothy and Titus, though they were to provide for a succession of sound teachers,[5] were to ordain men to succeed them in their apostolic office in the local Churches. All that we can fairly conclude is that St. Paul after ordaining, or with a view to ordaining, the local ministers, bishops and deacons, appointed delegates to exercise the apostolic office of supervision in his place, both before and after his death: and it must be added that the needs which required this extension of the apostolic ministry were not transitory ones. They were the needs of 'the

---

[1] 2 Tim. iv. 1-8.

[2] The presbyters of 1 Tim. iv. 14 are presumably the presbyters of Ephesus, but see Holtzmann *Pastoralbriefe* p. 231. On the other hand 'the good confession' (1 Tim. vi. 12) apparently refers to Timothy's baptismal profession. Note esp. the ἐκλήθης; and cf. Kühl. *l.c.* p. 29.

[3] 2 Tim. iv. 9, Hebr. xiii. 23.

[4] Titus iii. 12, 2 Tim. iv. 10.

[5] 2 Tim. ii. 2.

last times'—the constant phenomena of moral failure and doctrinal and moral instability and disorder. It should be added that no definite title is assigned to Timothy and Titus, though their function is spoken of as a 'ministry' and as 'the work of an evangelist,' and in Timothy's case at least is distinguished from that of the presbyters by the attribute of comparative youthfulness.¹ No doubt the necessity for fixed titles grew greater with lapse of time and increase of controversy.

Thirdly, the Pastoral Epistles give us a clear view of St. Paul's conception of the ministerial office. Over and above what constitutes the gift of the Christian life, the apostolic 'minister'² is qualified for his work by a special ministerial gift or 'charisma'—'a spirit of power and love and discipline'—imparted to him after his fitness has been indicated by a prophetic intimation, in a definite and formal manner, by means of the laying-on of the hands of the apostle, by means also of a prophetic utterance, accompanied with the laying-on of the hands of the presbytery.³

(iii) On the idea of ordination.

¹ 1 Tim. iv. 6, 2 Tim. iv. 5. It should be noticed that St. Paul calls his own ministry also a διακονία (1 Tim. i. 12) and speaks of himself as a διδάσκαλος ἐθνῶν, as well as κῆρυξ καὶ ἀπόστολος (ii. 7, 2 Tim. i. 11). It is most likely, I think, that Timothy and Titus would have been known as evangelists.
² I assume that what St. Paul says of Timothy he could have said of Titus also—no great assumption, as their offices are so wholly similar.
³ 2 Tim. i. 6, 7: ἀναμιμνῄσκω σε ἀναζωπυρεῖν τὸ χάρισμα τοῦ θεοῦ, ὅ ἐστιν ἐν σοὶ διὰ τῆς ἐπιθέσεως τῶν χειρῶν μου· οὐ γὰρ ἔδωκεν ἡμῖν ὁ θεὸς πνεῦμα δειλίας, ἀλλὰ δυνάμεως καὶ ἀγάπης καὶ σωφρονισμοῦ. (The ἡμῖν here refers surely to St. Paul and Timothy classified together in the ministry.) 1 Tim. iv. 14: μὴ ἀμέλει τοῦ ἐν σοὶ χαρίσματος ὃ ἐδόθη σοι διὰ προφητείας μετὰ ἐπιθέσεως τῶν χειρῶν τοῦ πρεσβυτερίου. 1 Tim. i. 18: κατὰ τὰς προαγούσας ἐπὶ σὲ προφητείας. This last expression may be compared with that of Clement of Alexandria *Quis Dives* 42, where he describes St. John as κλήρῳ ἕνα γέ τινα κληρώσων τῶν ὑπὸ τοῦ πνεύματος σημαινομένων. But the διὰ προφητείας of the second passage seems

250   *Christian Ministry.*   [CHAP.

In this process there were features which were not destined to be permanent. Thus the prophetic indication of the person to be ordained ceased; and the prophecy, which St. Paul speaks of as the medium through which with the laying-on of his hands the spiritual gift was communicated, passed from being an inspired utterance into an ordinary prayer or formula of ordination. But it is only a very arbitrary criticism which can fail to see here, with slight miraculous and transitory modifications, the permanent process of ordination with which we are familiar in later church history, and that conception of the bestowal in ordination of a special 'charisma,' which at once carries with it the idea of 'permanent charetcar,'[1] and that distinction of clergy and laity

to refer better to a prophetic utterance or prayer, which was part of the actual process of ordination. Prophetic prayer seems implied in 1 Cor. xiv. 14, 15. See App. Note I. The 'presbytery' can hardly be (as Theod. Mops. *in loc.* cf. Chrys.) ὁ τῶν ἀποστόλων σύλλογος.

[1] The 'charisma' is described as a permanent endowment which having been once received requires only to be 'stirred up,' like baptismal grace. The idea expressed by χάρισμα in the Pastoral Epistles is exactly the same as that expressed by πνεῦμα (not τὸ πνεῦμα) in St. John xx. 22. Cf. 1 Cor. xiv. 12, where πνεύματα = πνευματικὰ χαρίσματα. On the life-long character of church office see Dr. P. D. Müller *Verfassung der chr. Kirche* p. 19, Holtzmann p. 204.

Since Baur (*Die sogenannten Pastoralbriefe des Apostels Paulus*, 1835) denied the Pauline authorship of the Pastoral Epistles and emphasized as a ground for this rejection their hierarchical character, a prolonged controversy has been carried on in Germany—the one party emphasizing everything ecclesiastical, hierarchical, and sacerdotal in these documents, and denying their Pauline authorship on that account; the other party minimizing these characteristics, and then vindicating their Pauline authorship. Thus on their premises the party of denial (of whom Holtzmann is the ablest recent representative) has a motive to exaggerate the sacerdotalism of the Pastoral Epistles and the party of vindication (as represented recently in the able work of Kühl *Gemeindeordnung in den Past.brief.*) a motive to minimize it. Thus Holtzmann is exaggerating when he sees in οἱ λοιποί of 1 Tim. v. 20 an expression for the laity (as was Baur when he saw in Timothy and Titus the prototypes of archbishops), but on the other hand he seems to me to say no more than is true in the following passage (*l.c.* p. 231) : "Es ist also keine Frage,

which is involved in the possession of a definite spiritual grace and power by those who have been ordained. It is also arbitrary to deny that St. Paul, when he appointed Timothy and Titus to ordain other ministers, as we gather, by a similar process,[1] would have hesitated to use the same language about the subsequent ordinations made by them or to attach to them the same ideas.

The final conclusions which are to be drawn from what St. Paul tells us about the church ministry shall be reserved till we have finished our review of the New Testament literature.[2]

II. There is very little additional information to be derived from the other apostolic Epistles, but there are indications which must not be neglected. It will

II. Evidence of the other Epistles.

---

dass der Ausdruck χάρισμα in den Pastoralbriefen die bestimmtere Bedeutung einer, vermittels der Ordination übertragenen, Amtsgabe besitzt. Erst bei solcher Auffassung versteht sich endlich auch die beidemal stehende Formel τὸ χάρισμα ἐν σοί, weil ein mit der Begabung zugleich übertragenes Amtsrecht allerdings seinem Träger mehr einwohnt, als blos beilegt. Fiele die Handauflegung 1 Tim. v. 22 mit den bisher besprochenen Stellen in eine Kategorie, so würde Timotheus hier überdies noch davor gewarnt werden, die ihm inhärirende Gabe vorschnell weiter zu tradiren." So he quotes Weizsäcker (p. 233): " Man sieht, hier ist eine ganze festgeschlossene Kette von Begriffen, in welcher kein Ring fehlt; der Inhalt des Ganzen aber ist das Amt als Inhaber der reinen Lehre und des rechten Geistes, verbürgt durch eine förmliche und sichere Uebertragung." "Das Amt ist daher im eigentlichen Sinne die Lebensbedingung für den Bestand und Geist der Gemeinde."

[1] 1 Tim. v. 22: χεῖρας ταχέως μηδενὶ ἐπιτίθει.

[2] It ought to be added that St. Paul recognises a ministry of women in the Church; see Rom. xvi. 1: Φοίβην τὴν ἀδελφὴν ἡμῶν, οὖσαν [καὶ] διάκονον τῆς ἐκκλησίας τῆς ἐν Κεγχρεαῖς. But it is a ministry which is concerned with works of mercy and, if with teaching also, only in private (Acts xviii. 26). St. Paul clearly excludes women from public teaching (1 Cor. xiv. 34, 35; 1 Tim. ii. 11, 12). A woman may have the gift of prophecy (1 Cor. xi. 5) but is not apparently allowed even to exercise that in public. There is no reason why the 'apostle,' Ἰουνίαν (Rom. xvi. 7), should be a woman. The widows of 1 Tim. v. 9 are the recipients of support from the Church—ministered to rather than ministers.

be borne in mind that, though the apostolic office was essentially ecumenical, yet a distribution, not of area but of races, had been arrived at among the Apostles. It was recognised that St. Paul had been divinely "entrusted with the gospel of the uncircumcision, even as Peter with the gospel of the circumcision," and it was accordingly agreed that Paul and Barnabas should evangelize the heathen, while James, Peter, and John preached the same Gospel amongst the Jews.[1] We shall look then in the Epistles of James, Peter, John, and "Jude, the brother of James," for information about the ministry in the Jewish Christian communities, as well as in the Pauline Epistle to the Hebrews. And so in fact we find throughout those documents evidences more or less pronounced, not only of the apostolic ministry which the writers represent, but also of a local ministry in the several communities.[2] By what title are these local ministers known? In

[1] Gal. ii. 7-9.
[2] Thus James writes himself as a teacher with the authority which we know him on other grounds to have held in specially Jewish circles, and speaks (iii. 1) of local teachers and (vi. 14) more unmistakably of presbyters.

Peter writes as an "apostle of Jesus Christ" (1 Pet. i. 1, cf. 2 Pet. i. 1), but identifies himself as a presbyter with the local presbyters (1 Pet. v. 1-5) as sharing the same pastoral office. He speaks also (1 Pet. iv. 10, 11), in language which reminds us of St. Paul's, of the Church as differentiated by different 'charismata' for different ministries intended for the common good. Each man's charisma makes him a "steward of the manifold grace of God." The stewardships or charismata of which he specially speaks are those of speaking in God's name and of ministering. If, as is probable, these refer to the presbyterate and the diaconate, we have here another case to add to those of Eph. iv. 11 and 1 Tim. v. 17 of the presbyterate being considered a teaching office.

St. Jude indicates that Korah, the author of revolt against the Old Testament priesthood, had, as well as the self-seeking pastors whom Ezekiel denounced, his followers in the Church of the new covenant (Jude 11, 12).

The Epistle to the Hebrews speaks of 'leaders' ($\dot{\eta}\gamma o\acute{\upsilon}\mu\epsilon\nu o\iota$) in the Christian Church who had spoken the word of God and were passed away, alluding

St. Paul's Epistles, as we have seen, they are called first 'presidents,' then 'bishops,' and later in the Pastoral Epistles also 'presbyters.' Now while the first of these titles is of the most general significance, the second, though it is used in the Old Testament and its use in the Christian Church was certainly influenced by this fact, was of common acceptance in the Greek of the empire to express 'commissioners' or 'superintendents' of many different sorts.[1] The title 'presbyter' on the other hand was a specially Jewish title, and was in familiar use at any rate in Jerusalem. St. James is pre-eminently a Jew of *St. James.* Jerusalem writing to Jews,[2] and accordingly he uses the term 'presbyters' for the local church rulers among the Jews of the dispersion; but on the other hand, while Jewish presbyters had been merely judicial officers, and not officers of worship, nor teachers, the Christian presbyters have assigned to them by St. James a 'ministry of healing,'[3] both of body and soul,

apparently to apostolic teachers (cf. Acts xv. 22, Luke xxii. 26), and he uses the same expression of the rulers of the Church still living, who exercise the office of pastors over the Hebrews, "watching for their souls as those who shall give account" (Heb. xiii. 7, 17), and he bids the Hebrews to "greet them" (xiii. 24). This title will be considered further in connection with Clement's letter.

[1] See App. Note K. on the origin of the terms 'episcopus' and 'presbyter,' in connection with recent criticism.

[2] See especially the use of the word 'synagogue' (James ii. 2) for the Christian place of meeting.

[3] The 'elders of the Church' (James v. 14-16) are assumed to have the gift of healing by means of unction, accompanied by their 'prayer of faith' (cf. St. Mark vi. 13). But as sickness is the symbol, and often the effect, of sin (cf. 1 Cor. xi. 30), so the healing is spiritual as well as physical—it is spiritual absolution with the miraculous sanction and evidence still attached (cf. St. Mark ii. 10): "if he have committed sins, it shall be forgiven him." Then follows a general admonition to confess sins mutually one to another. This probably implies that the sick man would have confessed his sins to the presbyters whom he had summoned. See Origen *in Levit.* ii. 4. Generally great

with accompanying prayer, which has no analogy in the Jewish presbyterate, while it accords naturally with the general pastoral functions assigned to them by St. Peter.¹

St. Peter.

St. John.

It may surprise us that, whereas St. John is specially connected in authentic tradition with the establishment of the 'monarchical episcopate' and with the general development of the ministry, we have hardly any information on the subject in his writings. If, indeed, the Apocalypse dates from the end of his life, we shall naturally see in the 'angels' of the seven Churches of Asia some indirect reference to the responsible bishops.² But the mention of these angels cannot be put in evidence, because their primary meaning seems to be symbolical;³ they seem to be sym-

(The 'angels' prob. symbolic.)

---

light has been thrown on this practice of mutual confession among Christians by the passages in the *Didache*, iv. 14 and xiv. 1 : "On the Lord's day gather yourselves together and break bread and give thanks (εὐχαριστήσατε), having first confessed your sins, that your sacrifice may be pure." The practice was derived from the Jewish synagogue ; cf. Sabatier *La Didachè* pp. 47, 48. Cf. also 1 John i. 9 and Westcott *in loc.*

¹ 1 Pet. v. 1-5. St. Peter also (if he does not actually use the word ἐπισκοπεῖν in ver. 2, where the reading is doubtful) implies the use of the term ἐπίσκοπος by using it of Christ the "chief pastor" (ii. 25, cf. v. 4).

² Cf. Origen *in Luc.* xiii.

³. The angels have been generally taken to be bishops, the use of 'angels' in Mal. ii. 7 and Eccles. v. 6 being quoted. If this is so, they are addressed as embodying the Church, and Ignatius' language may be compared where he speaks (*ad Trall.* 1) of "seeing the whole community in the bishop," and when he passes imperceptibly (*ad Polyc.* 5, 6) from addressing the bishop of Smyrna to addressing his Church. But the identification of the bishop with the Church in the Apocalypse goes further than this, and the fact that the female personage, Jezebel (ii. 20), seems clearly symbolical would suggest a symbolical meaning for the angels also. So also the use of the whole book leads us to see in the angels symbolic representations of different agencies, e.g. Milligan (on Rev. x. 1-3 in Schaff's *Pop. Comment.* on the N. T.) is certainly right in describing 'the strong angel' as "neither the Lord, nor a mere creature executing His will, but a representation of His action. The angel by whom such representation is effected has naturally the attributes of the Being whose action he embodies." The more in fact one studies the Apoca-

bols of the temper or spirit of the different Churches. In the same way, as we have other reasons for believing St. John to have instituted bishops, we shall probably be inclined to see in Diotrephes, with his ambitious self-exaltation and his power 'to cast out of the Church'[1] brethren who had come from St. John, one of these local bishops who was misusing his authority. But here again the indication is too ambiguous to constitute evidence of itself. It remains for us then to seek such additional information, especially on the origin of the local ministry, as can be derived from the Acts of the Apostles.

III. In the Acts of the Apostles we are presented first of all with a very clear picture of the apostolic ministry. Just exception can indeed be taken to

III. Evidence of the Acts. (a) The apostolate, divinely appointed,

---

lypse, the more the symbolical character of personages, numbers, and events is impressed upon one. So the angels of the seven Churches seem to be ideal personifications of the temper or genius of the Churches. See Lightfoot *Dissert.* pp. 199, 200; Simcox *Early Ch. Hist.* p. 172 n.[1]; Milligan *in loc.* For the other sense see Trench *Epp. to the Seven Ch.* and Godet in *Expositor*, Jan. 1888, p. 67. Among the ancients, Arethas of Caesarea, using Andreas and other more ancient authors, interprets the angels first as guardian angels (who are addressed on behalf of the Churches, as masters on behalf of their pupils: εἰδὼς ὡς οἰκειοῦσθαι φιλεῖ τὰ τοῦ μαθητοῦ ὁ διδάσκαλος, εἴτε κατορθώματα, εἴτε ἡττήματα), and then as the Churches themselves (ἄγγελον τῆς Ἐφέσου τὴν ἐν αὐτῇ ἐκκλησίαν λέγει); see Cramer's *Catena Graec. Patr. in N.T.* viii. p. 200. So also the writer who passes for Victorinus of Petau, the earliest commentator on the book; he clearly interpreted the angels as symbolical of classes of individuals, for he paraphrases the letter to the angel of Ephesus thus: "ad eos scripsit [Ioannes] qui et laborant et operantur et patientes sunt et cum videant homines quosdam in ecclesia dispensatores praeposteros, ne dispersio fiat, portant, . . . Haec universa ad laudem spectant et laudem non mediocrem sed tales viros et talem classem et tales electionis homines oportet omnimodo admoneri." So he deals with the other letters: "aut ad eos scripsit . . . aut ad eos . . . aut ad eos, etc." Origen *in Num.* xx. 3 interprets of angels in the strict sense (and hence Andreas, as above), and so Jerome on Mic. vi. init.

[1] 3 John 9-10. Diotrephes seems clothed with official power.

M. Renan's phrase when he describes "the divine institution of the hierarchy" as a "favourite thesis" of St. Luke,[1] just so far as the phrase seems to carry with it too much implication of conscious design in writing; but it cannot be fairly denied that the divine authority of a hierarchy in the Christian Church does appear conspicuously enough in the course of St. Luke's narrative.

From the first the disciples appear as a body amongst whom eleven, or after Matthias' election twelve, are held to possess a ministerial office and commission direct from Christ.[2] Upon the whole body, thus differentiated into ministers and people, the Holy Ghost descends and the Church begins her life as the Spirit-bearing body, with the Apostles for her authoritative teachers and for her centre of unity. This is sufficiently implied in the phrase which describes the first new converts as "continuing steadfast in the Apostles' teaching and fellowship, in the breaking of the bread and the prayers."[3] They are prominent in the early history as representing Christ, acting in His name to work physical miracles of healing on 'those without,' of judgment also on 'those within.'[4] Again, they have the authority to ordain to

with authority;

---

[1] *Les Apôtres* p. xxxix. Cf. Sabatier *La Didachè* p. 155 : " Déjà du temps de saint Luc on faisait précéder les décisions du concile de Jérusalem d'un préambule gros de toutes les prétentions hiérarchiques romaines" (i.e. such as M. Sabatier thinks were derived from the influence of the Roman Church upon Christianity).

[2] Acts i. 25 : διακονία καὶ ἀποστολή.

[3] Acts ii. 42 : τῇ διδαχῇ τῶν ἀποστόλων καὶ τῇ κοινωνίᾳ, τῇ κλάσει τοῦ ἄρτου καὶ ταῖς προσευχαῖς, the phrase τῶν ἀποστόλων seems to characterize the whole sentence.

[4] Acts v. 1-11. These judgments brought a great fear not only on the Church but on all who heard of them (ver. 11)—a fear of the Apostles,

v.] *The Ministry in the Apostolic Age.* 257

those various ministries of the Church the origin of which will be considered shortly: thus the Church at Jerusalem set the seven (we are told) "before the Apostles, and when they had prayed, they laid their hands on them."[1] When we hear afterwards of those later-added Apostles, Barnabas and Saul, 'appointing elders' in the Churches they founded,[2] we cannot doubt (especially in view of the evidence of the Pastoral Epistles) that the method of appointment was the same method of laying on hands with prayer; and we shall not be surprised that St. Paul should describe the presbyters at Ephesus, appointed as they must have been by his hands, as none the less instituted by the Holy Ghost.[3] It is indeed not only in the case of the appointment of the ministry that we are led to associate the action of the Holy Ghost with the laying-on of apostolic hands. The narrative of the Acts elsewhere assures us that the Apostles laid their hands on all Christians after their baptism, in

and power to give the Holy Ghost by laying-on of hands,

in confirmation

---

apparently. Hence it seems natural to interpret the words of ver. 13: "of the rest durst no man join himself to them" (κολλᾶσθαι αὐτοῖς), as meaning 'of the rest durst no man associate himself with the Apostles, as being on their level.' (Cf. Alford.) If it means 'no man durst join the Church,' there seems an unintelligible contradiction in the words which follow: "believers were the more added to the Lord, multitudes." The obstacle to this rendering is that κολλᾶσθαι more naturally means to join the society, or to become an adherent; see Acts xvii. 34.

[1] Acts vi. 6.

[2] Acts xiv. 23: χειροτονήσαντες δὲ αὐτοῖς κατ' ἐκκλησίαν πρεσβυτέρους. With reference to this word χειροτονεῖν Holtzmann remarks (*l.c.* p. 219): "sprechen philologische Gründe allerdings mehr für die Bedeutung 'erwählen' schlechthin als für 'durch Stimmabgabe erwählen lassen,'" i.e. it had become a quite general word for 'to elect.'

[3] Acts xx. 28: προσέχετε . . . παντὶ τῷ ποιμνίῳ, ἐν ᾧ ὑμᾶς τὸ πνεῦμα τὸ ἅγιον ἔθετο ἐπισκόπους. (The ἔθετο recalls 1 Cor. xii. 28: οὓς μὲν ἔθετο ὁ θεὸς ἐν τῇ ἐκκλησίᾳ πρῶτον ἀποστόλους, κ.τ.λ.) The Holy Ghost had made them bishops by the special χάρισμα bestowed upon them (and perhaps also by prophetic indication).

R

order by this means to impart to them that gift of the Holy Ghost which is the essence of the Christian life.¹ The laying-on of hands in ordination is (as we should gather from the Acts and Pastoral Epistles taken together) a determination of this same divine gift to a special ministerial function, or the bestowal of a superadded power. Further we are led to believe that this function of the laying-on of hands belonged exclusively to the Apostles, with those 'prophets and teachers' who seem to have been associated in their apostolic office.²

This gift of the Holy Ghost, which is imparted to every Christian, was in the first days of the Church commonly accompanied by miraculous signs, such as 'prophesyings' and 'tongues,' and where the divine

---

¹ Acts xix. 6, and especially Acts viii. 15-19. This is the clearest expression of the apostolic ἐξουσία to impart the Holy Ghost by laying-on of hands: διὰ τῆς ἐπιθέσεως τῶν χειρῶν τῶν ἀποστόλων δίδοται τὸ πνεῦμα. I have assumed that this bestowal of the Holy Ghost was only *accompanied* by the special charismata of prophesying, tongues, etc., while its essence lay in the bestowal of that presence, which is permanent in the Christian Church, and which makes the Christian the temple of God. The miraculous χαρίσματα passed away, but the underlying gift remained, mediated by the same 'laying-on of hands.' I do not think this can be fairly questioned. In the Acts those who had not yet received 'the laying-on of hands' are represented not as being without certain miraculous powers, but as not possessing the Spirit. See viii. 16, xix. 3-7. The possession of the Spirit undoubtedly constitutes the essence of Christianity, with or without miraculous powers; see Gal. iii. 2 and Rom. viii. 9-17, where St. Paul speaks of it as received at a definite moment and as a permanent possession (ἐλάβετε, οἰκεῖ ἐν ὑμῖν). Cf. Hebrews vi. 2 for the close association of baptism with the laying-on of hands, and Tertullian *de Bapt.* 6: "non quod in aquis Spiritum sanctum consequamur, sed in aqua emundati sub angelo Spiritui sancto praeparamur . . . Dehinc manus imponitur per benedictionem advocans et invitans Spiritum sanctum . . . Tunc ille sanctissimus Spiritus super emundata et benedicta corpora libens a Patre descendit." *de Resurr. Carn.* 8.: "caro manus impositione adumbratur, ut et anima Spiritu illuminetur."

² It is presumable that the men who could lay-on hands in Acts xiii. 1-3 could also do so for the ordinary purpose of 'confirmation.' Otherwise Acts viii. 17-19 implies the limitation of this function to the Apostles.

v.]   *The Ministry in the Apostolic Age.*   259

gift evidenced by such outward miracles preceded baptism and the laying-on of hands, the instrumentality by which the gift was ordinarily communicated did indeed follow, at least so far as baptism is concerned, but it became, we must suppose, not the bestowal of a gift but the recognition of it.[1] In the same way the 'laying-on of hands' by the prophets and teachers at Antioch upon Saul and Barnabas, who had been themselves already classed under the same names, can hardly be regarded as more than the recognition by the Church, under the divine inspiration there recorded, of a mission which, at least in St. Paul's case, we have every reason to know came directly from Christ.[2] There may, in fact, have been many cases where the 'gift of government' evidenced by we know not what signs, or the more obvious gift of prophetic inspiration, anticipated the appointment to the church office. But the ceremony of ordination, where it was not the channel of the grace, was its recognition. The language however of St. Paul's Epistle to Timothy and of the Acts makes the imposition of apostolic hands in ordinary cases, whether of ordination or of 'confirmation,' nothing less than the instrument of divine bestowal.

Once more, the narrative of the Acts brings before us in action that power of binding and loosing, that is of legislation with a supernatural sanction, with which Christ endowed His Church. Questions were raised at Antioch as to the obligation of the *and power to bind and loose.*

---

[1] Acts x. 44-48; cf. xi. 15-17.
[2] Acts xiii. 1-3; cf. Gal. i. 1, Acts ix. 15, xxii. 14-21, xxvi. 16.

Jewish law on Gentile converts. Accordingly Paul and Barnabas with others were sent up by 'the brethren' to confer on this subject with the Apostles at Jerusalem who appear as associated in this function with the elders. There ensued an apostolic conference, resulting in a formal decision by which certain things were loosed and certain others bound—i.e. by which a certain amount of conformity to Jewish scruples was required, at least for the time, and in other respects the prescriptions of the law were declared to be not binding on Gentile Christians. This decision, issued in the name of "the apostles and elder brethren," was sent to those whom it concerned in Antioch and Syria and Cilicia, with the unmistakable declaration: "it seemed good to the Holy Ghost and to us, to lay upon you no greater burdens than these necessary things."[1]

(b) The sub-apostolic office

So far then, it must be admitted that the narrative of the Acts gives us a very clear picture of the apostolic office and authority. But, on the other hand, the indications given us of the position of those

of prophets and teachers.

'prophets and teachers,' and other associates of the Apostles of whom we also hear, are somewhat indefinite.[2] James, though he apparently was not one of the twelve, is clothed with apostolic authority,[3] and (as we shall have occasion to note further) when the Apostles go forth to exercise their universal mission, remains to represent the apostolic office in the Church of Jerusalem. How was he appointed? Probably

---

[1] Acts xv. 1-29; cf. xvi. 4.   [2] Acts xi. 27, xiii. 1, xv. 32, xxi. 10.
[3] See esp. Acts xv. 13-21.

not by the Apostles. Probably his authority would have been understood to have been given to him when Christ appeared to him after His resurrection.[1] And it must be remembered that, though 'the Lord's brethren' had not been among the disciples who believed before the passion, there had been others who had not only believed but had been commissioned as representatives of Christ. Besides the twelve there had been the seventy, and among the 'hundred and twenty' disciples who awaited the day of Pentecost there must have been many of these who had received a commission in some respects like that of the Apostles. Tradition assigns this position to Luke and Barnabas among others.[2] We are not then going beyond probabilities if we consider that the original ministerial equipment of the Church before the day of Pentecost consisted of others besides the twelve. Many of these may be amongst the prophets and teachers whom we hear of in the Acts, not as teaching only or foretelling, but as "ministering to the Lord,"—performing, that is, acts of worship—and laying on hands to give the recognition of the Church to the mission of Barnabas and Saul.[3] There were,

---

[1] 1 Cor. xv. 7. Cf. Dr. Ch. Wordsworth's *Remarks on Dr. Lightfoot's Essay* p. 19. The tradition in Clement of Alexandria represents James as appointed by the Apostles. But Hegesippus, who is a much better authority, speaks of him as "succeeding to the government of the Church with the Apostles." This will appear further on.

[2] For Barnabas see Clem. Alex. ap. Euseb. *H.E.* ii. 1. For Luke see Epiph. *Haer.* li. 11.

[3] The Christian prophets in thus combining the ministry of worship with that of preaching recall the functions of Elijah and Samuel. With the phrase λειτουργούντων τῷ κυρίῳ, cf. the *Didache* xv. 1: τὴν λειτουργίαν τῶν προφητῶν καὶ διδασκάλων. This laying-on of hands, if only in recognition of a divinely-given mission, would probably imply a power to do it in other cases. It

however, other fellow-labourers with the Apostles, who certainly did not belong to the original equipment of the Church. These we should certainly suppose would have received ordination from those who did. Such would have been St. Paul's sons in the faith, Timothy and Titus, as to the ordination of the former of whom by St. Paul we have positive information, which we naturally extend to similar cases.[1] Such ordination again we should suppose Apollos to have received;[2] nor is the silence of the Acts on the subject any objection to this view, for that narrative is silent also about his baptism and reception of the laying-on of hands,[3] which yet are not only mentioned but emphasized in exactly parallel cases.[4] It will however be of course acknowledged that miraculous evidence of the divine will, such as the Church could recognise, went far to reduce the ceremony of ordination to a lower level of importance than it held in ordinary cases.

(c) The local ministry

Leaving now the order of apostles, with its extension to prophets and teachers and other apostolic legates, it remains to collect the information given us in the Acts as to the origin of the local ministry.

should be noticed that, while Paul and Barnabas are here called 'prophets and teachers,' they are afterwards called 'apostles' (xiv. 4).

[1] Cf. Judas Barsabbas and Silas (Acts xv. 22, 32). Silas becomes St. Paul's companion (ver. 40), and is coupled with Timothy in 2 Cor. i. 19 and in the inscriptions of 1 and 2 Thess.

[2] St. Paul classes him with the Apostles as 'steward of the divine mysteries,' etc. (1 Cor. iv. 1-6).

[3] Acts xviii. 24-28.

[4] Acts xix. 1-6. These men had been baptized "into John's baptism" (cf. xviii. 25 of Apollos: "knowing only the baptism of John"). St. Paul gave these Christians baptism and confirmation. So again St. Paul himself had received baptism (ix. 17).

We find the existence of presbyters in the Church at Jerusalem assumed.¹ This is probably to be accounted for by the fact that there Jewish 'presbyters' were an institution of old standing and that the Christian 'synagogue' naturally had the like. It is however very easy to exaggerate the Jewish character of these church officers. Later evidence leads us to believe that they were definitely appointed to their office by the Apostles² and that, while they shared their legislative counsels at Jerusalem and were associated in their legislative authority in a matter of church discipline, they were not, as amongst the Jews, merely disciplinary officers. St. James, as we have seen, assigns to them a ministry of physical and spiritual healing; St. Peter allots to them the general pastoral function; and in accordance with these indications St. Paul tells them at Ephesus that it is the Holy Ghost who has given them their office and, calling them by the name of overseers or bishops, implies that the government and nourishment of the Church,³ in the general sense, belonged to them. So the earliest subapostolic evidence concurs in allotting to them a definitely spiritual ministry.⁴ Here in fact, as elsewhere, the Church adopted a Jewish nomenclature,

of presbyters

(='bishops')

---

¹ Acts xi. 30, xv. 2, 4, 6, 23, xvi. 4, xxi. 18.
² Acts xiv. 23.
³ Acts xx. 28-31. They are to act as *pastors*, and this implies the double idea of feeding and governing. The former is more closely associated with the word βόσκειν than with ποιμαίνειν (St. John xxi. 15-17), but it cannot be excluded from the latter: see Jude 12 ἑαυτοὺς ποιμαίνοντες = feeding themselves.
⁴ Clem. *ad Cor.* 44: the offering of the eucharistic gifts. The *Didache* (xv. 1) attaches the election of the bishops and deacons with an οὖν to the account of the eucharistic service, and associates their λειτουργία with that of the prophets and teachers.

but infused into the thing to which the old name was given its new spirit, and the hostility of the Jews to the Church certainly facilitated the process of distinguishing the ideas attached to the offices of the new Jerusalem from those which belonged to the old.

and deacons. Besides the presbyters we hear of the institution in the Church at Jerusalem of an inferior office. The occasion of its institution was the complaint of Hellenistic Christian Jews that "their widows were neglected in the daily ministration," apparently of food. In order, therefore, that this ministration of Christian charity might be carefully supervised without any hindrance to the Apostles in their higher 'ministry of the word,' a new office was created with a view to these 'works of mercy.' Seven, apparently Hellenistic Christians,[1] 'full of the Spirit and of wisdom,' are chosen by the community according to apostolic direction and ordained by the Apostles with the laying-on of hands and prayer.[2] In these seven we must see (with most authorities, ancient and modern) the prototype of the deacons.[3] In the case of some

[1] To judge from their names being Greek; but cf. Lightfoot *Dissert.* p. 188.

[2] Acts vi. 1-6.

[3] So Irenaeus iii. 12. 10, iv. 15. 1, etc., among ancients: so with most moderns Lightfoot and Renan: "On donna," says Renan *Les Apôtres* p. 120, "aux administrateurs ainsi désignés le nom syriaque de Schammaschîn, en grec διάκονοι. On les appelait aussi quelquefois 'les Sept' pour les opposer aux 'Douze.'" On the other hand St. Chrysostom *in loc.* speaks doubtfully, but implies on the whole that this office antedated both the presbyterate and the diaconate, and was in fact special for this particular need. So Œcumenius : οὐ κατὰ τὸν νῦν ἐν ταῖς ἐκκλησίαις βαθμόν. Cf. recently Müller *Verfassung etc.* p. 10. See Lightfoot (*Dissert.* p. 182), who also notes that the office here instituted cannot have been suggested by the ὑπηρέτης of the synagogue, who was more like a parish clerk. See St. Luke iv. 20. Schürer *Gemeindeverfassung der Juden* p. 28.

of these first appointed deacons, their peculiar gifts as preachers [1] sufficed to throw into the shade their humbler functions, but it is to be noticed that, though St. Philip can evangelize Samaria and baptize, he does not share the apostolic power to lay on hands.[2]

We are now in a position to sum up the results derived from our investigation of the origin, nature, and development of the Christian ministry, as it is presented in the writings of the apostolic period.

Summary.

(1) In the first place we have found that the conception of the apostolate which was derived from the Gospels is confirmed in the apostolic history. The Apostles are empowered by Christ and inspired by the Spirit as the primary witnesses of Christ's resurrection, stewards of the divine mysteries, ambassadors and ministers of the effected reconciliation of man to God. Their function is the ministry of the word or divine message, and inasmuch as the word is the basis of a covenant with a Church which is to be its 'pillar and ground,' so this apostolic ministry is not merely one of preaching. It involves the founding and governing of Churches with Christ's authority, the administration-in-chief of discipline, and the accompanying authority to bind and loose with divine

(1) The apostolate.

---

[1] Philip is called 'the evangelist' (Acts xxi. 8). This title is generally used in closer connection with the apostolic office, which Philip had not; cf. Eph. iv. 11 : 2 Tim. iv. 5 : Euseb. *H. E.* iii. 37. Either we must suppose the word to have had, like 'presbyter' and 'deacon,' a wider as well as a stricter use, or may suppose that Philip became later what, at the period described in Acts vi, he was not.

[2] Acts viii. 12-16.

sanction. It involves also a ministry of grace. Besides administering the chief sacraments committed to them by Christ, the Apostles appear (with a reservation to be mentioned afterwards) as alone possessing power to communicate the gift of the Holy Ghost by the laying-on of hands. By means of this rite they bestowed both that fundamental grace of the Spirit's indwelling, which made a Christian the temple of God and frequently carried with it in the first age a variety of special powers or 'charismata,' and also that particular 'charisma' which empowered men for the sacred ministry. The Apostles thus appear as the ordainers of an official clergy in the Churches, by communicating to them through the laying-on of hands an empowering gift of the Holy Ghost. The presbyters in some, or all, cases of ordination assisted at this rite, but, as the evidence suggests, to give their assent and witness, not as chief agents.

(2) The sub-apostolic ministry.

(2) This apostolic ministry is in its essence universal. It is true that an agreement was made, assigning to Paul and Barnabas the evangelization of the Gentiles, while James, Peter, and John kept themselves to the Jews; it is true, further, that of these last-named 'Apostles,' St. James was very early localized at Jerusalem; still, in its primary character, the apostolate is not a localized but a 'general ministry of the word.' And in this general ministry others share. St. James himself was not an apostle in the sense of being one of the twelve. Further, side by side with the Apostles, we hear of 'prophets' and, subordinate to them, of 'teachers' and 'evangelists,'

all of whom seem to have shared the apostolic function of teaching. Again, though they never appear as clothed with the same primary authority as the twelve, yet 'prophets and teachers' share also the ministry of worship and the laying-on of hands. We recognise then an extension of the apostolic function in some of its main features (*a*) to 'prophets,' whose authority was guaranteed by the permanent possession of those miraculous powers which in the first age witnessed to the inner presence of the Spirit, and who presumably had received either Christ's own commission before He left the earth, or (like Paul and Barnabas) the recognition by the laying-on of hands of those who were apostles and prophets before them of that divine mission which their miraculous 'gifts' evidenced; (*b*) to apostolic men like Timothy and Titus, known probably as 'teachers' and 'evangelists,' who without, as far as we know, sharing miraculous power, had yet imparted to them by the laying-on of apostolic hands what was essentially apostolic authority to guard the faith, to found and rule Churches, to ordain and discipline the clergy.

(3) Under this general ministry of the Apostles and their fellow-workers we find a local ministry of 'presbyters' or 'bishops,' who are appointed by the Apostles and ordained by the laying-on of hands to share in some particular community the pastorate and stewardship which Christ instituted in His Church. They are the local ministers of discipline — this being the function which was attached of old to the Jewish presbyterate—but they are as well the 'super-

(3) Presbyter-bishops.

intendents' in general of local affairs, the administrators of the Churches; and as the Churches are spiritual societies, so their function is spiritual. These local pastors are called also 'teachers' in the Epistle to the Ephesians, and we have no reason to suppose that they were not from the first, in a sense, 'ministers of the word,' though in subordination to apostles, prophets, and teachers. Again, since the earliest subapostolic writers speak of 'the offering of the gifts' and the ministry of the Eucharist as the special function of the 'bishop,' and St. James presents the presbyters to us as exercising a ministry of healing, both physical and spiritual, we need not hesitate to regard them as having been from the first ministers of the sacraments.

(4) Deacons

(4) We are also presented with a subordinate ministry of deacons. If their primary function was to administer alms, yet they are also presented to us as baptizing and teaching,—at least when they were endowed with qualifying gifts, though probably this function did not belong to their office. Besides we

and deaconesses.

find a female 'diaconate' as well as instances of 'prophetesses' in the Church, who however do not seem to have exercised any public ministry. We also hear of other leading Christians who specially addicted themselves to works of mercy and received a corresponding authority.

(5) The conception of ordination.

(5) Finally the Pastoral Epistles give us an unmistakable picture of the conception attached by the Apostle St. Paul to the ceremony of ordination. He regarded the laying-on of his hands as the instrumen-

tality through which Timothy received a special empowering gift of the Holy Ghost, which in virtue of this ceremony was 'in him' as a thing he might neglect or use, but which was in him in any case as at once his power and his responsibility. And we cannot but extend this conception to the ordinations of other clergy which Timothy is commissioned in his turn to make by the same ceremony of the laying-on of hands. Here we have the sacerdotal conception of a special order in the Church, differentiated by a special endowment.

Two points may be mentioned in which the witness of the New Testament needs supplementing by the witness of the Church. *Evidence is lacking as to*

First. We have no clear information as to the limitation of the functions of the different orders in the Church, except so far as that the 'viri apostolici' alone have the power to communicate the gift of the Holy Ghost by laying-on of hands. We have no clear information as to who exactly can celebrate the Eucharist and who can baptize. But we must remember that the New Testament does witness to a binding or loosing power in the Church and to a continuity in the Church's life. This enables us to rest satisfied with the fact that the principle of a ministry with different grades of function and power is given us in the apostolic age, and to accept in detail the mind of the Church, as soon as it declares itself, as representing the mind of the Spirit. *(i) exact division of functions:*

Second. We have no determining evidence as to the exact form which the ministry of the future was *(ii) form of the future ministry.*

to take. True the ministry of 'bishops' and deacons does appear in the New Testament as an almost essentially subordinate ministry, and we have clear evidence that the apostolic office admitted of being extended and localized, as in the case of St. James and (more or less) of St. Timothy and St. Titus; but all that the New Testament can be said to give us clearly is the principle that the church ministry is a thing received from above with graduated functions in different offices, so that it follows as a matter of course that there would always be persons who had the power to minister and persons who had also the power to ordain other ministers; with the corresponding position that only those who had the power communicated to them could exercise the function. What we do not get, then, is a distinct instruction as to what *form* the ministry was to take. Were the local bishops to receive additional powers, such as would make them independent of any higher order? Or were the apostles and apostolic men, like Timothy and Titus, to perpetuate their distinct order? and, if so, was it to be perpetuated as a localized or as a general order? These questions are still open.

CHAPTER VI.

THE MINISTRY IN THE SUBAPOSTOLIC AGE.

Two moments in the history of the Christian ministry have hitherto come under our notice. First, we have traced back the ministry of bishops, presbyters, and deacons, as church history makes us familiar with it, to the dim period of the middle of the second century. Secondly, we have seen it take its rise at the apostolic fountain-head. We have, so to speak, watched the Divine Founder of the Church separate and educate and institute the apostolate, and we have watched the Apostles at work, after the withdrawal of His visible presence, with the full consciousness of divine commission and authority. And in doing this we could not but perceive that, while in a certain sense they exercised a unique function —so far, that is, as they were the original witnesses and heralds of the revelation given in Christ,— in another sense they held a stewardship and pastorate of souls, a function of government and a corresponding power, which they intended to perpetuate in the life of the Church : the Church was not to develop her ministry from below, but to receive it from above by apostolic authorization. Thus we have found in the records of the New Testament the origin and title-deeds of a permanent ministry in the Church, the outcome of the apostolate, and we have found in the latter half of the second century that this ministry has taken shape in the episcopal successions of the Churches, which claim to perpetuate the apostolate in certain of its most fundamental functions. Now we approach another group of questions. What are the links which connect the ministry of the apostolic age with that of the age of Irenaeus? are they such as to justify the claims which Irenaeus makes for the episcopate? In particular, does the history, so far as we can trace it, suggest that the apostolic authority was perpetuated from the first in a special office superior to that of the presbyters, though it came shortly to be known by a title at first synonymous with the presbyterate, viz. the episcopate? Or does the evidence, on the other hand, lead us to believe that the permanent functions of government and ordination hitherto exercised by apostles and apostolic men were, so to speak, put into commission in the local colleges of presbyter-bishops, and that subsequently these supreme functions, hitherto belonging to all in common, came to be limited to one who alone retained the title of bishop? There is of course a third possibility, viz. that the functions exclusively discharged by the general or apostolic order in the first days (for instance, that of the laying-on of hands) lapsed altogether, and the Church of the second century, so to speak, redeveloped an apostolic order of bishops from below. With a view to answering the questions thus presented, we proceed to examine

Questions connected with the subapostolic ministry.

VI.] *The Ministry in the Subapostolic Age.* 273

the historical links afforded by the subapostolic documents. Links of evidence.

I.

The first link is that supplied by the episcopate in Jerusalem derived from James. "James," says Hegesippus, "receives the Church in succession with the Apostles."[1] This corresponds to the evidence of the New Testament. James ranks with the Apostles;[2] but, unlike the Apostles, he is localized in Jerusalem, where he presides with the presbyters,[3] and where at the apostolic conference he seems to hold the office of president and speaks with some degree of decisive authority, suggesting and probably framing the apostolic decree.[4] Thus it has been common from the earliest times to see in James the 'bishop of Jerusalem' in the later sense, i.e. a localized apostolic ruler of the Church, and this commends itself to most modern critics.[5] But though localized, his personal reputation and apostolic character made him a universal authority with Jewish Christians.[6] This is

1. The episcopate at Jerusalem.
James the head of a line of bishops,

---

[1] ap. Euseb. *H. E.* ii. 23 : διαδέχεται τὴν ἐκκλησίαν μετὰ τῶν ἀποστόλων.

[2] Gal. i. 19, ii. 9 ; Acts xv.

[3] Gal. i. 19 ; Acts xii. 17, xxi. 18.

[4] Acts xv. 13, 19, 20. See Lightfoot *Dissert.* p. 197.

[5] Clement of Alexandria (ap. Euseb. *H. E.* ii. 1) says : "Peter and James and John, after the assumption of the Saviour, though even the Lord had assigned them special honour, did not claim distinction, but elected James the Just bishop of Jerusalem." "As early as the middle of the second century," says Dr. Lightfoot (p. 208), "all parties concur in representing him as a bishop in the strict sense of the term." He refers to Hegesippus ap. Euseb. *H. E.* ii. 23, iv. 22, and to the Clementines, *Hom.* xi. 35, *Ep. Petr.* init., *Ep. Clem.* init., *Recog.* i. 43, 68, 73, etc. He himself concurs : James "can claim to be regarded as a bishop" (p. 197). He gave, says Mr. Simcox (*Early Ch. Hist.* p. 50), "it is scarcely inaccurate to say, the first example of a diocesan bishop." Cf. Müller *Verfassung* p. 12.

[6] Gal. ii. 11-14 illustrates St. James' influence, however little those who

S

the historical basis for the 'archiepiscopal' and even papal dignity assigned to him in the Ebionite traditions.[1] When the hostility of the extreme Jewish nationalists led to his being put to death for 'breaking the law' just before the siege of Jerusalem, Symeon was elected to take his place, who, like James, was a relative of Jesus Christ. Hegesippus (whom Eusebius speaks of as "having been born in the time of the first succession from the Apostles," i.e. probably before Symeon's death) apparently recorded his election *by the Apostles themselves*,[2] and certainly

'came from' him acted as he would have had them act; cf. the opening of his own epistle. Hegesippus gives a sacerdotal colour to his office; see Harnack *Expositor*, May 1887, p. 327. He was held in high regard amongst non-Christian Jews, and was known from the protection given by his constant intercessions as the περιοχὴ τοῦ λαοῦ; see Heges. ap. Euseb. *H. E.* ii. 23; Josephus *Ant. Jud.* xx. 9. 1; cf. Simcox *l.c.* p. 123.

[1] *Recog.* i. 73 and *Ep. Clem.* init. "bishop of bishops," and "archbishop." He exercises a quasi-papal authority over Peter; *Ep. Clem.* 1, *Recog.* i. 17, 72.

[2] ap. Euseb. *H. E.* iii. 32, iv. 22; cf. Lightfoot *Dissert.* pp. 202, 208. Eusebius says, iii. 11: "After the martyrdom of James and the taking of Jerusalem which immediately ensued, it is recorded (λόγος κατέχει) that those of the Apostles and of the Lord's disciples who were still alive came together from all parts, with those who were related to our Lord; for of them also there were still several alive: and that they all held conference together as to whom they ought to select as worthy to succeed to James (ἄξιον τῆς Ἰακώβου διαδοχῆς). And that they all with one mind approved of Symeon the son of Clopas ... as worthy of the throne of the parish there, who was a cousin as they say of the Saviour. For Hegesippus relates that Clopas was a brother of Joseph." The authority for this meeting may fairly, as Rothe maintains and Dr. Lightfoot admits, be assigned to Hegesippus.

The question arises—granted this meeting historical, as it well may be, can it be supposed that it not only elected a bishop of Jerusalem but also issued a general decree for the establishment of episcopacy? Such a 'second apostolic council' forms the basis for the supposed apostolic legislation of the *Constitutions*, and the establishment of 'monepiscopacy' seems to be assigned to it by Ambrosiaster on Eph. iv. 12 ("prospiciente concilio"). Jerome probably has the same meaning when he assigns the establishment of episcopacy to a formal 'decretum,' apparently of the Apostles (see on Tit. i. 5). Besides this Rothe (*Anfänge* pp. 351-392) quotes for the council the expression of Ignatius, τὰ διατάγματα τῶν ἀποστόλων (*ad Trall.* 7), and the ex-

VI.] *The Ministry in the Subapostolic Age.* 275

distinctly identifies his office with that of James and calls it a bishopric. He also mentions that there was a disappointed rival for the see called Thebuthis, who subsequently raised a schism and 'made a beginning of corrupting the virgin purity of the Church' with false doctrines. No one apparently supposes that the Jerusalem episcopate from this date was not continuous.[1] It is plain then that here at any rate the episcopal office was not only developed under apostolic patronage, but was in direct continuity with the apostolate, as represented by James, who, though not one of the twelve, ranked and acted with them: and whether the presbyters at Jerusalem were ever known as 'bishops' or no, certainly the episcopal authority never belonged to them.

But this earliest episcopate at Jerusalem had one unique feature. It was held by relatives of Christ. Symeon, our authority tells us, was chosen as "the cousin of the Lord"; he was "a descendant of David and a Christian."[2] And we have other evidence of a tendency in the Jewish Christian Church of Palestine to prefer for ecclesiastical offices of authority those who could thus claim royal blood. Thus St. Jude's

who at first were of the family of Christ:

---

pression of the second of Pfaff's fragments, attributed to Irenaeus, αἱ δεύτεραι τῶν ἀποστόλων διατάξεις. He also thinks that the ambiguous language of Clement's letter (c. 44) supports the same view. He holds that it was on this occasion that the Apostles so distributed the work amongst them as that Asia, according to a tradition mentioned by Origen (ap. Euseb. *H. E.* iii. 1), "was assigned to John." This evidence is discussed fully by Dr. Lightfoot *Dissert.* p. 204 f. and most people will agree with him that it affords a very insecure basis for the idea of a formal second council of the Apostles legislating for the establishment of episcopacy.

[1] Eusebius' list of subsequent bishops of Jerusalem (*H. E.* iv. 5) is not apparently derived from Hegesippus. See Lightfoot *l.c.* p. 209 n.²

[2] Euseb. *H. E.* iv. 22: ὃν προέθεντο πάντες, ὄντα ἀνέψιον τοῦ κυρίου, δεύτερον.

276   *Christian Ministry.*   [CHAP.

<small>others of this family held a less localized authority.</small> grandsons "of the family of the Lord," who were compelled (as Hegesippus tells us) to appear before Domitian in order to satisfy him that the empire was in no peril from their royal claims, when they were dismissed, became "rulers of the Churches," or "rulers of every Church."[1] This last expression (which seems to be Hegesippus' own) would probably indicate that, while there was a local episcopate at Jerusalem, there was a more general authority assigned, amongst the Jewish Christians of Palestine, to these members of the royal family of Christ—not, however, as the case of Symeon would assure us, by mere right of birth, but by due appointment. Chief authority in the Church was not yet, even among Jewish Christians, in all cases a localized or diocesan authority. And this is the evidence of the next document to be considered.

II.

<small>II. The Didache.</small>

<small>Its general character.</small>

The *Teaching of the Twelve Apostles* or, as it was probably originally called, the *Teaching of the Apostles*,[2] is a document which we may assume to belong at latest to the first century, and to have been composed by a Jewish Christian for a Jewish Christian community. There are also several indications justify-

---

[1] See ap. Euseb. *H. E.* iii. 20 and 32. In the first case Eusebius, apparently quoting Hegesippus in the oratio obliqua, says that they ἡγήσασθαι τῶν ἐκκλησιῶν. In the second passage he quotes his actual words: προηγοῦνται πάσης ἐκκλησίας. This is therefore the more trustworthy expression. Dr. Hatch says (*B. L.* p. 89) "they presided in other Churches"; but Hegesippus seems to give them a more general authority.

[2] See Dr. Warfield *Bibliotheca Sacra*, Jan. 1886, p. 110.

VI.] *The Ministry in the Subapostolic Age.*   277

ing the supposition that it belongs to Syria or Palestine—probably to some district remote from the centre of apostolic influence.[1] The theology which it represents is of a very inadequate nature, when compared with the teaching of the New Testament, and suggests in fact nothing so much as the condition of belief of those Hebrew Christians to whom the Epistle to the Hebrews was directed, in order to lift them out of the stage of rudimentary knowledge in which they were into some more adequate conceptions of the person of Christ, of His priesthood and mediation in the Church. It will cause no surprise that there should have existed in the latter part of the first century communities of Jewish Christians with very imperfect doctrinal instruction, perhaps in some outlying district of Syria; and, though we shall not look to a writing emanating from amongst them for much light on Christian theology, we shall look with great interest to their form of church organization.

In the *Didache* then we are presented with a form of church ministry which ought not to perplex any one acquainted with the Acts of the Apostles. We have as local officers bishops and deacons, who are elected specially with a view to the conduct of worship in the community.[2] But, as in the apostolic

Its church organization:

local bishops and deacons,

---

[1] "I should conjecture [the *Didache*], on account of its strongly Jewish character, to have had its birth in the country east of the Jordan, where Christian Jews were numerous" (Salmon *Introd.* pp. 612); but see further on the whole subject of the *Didache* App. Note L.

[2] xv. 1: χειροτονήσατε οὖν ἑαυτοῖς ἐπισκόπους καὶ διακόνους. This οὖν connects the election of the officers with c. xiv about the Sunday celebration of the 'pure sacrifice.' It will be noticed that nothing is said about the bishop in the passage (xiii. 4) about almsgiving. We should not however be right in assuming that the bishop had nothing to do with this, any more than con-

church, these local officers are not the chief figures in the organization. Over them are 'apostles,' 'prophets,' and 'teachers,' who exercise a ministry not yet localized in any particular Church.[1] The apostles are not indeed the twelve; they correspond to what we should suppose is meant by the 'evangelist' of the New Testament; they are 'ambulatory' messengers of the Gospel,[2] and are almost identified with the prophets,[3] who are better defined figures than either apostles or teachers. These representatives of the Church at large, when they visit a community of Christians, are first of all to be tested by the standard of right teaching and of moral character.[4] The true apostle is to be distinguished by the absence of any selfish motive any sign of an inclination to fasten himself upon a Church or to abandon the holy poverty of his vocation is to stamp him as a false prophet. The prophet too is to be tested by his character and conformity to the truth which he teaches, but when once he has been approved, his inspired utterances are not to be subjected to any criticism. This would be a sin which cannot be for-

[margin: with apostles, prophets, and teachers over them.]

cluding from c. vii that the bishop had nothing to do with baptizing. The community in fact is addressed as a whole. They are directed to baptize, to fast, to give alms, to pray, to come together on the Lord's Day and confess their sins and celebrate their thank-offering, and then, with a view to the due performance of all these functions, they are directed to elect for themselves bishops and deacons.

[1] xi. 3, xiii. 2.

[2] They are perhaps like the 'apostles' of Rom. xvi. 7, Andronicus and Junias. For the use of the word 'teacher' we may compare the *Ep. ad Diognet.* 11: ἀποστόλων γενόμενος μαθητὴς γίνομαι διδάσκαλος ἐθνῶν. (This chapter, however, is not part of the original letter.)

[3] The apostle who stays in a Church more than two days is called a 'false prophet' (xi. 5); again (xi. 6) if he ask for money, he is a 'false prophet.'

[4] c. xi.

given. He is to be listened to with reverent acceptance and allowed the freedom, which the old prophets had, to perform exceptional acts 'for a sign' or in a mystery.[1] He has freedom also to give thanks in the eucharistic celebration without the restriction of any set form;[2] and receives the first fruits of all the produce of the community, because the prophets are the Christian 'high-priests.'[3] Clearly then these prophets, with the apostles and teachers, occupy the first rank in the church ministry, but, as we saw reason in the apostolic age to believe that the local 'clergy' shared fundamentally the same spiritual ministry as the apostles, only in a subordinate grade, so here we have it specified that the bishops and deacons exercise the same ministry as the prophets and teachers, and are therefore not to be 'overlooked.'[4]

So far then the indications of this document suggest a state of church government closely akin to what we should suppose would have existed in apostolic and subapostolic days in any community not under the direct supervision of the twelve. There are bishops and deacons, and over them prophets and

---

[1] iv. 1, xi. 11. I do not wish to express any certainty about the meaning of these words; see Taylor *Teaching of the Twelve Apostles*, pp. 82-92.

[2] x. 7: τοῖς δὲ προφήταις ἐπιτρέπετε εὐχαριστεῖν ὅσα θέλουσιν.

[3] xiii. But ver. 4: 'if you have no prophet, give to the poor.' It is probably implied that the prophet will himself, when he is present, minister to the wants of the poor. He could not take the first fruits for himself only without coming under the category of a 'false prophet.'

[4] C. xv, after providing for the election of fit persons as bishops and deacons, ἀξίους τοῦ κυρίου, ἄνδρας πραεῖς καὶ ἀφιλαργύρους καὶ ἀληθεῖς καὶ δεδοκιμασμένους, continues: ὑμῖν γὰρ λειτουργοῦσι καὶ αὐτοὶ τὴν λειτουργίαν τῶν προφητῶν καὶ διδασκάλων· μὴ οὖν ὑπερίδητε αὐτούς· αὐτοὶ γάρ εἰσιν οἱ τετιμημένοι ὑμῶν μετὰ τῶν προφητῶν καὶ διδασκάλων. I shall remark further on this word τετιμημένοι in connection with the Epistle of Clement.

teachers and apostles in the sense of evangelists,—men belonging to a ministry as yet unlocalized, and, in the case of the prophets at least, inspired. But two points specially require notice.

The prophet

(1) It is specified that the prophet has the right to 'settle' in any of the Churches he visits.[1] It is just in this context that he is declared to be the proper recipient of all first fruits and the 'high-priest' of the community. Can we doubt then that, in the event of this prophetic teacher taking up his permanent residence in any Church, with his authority as an inspired man, with his free power of eucharistic celebration, and with his 'high-priestly' dignity, he would have become (by whatever name he was called) the bishop of the community in the later sense? As then we have in St. James the first instance of a member of the apostolic ministry localized in a single Church, so the *Teaching* seems to give us an indication that the settling of prophets would have been at least one way in which the transition was effected from the apostolic ministry to that of the later Church. What in fact was Polycarp of Smyrna, or Ignatius of Antioch, but a prophet who had become a bishop?[2] Thus the *Teaching* gives no countenance to the idea that in the region which it represents the 'bishops' (i.e. presbyters) and deacons would

(1) by 'settling' would become a diocesan bishop:

---

[1] xiii. 1: πᾶς δὲ προφήτης ἀληθινός, θέλων καθῆσαι πρὸς ὑμᾶς, ἄξιός ἐστι τῆς τροφῆς αὐτοῦ, κ.τ.λ.

[2] Ignatius claims the gift of prophecy: *ad Philad.* 7. For Polycarp see *Mart. Polyc.* 16: "having been an apostolic and prophetic teacher, bishop of the holy Church in Smyrna," and cf. c. 5, where he foresees his own martyrdom by means of a vision. On 'teachers' becoming bishops, see Kühl *Gemeindeord.* p. 131.

ever have held the place of chief authority in the Church.

(2) The community in the *Teaching* are exhorted to elect their bishops and deacons; we have here a more democratic mode of election than is general.[1] Nothing is said of any control over the election, or of any ordination from above by laying-on of hands. Now some modern critics show a tendency to exalt the *Didache* in this respect as a source of evidence over the Pastoral Epistles and the Acts of the Apostles; and undoubtedly, if we are to take this anonymous writing of very ambiguous doctrinal character and exalt it as a criterion of what early Christianity meant over writings whose genuineness and apostolic authority there is no good reason to doubt, we shall probably see grounds for believing that the subapostolic Church rated not only church orders, but also Baptism and the Eucharist at a very low estimate. Believing, however, the Pastoral Epistles and the Acts to be genuine documents, we naturally prefer to look at so questionable a writing as the *Didache* in the light of apostolic practice and injunction. The question we ask is this: Is the evidence of the *Didache* incompatible with the evidence about ordination which we derive from apostolic sources? The answer is, we think, in the negative. The *Didache*

<small>(2) must have before held the power of laying on hands.</small>

---

[1] In the Acts and the Pastoral Epistles the man of apostolic authority appoints elders: so also in Clement's Epistle they are appointed from above, "with the consent of the whole Church" (c. 44). Here the Church simply elects, and the same is the case in the Egyptian *Church Ordinances*, where very small communities of twelve are contemplated electing their bishop (in the later sense). It should not of course be forgotten that the election of 'the seven' in the Acts was made by the community.

is silent about ordination, but it is silent also about all 'laying-on of hands.' Yet we know that there was closely associated in the minds of the early Church, and especially of its Jewish members, with the doctrine of baptisms that of the laying-on of hands.[1] The silence of the *Didache* about ordination then, like other instances of silence, proves too much, if it is to be taken as equivalent to ignorance. It can be accounted for easily enough with a little consideration. The *Didache* appears to be a manual of directions for the local church. It does not presume to dictate to the prophets.[2] It says, therefore, nothing about the functions which do not belong to the local church with the local officers. Now all the evidence of the apostolic documents leads us to believe that the function of the laying-on of hands did not belong to the local officers, but to apostles and apostolic legates and also, as appeared, to certain prophets and teachers, the associates of apostles. As, therefore, we find the prophets in the *Didache* performing that 'liturgy' which is assigned to them also in the Acts,[3] what is more reasonable than to suppose that to them would have belonged as well that 'laying-on of hands' which in the same passage of the Acts is also assigned to them? We may well believe then that in the communities represented by the *Didache*, the bishops and deacons would have been elected by the whole body but ordained with laying-on of hands by some one of the prophetic 'high priests' on their occasional visits.

[1] See esp. Hebr. vi. 2. [2] x. 7, xi. 7, 11. [3] Acts xiii. 2.

The picture which is here given us of Churches in the subapostolic age still governed by a local body of bishops,[1] while the higher authority in the word and sacraments remained with men who exercised an 'ambulatory' ministry, may be compared with the picture that Eusebius draws of the activity of evangelists in immediate succession to the Apostles. He describes how they went among the heathen, laying the foundations of the faith in some places, and appointing pastors in others to whom they entrusted 'the husbandry' of those just brought within the pale, while they themselves went forth into new fields; how they had still many extraordinary powers working in them; and how it would be "impossible for him to enumerate by name all those who in the first succession to the Apostles became pastors or evangelists in the Churches over the whole world."[2] We have only to suppose that these missionaries with their miraculous gifts not only founded Churches but also for a time, like the Apostles to whom they succeeded, supervised them on occasional visits, and we have a picture, with merely the substitution of the title evangelist, very like that which the *Didache* presents. And it must not be forgotten that the earliest recorded traditions of the Syriac Church pointed back not, like those of Asia and of the West, to twelve Apostles, but to seventy-two, as having founded the successions of the priesthood in their communities.[3]

Cf. the ministry of Eusebius' evangelists.

---

[1] Who are of course equivalent to presbyters though they are not called so. See App. Note K.
[2] Euseb. iii. 37. These evangelists are described as τὴν πρώτην τάξιν τῆς τῶν ἀποστόλων ἐπέχοντες διαδοχῆς.
[3] See above, p. 131 and note.

<small>Prophets cease, as such, to hold the ministry.</small>

It only remains to add that this is the latest document which presents us with prophets exercising any ministerial function as such. It is true that later we have bishops like Ignatius and Polycarp who in fact are prophets—but they exercise their functions not as prophets but as bishops. The power of prophecy had not died out when Hermas saw his visions, or when Irenaeus wrote against heresies, or when Ammia and Quadratus prophesied[1]; but the prophets held no official rank. So far as they had in early times been the chief teachers of the Church, their 'high-priestly' functions and their teaching 'chair' passed to the bishops:[2] in a minor sense, the 'readers of holy Scripture in the congregation'[3] were

---

[1] Euseb. v. 17. See App. Note H.

[2] The high-priesthood ascribed by Hippolytus to the bishops (*Ref. Omn. Haer.* prooem. quoted in App. Note G) seems to be specially connected with *teaching authority*: he speaks of a "grace and high-priesthood and teaching" which the bishops hold in succession to the Apostles. So Polycrates describes St. John as a "priest, wearing the mitre, and witness and teacher" (ap. Euseb. *H. E.* iii. 31). So again the καθέδρα of the bishops was first of all the chair of the teacher. Thus in the Clementines (*Ep. Clem.* 2) St. Peter speaks: Κλήμεντα τοῦτον ἐπίσκοπον ὑμῖν χειροτονῶ, ᾧ τὴν ἐμὴν τῶν λόγων πιστεύω καθέδραν. So in Irenaeus the office of the bishop is conceived of primarily as carrying with it the "charisma veritatis certum" (iv. 26. 2), and this coincides with Hegesippus' view of the episcopal succession. It is also noticeable that the right of extempore eucharist seems to have passed to the bishop, as in Justin Martyr *Apol.* i. 67; cf. *Did.* x. 7.

[3] The prayer for the ordination of a reader in *Apost. Const.* viii. 22 invokes upon him "the prophetic spirit" (cf. the Gk. Vers. of the Syriac *Didascalia* quoted by Harnack, *Texte u. Untersuch.* band ii. h. 3. p. 77); and the western writers on church offices from Isidore down into the later middle ages regard the reader's office as a continuation of that of the prophet: thus Isidore *de Eccl. Off.* ii. 11 (Hittorp. p. 23) writes: "lectorum ordo formam et initium a prophetis accepit." These words are repeated by Rabanus Maurus *de Inst. Cler.* i. 11 (p. 317) and by (pseudo) Albinus Flaccus *de Div. Off.* (p. 70). Amalarius *de Eccl. Off.* ii. 8 (p. 163) regards the office as a continuation of another charisma: "hoc ministerium continetur in dono gratiae Dei de quo dicit apostolus: alii sermo scientiae secundum eundem Spiritum." In the *Church Ordinances* (c. 17) the reader ranks above the deacons and is said to "work the place of an evangelist." The so-called second Epistle of Clement

accounted their successors. This then is the last time that we are presented with the apostolic ministry exercised by men who are called prophets. If we ask the question, how these prophets were appointed to their ministry, we cannot obtain a very definite answer. We do not know exactly what rights were understood to belong to those who had these miraculous gifts as pledges of divine favour and mission, but the evidence of the Acts as to the laying-on of hands, which gave, or confirmed, the mission even of St. Paul and St. Barnabas, will not allow us to suppose that the inspiration of these later prophets would have enabled them to dispense with ecclesiastical ordination by apostles or apostolic men. It is however evident enough in the *Didache* that there was a considerable admixture of self-seeking impostors in the ranks of these later apostles and prophets, and it is very easy to see that the system of an unlocalized prophetic ministry was not one which could have been safely allowed to become permanent in the Churches.[1] As it is, we have evidence such as cannot be resisted that the transition to the localized episcopate was effected by no less an authority than that of apostles.

seems to be the homily of a reader; cf. also the reff. to 'reading' in the N. T. 1 Tim. iv. 13 and Apoc. i. 3, and on the whole subject see Harnack *l.c.* p. 57. Such readers held of course an office of great importance when illiterate bishops were contemplated (*Apost. Const.* ii. 1, *Ch. Ordin.* 16).

[1] The same suggestion of spiritual expediency would have promoted the transition from the state of things which we find in the *Didache* to that which we find in Ignatius' letters, which in a later age led to the drawing tight of diocesan restrictions: see above p. 162 n.[2] on the wandering bishops from Ireland and elsewhere. This wandering ministry gave every opportunity for imposture, and we ought not perhaps to be surprised to find a similar danger and similar abuses in the subapostolic age. As to the bearing of such dangerous periods on the security of the apostolic succession, enough perhaps was said in the second chapter.

III.

III. St. John institutes the diocesan episcopate,

At the time when the prophets and teachers of whom the *Didache* speaks were going on their journeys from Church to Church, St. John was living at Ephesus; and Polycrates, who was bishop there within the second century, speaks of him "who lay upon the Lord's breast" as having become "a priest, wearing the mitre, and witness and teacher" before he fell asleep in Ephesus.[1] What then was the nature of St. John's activity during this last period of his life? A tradition which cannot be set aside connects with his name not only the writing of the fourth Gospel but also the establishment of episcopacy in its later sense. "Listen," says Clement of Alexandria, "to a legend, which is no legend but very history, which has been handed down and preserved about John the Apostle. When on the death of the tyrant he returned from the isle of Patmos to Ephesus, he used to go away when he was summoned to the neighbouring districts as well, in some places to establish bishops, in others to organize whole Churches, in others to ordain to the clergy some one of those indicated by the Spirit."[2] The reference here is to bishops in the later sense: and Clement means that St. John ordained one bishop in each place, for the history

---

[1] ap. Euseb. *H. E.* iii. 31: ἐγενήθη ἱερεὺς πέταλον πεφορεκὼς καὶ μάρτυς καὶ διδάσκαλος.

[2] *Quis Dives* 42. These last words vividly recall the apostolic age, cf. 1 Tim. i. 18, Acts xiii. 2. They "seem to convince us that St. Clement reproduces the usage [of St. John's age] faithfully" (Simcox *Early Ch. Hist.* p. 183). See Lightfoot *Ignatius* i. 380 on Clement's special means of knowledge through his "Ionian" teacher.

which he goes on to narrate turns on the conduct of one of those appointed bishops who 'presided over' a certain city, which St. John visited once and again on occasions of necessity.[1] Here then we have St. John organizing episcopacy in the district about Ephesus. This testimony is confirmed by Tertullian: "We have," he says, "the Churches who have John for their teacher. For the series of bishops (of the Churches of Asia) if taken back to its origin will rest upon his authorization."[2] So, earlier than Tertullian, the author of the Muratorian fragment speaks of St. John as urged to write his Gospel by "his fellow-disciples and bishops." Once again Irenaeus, who represented all the traditions of Asia, who had been Polycarp's disciple 'in his first youth' and kept up so vivid a memory of those early days, tells us that his master "was not only made a disciple by apostles and held converse with many who had seen Christ, but was also established in Asia by apostles as bishop in the Church of Smyrna."[3] In the term "apostles" Irenaeus certainly means to include St. John. Here is then a great body of testimony connecting the episcopacy of the Churches of Asia with St. John. It suggests strongly that St. John regarded it as his apostolic function to perpetuate a church ministry.

[1] Clement calls him also ὁ πρεσβύτερος, but perhaps in its natural sense, as he calls him ὁ πρεσβύτης later on. However, we have seen already that the word πρεσβύτερος was used to include bishops by Clement and Irenaeus and later writers.

[2] *adv. Marc.* iv. 5. Later however the Asiatic Church received Timothy as the first bishop of Ephesus, i.e. they carried back the succession behind John. See Labbe *Collect. Concil.* iv. p. 1620.

[3] Euseb. *H.E.* iv. 14, cf. Tertull. *de Praescr.* 32: "Smyrnaeorum ecclesia Polycarpum ab Ioanne collocatum refert."

with other surviving Apostles.

And in this last period of the apostolic ministry we must not isolate St. John. Irenaeus, as noticed above, speaks of Polycarp as instituted by *apostles.* Ignatius speaks of episcopacy as the ordinance of *the Apostles.* "When," Dr. Lightfoot says, "after the destruction of Jerusalem St. John fixed his abode at Ephesus, it would appear that not a few of the oldest surviving members of the Palestinian Church accompanied him into 'Asia,' which henceforward became the headquarters of apostolic authority. In this body of emigrants Andrew and Philip among the twelve,[1] Aristion and John the presbyter among other personal disciples of the Lord, are specially mentioned." "A life-long friendship would naturally draw Philip the Apostle of Bethsaida after John, as it also drew Andrew. And, when we turn to St. John's Gospel, we can hardly resist the impression that incidents relative to Andrew and Philip had a special interest, not only for the writer of the Gospel, but also for his hearers. Moreover the Apostles Andrew and Philip appear in this Gospel as inseparable companions."[2] There is then reason to connect the establishment of the Asiatic episcopacy with the combined action of several of the Apostles.

Ignatius testimony.

Even, however, if we had not such direct testimony as has just been recorded to this organization of

---

[1] Andrew is mentioned among the 'condiscipuli' of St. John who urged him to write his Gospel in the *Canon Murator.* Philip, one of the twelve, is mentioned by Polycrates ap. Euseb. *H.E.* iii. 31: "Philip . . . who sleeps in Hierapolis, and his two daughters, having grown old in virginity, and his other daughter, having lived (πολιτευσαμένη) in the Holy Ghost, sleeps in Ephesus." Dr. Lightfoot's argument that this Philip was really the Apostle and not the evangelist (*Colossians* p. 45 note) is convincing.

[2] *Colossians* p. 45 and n.[3]

episcopacy by the Apostles who survived the destruction of Jerusalem,[1] the claim which Ignatius makes for episcopacy in the beginning of the second century would force us to postulate it. In passing to the consideration of the evidence which his letters afford for the history of the ministry, we cannot but congratulate ourselves that now for the third time in the history of literary controversy their genuineness has been vindicated by an English scholar. It is perhaps hardly too much to say that Dr. Lightfoot has now at last brought the controversy to an end.[2]

---

[1] It may well be considered that up to the time of the destruction of Jerusalem—that 'end of the age' for the Jewish Church—all ecclesiastical arrangements had a provisional character.

[2] Since the revival of learning, when scholars first began to perceive that the mediaeval 'Ignatian letters' were not the same as those quoted by the Fathers, down to the present time, the writings of Ignatius have been a field for controversy constantly renewed. The decision of the controversy, at least for the time, has (as was said) thrice been due to English scholars. First in 1644 the critical insight and genius of Ussher led to the recovery, though only in Latin, of the seven shorter letters in the form now recognised as genuine and banished for ever their mediaeval—interpolated or spurious—representatives. Next, when after the appearance of the Greek text (in the main) in 1646 the presbyterians, especially the French presbyterians, represented by Daillé (1666), were alarmed at the witness of the letters of Ignatius in favour of the cause of episcopacy and did their best to prove them spurious, the great Bishop Pearson wrote his *Vindiciae Ignatianae* (1672)—"incomparably," Dr. Lightfoot says (*Ignatius* i. p. 320), "the most valuable contribution to the subject which had hitherto appeared, with the single exception of Ussher's work," —and on the main issue seemed almost to have put the question at rest for those open to conviction. But once again, after an interval of more than two centuries, Cureton's publication in 1845 of some Syriac abridgements of some of the letters or extracts from them (as we may now pronounce them to be), which he maintained to be the only original letters, stirred the embers of the old discussion and the question was again rife which version, if any, represented the real Ignatius; and now once more the vindication of the genuineness of the 'shorter Greek' letters has fallen to an English scholar, Dr. Lightfoot, the prince we may be proud to call him of living historical critics in the department of church history. Dr. Lightfoot does not indeed stand alone in his work of renewed vindication. Zahn's *Ignatius von Antiochien*, which appeared in 1873, is described by Dr. Lightfoot himself (*l.c.* p. 272) as "quite the most important contribution to the solution of the Ignatian

Ignatius, bishop of Antioch, appears as a condemned prisoner moving by a route through Asia to his death at Rome, in the custody of a maniple of ten soldiers, whom for their harshness he calls "ten leopards."[1] But his progress is converted into a sort of triumph. The Churches hear where he can be seen, and at Smyrna deputations arrive from Ephesus, Magnesia, and Tralles

question which has appeared since Cureton's discovery," and as having "dealt a fatal blow at the claims of the Curetonian letters." But the chief merit rests with the English scholar. Dr. Harnack speaks of his work as "the most learned and careful (sorgfälligste) patristic monograph of the century," and is in common with almost all scholars convinced by the array of historical, linguistic, and general evidence on behalf of the letters which has been produced. He speaks of their genuineness as "certain," and of the "inner grounds for it" as "overpowering" (*Expositor*, Jan. 1886, pp. 10, 15).

Harnack however, while accepting Dr. Lightfoot's conclusion that Ignatius, bishop of Antioch, was the author of these letters, disputes the position that Ignatius wrote these letters and suffered martyrdom in the time of Trajan. He would bring the letters down from A.D. 110-118 to some date probably after A.D. 130. The earlier date he speaks of as a "mere possibility, which is highly improbable, because it is not supported by any word in the Epistles and because it rests only upon a late and very problematic witness" (*Expositor*, March 1886, p. 190). As regards however (1) the internal witness to date, Dr. Lightfoot has certainly the advantage over Harnack in the discussion of the nature of the heresy which Ignatius is opposing. In the Epistles to the Ephesians, Trallians, and Smyrnaeans a docetic heresy is in question, in the Epistle to the Philadelphians a Judaistic. But in the Epistle to the Magnesians, at least, we learn that these do not represent separate and distinct tendencies. The heresy there in question is Judæo-docetic—a type of heresy which recalls that with which St. Paul contended at Colossae and Ephesus. And throughout the Epistles the same general terms are used in speaking of either heretical tendency. There are no signs of two movements which Ignatius was resisting. Harnack admits that Lightfoot "can appeal on behalf of [his position] to the consensus of most scholars of modern times." But then the Judæo-docetic heresy points strongly to the earlier date. See Lightfoot i. pp. 361-3; Harnack *l.c.* pp. 175-185. As regards (2) the external evidence, Harnack quite underrates the force of Origen's testimony to the early date. Origen quotes and mentions Ignatius the martyr as "second bishop of Antioch after the blessed Peter, who fought with beasts in the persecution at Rome" (*in Luc.* vi). This must refer (see Lightfoot ii. p. 470) to the persecution under Trajan. On the whole we may accept the traditional connection of Ignatius' martyrdom with Trajan's reign with great confidence.

[1] *ad Rom.* 5: δέκα λεοπάρδοις, ὅ ἐστι στρατιωτικὸν τάγμα· οἳ καὶ εὐεργετούμενοι χείρους γίνονται.

and join the flock of Polycarp in doing him honour. While he is at Smyrna he writes four of the extant letters—to the Ephesians, to the Magnesians, to the Trallians, and to the Romans. The other three were written from Troas, whither an Ephesian deacon had accompanied him, and were addressed to Churches through which he had just passed to Philadelphia and Smyrna, and to Smyrna's bishop, Polycarp. He passes from Neapolis to Philippi, where he is again welcomed by the Church and escorted on his way, and so he goes on towards Rome and we lose sight of him.[1] Here then we have a very notable witness. He is a man who, though he loves to describe himself as "only now beginning to be a disciple," is probably old in years.[2] He would have been verging upon man's estate at least when St. Paul wrote his great Epistles; he would have been in full manhood when the last days came upon Jerusalem. If the traditions of his relation to St. John cannot be depended upon, at any rate we must admit that he can bear unexceptionable testimony to apostolic intentions, and, unlike some of the subapostolic witnesses, he is one who, whatever age he had belonged to, would have been remarkable for his character and powers. The doctrinal and ecclesiastical interest of his letters has sometimes led to the moral beauty and power which they exhibit being overlooked. They reveal a man on fire with

His qualifications as a witness.

---

[1] Lightfoot i. pp. 34-37.

[2] He writes to Polycarp "in language which is most appropriate on the lips of an old man speaking to one who is many years his junior" (Lightfoot i. p. 425). Now Polycarp, if he had received his appointment in the Church of Smyrna, as Irenaeus says, from apostles, must, even if ordained at thirty, have been well on in life in A. D. 110.

love, filled with the Spirit, one whom it would be absurd to call a literalist, a formalist, or a mere lover of organization. In spite of his Italian name, he is a thorough oriental, with a mystical, meditative spirit, who sees things according to their inner forces and hidden powers—witness his sayings of intense conviction about the silent workings of God[1] and of holiness, his spiritual conception of Christianity and of the eucharistic gifts,[2] his perception of the sanctity of common life.[3] Again he is beyond question the greatest theologian among the 'apostolic fathers,' with his deep insight into the Incarnation as a principle, a fact, a doctrine, and with his power to hold in balance its great antithesis in all its applications—the antithesis of the spiritual and the material, of the Word made Flesh.[4]

This man then is on his way to death. Time is passing away from him, and he has but few moments in which to give as his last message to the Churches, what he thinks of most urgent importance for them in view of that age of restless speculation and wild imaginative idealism, the solvent forces of which they were just beginning to feel. Under these circumstances he applies himself to strengthening two great fortresses of the Church's life. The first is the

---

[1] See *ad Eph.* 6, 15, 19, *ad Philad.* 1, *ad Magn.* 8, *ad Trall.* 4.

[2] Whatever external conditions church unity requires, its essence is an inward fact. God Himself is the inner principle of union; *ad Trall.* 11, *ad Magn.* 15. For the eucharistic gifts, see *ad Eph.* 20, cf. 1 and 5, *ad Trall.* 8, *ad Rom.* 7.

[3] *ad Eph.* 8 : ἃ γὰρ κατὰ σάρκα πράσσετε, ταῦτα πνευματικά ἐστιν.

[4] Cf. his constant balancing of σαρκικῶς and πνευματικῶς, *ad Eph.* 10, *ad Magn.* 1, 13, *ad Trall.* 12, *ad Smyrn.* 1, 12, *ad Polyc.* 2 ; cf. Lightfoot ii. p. 48.

Incarnation—as a fact in history, as a thing sacramentally perpetuated, as a principle to be meditated upon, formulated, and fought for.[1] The second is the Ministry—the visible organization of bishops, presbyters, and deacons, by which the Church, the home of God's redemption, is to be known, and by which it is made plain that the Christian religion is not a dream or a speculation but a manifested life, social, organized, and disciplined, under the authority of a divinely-given rule.

In his assertion of the prerogative of the threefold ministry Ignatius is almost violently emphatic, as may be seen from the following passages from his letters[2]:—

The claim he makes for the threefold ministry.

"It is meet therefore ... that being perfectly joined together in one submission, submitting yourselves to your bishop and presbytery, ye may be sanctified in all things."

"I was forward to exhort you, that ye run in harmony with the mind of God: for Jesus Christ also, our inseparable life, is the mind of the Father, even as the bishops that are settled in the farthest parts of the earth are in the mind of Jesus Christ. So then it becometh you to run in harmony with the mind of the bishop; which thing also ye do. For your honourable presbytery, which is worthy of God, is attuned to the bishop, even as its strings to a lyre."

---

[1] The emphasis upon the physical fact of Christ's incarnation, birth, death, resurrection, as against Docetism, is of course constant (*ad Magn.* 11, *ad Trall.* 9, *ad Smyrn.* 1); see Lightfoot i. pp. 359, 360. For the close connection of the Incarnation with the Eucharist, see *ad Smyrn.* 7. For Ignatius' tendency to formulate the antithesis it involves as a doctrine, see *ad Eph.* 7, *ad Polyc.* 3, cf. *ad Eph.* 20.

[2] From Dr. Lightfoot's translation.

"Let no man be deceived. If any one be not within the precinct of the altar, he lacketh the bread [of God]. For, if the prayer of one and another hath so great force, how much more that of the bishop and of the whole Church.... Let us therefore be careful not to resist the bishop, that by our submission we may give ourselves to God. And in proportion as a man seeth that his bishop is silent, let him fear him the more. For every one whom the Master of the household sendeth to be steward over His own house, we ought so to receive as Him that sent him. Plainly therefore we ought to regard the bishop as the Lord Himself."

"Assemble yourselves together in common, every one of you severally, man by man, in grace, in one faith and one Jesus Christ, who after the flesh was of David's race, who is Son of Man and Son of God, to the end that ye may obey the bishop and the presbytery without distraction of mind; breaking one bread, which is the medicine of immortality and the antidote that we should not die."[1]

---

[1] *ad Eph.* 2 : πρέπον οὖν ἐστιν κατὰ πάντα τρόπον δοξάζειν Ἰησοῦν Χριστὸν τὸν δοξάσαντα ὑμᾶς, ἵνα ἐν μιᾷ ὑποταγῇ κατηρτισμένοι, ὑποτασσόμενοι τῷ ἐπισκόπῳ καὶ τῷ πρεσβυτερίῳ, κατὰ πάντα ἦτε ἡγιασμένοι.

3, 4 : προέλαβον παρακαλεῖν ὑμᾶς, ὅπως συντρέχητε τῇ γνώμῃ τοῦ θεοῦ : καὶ γὰρ Ἰ. Χ., τὸ ἀδιάκριτον ἡμῶν ζῆν, τοῦ πατρὸς ἡ γνώμη, ὡς καὶ οἱ ἐπίσκοποι οἱ κατὰ τὰ πέρατα ὁρισθέντες ἐν Ἰ. Χ. γνώμῃ εἰσίν. Ὅθεν πρέπει ὑμῖν συντρέχειν τῇ τοῦ ἐπισκόπου γνώμῃ, ὅπερ καὶ ποιεῖτε. τὸ γὰρ ἀξιονόμαστον ὑμῶν πρεσβυτέριον, τοῦ θεοῦ ἄξιον, οὕτως συνήρμοσται τῷ ἐπισκόπῳ ὡς χορδαὶ κιθάρᾳ.

5, 6 : μηδεὶς πλανάσθω· ἐὰν μή τις ᾖ ἐντὸς τοῦ θυσιαστηρίου ὑστερεῖται τοῦ ἄρτου [τοῦ θεοῦ]. εἰ γὰρ ἑνὸς καὶ δευτέρου προσευχὴ τοσαύτην ἰσχὺν ἔχει, πόσῳ μᾶλλον ἥ τε τοῦ ἐπισκόπου καὶ πάσης τῆς ἐκκλησίας ... σπουδάσωμεν οὖν μὴ ἀντιτάσσεσθαι τῷ ἐπισκόπῳ, ἵνα ὦμεν θεῷ ὑποτασσόμενοι. Καὶ ὅσον βλέπει τις σιγῶντα ἐπίσκοπον, πλειόνως αὐτὸν φοβείσθω· πάντα γὰρ ὃν πέμπει ὁ οἰκοδεσπότης εἰς ἰδίαν οἰκονομίαν, οὕτως δεῖ ἡμᾶς αὐτὸν δέχεσθαι ὡς αὐτὸν τὸν πέμψαντα· τὸν οὖν ἐπίσκοπον δηλονότι ὡς αὐτὸν τὸν κύριον δεῖ προσβλέπειν.

"Forasmuch then as I was permitted to see you in the person of your godly bishop Damas, and your worthy presbyters Bassus and Apollonius and my fellow-servant the deacon Sotion, of whom I would fain have joy, for that he is subject to the bishop as unto the grace of God and to the presbytery as unto the law of Jesus Christ:—Yea, and it becometh you also not to presume upon the youth of your bishop, but according to the power of God the Father to render unto him all reverence, . . . yet not to him, but to the Father of Jesus Christ, even to the Bishop of all. . . . For a man does not so much deceive this bishop who is seen, as cheat that other who is invisible."

"It is therefore meet that we not only be called Christians, but also be such; even as some persons have the bishop's name on their lips, but in everything act apart from him. Such men appear to me not to keep a good conscience, forasmuch as they do not assemble themselves together lawfully according to commandment."

"Be ye zealous to do all things in godly concord, the bishop presiding after the likeness of God and the presbyters after the likeness of the council of the Apostles, with the deacons also who are most dear to me, having been entrusted with the diaconate of Jesus Christ."

"As the Lord did nothing without the Father,

20: οἱ κατ' ἄνδρα κοινῇ πάντες ἐν χάριτι ἐξ ὀνόματος συνέρχεσθε ἐν μιᾷ πίστει καὶ ἐν Ἰ. Χ. τῷ κατὰ σάρκα ἐκ γένους Δαβίδ, τῷ υἱῷ ἀνθρώπου καὶ υἱῷ θεοῦ, εἰς τὸ ὑπακούειν ὑμᾶς τῷ ἐπισκόπῳ καὶ τῷ πρεσβυτερίῳ ἀπερισπάστῳ διανοίᾳ· ἕνα ἄρτον κλῶντες, ὅ ἐστιν φάρμακον ἀθανασίας, ἀντίδοτος τοῦ μὴ ἀποθανεῖν.

[being united with Him] either by Himself or by the Apostles, so neither do ye anything without the bishop and the presbyters. And attempt not to think anything right for yourselves apart from others; but let there be one prayer in common, etc."

"Do your diligence therefore that ye be confirmed in the ordinances of the Lord and of the Apostles, that ye may prosper in all things whatsoever ye do in flesh and spirit . . . in the Son and Father and in the Spirit, . . . with your revered bishop, and with the fitly wreathed spiritual circlet of your presbytery, and with the deacons who walk after God. Be obedient to the bishop and to one another, as Jesus Christ was to the Father [according to the flesh], and as the Apostles were to Christ and to the Father, that there may be union both of flesh and of spirit."[1]

---

[1] *ad Magn.* 2, 3 : Ἐπεὶ οὖν ἠξιώθην ἰδεῖν ὑμᾶς διὰ Δαμᾶ τοῦ ἀξιοθέου ὑμῶν ἐπισκόπου καὶ πρεσβυτέρων ἀξίων Βάσσου καὶ Ἀπολλωνίου καὶ τοῦ συνδούλου μου διακόνου Ζωτίωνος, οὗ ἐγὼ ὀναίμην, ὅτι ὑποτάσσεται τῷ ἐπισκόπῳ ὡς χάριτι θεοῦ καὶ τῷ πρεσβυτερίῳ ὡς νόμῳ Ἰ. Χ. Καὶ ὑμῖν δὲ πρέπει μὴ συγχρᾶσθαι τῇ ἡλικίᾳ τοῦ ἐπισκόπου, ἀλλὰ κατὰ δύναμιν θεοῦ πατρὸς πᾶσαν ἐντροπὴν αὐτῷ ἀπονέμειν, καθὼς ἔγνων καὶ τοὺς ἁγίους πρεσβυτέρους οὐ προσειληφότας τὴν φαινομένην νεωτερικὴν τάξιν, ἀλλ' ὡς φρονίμῳ ἐν θεῷ συγχωροῦντας αὐτῷ· οὐκ αὐτῷ δὲ, ἀλλὰ τῷ πατρὶ Ἰ. Χ. τῷ πάντων ἐπισκόπῳ. . . . ἐπεὶ οὐχ ὅτι τὸν ἐπίσκοπον τοῦτον τὸν βλεπόμενον πλανᾷ τις, ἀλλὰ τὸν ἀόρατον παραλογίζεται.

4 : Πρέπον οὖν ἐστὶν μὴ μόνον καλεῖσθαι Χριστιανοὺς ἀλλὰ καὶ εἶναι· ὥσπερ καί τινες ἐπίσκοπον μὲν καλοῦσιν, χωρὶς δὲ αὐτοῦ πάντα πράσσουσιν· οἱ τοιοῦτοι δὲ οὐκ εὐσυνείδητοί μοι εἶναι φαίνονται διὰ τὸ μὴ βεβαίως κατ' ἐντολὴν συναθροίζεσθαι.

6 : ἐν ὁμονοίᾳ θεοῦ σπουδάζετε πάντα πράσσειν, προκαθημένου τοῦ ἐπισκόπου εἰς τύπον θεοῦ καὶ τῶν πρεσβυτέρων εἰς τύπον συνεδρίου τῶν ἀποστόλων, καὶ τῶν διακόνων, τῶν ἐμοὶ γλυκυτάτων πεπιστευμένων διακονίαν Ἰ. Χ.

7 : Ὥσπερ οὖν ὁ κύριος ἄνευ τοῦ πατρὸς οὐδὲν ἐποίησεν [ἡνωμένος ὤν] οὔτε δι' ἑαυτοῦ οὔτε διὰ τῶν ἀποστόλων· οὕτως μηδὲ ὑμεῖς ἄνευ τοῦ ἐπισκόπου καὶ τῶν πρεσβυτέρων μηδὲν πράσσετε, μηδὲ πειράσητε εὔλογόν τι φαίνεσθαι ἰδίᾳ ὑμῖν· ἀλλ' ἐπὶ τὸ αὐτὸ μία προσευχὴ κ.τ.λ.

13 : Σπουδάζετε οὖν βεβαιωθῆναι ἐν τοῖς δόγμασιν τοῦ κυρίου καὶ τῶν ἀποστόλων, ἵνα πάντα ὅσα ποιεῖτε κατευοδωθῆτε σαρκὶ καὶ πνεύματι, πίστει καὶ ἀγάπῃ, ἐν υἱῷ καὶ πατρὶ καὶ ἐν πνεύματι, ἐν ἀρχῇ καὶ ἐν τέλει, μετὰ τοῦ ἀξιοπρεπεστάτου ἐπισκόπου ὑμῶν καὶ ἀξιοπλόκου πνευματικοῦ στεφάνου τοῦ πρεσβυτερίου ὑμῶν καὶ τῶν

"When ye are obedient to the bishop as to Jesus Christ, it is evident to me that ye are living not after men but after Jesus Christ.... It is therefore necessary, even as your wont is, that ye should do nothing without the bishop; but be ye obedient also to the presbytery, as to the Apostles... And those likewise who are deacons of the mysteries of Jesus Christ must please all men in all ways. For they are not deacons of meats and drinks but servants of the Church of God. It is right therefore that they should beware of blame as of fire. In like manner let all men respect the deacons as Jesus Christ, even as they should respect the bishop as being a type of the Father and the presbyters as the council of God and as the college of apostles. Apart from these there is not even the name of a Church."

"This will surely be, if ye be not puffed up and if ye be inseparable from [God] Jesus Christ, and from the bishop and from the ordinances of the Apostles. He that is within the sanctuary is clean; but he that is without the sanctuary is not clean, that is, he that doeth aught without the bishop and presbytery and deacons, this man is not clean in his conscience."

"Fare ye well in Jesus Christ, submitting yourselves to the bishop as to the commandment, and likewise also to the presbytery."[1]

κατὰ θεὸν διακόνων. ὑποτάγητε τῷ ἐπισκόπῳ καὶ ἀλλήλοις, ὡς I. X. τῷ πατρὶ [κατὰ σάρκα] καὶ οἱ ἀπόστολοι τῷ X. καὶ τῷ πατρί, ἵνα ἕνωσις ᾖ σαρκική τε καὶ πνευματική.

[1] ad Trall. 2, 3 : "Ὅταν γὰρ τῷ ἐπισκόπῳ ὑποτάσσησθε ὡς 'Ι. X., φαίνεσθέ μοι

"For as many as are of God and of Jesus Christ, they are with the bishop; and as many as shall repent and enter into the unity of the Church, these also shall be of God. ... Be not deceived, my brethren, if any man followeth one that maketh a schism, he doth not inherit the kingdom of God. If any man walketh in strange doctrine, he hath no fellowship with the passion. Be ye careful therefore to observe one Eucharist (for there is one flesh of our Lord Jesus Christ and one cup unto union in His blood; there is one altar, as there is one bishop, together with the presbytery and the deacons my fellow-servants)."[1]

"Shun divisions, as the beginning of evils. Do ye all follow your bishop, as Jesus Christ followed the Father, and the presbytery as the Apostles; and to the deacons pay respect, as to God's commandment.

οὐ κατὰ ἀνθρώπους ζῶντες, ἀλλὰ κατὰ Ι. Χ. . . . ἀναγκαῖον οὖν ἐστίν, ὥσπερ ποιεῖτε, ἄνευ τοῦ ἐπισκόπου μηδὲν πράσσειν ὑμᾶς· ἀλλ' ὑποτάσσεσθε καὶ τῷ πρεσβυτερίῳ, ὡς [τοῖς] ἀποστόλοις Ι. Χ. . . . δεῖ δὲ καὶ τοὺς διακόνους ὄντας μυστηρίων Ι. Χ. κατὰ πάντα τρόπον πᾶσιν ἀρέσκειν· οὐ γὰρ βρωμάτων καὶ ποτῶν εἰσὶν διάκονοι, ἀλλ' ἐκκλησίας θεοῦ ὑπηρέται· δέον οὖν αὐτοὺς φυλάσσεσθαι τὰ ἐγκλήματα ὡς πῦρ. Ὁμοίως πάντες ἐντρεπέσθωσαν τοὺς διακόνους ὡς Ι. Χ. ὡς καὶ τὸν ἐπίσκοπον ὄντα τύπον τοῦ πατρός, τοὺς δὲ πρεσβυτέρους ὡς συνέδριον θεοῦ καὶ ὡς σύνδεσμον ἀποστόλων· χωρὶς τούτων ἐκκλησία οὐ καλεῖται.

7: τοῦτο δὲ ἔσται ὑμῖν μὴ φυσιουμένοις καὶ οὖσιν ἀχωρίστοις [θεοῦ] Ι. Χ. καὶ τοῦ ἐπισκόπου καὶ τῶν διαταγμάτων τῶν ἀποστόλων. ὁ ἐντὸς θυσιαστηρίου ὢν καθαρός ἐστιν, ὁ δὲ ἐκτὸς τοῦ θυσιαστηρίου ὢν οὐ καθαρός ἐστιν· τουτέστιν, ὁ χωρὶς ἐπισκόπου καὶ πρεσβυτερίου καὶ διακόνου πράσσων τι, οὗτος οὐ καθαρός ἐστιν τῇ συνειδήσει.

13: ἔρρωσθε ἐν Ι. Χ., ὑποτασσόμενοι τῷ ἐπισκόπῳ ὡς τῇ ἐντολῇ, ὁμοίως καὶ τῷ πρεσβυτερίῳ.

[1] ad Philad. 3, 4: ὅσοι γὰρ θεοῦ εἰσὶν καὶ Ι. Χ. οὗτοι μετὰ τοῦ ἐπισκόπου εἰσίν· καὶ ὅσοι ἂν μετανοήσαντες ἔλθωσιν ἐπὶ τὴν ἑνότητα τῆς ἐκκλησίας, καὶ οὗτοι θεοῦ ἔσονται . . . μὴ πλανᾶσθε, ἀδελφοί μου· εἴ τις σχίζοντι ἀκολουθεῖ βασιλείαν θεοῦ οὐ κληρονομεῖ· εἴ τις ἐν ἀλλοτρίᾳ γνώμῃ περιπατεῖ, οὗτος τῷ πάθει οὐ συγκατατίθεται. Σπουδάσατε οὖν μιᾷ εὐχαριστίᾳ χρῆσθαι· μία γὰρ σὰρξ τοῦ κυρίου ἡμῶν Ι. Χ., καὶ ἓν ποτήριον εἰς ἕνωσιν τοῦ αἵματος αὐτοῦ· ἓν θυσιαστήριον, ὡς εἷς ἐπίσκοπος, ἅμα τῷ πρεσβυτερίῳ καὶ διακόνοις, τοῖς συνδούλοις μοι.

VI.] *The Ministry in the Subapostolic Age.* 299

Let no man do aught of things pertaining to the Church apart from the bishop. Let that be held a valid Eucharist which is under the bishop or one to whom he shall have committed it. Wheresoever the bishop shall appear, there let the people be; even as where Jesus may be, there is the universal Church. It is not lawful apart from the bishop either to baptize or to hold a love-feast; but whatever he shall approve, this is well-pleasing also to God; that everything which ye do may be sure and valid."

"It is good to recognise God and the bishop. He that honoureth the bishop is honoured of God; he that doeth aught without the knowledge of the bishop rendereth service to the devil."[1]

The following points in Ignatius' teaching about the ministry require to be emphasized:— *The ministry is*

(1) He has an intensely clear perception that the 'mind of God' for man's salvation has expressed itself not in any mere doctrine but in a divinely instituted society with a divinely authorized hierarchy. This is the 'mind of God,' this is 'the commandment,' so clearly that he who would obey the commandment and run in harmony with the divine purpose must perforce have merged his individuality *(1) of divine authority;*

---

[1] *ad Smyrn.* 8: τοὺς δὲ μερισμοὺς φεύγετε, ὡς ἀρχὴν κακῶν. πάντες τῷ ἐπισκόπῳ ἀκολουθεῖτε, ὡς Ἰ. Χ. τῷ πατρί, καὶ τῷ πρεσβυτερίῳ ὡς τοῖς ἀποστόλοις. τοὺς δὲ διακόνους ἐντρέπεσθε, ὡς θεοῦ ἐντολήν. μηδεὶς χωρὶς τοῦ ἐπισκόπου τι πρασσέτω τῶν ἀνηκόντων εἰς τὴν ἐκκλησίαν. ἐκείνη βεβαία εὐχαριστία ἡγείσθω ἡ ὑπὸ τὸν ἐπίσκοπον οὖσα, ἢ ᾧ ἂν αὐτὸς ἐπιτρέψῃ. ὅπου ἂν φανῇ ὁ ἐπίσκοπος, ἐκεῖ τὸ πλῆθος ἔστω· ὥσπερ ὅπου ἂν ᾖ Ἰ. Χ., ἐκεῖ ἡ καθολικὴ ἐκκλησία. οὐκ ἐξόν ἐστιν χωρὶς τοῦ ἐπισκόπου οὔτε βαπτίζειν οὔτε ἀγάπην ποιεῖν· ἀλλ' ὃ ἂν ἐκεῖνος δοκιμάσῃ, τοῦτο καὶ τῷ θεῷ εὐάρεστον, ἵνα ἀσφαλὲς ᾖ καὶ βέβαιον πᾶν ὃ πράσσετε.
9: καλῶς ἔχει θεὸν καὶ ἐπίσκοπον εἰδέναι· ὁ τιμῶν ἐπίσκοπον ὑπὸ θεοῦ τετίμηται· ὁ λάθρα ἐπισκόπου τι πράσσων τῷ διαβόλῳ λατρεύει.

in the fellowship of the Church and submitted his wilfulness to her government.

(2) essentially threefold;

(2) He regards the authoritative hierarchy of the Church as essentially threefold—a ministry of bishops, presbyters, and deacons. It is not merely, as has been suggested, that he exhorts men to be, or to be more decidedly, members of the church organization which happens to have a ministry of bishops, priests, and deacons. He insists polemically that this particular form of ministry is essential to the existence of a Church: "without these three orders" (so Dr. Lightfoot renders his words) "no Church has a title to the name."[1]

(3) undisputed;

(3) Ignatius' testimony presents us with the 'monarchical episcopate' as 'firmly rooted,' 'completely beyond dispute.'[2] We cannot doubt that he bases its authority on *the ordinances of the Apostles*.'[3]

---

[1] *ad Trall.* 3 χωρὶς τούτων ἐκκλησία οὐ καλεῖται, and see Lightfoot *in loc.* Cf. also Zahn *Ignat. von Antioch.* p. 300: "was ohne die Träger des dreifachen Kirchenamtes ist, heisst nicht Kirche." He however goes on: "aber den Gegensatz bildet nicht eine Gemeinde, welche dieser Institute oder eines derselben entbehrt, sondern ein kirchliches Handeln, wie Abendmahlsfeier oder sonstige gottesdienstliche Versammlungen, welches ohne Wissen und Willen, ohne directe oder indirecte Leitung des an der Spitze stehenden Bischofs und der ihm untergeordneten Presbyter und Diaconen vor sich geht." Cf. Lightfoot i. p. 382. It is quite true that Ignatius has no 'presbyterian' form of government in view, but it seems to me beyond fair question that he insists upon episcopacy as the *only* church government, and would have refused to recognise any other.

It must be noticed that Ignatius claims prophetic gifts and as a prophet has received special communications on the subject of church order. He claims (*ad Philad.* 7) to have spoken with the voice of God: "It was the preaching of the Spirit, who spake on this wise; 'do nothing without the bishop; keep your flesh as a temple of God; cherish union; shun divisions; be imitators of Jesus Christ, as He Himself also was of the Father.'"

[2] Harnack *Expositor*, Jan. 1886, p. 16. Lightfoot disposes of the notion that νεωτερικὴ τάξις (*ad Magn.* 3) refers to the episcopate as a 'newly instituted order.'

[3] *ad Trall.* 7: οὖσιν ἀχωρίστοις [θεοῦ] Ἰησοῦ καὶ τοῦ ἐπισκόπου καὶ τῶν διαταγ-

VI.] *The Ministry in the Subapostolic Age.* 301

(4) Besides regarding episcopacy as of the essence of a Church and as of apostolic authority, he speaks of it as co-extensive with the Church, that is, as existing everywhere. He speaks of the bishops as *established in the farthest parts of the earth*.[1] He knows of no nonepiscopal area. This of course is evidence to which it will be necessary to pay attention when we come to consider the state of the western Churches, especially that of Philippi, through which he was to pass, and that of Rome, which he addresses in such high praise as "enlightened through the will of Him who willed all things that are, ... in flesh and in spirit united unto His every commandment."[2]

(4) universal in the Church.

(5) Lastly, it is of great importance to see what answer Ignatius suggests to the question whether the monarchical episcopate came into existence by elevation out of the presbyterate, or whether it inherited functions which had belonged hitherto only to apostles and those who were fellow-workers with apostles or who subsequently had shared their authority. Now all the indications of Ignatius' letters seem

(5) The episcopate represents the 'monarchy' of Christ.

μάτων τῶν ἀποστόλων. "The reference [of the last four words] is doubtless to the institution of episcopacy" (Lightfoot *in loc*). Cf. *ad Trall.* 12, where he orders the Church and presbyters to comfort their bishop to the honour of the Father and of Jesus Christ and of the Apostles. Kühl has no grounds for his attempt to make Ignatius struggle to promote a new ideal; see *Gemeindeord.* pp. 132, 133.

[1] *ad Eph.* 3 οἱ ἐπίσκοποι οἱ κατὰ τὰ πέρατα ὁρισθέντες; cf. *ad Rom.* 6 τὰ πέρατα τοῦ κόσμου. "Ignatius would be contemplating regions as distant as Gaul on the one hand and Mesopotamia on the other" (Lightfoot *in loc*). He ascribes equal catholicity to the Church and to the episcopate.

[2] *ad Rom.* inscr.; see also c. 4, where he specially speaks of the Roman Church as having received commandments from the Apostles Peter and Paul, and cf. Lightfoot i. p. 357.

to assure us that the latter is the true view. That is to say, the presbyters in the Church of Asia, as in the Churches of Palestine and Syria, never had held the office which Ignatius calls episcopal. They had indeed borne the name (which perhaps St. John's authority transferred to those whom he put in chief charge of the Churches[1]) but they had never held the office. The reasons for this view are these.

Ignatius attributes to the bishops an authority *essentially monarchical*. He does not speak of them as succeeding to the Apostles, but he regards them as representing Christ or the Father, while the presbyters, the companions of the bishop, are like the circle of the twelve round their Master.[2] Thus

[1] This transference of the title 'episcopus' need not surprise us. It will be noticed that St. Peter classes himself, though he is an apostle, among the presbyters (1 Peter v. 1; cf. Lightfoot *Dissert.* p. 198 on St. Paul's relation to the presbyterate at Corinth). Thus, when the 'vir apostolicus' like Timothy was put in charge of a Church, he doubtless became a presbyter among presbyters, though he was their ruler, and would have been reckoned with them as holding the ἐπισκοπή. But, where there was a distinction of office and power, a distinction of names was desirable, and it was most natural that the localized representative of apostolic authority, like 'bishops' James and Symeon, should have the title 'episcopus' reserved to him (while the title presbyter remained common to all who sat on the raised bench of church rulers), for it is in itself much more applicable to a single president than to the members of a college. (It is perhaps just worth notice that the term ἐπισκοπή is first used, though with reference to the Psalm, for the apostolic office in Acts i. 20). The titles 'apostle,' 'evangelist,' 'teacher,' 'prophet,' were on the other hand, for different reasons, not suitable to describe the chief pastors of a particular Church. We have a parallel to this transference of a title from a lower to a higher use in the history of the term *imperator*. So it may be noticed that the term χειροτονία passed upward from meaning election—by the members of the Church (*Did.* xv. 1) as well as by the Apostles, (Acts xiv. 23)—to meaning ordination, while the phrases χειρῶν ἐπίθεσις, χεῖρας ἐπιτιθέναι, as represented by χειροθετεῖν, came to have the lower meaning of benediction. Thus *Apost. Const.* viii. 28: ὁ πρεσβύτερος χειροθετεῖ, οὐ χειροτονεῖ.

[2] The comparison of the presbyters to the Apostles is the regular comparison in Ignatius. The comparisons for the bishop and deacons are more variable; see Lightfoot on *ad Trall.* 3. The bishop represents indifferently Christ or the Father: see *ad Magn.* 6, *ad Trall.* 2, 3, (cf. 13), *ad Smyrn.* 8.

each Church with its bishop and presbytery is like a little theocracy, in which the bishop represents the authority of God and is a fresh embodiment of that divine presence which was in the world when Christ moved about with His Apostles round Him. This appears to have been a Jewish way of representing the succession in the Church. We recall how Hegesippus spoke of James as "receiving the Church in succession with the Apostles," implying that he and the Apostles *succeeded to Christ*; so those who were of Christ's family were supposed to represent Him in Palestine as the King of the house of David; so in the Clementines the bishop ordained by Peter is given not only the chair of the Apostle but also 'the chair of Christ,'[1] and this way of conceiving the succession appears later in the *Apostolical Constitutions*.[2] Thus,

There are also vaguer phrases according to which the bishop represents "the grace of God," and the presbyters "the law of Jesus Christ" (*ad Magn.* 2). The deacons in a sense represent Christ as ministering (*ad Magn.* 6, *ad Trall.* 3); cf. Lightfoot i. p. 382.

[1] *Ep. Clem.* 17, *Hom.* iii. 70; and twelve presbyters are instituted, i.e. the number of the Apostles (*Recog.* iii. 66, vi. 15, xi. 36).

[2] *Apost. Const.* ii. 26, 28: "Let the presbyters be esteemed by you to represent us the Apostles; let them be teachers of the knowledge of God, since our Lord also, when He sent us, said: 'Go ye, etc.'" "Let a double portion be set apart for the presbyters as for such as labour continually about the word of the doctrine in honour of the Apostles of our Lord, whose place also they sustain as counsellors of the bishop and the crown of the Church." It will be remembered that in the Maronite office for the ordination of bishops and in a passage of Ephraem Syrus the succession is traced from God on Mount Sinai, through Moses and Aaron, to John the Baptist, and so through Christ, to His Apostles and the bishops. In each generation there have been persons who (more or less) represented God and his authority. This is a somewhat Judaistic way of conceiving the succession. It comes from emphasizing authority rather than grace; Ignatius however cannot in general be accused of any Judaism in his mode of representing Christ's relation to His Church. See esp. *ad Rom.* 3: "For our God Jesus Christ, being in the Father, is the more plainly visible."

It is to be noticed that Dr. Hatch in describing this theocratic conception of the episcopal office says (*B. L.* p. 89): "Upon this theory of ecclesiastical

304   *Christian Ministry.*   [CHAP.

Relation of this to the apostolic succession.

if the presbyters by this comparison represent the Apostles, they represent them as they were *before Christ's ascension*, not after it,—as they were when Christ was among them. After that each one of the Apostles became in his turn a representative of Christ, and that in a sense which gave him an authority far greater than Ignatius would dare to claim for himself or any of his contemporaries.[1] In a sense, then, the Apostles according to Ignatius have no successors; in a sense, again, the presbyters in their relation to the bishop succeed to them in their relation to Christ when He was on earth; but in yet another sense the bishops alone succeed to that office of representing Christ and speaking with the authority of God which had been the special prerogative of the Apostles. Thus, though the bishops are represented by Ignatius as successors not of the Apostles but rather of Christ or God, they are clothed with that monarchical authority, which had belonged to the Apostles (whose representatives they became in relation to each particular church) but never to the presbyters: only the bishops are limited to one church, whereas the former holders of their authority had not been. Once again the office of the bishop in Ignatius is distinguished from the presbyterate, when he speaks of the "youthful rank"

The authority of the episcopate never held by the presbyters.

organization the existence of a president was a necessity; and the theory seems to go back to the very beginnings of the Christian societies." I do not know how this admission is worked in with his general theory of the origin of church organization.

[1] *ad Rom.* 4 : οὐχ ὡς Πέτρος καὶ Παῦλος διατάσσομαι ὑμῖν· ἐκεῖνοι ἀπόστολοι, ἐγὼ κατάκριτος. Cf. *ad Trall.* 3, *ad Philad.* 5. See further, on this idea of succession to Christ, Dr. Liddon in *A Father in Christ* [2nd ed.] p. xxv f.

VI.] *The Ministry in the Subapostolic Age.* 305

of one who held it and bids his flock reverence him none the less, in words which recall St. Paul's exhortation to his apostolic legate to let no man despise his youth.[1] The office of presbyter, we know, was not yet divorced from the qualifications and associations of age.[2] The bishops then in Ignatius succeed to an authority which had been apostolic and had never belonged to the presbyters.[3]

We are now in a position to sum up the results of our investigation as far as concerns the Churches of Palestine, Syria, and Asia. All the indications we have would lead to the belief that the chief authority of government, ministry, and ordination passed from the Apostles and those who ranked with them to the bishops of the period of Ignatius without ever having belonged to the presbyters. James, 'the first bishop,'

Summary of results from Palestine, Syria, Asia.

---

[1] *ad Magn.* 3.

[2] The πρεσβύτεροι are still put in contrast to νεώτεροι or νέοι by Polycarp *ad Phil.* 5, as well as by Clement *ad Cor.* 1. So in the *Church Ordinances* 16, 17. There is no requirement of age for the bishop, but there is for the presbyters, c. 18 ἤδη κεχρονικότας ἐπὶ τῷ κόσμῳ.

[3] Dr. Lightfoot emphasizes the absence of sacerdotalism in Ignatius. See i. p. 381: "There is not throughout these letters the slightest tinge of sacerdotal language in reference to the Christian ministry." I think I have said enough on this subject already. Ignatius' words—*ad Smyrn.* 8: "Let that be held a valid Eucharist which is under the bishop or one to whom he shall have committed it"—are hardly what is commonly called unsacerdotal. There is indeed a striking absence of the false sacerdotalism which identifies church office with spiritual nearness to God, see *ad Smyrn.* 6: τόπος μηδένα φυσιούτω· τὸ γὰρ ὅλον ἐστὶν πίστις καὶ ἀγάπη, ὧν οὐδὲν προκέκριται. A passage (*ad Philad.* 9), in which he contrasts the priests of the old covenant with 'the High-priest' of the new, may suggest a reason for his repudiating sacerdotal terms about the Christian ministry. The term had still associations too Judaic to be admissible. In regard to the unseen Christ there was no danger of mistake, and the recognition of His High-priesthood guaranteed the sacerdotal character of His Church in the general sense. We may notice that he speaks of the bishops, presbyters, and deacons at Philadelphia as appointed in accordance with the mind of Jesus Christ and established by Him with the Holy Spirit in confirmation of their office; see *ad Philad.* inscr.

U

is a man of apostolic rank and authority settled in Jerusalem, and his office devolved upon a line of bishops after him, who were in the Church of Jerusalem what he had been, except so far as his position had depended upon his personal character and relation to our Lord. The *Didache* presents us with a chief ministry in the Church not yet localized, the holders of this Christian 'high-priesthood' being known as 'prophets' and associated with other evangelists known as 'apostles' or 'teachers.' The authority, however, of the survivors of the twelve seems to have promoted a transition to a state of things in which we have a ruler-in-chief localized in each community, like Ignatius in Syria, Polycarp at Smyrna, and the other bishops whom Ignatius' letters present to us. These rulers, though they bear a name transferred from the presbyterate, hold that office of representing the supreme authority of Christ and of the Father, which had belonged to James and his successors at Jerusalem, to prophets and teachers, and to apostolic legates, but never to the presbyters. There was not indeed such a localized ruler in every Church in the age immediately after the destruction of Jerusalem; but there is no reason why we should not believe such a tradition as assigns to St. Peter the foundation of the episcopate at Antioch, i.e. there is no reason against believing that there was from the first a representative of apostolic authority localized at Antioch, or indeed at the other chief centres of Christian life. But, even if this and similar traditions present us with the facts somewhat idealized, as is the habit of tradition, at least they do not misrepresent the facts. It would certainly appear that the episcopal authority at Antioch and elsewhere was derived direct from that of 'apostles and prophets' and had never passed through the presbyterate. It was an authority which represents devolution from above and not delegation from below.

It will not have been forgotten with what strength of conviction the western traditions of the later half of the second century represent the authority of the episcopal successions then existing as derived from the Apostles. It is enough to recall the testimony of Irenaeus, corroborated as it is by that of the earlier Hegesippus, as to the list of bishops of Rome, running back through Clement to Linus who was entrusted with the episcopate by the Apostles Peter and Paul after they had founded the Church, and the assertion of Dionysius of Corinth (writing about A.D. 170) that his namesake the Areopagite had been the first to be entrusted with the episcopate at Athens.[1] The confidence of these immemorial traditions at this early date is at least very impressive. "Episcopacy," Dr. Lightfoot says, "is so inseparably interwoven with all the traditions and beliefs of men like Irenaeus and Tertullian, that they betray no knowledge of a time when it was not.... Their silence [as to any controversy about it] suggests a strong negative presumption, that while every other point of doctrine or practice was eagerly canvassed, the form of church government alone scarcely came under discussion."[2]

The West. Strong tradition in favour of the succession of bishops from the Apostles.

[1] Euseb. *H.E.* iv. 23: πρῶτος τῆς ἐν Ἀθήναις παροικίας τὴν ἐπισκοπὴν ἐγκεχείριστο.

[2] *Dissert.* p. 227. It should be noticed that the views of Ambrosiaster,

308   *Christian Ministry.*   [CHAP.

Historical links:

We have then now to enquire how far this 'confidence of boasting' about the apostolic succession is justified by the indications which history gives us of the development of the ministry in the Churches of Europe between the period of apostolic presidency and the age of Irenaeus and Dionysius.

The historical links are afforded by three documents: the Epistle of Clement to the Corinthians, that of Polycarp to the Philippians, and the *Shepherd* of Hermas.

IV.

IV. Epistle of Clement. The writer.

Clement, who is the real writer of the Epistle which commonly bears his name,[1] though he merges his personality in his Church and writes as Jerome says "ex persona ecclesiae Romanae," is a very different man from the intense, abrupt, fervid Ignatius. But, though he writes in a very different tone, it is with the same general purpose as moved Ignatius—it is to uphold the authority of the church ministry against schismatic aggression. Whatever may have been his origin,[2] Clement is a thorough Roman in his respect for the principle of order, and he insists upon it with a strong yet gentle reasonableness, or (to quote a phrase which occurs twice in his letter) with an "intense moderation."[3]

Jerome, etc. as to the original government of the Churches by equal presbyter-bishops and the subsequent creation of the monarchical episcopate do not seem to rest on tradition, but to be based on philological and exegetical grounds like the views of later scholars.

[1] As Dionysius of Corinth first assures us.
[2] Lightfoot thinks he was a Hellenist Jew.
[3] See Lightfoot *Ignat.* i. p. 2.

VI.] *The Ministry in the Subapostolic Age.* 309

There is not much of theological insistence in Clement's letter, for he has no pressing heresy to combat.¹ His mind's eye is constantly fixed in admiration on the divine order and harmony in things and on the duty which lies upon all men of respecting this principle in the several departments of life. For the order of civil government he has a Roman's veneration, and (though his Church was still passing through the fiery furnace of Domitian's persecution) he realizes with no difficulty at all the duty St. Paul insists upon of praying for kings and all who are in authority and gives the Roman state the full support of his Church's intercessions.² He emphasizes again how the strength of the army depends upon each man knowing, and submissively keeping, his place in the common order.³ In the wider area he loves to think of order as 'heaven's first law,' as the life of the whole of nature and the joy of the angelic hosts.⁴ His mind is akin to Richard Hooker's as he meditated when he lay a-dying "the number and nature of angels and their blessed obedience and order, without which peace could not be in heaven; and oh that it might be so on earth!" Then finally in the kingdom of God's redemptive love there is order also. On this are based the special exhortations to the

¹ The contents of cc. 24-26, however, may indicate a renewed tendency among the Corinthians to disbelief in the resurrection. In his theology Clement shows his true character as a harmonizer—both by holding together the teaching of St. John, St. Paul, and St. James, and by emphasizing the motives which Christian theology suggests, making for self-suppression and peace (see c. 16.).
² cc. 60, 61. See Lightfoot's *Clement of Rome* p. 269. The date of the Epistle is about A.D. 95.
³ c. 37. ⁴ cc. 20, 34, 60.

suppression of selfish ambition and rivalry which Clement's Church addresses under his guidance to the Church at Corinth.¹ For, led by one or two reckless and ambitious young men,² they had rebelled against their legitimate hierarchy, had causelessly deposed some of their presbyters, and (whether or no they had other presbyters taking part in the rebellion) had raised a schism against them and left their obedience. The evil had not been of short standing, but the Roman Church had not hitherto been able to bring pressure to bear upon them owing to the "sudden and successive calamities and disasters" she was passing through under the persecuting rule of Domitian.

<small>Occasion of the letter;</small>

<small>its substance.</small>

The Epistle runs to this effect. The Corinthians are bidden to bear in mind the shame it will be if a reputation such as their Church has borne is allowed to be overthrown by the ambitions of two or three and the foolish party spirit of the rest. They used to be men walking after the ordinances of God, in due submission to their spiritual rulers, holding in abomination all sedition and schism. But now there is a reversal of all this. There is amongst them a renewed outbreak of the old danger of party-spirited adherence to particular leaders,³ against which St. Paul had warned them. But the last evil is worse than the first, for their proclivities are directed now not to apostolic men but to self-interested schismatics.

---

¹ He does not shrink from adducing examples of pagan self-sacrifice in the cause of unity: πολλοὶ ἐξεχώρησαν ἰδίων πόλεων ἵνα μὴ στασιάζωσιν ἐπὶ πλεῖον.

² Their youth seems to follow from the emphasis Clement lays (c. 3.) on the reverence due from youth to age.

³ c. 47 προσκλίσεις.

They should recognise how in Scripture and history, ancient and recent, all evils have come of jealousy or self-interest such as stir party leaders and their followers—even as in their own generation such temper had caused St. Peter and St. Paul to be put to death—while all good, on the other hand, had come of obedience and humility. They should recognise how the divine principle of order prevails in nature, in civil and military government, in the organism of the human body, in the very mission of Christ—a divine principle which upon all men and things makes everywhere the claim of submission and obedience. Above all, this must be recognised in the Church. In the Jerusalem of the old covenant there is a divine law of service—a divine prescription of times and places and persons—and the principle has passed into the new covenant. Here too he that would serve God and offer his worship with acceptableness must submit to requirements of time and place and the appropriation of special functions to special orders. High-priest, priest, Levite, and layman must observe the appointed rule of His service. Specially of old there had been a divinely ordained ministry of Moses' appointment certificated by a special miracle of the budding rod, and the sanction of a miraculous punishment on those who invaded its peculiar privileges.

So too under the Christian covenant the Apostles instituted in the churches they founded a ministry of bishops and deacons, in continuation of their own mission from Christ and in fulfilment of prophecy;

and further, in view of the strife which they foresaw would arise over the episcopal office, they made provision for a succession in this ministry. Now it was men appointed in accordance with this apostolic provision by men of repute in the Church with the consent of the whole body, and who had fulfilled their ministry without reproach—it was such men whom the Corinthians had now deposed from their sacred functions. What a sin was such deposition! What a judgment it must bring on those who are guilty of it!

So seriously and authoritatively does the Roman community bid the Corinthians hear God's will speaking by them, to consider their ways and be wise: and the letter passes into a prayer, the prayer of one who 'lifts up his hands without wrath or doubting' in orderly and harmonious intercession — intercession which seems to represent the form which under Clement's auspices was being given to the 'prayer of the oblation' in the Roman Church.

Passages bearing on the ministry. We proceed to quote the passages which have an immediate bearing on the principle and form of the ministry.

Formerly "ye did all things without respect of persons, and ye walked after the laws of God, submitting to your rulers and rendering to the presbyters among you their appropriate honour;[1] and upon your

---

[1] c. 1: ὑποτασσόμενοι τοῖς ἡγουμένοις ὑμῶν καὶ τιμὴν τὴν καθήκουσαν ἀπονέμοντες τοῖς παρ' ὑμῖν πρεσβυτέροις. Lightfoot translates the last word "the older men," but the word is used of the church officers in cc. 47 and 57, and must be given the same meaning here (see Gebhardt and Harnack *in loc.*). The use of τιμή is almost technical, see *Didache* xv. 2 : αὐτοὶ γάρ [bishops and deacons] εἰσιν οἱ τετιμημένοι ὑμῶν μετὰ τῶν προφητῶν καὶ διδασκάλων, and cf. 1 Tim. v. 17. It is no objection to this that the 'presbyters' are opposed to

VI.] *The Ministry in the Subapostolic Age.* 313

young men ye enjoined a modest and grave state of mind, and your women ye commanded to do all in a blameless and grave and pure conscience."

But now all is changed: "men were stirred up, the mean against the honourable, the ill-reputed against the highly-reputed, the foolish against the wise, the young against the elders"[1] (Is. iii. 5).

"Let us fear the Lord Jesus whose blood was given for us; let us reverence our rulers, let us honour our presbyters, let us instruct our young men in the lesson of the fear of God, let us bring back our women to the standard of good behaviour."[2]

"Let us enlist ourselves with all earnestness in His faultless ordinances. Let us consider those who are enlisted under our rulers,[3] with what order, with what submission, with what subordination they accomplish what is enjoined. All are not prefects, nor rulers of thousands, nor rulers of hundreds, nor rulers of fifties, and so forth, but each one in his own order accomplishes what is enjoined by the king and the rulers. The great cannot exist without the small or the small

---

the 'young men': the same antithesis appears in 1 Peter v. 1-5 and Polyc. *ad Phil.* 5, 6, where there can be no doubt of the reference to office. The word still retained the associations of age: very likely in the earliest Church, where clergy were not debarred from ordinary work, an elder man, where his reputation was satisfactory, commonly became a presbyter in office. Here the antithesis of elder and younger is partly due to the fact that the rebels seem to have been young men. Hermas exactly in the same way (as will be noticed) distinguishes προηγούμενοι from πρωτοκαθεδρῖται(=πρεσβύτεροι). This is, I think, enough to remove any doubt that may be felt as to Clement's language, which again recurs in c. 21.

[1] τοὺς πρεσβυτέρους, but the reference is to Isaiah.

[2] c. 21: τοὺς προηγουμένους ἡμῶν αἰδεσθῶμεν, τοὺς πρεσβυτέρους τιμήσωμεν (Lightfoot again "elders"). Here again 'rulers' are specified besides 'presbyters' as the authorities in the Church.

[3] τοῖς ἡγουμένοις ἡμῶν, i.e. our secular rulers.

without the great; there is a certain mixture in all things and therein is utility. Let us take our body as an instance. The head is nothing without the feet, etc. . . . All parts conspire and accept one obedience for the preservation of the whole body. Therefore let our whole body be preserved in Christ Jesus, and let each man submit to his neighbour, even as he was appointed in the special grace given him."[1]

"All this then being manifest to us, even as we have gazed into the depths of the divine knowledge, we ought to do all that the Lord commanded to be performed in order, at appointed times. The offerings and ministrations he commanded to be performed, and not at random or without order, but at definite times and hours. Where and by whom He wills that they should be performed, He Himself ordained by His supreme choice, so that all being done holily in well-pleasing might be acceptable to His will. Those then who accomplish their offerings at the appointed times are acceptable and blessed, for following the laws of the Master they fall into no sin. For to the high-priest his own proper ministrations have been assigned, and to the priests their proper place ordained, and their proper ministries enjoined upon the Levites; the layman has been bound by the layman's ordinances.[2] Let each of us, brethren, in his own order

---

[1] cc. 37, 38. The last words are καθὼς καὶ ἐτέθη ἐν τῷ χαρίσματι αὐτοῦ.

[2] c. 40: Προδήλων οὖν ἡμῖν ὄντων τούτων, καὶ ἐγκεκυφότες εἰς τὰ βάθη τῆς θείας γνώσεως, πάντα τάξει ποιεῖν ὀφείλομεν ὅσα ὁ δεσπότης ἐπιτελεῖν ἐκέλευσεν κατὰ καιροὺς τεταγμένους· τάς τε προσφορὰς καὶ λειτουργίας ἐπιτελεῖσθαι, καὶ οὐκ εἰκῇ ἢ ἀτάκτως ἐκέλευσεν γίνεσθαι, ἀλλ' ὡρισμένοις καιροῖς καὶ ὥραις· ποῦ τε καὶ διὰ τίνων ἐπιτελεῖσθαι θέλει, αὐτὸς ὥρισεν τῇ ὑπερτάτῳ αὐτοῦ βουλήσει, ἵν' ὁσίως πάντα γινόμενα ἐν εὐδοκήσει εὐπρόσδεκτα εἴη τῷ θελήματι αὐτοῦ. οἱ οὖν τοῖς προστεταγ-

make his Eucharist to God in gravity, abiding in a good conscience, not transgressing the appointed rule of his ministration. Not everywhere, brethren, are offered the daily sacrifices or freewill-offerings or sin- and trespass-offerings, but in Jerusalem alone; and there is offering made not in every place but before the holy place at the altar, after the offering has been inspected by the high-priest and the aforesaid ministers. They then who do anything contrary to what His will has thought fitting have death for their penalty. See, brethren, in as much as we have been thought worthy of more knowledge, to so much greater a peril are we subject.[1]

μένοις καιροῖς ποιοῦντες τὰς προσφορὰς αὐτῶν εὐπρόσδεκτοί τε καὶ μακάριοι· τοῖς γὰρ νομίμοις τοῦ δεσπότου ἀκολουθοῦντες οὐ διαμαρτάνουσιν. τῷ γὰρ ἀρχιερεῖ ἴδιαι λειτουργίαι δεδομέναι εἰσὶν καὶ τοῖς ἱερεῦσιν ἴδιος ὁ τόπος προστέτακται καὶ Λευίταις ἴδιαι διακονίαι ἐπίκεινται· ὁ λαϊκὸς ἄνθρωπος τοῖς λαϊκοῖς προστάγμασιν δέδεται.

It will be apparent, as this and the following chapters are read, that the Church of the new covenant is spoken of under terms of the old, so instinctively alive is Clement to the continuity of principle between the two. "Non negare possum," says Lipsius, "v.t. hierarchiam quae vocatur, hoc loco ad Christianorum societatem accommodari." As the layman is the Christian layman, it is natural to suppose that there was a threefold ministry corresponding to the high-priest, priest, and Levite, but it must be observed that an analogy is claimed in respect of place and time, as well as of ministers, and, as it cannot be pressed in the former case, so also it cannot in the latter. But the language is certainly more natural if Clement had in view a threefold Christian ministry.

[1] c. 41: Ἕκαστος ἡμῶν, ἀδελφοί, ἐν τῷ ἰδίῳ τάγματι εὐχαριστείτω θεῷ ἐν ἀγαθῇ συνειδήσει ὑπάρχων, μὴ παρεκβαίνων τὸν ὡρισμένον τῆς λειτουργίας αὐτοῦ κανόνα, ἐν σεμνότητι. οὐ πανταχοῦ, ἀδελφοί, προσφέρονται θυσίαι ἐνδελεχισμοῦ ἢ εὐχῶν ἢ περὶ ἁμαρτίας καὶ πλημμελείας, ἀλλ' ἢ ἐν Ἱερουσαλὴμ μόνῃ· κἀκεῖ δὲ οὐκ ἐν παντὶ τόπῳ προσφέρεται, ἀλλ' ἔμπροσθεν τοῦ ναοῦ πρὸς τὸ θυσιαστήριον, μωμοσκοπηθὲν τὸ προσφερόμενον διὰ τοῦ ἀρχιερέως καὶ τῶν προειρημένων λειτουργῶν· οἱ οὖν παρὰ τὸ καθῆκον τῆς βουλήσεως αὐτοῦ ποιοῦντές τι, θάνατον τὸ πρόστιμον ἔχουσιν. ὁρᾶτε, ἀδελφοί· ὅσῳ πλείονος κατηξιώθημεν γνώσεως, τοσούτῳ μᾶλλον ὑποκείμεθα κινδύνῳ.

I have translated εὐχαριστείτω 'make his Eucharist.' Clement uses the word in a general sense for 'to give thanks' in c. 38. But here he is describing that formal act of thanksgiving in which the whole Church approaches in due order before God, and that is the Eucharist in the technical sense. The verb has its technical meaning in the *Didache* (ix. 1, x. 1, 7,

The Apostles were sent to us with the Gospel from the Lord Jesus Christ, Jesus the Christ was sent forth from God. Christ then is from God and the Apostles from Christ; it took place in both cases in due order by the will of God. They then having received commandments, and having been fully assured through the resurrection of the Lord Jesus Christ and confirmed in the word of God, with full assurance of the Holy Spirit went forth preaching the Gospel that the kingdom of God was about to come. Preaching then in country and town they appointed their firstfruits, when they had tested them in the Spirit, for bishops and deacons of those who were about to become believers. And this was no new thing, for of old it had been written about bishops and deacons. For thus says the Scripture: 'I will appoint their bishops in righteousness and their deacons in faith' (Is. lx. 17).[1] And what wonder is it if those who were entrusted in Christ from God with so great a work appointed these aforesaid officers? Since even the blessed Moses, the 'faith-

xiv. 1) in close connection with its general meaning (ix. 2, x. 2) and the substantive εὐχαριστία also occurs (ix. 1) in its technical sense. It appears however that the author of the *Church Ordinances* read εὐαρεστείτω, and this is the reading of the Constantinople MS and of the Syriac version. Thus Harnack prefers it (*Texte u. Untersuch.* band ii. heft 5, p. 27). On the other hand the alteration of εὐχαριστείτω into εὐαρεστείτω is more probable than *vice versa*, and Lightfoot retains εὐχαριστείτω as "doubtless the right reading."

[1] c. 42 : Οἱ ἀπόστολοι ἡμῶν εὐηγγελίσθησαν ἀπὸ τοῦ κυρίου Ἰησοῦ Χριστοῦ, Ἰ. ὁ Χ. ἀπὸ τοῦ θεοῦ ἐξεπέμφθη. ὁ Χριστὸς οὖν ἀπὸ τοῦ θεοῦ, καὶ οἱ ἀπόστολοι ἀπὸ τοῦ Χριστοῦ· ἐγένοντο οὖν ἀμφότερα εὐτάκτως ἐκ θελήματος θεοῦ. παραγγελίας οὖν λαβόντες καὶ πληροφορηθέντες διὰ τῆς ἀναστάσεως τοῦ κ. Ἰ. Χ. καὶ πιστωθέντες ἐν τῷ λόγῳ τοῦ θεοῦ, μετὰ πληροφορίας πνεύματος ἐξῆλθον εὐαγγελιζόμενοι τὴν βασιλείαν τοῦ θεοῦ μέλλειν ἔρχεσθαι. κατὰ χώρας οὖν καὶ πόλεις κηρύσσοντες καθίστανον τὰς ἀπαρχὰς αὐτῶν, δοκιμάσαντες τῷ πνεύματι, εἰς ἐπισκόπους καὶ διακόνους τῶν μελλόντων πιστεύειν. καὶ τοῦτο οὐ καινῶς κ.τ.λ.

ful servant in all the house,' indicated all that was enjoined upon him in the sacred books." Here follows a description of Moses' conduct (Numb. xvii) when "envy arose as to the priesthood and the tribes made revolt because they were ambitious of that glorious title." Moses knew beforehand, he says, that Aaron's rod would bud. But he acted as he did to prevent disorder in Israel, and for God's glory.[1] So in the same way, he continues: "Our Apostles also knew through our Lord Jesus Christ that there would be contention about the title of the episcopate. Therefore on this account, having received perfect fore-knowledge, they appointed the aforesaid [bishops and deacons], and subsequently gave an additional injunction [? or 'established a supervision'] in order that, if they fell asleep, other approved men might succeed to their ministry. They, then, who were appointed by those [Apostles] or subsequently by other distinguished men with the consent of the whole Church, and who have exercised their ministry blamelessly to the flock of Christ with humility, quietly and without display, and have had good witness borne them by all again and again, these we do not think to be justly cast out of their ministry. For it will be no small sin to us if we cast out of the episcopate those who have blamelessly and holily offered the oblations. Blessed are those presbyters

---

[1] c. 43: ζήλου ἐμπεσόντος περὶ τῆς ἱερωσύνης καὶ στασιαζουσῶν τῶν φυλῶν ὁποία αὐτῶν εἴη τῷ ἐνδόξῳ ὀνόματι κεκοσμημένη κ.τ.λ. Moses is afterwards said to lay the rods ἐπὶ τὴν τράπεζαν τοῦ θεοῦ, and then to explain that the rod of whichever tribe should bud, ταύτην ἐκλέλεκται ὁ θεὸς εἰς τὸ ἱερατεύειν καὶ λειτουργεῖν αὐτῷ. But Moses foreknew (προῄδει) the result.

who passed on their journey before, for they made their departure with good fruit and completeness; for they have no cause for fear lest any one remove them from their determined place. For we perceive that you have removed some, though their conversation was honourable, out of the ministry which had been observed by them without reproach."[1]

[1] c. 44: Καὶ οἱ ἀπόστολοι ἡμῶν ἔγνωσαν διὰ τοῦ κυρίου ἡμῶν Ἰ. Χ. ὅτι ἔρις ἔσται ἐπὶ τοῦ ὀνόματος τῆς ἐπισκοπῆς. διὰ ταύτην οὖν τὴν αἰτίαν πρόγνωσιν εἰληφότες τελείαν κατέστησαν τοὺς προειρημένους, καὶ μεταξὺ ἐπινομὴν ἔδωκαν ὅπως, ἐὰν κοιμηθῶσιν, διαδέξωνται ἕτεροι δεδοκιμασμένοι ἄνδρες τὴν λειτουργίαν αὐτῶν. τοὺς οὖν κατασταθέντας ὑπ' ἐκείνων ἢ μεταξὺ ὑφ' ἑτέρων ἐλλογίμων ἀνδρῶν συνευδοκησάσης τῆς ἐκκλησίας πάσης, καὶ λειτουργήσαντας ἀμέμπτως τῷ ποιμνίῳ τοῦ Χ. μετὰ ταπεινοφροσύνης, ἡσυχῶς καὶ ἀβαναύσως, μεμαρτυρημένους τε πολλοῖς χρόνοις ὑπὸ πάντων, τούτους οὐ δικαίως νομίζομεν ἀποβάλλεσθαι τῆς λειτουργίας. ἁμαρτία γὰρ οὐ μικρὰ ἡμῖν ἔσται ἐὰν τοὺς ἀμέμπτως καὶ ὁσίως προσενεγκόντας τὰ δῶρα τῆς ἐπισκοπῆς ἀποβάλωμεν. μακάριοι οἱ προοδοιπορήσαντες πρεσβύτεροι, οἵτινες ἔγκαρπον καὶ τελείαν ἔσχον τὴν ἀνάλυσιν· οὐ γὰρ εὐλαβοῦνται μή τις αὐτοὺς μεταστήσῃ ἀπὸ τοῦ ἰδρυμένου αὐτοῖς τόπου. ὁρῶμεν γὰρ ὅτι ἐνίους ὑμεῖς μετηγάγετε καλῶς πολιτευσαμένους ἐκ τῆς ἀμέμπτως αὐτοῖς τετιμημένης λειτουργίας.

(a) The meaning of ἐπινομὴν ἔδωκαν, if the reading is right, is very uncertain. (It is the reading of A, while C reads ἐπιδομήν and the Syr. supports ἐπὶ δοκιμῇ.) Undoubtedly the first thing is to fix as far as we can the general sense of the context. I venture to think then that τὴν λειτουργίαν αὐτῶν refers certainly to the ministry of the bishops (and deacons): throughout the chapter λειτουργία, λειτουργεῖν are used for their office. If this is settled it matters less to whom ἐὰν κοιμηθῶσιν refers, but I think as the sentence is carelessly constructed that it probably refers to the Apostles. See Liddon's *Father in Christ* pp. 33, 34. The Apostles then made some arrangement to secure a succession to the office of the presbyter-bishops, if they (the Apostles) had passed away and were therefore no longer able to appoint new ones. The result of this precaution had been that, in the interval since the appointment of the first presbyters by the Apostles, other presbyters had been duly appointed by certain "distinguished men" in the Church. It seems to me certain that these ἐλλόγιμοι ἄνδρες, who in accordance with the apostolic arrangement had since their death appointed "approved men," are not the same as the "approved men," but different. The apostolic arrangement must have consisted in providing that there should be after their death this body of "distinguished men" in the Church to appoint presbyters and deacons. See Kühl *Gemeindeordnung* p. 135-8. May not ἐπινομὴν ἔδωκαν mean 'they instituted a jurisdiction' or 'supervision'? Cf. the schol. on Pindar *Pyth.* xi. 7 (quoted in Stephanus *Thesaurus Ling. Graec.* s.v. ἐπίνομος) ἐπίνομον τὸν σύννομον ταῖς Θήβαις τὸν ἐπὶ τοῦ αὐτοῦ νομοῦ καὶ τῆς αὐτῆς ἐπινομῆς. Otherwise ἐπινομή is used (1) very frequently by Galen *de Fasciis* to mean the revolutions or additional applications of a bandage. He describes first

VI.]   *The Ministry in the Subapostolic Age.*   319

"It is shameful, dearly beloved, yes utterly shameful and unworthy of the life in Christ, that it should be reported that the very steadfast and ancient Church of the Corinthians, for the sake of one or two persons, is making sedition against its presbyters."[1]

"Who therefore [with reference to Moses' conduct, Exod. xxxii. 30 f.] is noble among you? Who is compassionate? Who is fulfilled with love? Let him say: 'If by reason of me there be faction and strife and schisms, I retire, I depart, whither ye will, and I do that which is ordered by the people: only let the flock of Christ be at peace with its duly-appointed presbyters.'"[2]

the original direction in which it is to be applied (ἐπινέμησις), and then directs that it should be rolled on in the same direction—αἱ δὲ ἐπινομαὶ κατὰ τῶν αὐτῶν. See Kühn *Medici Graeci* vol. xviii. pp. 787. 16, 791. 11, 792. 1, 793. 11, 795. 1, 12, etc. (2) by Plutarch for the advance of a fire, 'depastio ignis.' Whether or no ἐπινομή can mean jurisdiction or supervision—and one may wish it were permissible to substitute ἐπιτροπήν (= tutelam dederunt)—it does seem to me that the meaning of the apostolic arrangement is made manifest by its result, namely, that there had existed since the Apostles a body of 'distinguished men' to appoint to the local church offices, with the consent of the whole Church.

(b) οὐ δικαίως νομίζομεν ἀποβάλλεσθαι κ.τ.λ.   St. Clement uses somewhat minimizing language of the highest goods and the worst evils, cf. c. 19, where he speaks of the character of the saints having "improved us." In this moderation of tone he contrasts with Ignatius.

(c) προσφέρειν τὰ δῶρα. Cf. *Apost. Const.* viii. 12 : οἱ διάκονοι προσαγέτωσαν τὰ δῶρα τῷ ἐπισκόπῳ. Knowing as we do that Irenaeus and Justin Martyr alike regarded the 'sacrifice' of the Eucharist as centering round the oblations of the bread and wine, and having in view the fact that Clement is here speaking of the Church's 'liturgy' as the spiritual counterpart of the sacrificial 'liturgy' of the old covenant, it seems to me impossible to doubt that the words δῶρα προσφέρειν here refer to the offering of the eucharistic gifts. Cf. Harnack *Texte u. Untersuch.* band ii, heft 5, p. 144, note 73: "Beyond a doubt the προσφέρειν δῶρα τῷ θεῷ, in the sense of offering sacrifices (Opferdarbringung), appears as the most important function of the episcopus."

(d) For τοῦ ἱδρυμένου αὐτοῖς τόπου cf. c. 40 τοῖς ἱερεῦσιν ἴδιος ὁ τόπος.

[1] c. 47.
[2] c. 54 μετὰ τῶν καθεσταμένων πρεσβυτέρων.

"Ye therefore that laid the foundation of the sedition, submit yourselves unto the presbyters and receive chastisement unto repentance, bending the knees of your heart."[1]

"It is right for us to give heed to so great and so many examples and to submit the neck and, occupying the place of obedience, to take our side with them that are the leaders of our souls."[2]

Results:

It remains for us to sum up the evidence of Clement's Epistle so far as it affects the ministry.

(1) The ministry has (a) authority in government;

(1) St. Clement speaks of the ministry in the Church from two points of view. It represents the authority of government, and so claims obedience;

(b) a distinct function in the 'liturgy.'

but it also has its special function in relation to worship. The 'liturgy' of the Christian Church is the perpetuation in principle of the 'liturgy' of the Jews, and, like the Church of the old covenant, she approaches God as one body, differentiated in function, with grades of privilege and dignity, by the appointment of God.[3] Thus it is the special function of the bishops to "offer the gifts." It is often said that Clement regards the distinction of offices in the Church as only matter of 'order,' not of exclusive power. He does however speak of each member of the Church as qualified for his special function by a special

---

[1] c. 57.

[2] c. 63: τὸν τῆς ὑπακοῆς τόπον ἀναπληρώσαντας, προσκλιθῆναι τοῖς ὑπάρχουσιν ἀρχηγοῖς τῶν ψυχῶν ἡμῶν. For τόπος see cc. 40, 44, and Lightfoot *in loc*. The layman too has his τόπος (c. 40 and cf. 1 Cor. xiv. 16).

[3] It corresponds to the high value which Clement clearly sets upon the Church's worship that he should give us, as apparently he does, the eucharistic intercession, with which he was accustomed to lead the worship of his Church (cc. 59-61). His language seems in parts to have influenced the Liturgy of St. Mark; see Lightfoot *Clement* pp. 269, 289.

VI.] *The Ministry in the Subapostolic Age.* 321

charisma;[1] and, though he speaks of mutual subordination as the principle of 'utility,' yet he illustrates it not only by the distinction of grades in the Roman army, but by the differentiation of limbs in the human body, and by the divinely-ordained hierarchy of the Jewish Church. There is no reason whatever to believe that the 'charisma' of any 'member of the body' who was not a presbyter-bishop would have qualified him to offer the gifts.

(2) Clement expresses very plainly the fundamental principle of the apostolic succession. The Church's officers are appointed from above. The body of the Church indeed has the privilege of assent or dissent in their appointment,[2] and Clement may be held to imply that under circumstances of misconduct it could legitimately depose them,[3] but he clearly never conceives that it could appoint them. The ministers of the Church must derive their authority from that one mission by which Christ came forth from God and the Apostles from Christ: in virtue of which these same Apostles appointed bishops and deacons in the Churches which they first founded, and afterwards took measures to secure the perpetuation of their office in due *succession.* Clement then gives us the two principles which involve the whole doctrine of the apostolic succession: the principle

(2) It is derived by succession from the Apostles.

[1] c. 38: καθὼς καὶ ἐτέθη ἐν τῷ χαρίσματι αὐτοῦ.
[2] c. 44.
[3] This is probably implied in the rebuke for having deposed blameless presbyters (c. 44); cf. also 54: ποιῶ τὰ προστασσόμενα ὑπὸ τοῦ πλήθους, though here the supposed speaker is not necessarily a presbyter. But it would probably be the case that the Church could depose the presbyters only by an appeal to a higher authority, cf. 1 Tim. v. 19, 20.

X

that the Church is a differentiated body in which different individuals exercise different and clearly defined functions, and the principle that power to exercise these functions, so far as they are ministerial, is derived by succession from the Apostles.

<small>(3) There is an order superior to presbyters;</small>

(3) It is generally supposed[1] that in Clement's Epistle we have only two orders of ministers, viz. presbyter-bishops and deacons, recognised in the Church. But this supposition—though there need be no objection to it on the ground of principle—does not seem to account for all the phenomena which the Epistle presents. It is quite true that presbyters are also called bishops, and that there is no local authority in the Church at Corinth above the presbyters. Clement's language about submission to them postulates this. It may also be acknowledged that it is an unwarrantable hypothesis that the see of the chief pastor was vacant when Clement wrote. But it does not therefore follow that there is not in this Epistle, as in the *Didache*, the recognition of a superior authority though it has yet no localized representation in the particular Church addressed. On the contrary Clement's language seems to suggest and even to require some such supposition. Besides the presbyters whom the Corinthians are to 'honour,' there is mention *on two occasions*[2] of their rulers whom they are to reverence and obey. This repeated mention of 'rulers' as distinct from 'presbyters,' more particu-

---

[1] As by Dr. Lightfoot *Dissert.* pp. 216, 218; and Dr. Langen *Gesch. der röm. Kirche* i. p. 82.

[2] cc. 1, 21. Hermas makes a similar distinction (*Vis.* iii. 9). See Hilgenfeld in *Zeitschr. für wiss. Theol.*, 1886, p. 23.

larly as we find the same distinction in the *Shepherd* of Hermas, cannot be overlooked; and the title 'ruler' is already familiar to us as applied to men of the highest order in the Church, like the prophets Judas and Silas, and those who first brought the Gospel to 'the Hebrews,' and the members of the royal family of Christ who 'ruled' in the Churches of Palestine.[1] Again there have been certain 'distinguished men,' who in accordance with the arrangement made by the Apostles have, since their death, appointed the presbyters. It appears then that Clement does recognise a body of men who at least appointed the presbyters at Corinth, and whom it is natural to identify with the 'rulers' mentioned elsewhere. 'Rulers' is a general term and we cannot tell what further official title they had, if any, but we must recollect that there is the same absence of a definite official title for the 'men of distinction' like Timothy and Titus, who probably filled exactly the same position during the lifetime of the Apostles. It is quite natural that they should have been known sufficiently well as individuals and as depositaries of apostolic authority to make an exact title a matter of indifference. Definite terminology is in the region of administration as of theology a gradual growth. It is enough that we

---

[1] Acts xv. 22; Euseb. *H.E.* iii. 32 προηγοῦνται πάσης ἐκκλησίας; Heb. xiii. 7. Here the ἡγούμενοι are those apostolic preachers who have passed away; but in ver. 17 the present authorities amongst the Hebrews, "who watch for their souls as men who shall give account," and whom they are to greet (ver. 24), are also called ἡγούμενοι. These would more naturally be local 'presbyters' but not necessarily, more especially as the Epistle is not written to any one community: see on these 'rulers' Harnack *Texte u. Untersuch* band ii, heft 1. pp. 95, 96. Later the expression is generally used for bishops (Euseb. *H.E.* iii. 36; *Apost Const.* ii. 46) but not always.

should recognise that certain men in the Church were understood to have the apostolic authority to ordain elders and presumably the powers of control which always accompanied that authority. This is the same class of men who in the *Didache* are known as 'prophets' or 'teachers,' and whose authority, under St. John's last arrangements, passed to the local presidents who were known as 'bishops.' They may have been already localized in other Churches of Greece, only (as it appears) there was not one on the spot at Corinth, though before the time of Hegesippus a regular succession of diocesan bishops was existing there as elsewhere. The fact that no one of this order was yet resident in Corinth may account for Clement's authoritative appeal to that Church.[1]

(4) which Clement represented in Rome.

(4) For, though Clement cannot have been *called* a 'bishop' in the later sense, his position in the earliest tradition is so prominent that he must in fact have been what would have been designated in later times by that name.[2] He merges his own authority, as

[1] It becomes natural then, as the prophet is called the Christian high-priest in the *Didache*, to see in Clement's analogical use of 'high-priest, priest, and Levite,' in speaking of the Christian ministry, a reference to the three orders, of whom the second and third are presbyter-bishops and deacons, but of whom the highest are these 'rulers' and 'distinguished men,' who correspond to the prophets of the *Didache*.

I do not wish to imply that the term ἐλλόγιμος ἀνήρ was at all a title reserved for these apostolic men. Clement uses it quite generally of the Corinthian Church (c. 62): ἀνδράσι πιστοῖς καὶ ἐλλογιμωτάτοις καὶ ἐγκεκυφόσιν κ.τ.λ. So he uses ἡγούμενοι also of secular rulers (c. 37, 61).

[2] The evidence of the Clementines is enough to show us that Clement's personality made a great impression on his own generation and those that succeeded, and it was as a church ruler and bishop that he impressed himself on the memory. It is Clement in the *Shepherd* who is to communicate the messages given to Hermas to the Churches of the other cities (εἰς τὰς ἔξω πόλεις, ἐκείνῳ γὰρ ἐπιτέτραπται). He appears in the third place in the succession of Roman bishops given by Irenaeus, and he doubtless held this place in

VI.] *The Ministry in the Subapostolic Age.* 325

he writes, in the Church which he represents but in the Church[1] not in the presbyterate, and the letter therefore affords no evidence at all as to Clement's relation to the other church officers. Thus, if we could get behind the scenes, we should probably find that the chief authority really belonged to him, and that he was one of those 'men of reputation,' one of those 'rulers,' who since the Apostles' death had exercised that part of their ministry which was to become permanent in the Church. One of this order must, we should suppose, always have existed in so eminent a Church as Rome. If not in name, we may well believe there was there in fact an episcopal succession from the first.

the 'succession' which Hegesippus drew up. It does not seem to me that the absence of specific mention of the bishop in Ignatius' letter to the Church of Rome is any evidence at all against there having been one. See Lightfoot *Ignat.* i. p. 381, also *Dissert.* p. 221, where he remarks: "the reason for supposing Clement to have been a bishop is as strong as the universal tradition of the next ages can make it." Clement cannot have been called a 'bishop' in the later sense of the term, because in his epistle he clearly calls the presbyters bishops, and this must reflect the usage of the Roman church. Perhaps, as suggested above, the distinction of men like him, who bore some measure of the apostolic authority, may have made a fixed title not yet indispensable. Clement of Alexandria (*Strom.* iv. 17. 105) quotes him as the "apostle Clement"; see Lightfoot *Clement* p. 12. His eucharistic prayer, as well as the teaching authority which breathes in his epistle, and which is probably his own, suggests the prerogative freedom of teaching and Eucharist which is assigned to the prophets in the *Didache* (x. 7, xi, xii).

[1] Dr. Salmon, *Introd.* p. 565 n., calls attention to the fact "how all through the first two centuries the importance of the bishop of Rome is merged in the importance of his Church;" for instance, how Dionysius of Corinth writes to the *Church* of Rome (Euseb. *H. E.* iv. 23), and how "when Victor attempted to enforce uniformity of Easter observance, it was still in the name of his Church that he wrote. . . . This is evidenced by the plural ἠξιώσατε in the reply of Polycrates" (Euseb. v. 24).

V.

V. The Epistle of Polycarp.

Its occasion.

The letter of Polycarp to the Philippians was written under the following circumstances. Ignatius, in company with others of the 'noble army of martyrs' bound with the 'sacred fetters,' had passed from Troas to Philippi on his way to Rome. There he had held intercourse with the Philippian Christians, and had bidden them, as he had bidden the other Churches, send a letter to the bereaved Church of Antioch. It was too far for them however to send a messenger; so they wrote to Polycarp of Smyrna to request that his messenger might take their letter, and to request him further to let them have any of Ignatius' letters—whether to his own Church or to others—that he might have in his possession. It was in assent to this request that Polycarp wrote the letter which has been preserved to us.

It implies absence of a bishop at Philippi;

This Epistle is remarkable for its exhibition of the saint's character, but remarkable also because of the light it throws on the constitution of the Church of Philippi. Polycarp writes no doubt as a bishop—"Polycarp and the presbyters with him"[1] —but he speaks of no bishop at Philippi, only of elders and deacons, and bids the Philippians obey "the elders and deacons as God and Christ," as if there

---

[1] Dr. Hatch (*B.L.* p. 88 n.⁵) denies that Polycarp is here distinguishing himself from his presbyters, but whatever the ambiguities of the phrase, it is cleared up by the letters of Ignatius to Polycarp and to the Church of Smyrna. Polycarp was admittedly bishop of Smyrna. He writes moreover in the first person.

was no higher officer in question there. The elders moreover are exhorted in terms which imply that the exercise of discipline and the administration of alms belongs to them.[1] It is of course possible that amongst the presbyters may have been one who was their president and was known as 'bishop,' but Polycarp's language does not suggest it,[2] nor is it a very reasonable hypothesis that the see was vacant.[3] Are we then to conclude that the only church authorities recognised at Philippi were the presbyters and the deacons? There is one consideration which seems to

---

[1] The following passages are here referred to: c. 5: Εἰδότες οὖν, ὅτι θεὸς οὐ μυκτηρίζεται ὀφείλομεν ἀξίως τῆς ἐντολῆς αὐτοῦ καὶ δόξης περιπατεῖν. ὁμοίως διάκονοι ἄμεμπτοι κατενώπιον αὐτοῦ τῆς δικαιοσύνης, ὡς θεοῦ καὶ Χριστοῦ διάκονοι καὶ οὐκ ἀνθρώπων· μὴ διάβολοι, μὴ δίλογοι, ἀφιλάργυροι, ἐγκρατεῖς περὶ πάντα, εὔσπλαγχνοι κατὰ τὴν ἀλήθειαν τοῦ κυρίου, ὃς ἐγένετο διάκονος πάντων. Here follow some admonitions to young men to be blameless and pure, self-controlled in their lives, keeping free from sensual sin; then he continues: διὸ δέον ἀπέχεσθαι ἀπὸ πάντων τούτων, ὑποτασσομένους τοῖς πρεσβυτέροις καὶ διακόνοις ὡς θεῷ καὶ Χριστῷ· τὰς παρθένους ἐν ἀμώμῳ καὶ ἁγνῇ συνειδήσει περιπατεῖν.

c. 6: Καὶ οἱ πρεσβύτεροι δὲ εὔσπλαγχνοι, εἰς πάντας ἐλεήμονες, ἐπιστρέφοντες τὰ ἀποπεπλανημένα, ἐπισκεπτόμενοι πάντας ἀσθενεῖς, μὴ ἀμελοῦντες χήρας ἢ ὀρφανοῦ ἢ πένητος· ἀλλὰ προνοοῦντες ἀεὶ τοῦ καλοῦ ἐνώπιον θεοῦ καὶ ἀνθρώπων, ἀπεχόμενοι πάσης ὀργῆς, προσωποληψίας, κρίσεως ἀδίκου, μακρὰν ὄντες πάσης φιλαργυρίας, μὴ ταχέως πιστεύοντες κατά τινος, μὴ ἀπότομοι ἐν κρίσει κ.τ.λ. Later on it is noticeable that the prophets who are mentioned after the Apostles are the Old Testament prophets who foretold Christ.

c. 9. They are exhorted "to obey the word of righteousness and to practise all patience," after the example of the blessed Ignatius and Zosimus and Rufus and others who had lived among them, as well as of the Apostles. Then (in c. 11, where the Greek fails us) mention is made of the case of a presbyter Valens, "qui presbyter factus est aliquando apud vos quod sic ignoret is locum qui datus est ei." It appears that he had sinned through avarice and impurity and want of truth, and had shown himself quite unfit for an office of government. "Valde ergo, fratres, contristor pro illo et pro coniuge eius, quibus det Dominus poenitentiam veram."

[2] Winterstein thinks that there must have been a 'bishop,' because only here are 'deacons' associated with presbyters, but this argument has no force for those who admit that the titles presbyter and episcopus were at one time synonymous. Polycarp of course would not call the presbyters bishops as St. Paul did (Phil. i. 1). The titles had become distinct. He speaks of presbyters and deacons only.

[3] See Lightfoot *Ignat.* i. p. 578.

which must be reconciled with Ignatius' visit. make this view almost untenable. We have already seen that Ignatius when he wrote his epistles from Smyrna certainly regarded episcopacy as extended 'to the ends of the earth'[1]: with equal certainty he regarded it as an essential of church organization—"without these [the three orders]," he had written, "no Church has a title to the name."[2] He moved from Smyrna to Troas, and his tone is still the same; there is the same insistence upon episcopacy. Can he have been ignorant of the condition of the Church at Philippi to which he was just going? He came thither and enjoyed, as we gather, the same cordial intercourse which he had held in other Churches.[3] He left behind him when he passed on a venerated name. Had he rebuked them or remonstrated with them in any way, we must certainly have caught an echo of it through their correspondence with Polycarp. It is impossible, on the other hand, to believe that Ignatius suddenly dropped the urgent tone about episcopacy which had been one of the two main topics of all that he wrote in Asia. Can we then consistently with the phenomena of Polycarp's

---

[1] *ad Eph.* 3.

[2] *ad Trall.* 3. I cannot think that Dr. Lightfoot is justified (*Ignat.* i. 382) in saying that "there is no indication that he is upholding the episcopal against any other form of church government, as for instance the presbyteral. ... If Ignatius had been writing to a Church which was under presbyteral government he would doubtless have required its submission 'to the presbyters and deacons.' As it is he is dealing with communities where episcopacy had been already matured and therefore he demands obedience to their bishops." It seems to me as clear as day that Ignatius regarded episcopacy as universal, and as the only legitimate form of church government.

[3] This we gather from the tone in which Polycarp's letter implies that the Philippians had written about him; see c. 13. Ignatius himself, we should notice, had written to Polycarp from Philippi (ἐγράψατέ μοι καὶ ὑμεῖς καὶ Ἰγνάτιος).

letter suppose a state of things at Philippi which would not have shocked the mind of Ignatius? The hypothesis of a superior order in the Church, such as Clement's letter has been seen to imply, of which no representative was yet localized in the Church at Philippi, seems to meet the conditions of the problem. This would suggest a special reason why the "apostolic and prophetic teacher and bishop" Polycarp[1] should address his exhortations to them, as it suggested a reason for the similar appeal of Clement to the Corinthians. This would postulate a state of things at Philippi which Ignatius could at once have recognised as agreeable to his standard of apostolic requirements. It is not unlikely that Ignatius himself had been not merely the bishop of Antioch but the only representative of episcopal authority in Syria,[2] just as later in the century it is not impossible that there was only one bishop in the Churches of South Gaul.[3] What we

Probable solution.

---

[1] For Polycarp's prophetic character see his *Martyrium* cc. 5 and 16: ἐν τοῖς καθ' ἡμᾶς χρόνοις διδάσκαλος ἀποστολικὸς καὶ προφητικὸς γενόμενος, ἐπίσκοπος τῆς ἐν Σμύρνῃ ἁγίας ἐκκλησίας.

[2] On the position of Ignatius in Syria see *ad Rom.* 2: τὸν ἐπίσκοπον Συρίας κατηξίωσεν ὁ θεὸς εὑρεθῆναι εἰς δύσιν, ἀπὸ ἀνατολῆς μεταπεμψάμενος. He also speaks of himself as representing "the Church in Syria" (*ad Eph.* 21, *ad Magn.* 14, *ad Rom.* 9, *ad Trall.* 13) as well as the Church in Antioch of Syria (*ad Philad.* 10, *ad Smyrn.* 11, *ad Polyc.* 7). Perhaps by 'Syria' would be meant only what after Hadrian's division was called Syria Coele or Magna Syria: see *Dict. Gr. and Rom. Geogr.* s.v. SYRIA. Dr. Lightfoot says (i. p. 383): "Of a diocese, properly so called, there is no trace.... The bishops and presbyters are the ministry of a city, not of a diocese. What provision may have been made for the rural districts we are not told." The suggestion above is that there was originally a ministry-in-chief unlocalized, and that only gradually was a representative of this ministry localized in every Church with the name of 'bishop.' There is however no evidence against the bishop of a city having had from the first the supervision of the Christians in the surrounding district, until chorepiscopi were appointed.

[3] See Eusebius' expression, *H. E.* v. 23 παροικίαι κατὰ Γαλλίαν ἃς Εἰρηναῖος ἐπεσκόπει. (The same expression however is used in the previous chapter of

would suggest is not exactly that Philippi was in the diocese of Thessalonica,[1] or of some other see, but that we have still to do with a state of things which is transitional between what is represented in the *Didache* and the localized episcopate which already existed probably in every town-church of Greece by the middle of the century.

VI.

VI. The *Shepherd* of Hermas.

Its date.

It only remains for us to consider the evidence of the *Shepherd*. This document is one of those in the case of which the internal evidence of date is in conflict with the external. For, on the one hand, all that Hermas says about the Christian ministry suggests such an early date as accords naturally with a mention of Clement—presumably the well-known Clement— as the person in the Roman Church whose duty it was to send to other cities the visions vouchsafed to Hermas. On the other hand, we have positive information from a contemporary that Hermas wrote the *Shepherd* at a period which cannot be earlier than A.D. 140.[2]

---

the different 'parishes' of Alexandria in the more modern sense; see App. Note B.) In the fourth century we know there was only one bishop in Scythia, and this was regarded as traditional; see Sozomen *H. E.* vi. 21: τοῦτο τὸ ἔθνος πολλὰς μὲν ἔχει καὶ πόλεις καὶ κώμας καὶ φρούρια· μητρόπολις δέ ἐστι Τόμις, πόλις μεγάλη καὶ εὐδαίμων, παράλιος ... εἰσέτι δὲ καὶ νῦν ἔθος παλαιὸν ἐνθάδε κρατεῖ τοῦ παντὸς ἔθνους ἕνα τὰς ἐκκλησίας ἐπισκοπεῖν.

[1] Thessalonica is reported by Origen to have had Gaius (Rom. xvi. 27) for its first bishop.

[2] The Muratorian fragment asserts: "Pastorem vero nuperrime temporibus nostris in urbe Roma Hermas conscripsit, sedente cathedra urbis Romae ecclesiae Pio episcopo fratre eius." This is too definite a statement by a contemporary for us to reject. But, accepting it, what are we to make

VI.]   *The Ministry in the Subapostolic Age.*   331

What then are the hints given us by Hermas as to the condition of the ministry?

(1) He speaks of "the presbyters who preside over the Church," and these must no doubt be identified with the occupants of the 'chief seat' whom he mentions elsewhere.[1] The 'chief seat' is elsewhere spoken of as an object of ambition to false prophets and others.[2] We also hear of deacons who abused their diaconate to make money, plundering widows and orphans.[3] So far then the government of the Church of Rome appears to be a government of presbyters, assisted by deacons in the administration of alms.

Its language about the ministry.

(2) We have also mention of church "rulers," and these in another passage are unmistakably distinguished, as in Clement's letter, from the occupants

of the reference in the *Shepherd* to a Clement whose duty it is to send Hermas' visions to foreign Churches (*Vis.* ii. 4)? It is, I think (following Dr. Salmon), impossible that the brother of Pius (who acceded, according to Lipsius, not before A.D. 140), writing apparently during his episcopate, can refer, as he does, to Clement the bishop as his contemporary at a time when he was himself a married man with a family (*Vis.* i. 3, ii. 3). Salmon rejects the statement of the fragment, but this seems most arbitrary. There remain only two alternatives, either to suppose (what is improbable) that the Clement referred to is another Clement and his office not the bishopric, or to suppose that Hermas is (for some reason) using Clement's name as a symbol. So Origen treats the names here (Grapte, Clement, Hermas) as allegorical; see *de Princip.* iv. 11. But this again is improbable. The uncertainty as to date renders the use of this writing difficult. The matter is discussed by Lightfoot *Dissert.* p. 16, and Salmon *Introd.* p. 571 f.

[1] *Vis.* ii. 4: γράψεις οὖν δύο βιβλαρίδια, καὶ πέμψεις ἐν Κλήμεντι καὶ ἐν Γραπτῇ. πέμψει οὖν Κλήμης εἰς τὰς ἔξω πόλεις, ἐκείνῳ γὰρ ἐπιτέτραπται· Γραπτὴ δὲ νουθετήσει τὰς χήρας καὶ τοὺς ὀρφανούς· σὺ δὲ ἀναγνώσῃ εἰς ταύτην τὴν πόλιν μετὰ τῶν πρεσβυτέρων τῶν προϊσταμένων τῆς ἐκκλησίας. (There is nothing to indicate Clement's relation to the presbyters.) Cf. *Vis.* iii. 9. 7 : ὑμῖν λέγω τοῖς προηγουμένοις τῆς ἐκκλησίας καὶ τοῖς πρωτοκαθεδρίταις.

[2] *Mand.* xi. 12: ὁ δοκῶν πνεῦμα ἔχειν ὑψοῖ ἑαυτὸν καὶ θέλει πρωτοκαθεδρίαν ἔχειν. Cf. *Sim.* viii. 7. 4. In the *Shepherd* the prophet has no official dignity in the Church, see App. Note I.

[3] *Sim.* ix. 26. 2. In 15. 4 we read of προφῆται τοῦ θεοῦ καὶ διάκονοι αὐτοῦ. Here the word is probably used in a general sense.

of the 'chief seat.'[1] So far the phenomena are exactly the same as those presented by Clement's letter.

(3) Thirdly, we have mention of "apostles and teachers who preached over the whole world and who taught with gravity and purity the word of the Lord." Both are spoken of as having "received the Holy Ghost," and both belong to the past generation.[2] Here again there is no difficulty.

in spite of ambiguities

(4) There is mention also of "bishops" who exercised hospitality and protected the desolate and the widows,[3] and in another place a list is given of the worthies of the church ministry, past and present, as follows: "Apostles and bishops and teachers and deacons, who walked according to the gravity of God and exercised their episcopate and taught and ministered with purity and gravity to the elect of God."[4] Now if these visions were seen and written down in the days of Clement we should naturally identify the 'bishops' with the 'presbyters who preside,' and suppose that the 'teachers' are inserted out of place or perhaps that the 'bishops' are called 'teachers' also, like the 'pastors' (i.e. presbyter-bishops) of Eph. iv. 11. On the other hand, if, as we are almost forced to

---

[1] *Vis.* ii. 2. 6: ἐρεῖς οὖν τοῖς προηγουμένοις τῆς ἐκκλησίας. Cf. iii. 9. 7: ὑμῖν λέγω τοῖς προηγουμένοις τῆς ἐκκλησίας καὶ τοῖς πρωτοκαθεδρίταις.

[2] *Sim.* ix. 25. 2. The apostles are distinguished from the teachers (*Sim.* ix. 16. 5 οἱ ἀπόστολοι καὶ οἱ διδάσκαλοι) and are mentioned alone (*Sim.* ix. 17. 1: they were the preachers to "the twelve tribes who inhabit the whole world," and are therefore presumably reckoned as twelve). But both apostles and teachers belong to the past generation and were the original proclaimers of the gospel (*Sim.* ix. 15. 4). Together they are symbolized under forty stones in the fabric of the tower which is the Church.

[3] *Sim.* ix. 27. 2: ἐπίσκοποι καὶ φιλόξενοι, οἵτινες ἡδέως εἰς τοὺς οἴκους ἑαυτῶν πάντοτε ὑπεδέξαντο τοὺς δούλους τοῦ θεοῦ ἄτερ ὑποκρίσεως· οἱ δὲ ἐπίσκοποι κ.τ.λ.

[4] *Vis.* iii. 5. 1.

believe, the writing dates from the days of Pius, we can hardly do otherwise than interpret bishops in the later sense and suppose that the 'teachers' are the presbyters here, to which again the passage of St. Paul just referred to would be a parallel. In this case we should naturally identify the 'bishops' with the 'rulers,' and should suppose that in the interval since Clement's Epistle these rulers had become localized in the different Churches as bishops and, though as such they would have sat among the presbyters on the 'chief seat' and been reckoned among them, they still can be classed apart as a separate order and spoken of either by the title of 'bishop,' which belonged to their local presidency, or by their general name of 'rulers.'

In any case it seems clear that this document adds considerably to the force of the argument derived from Clement's language, that even when the presbyters were the chief local authorities they were still in subordination to 'rulers,' who represented, since the apostles and teachers had passed away, the chief authority in the Church. *suggests an order superior to presbyters.*

In summing up the results derived from a consideration of the historical links which in the Western Church connect the age of the Apostles with that of Irenaeus, there are two theories which require notice besides the one which we have been led to adopt. *Summary for the West.*

There is the view (which is undoubtedly supported by the Epistle of Polycarp, taken alone) that the Churches in the West were governed simply by a council of presbyters, who had no superiors over them, *Possible theories: (i) equal colleges of presbyter-bishops;*

and who therefore must be supposed to have handed on their own ministry. There is no objection on ground of principle to this conclusion viewed in the light of the apostolic succession, as has been sufficiently explained already. These presbyter-bishops legitimately 'ordained' and fulfilled episcopal functions because those functions belonged to the equal commission they had all received. Subsequently at later ordinations this full commission was confined to one of their number and the rest received the reduced authority which belonged to the presbyterate of later church history. Such a process would not represent the elevation of any new dignity from below but the limitation of an old dignity to one instead of its extension to many, and that in accordance with the precedent set by the Apostle St. John. 'Monepiscopacy' takes the place of a diffused episcopacy.[1] It has however been pointed out that this supposition does not satisfy all the evidence of Clement's letter or of the *Shepherd*. It should also be added that it makes the strong tradition of the monepiscopal succession which meets us in the latter part of the second century, and the undisputed supremacy of the single bishop, almost unintelligible.

(ii) the bishop hidden in the presbyterate;

Secondly, there is a view based on the consideration that long after the existence of bishops in every Church, as distinct from presbyters, the term presbyter could still be used for both orders, as it is occasionally by Irenaeus and Clement and Origen.

---

[1] So Dr. Langen states the principle *Gesch. der röm. Kirche* i. p. 95, and Lightfoot (*Ignat.* i. p. 376 n.¹) expresses agreement with him.

Consequently it is maintainable that in the Church of Clement's day and of Polycarp's, at Corinth and at Philippi, there existed one amongst the presbyters who, though he held the unique powers which afterwards belonged to the episcopate, was still included under the common name.[1] While however this view cannot be disproved, it must be admitted that it is unsupported by the evidence of the documents we have been considering.

It remains to state the conviction to which we have been led, viz. that in the West no more than in the East did the supreme power ever devolve upon the presbyters. There was a time when they were (as the Epistles of Clement and Polycarp bear witness) the chief *local* authorities—the sole ordinary occupants of the chief seat. But over them, not yet localized, were men either of prophetic inspiration or of apostolic authority and known character—'prophets' or 'teachers' or 'rulers' or 'men of distinction'—who in the subapostolic age ordained to the sacred ministry and in certain cases would have exercised the chief teaching and governing authority. Gradually these men, after the pattern set by James in Jerusalem or by John in the Churches of Asia, became themselves local presidents or instituted others in their place. Thus a transition was effected to a state of things in which every Church had its local president, who ranked amongst the presbytery

(iii) the gradual localization of apostolic men—the best supported view.

---

[1] Dr. Salmon writes (*Introd.* p. 568): "It has been thought that although Clement's letter exhibits the prominence of a single person as chief in the Church of Rome, it affords evidence that there was no such prominence in the Church of Corinth. . . . But this inference is not warranted."

—a fellow-presbyter, like St. Peter—sitting with them on the chief seat, but to whom was assigned exclusively the name of 'bishop.' This transference and limitation of a name can hardly be a difficulty when we remember the vague use of official titles which meets us in early church history. In the organization, as in the theology, of the Church nomenclature was only gradually fixed.[1] The view here expressed of the development of the ministry has one great advantage, besides appearing to account for all the phenomena of the documents of the period: it accounts also for the strength of the tradition which gave authority to the episcopal successions when they first come into clear view, and for the unquestioned position which they held.[2] There is no trace of elevation in the records of the episcopate.

[1] Cf. Theodoret on 1 Tim. iii. 1 : τοὺς αὐτοὺς ἐκάλουν ποτὲ πρεσβυτέρους καὶ ἐπισκόπους, τοὺς δὲ νῦν καλουμένους ἐπισκόπους ἀποστόλους ὠνόμαζον· τοῦ δὲ χρόνου προϊόντος, τὸ μὲν τῆς ἀποστολῆς ὄνομα τοῖς ἀληθῶς ἀποστόλοις κατέλιπον, τὴν δὲ τῆς ἐπισκοπῆς προσηγορίαν τοῖς πάλαι καλουμένοις ἀποστόλοις ἐπέθεσαν. The idea that bishops were at first called apostles is derived from Theodore Mops. on 1 Tim. iii. 8. There is no early evidence to support it, though there were 'apostles' besides the twelve. In other respects, however, Theodore's account of the development of the ministry is very interesting. Timothy and Titus represent, he thinks, a class of subapostolic church rulers, who were put in charge of 'eparchies' or large districts, and held the supreme control with the authority to ordain, while the local Churches were ruled by presbyter-bishops : afterwards the increase in the number of the faithful led to the multiplication of the chief rulers, and their unwillingness to equal themselves to the Apostles, to their adoption of the name of bishops : in later days the episcopate, especially in the East, had come to be unduly multiplied. See Swete *Theodore of Mops. on the Minor Epp. of St. Paul*, ii. pp. 118-125.

[2] We should still have to acknowledge a little idealizing in Tertullian's statement that the local episcopate at Corinth and Philippi was of apostolic institution. See *de Praescr.* 36.

CHAPTER VII.

CONCLUSIONS AND APPLICATIONS.

THE task which remains for us is that of endeavouring to sum up the conclusions of a long investigation.

It appeared first of all that the record of history renders it practically indisputable that Jesus Christ founded a visible society or Church, to be the organ of His Spirit in the world, the depository of His truth, the covenanted sphere of His redemptive grace and discipline. Now such a society, as by its very nature it is to be universal and continuous, must have links of connection; and in the uninterrupted history of the Church, as it is spread out before us from the latter part of the second century, one such link has always existed in the apostolic successions of the ministry.[1] It appeared further that these successions have been regarded by the church writers, with an unanimity and to an extent which hardly admit of being exaggerated, as an essential element of her corporate life. Of course an essential ministry is a sacerdotal con-

The verdict of history on the Church;

the apostolic succession;

sacerdotalism;

---

[1] On the fundamental principle of the ministry I should like to take this last opportunity of referring to the *Theologia Naturalis* of Raymund of Sabunde, a very interesting theologian of the fifteenth century; cf. tit. 303: "quia vita spiritualis consistit in charitate et unitate, ideo convenientissime debuit ordinari, ut homines vice Christi administrent sacramenta salutis hominibus, ut magis fierent unum inter se."

Y

ception. Accordingly reasons have been given for believing that ideas now current as to the growth of sacerdotalism in the early centuries are greatly exaggerated. Undoubtedly there has been a certain growth and development in this respect, and the causes of it are not far to seek. The ministry existed in order to govern, and the lawlessness which made government necessary made the assertion of its authority more emphatic. Again, the growing secularity of the Church, consequent upon the popular acceptance of the Christian religion becoming increasingly easy, led inevitably to stress being laid, where there was special need and opportunity to lay it, upon the sanctity requisite for the clergy in their ministerial relation to God. Thus, no doubt, the gulf broadened between the clergy and laity; for, as that gulf is narrowest where the general level of Christian life and aspiration is highest, so the lowering of the average tone tends to the isolation of the priesthood of the ministry. Thus it would be impossible to deny a growth in the sacerdotal conceptions of the Church, but it is a growth which (as has been said) is very easily exaggerated. At least there antedated it the belief (which appears in the latter part of the second century with all the force of an immemorial tradition) that a ministry of bishops, priests, and deacons of apostolic descent and divine authorization is the centre of unity in each local Christian society, and is charged with the administration of that worship and discipline, and with the guardianship of that doctrine, which belong to the whole Church.

The chief authority lay with the bishop, and accordingly episcopal ordination was regarded—without a single exception which can be alleged on reasonable grounds—as essential to constitute a man a member of the clergy and give him ministerial commission. Thus what is commonly understood to be meant by the doctrine of the apostolic succession was a commonplace among Christian ideas, and was bound up with the whole fabric of the life of the catholic Church. Nor would this position be affected if we were to accept Jerome's testimony—though grave reasons were shown against accepting it—to the effect that in the early Church of Alexandria on the vacancy of the see, one of the presbyters succeeded to the episcopate after mere election by his fellows. This would only mean that the Alexandrian presbyters were by the terms of their ordination bishops *in posse*, even though their exercise of episcopal powers without special election would have been irregular and would not therefore, according to current teaching, have been accepted as valid. It would not mean—it was not understood by Jerome to mean—that a presbyter, who had been ordained without any such special conditions attached to his charge, could advance himself under any circumstances to episcopal functions. This supposed arrangement would not, therefore, have touched the principle of the succession, viz. that no ecclesiastical ministry can be validly exercised except such as is covered by a clearly understood commission, received in the regular devolution of ecclesiastical authority.

Was, then, this position which the Church took up about her orders justified by the original intentions of her Founder and His Apostles?

The witness of the Gospels;

In answer to this we were led to see that, however much ambiguity might attach to the record of the four Gospels if they were isolated documents, they certainly appear to warrant, if not to require, the position that Christ instituted in His Church a permanent and official apostolate.

the apostolic records.

Further the early records of the apostolic age present us with a picture of the Church governed by such an apostolate, invested without any doubt with a supernatural authority. As the Church grows, a local ministry of presbyter-bishops and deacons is developed in the different Churches. These local officers appear as sharing the apostolic ministry, though in subordinate grades, and as instituted by apostolic authority. It is only by giving the evidence of the *Didache* an importance denied to that of the Pastoral Epistles, the Acts of the Apostles, and Clement's Epistle, that the idea of a ministry elected simply by the congregation can find any countenance, and though the *Didache* taken by itself would admit of this interpretation it does not require it. At the period then represented by the Pastoral Epistles—when the Apostle St. Paul is writing especially about church organization and in view of the future—the church ministry consisted of presbyter-bishops and deacons, controlled by the superior authority of apostles and apostolic men.

Earlier the rich miraculous endowments of the

VII.]   *Conclusions and Applications.*   341

Church—endowments which witnessed to the reality of the Spirit's presence, which was ministered by apostolic hands—had more or less thrown into the background the more normal and permanent 'gift of government': but at every stage the Church is presented to us as an elaborate organization in which every member has his own position and function by divine appointment. It is certain that miraculous indications of the divine will in regard to any particular person would have rendered official appointment in accordance with such indications a very subordinate matter; but the force to be attributed to miraculous qualifications recognised by the community is not a practical question in reference to the later church ministry, nor did it appear probable that even such qualifications were allowed (in the case for instance of those prophets and teachers who shared the apostolic authority) to dispense with an appointment to office received either directly from Christ or from His Apostles.

The question then arose: What are the links of connection between the apostolic ministry as it is presented to us in the Pastoral Epistles and the ministry of bishops, priests, and deacons as it appears in church history? In particular do the single bishops in each community represent simply a localization of the authority of apostles, prophets, and teachers, which had been catholic or general, while the title 'bishop' was transferred from the lower to the higher grade of office: or was it the case that such apostolic authority as was needed for the permanent govern-

[margin: The links between the apostolic ministry and the episcopate.]

ment of the Church passed first to the local colleges of equal presbyter-bishops, and that after a time the general governing authority was confined to one only who was called 'bishop' by a limitation of the term —the rest receiving the reduced commission of presbyters?

In answer to this question it appeared that the latter hypothesis can indeed be defended in the case of certain parts of the Church, especially on the evidence of the Epistle of Polycarp and Jerome's statements about the Church of Alexandria, and that it is a hypothesis which in view of its common reception in the West it would be impossible to condemn as if it contradicted the principle of the apostolic succession: but it appeared also that the former alternative is by far the more probable. It has on its side the evidence of the history of the ministry in Palestine, Syria, and Asia; and, on closer inspection, the evidence which the Epistle of Clement gives us as to the development of the Church at Rome and Corinth, while it is not incompatible with the witness of Polycarp's letter. Thus the presbyters seem never to have held the powers later known as episcopal; but as Church after Church gained a local representative of apostolic authority, the title of bishop was very naturally confined in its use to distinguish this 'successor of the Apostles' among the local 'presbyters,' with whom he was associated.

It is, however, necessary to emphasize once again that there is considerable room for uncertainty as to the exact steps by which in this place or that the apostolic

VII.]   *Conclusions and Applications.*   343

ministry passed into the ordinary ministry of the Church. But there are matters of much more importance as to which there is no such uncertainty :—

(1) The ministry advanced always upon the principle of succession, so that whatever functions a man held in the Church at any time were simply those that had been committed to him by some one among his predecessors who had held the authority to 'give orders' by regular devolution from the Apostles.

(2) "It was by a common instinct that this [the threefold or episcopal] organization was everywhere adopted. It was as it were a law of the being of the Church that it should put on this form, which worked as surely as the growth of a particular kind of plant from a particular kind of seed. Everywhere there was a development which made unerringly for the same goal. This seems to speak of divine institution almost as plainly as if our Lord had in so many words prescribed this form of church government. He, the founder, the creator of the Church, would seem to have impressed upon it this nature."[1]

Mr. Darwin, writing about his theory of the process of evolution in nature, uses these words : " I fully admit that there are very many difficulties not satisfactorily explained by my theory of descent with modification, but I cannot possibly believe that a false theory would explain so many classes of facts as I think it certainly does explain. On these grounds I drop my anchor, and believe that the difficulties will

The doctrine of apostolic succession alone satisfies all the evidence.

---

[1] Stanton *Christian Ministry Historically Considered* in *Lectures on Church Doctrine*, series iii, pp. 16, 17. I have altered the tenses to adapt the quotation to the context, but with no change of sense.

slowly disappear."[1] It is interesting to notice what grounds of evidence a great scientific teacher thinks adequate to support a far-reaching doctrine: and it is impossible not to perceive what infinitely higher grounds we have for our theory of the apostolic succession. It not only 'explains many classes of facts,' but it, and it only (though of course the cogency of the positive evidence for it is different at different stages), appears to explain all the phenomena of the Christian ministry from the beginning. We, then, have better cause to 'drop our anchor.'

<small>Application of the principle</small>

It is not proposed to carry very far the application of the principles which have been enunciated and defended in this book. It is not for instance proposed to discuss whether such and such Churches or religious bodies which call themselves episcopal have really the historical succession, nor on the other hand to investigate the theories of ordination, more or less subversive, which have been current since the Reformation.

<small>(a) to invalidate non-episcopal ministries;</small>

But it will appear at once as a consequence of all this argument that the various presbyterian and congregationalist organizations, however venerable on many and different grounds, have, in dispensing with the episcopal successions, violated a fundamental law of the Church's life. It cannot be maintained that the acts of ordination, by which presbyters of the sixteenth or subsequent centuries originated the ministries of some of these societies, were covered by their commission or belonged to the office of presbyter which

---

[1] *Life and Letters of Charles Darwin* ii. p. 217. Cf. p. 286: "it seems to me that an hypothesis is developed into a theory solely by explaining an ample lot of facts."

they had duly received. Beyond all question they 'took to themselves' these powers of ordination, and consequently had them not. It is not proved—nay, it is not perhaps even probable—that any presbyter had in any age the power to ordain. But it is absolutely certain that for a large number of centuries it had been understood beyond all question that only bishops could ordain and that presbyters had not episcopal powers; and no exceptional dignity, belonging to any presbyter-abbot had ever enabled him to transcend the limits of his office. It follows then—not that God's grace has not worked, and worked largely, through many an irregular ministry where it was exercised or used in good faith—but that a ministry not episcopally received is invalid, that is to say, falls outside the conditions of covenanted security and cannot justify its existence in terms of the covenant.

This conclusion once accepted has of course an immediate bearing on the obligations of individuals who may find themselves members of presbyterian or congregationalist bodies; but it has also another and more general bearing on the relation of large communities of Christians to the properly constituted Church. How can you suppose, they indignantly ask, that we can accept conclusions which would falsify the prolonged experience we have had in our Churches of the systematic action of the grace of God? The answer to such pleading is surely this. We do not ask you to deny any spiritual experience of the past or the present. The blame for separations (the bearing on this of present experience) lies, on any fair showing, quite sufficiently with the Church to make it intelligible that God should have let the action of His grace extend itself widely and freely beyond its covenanted channels. We ask you then to be false to no part of experience but rather to be more completely true to experience in all its aspects. For must you not admit that viewed on the whole the results of our divisions have been disastrous; that the present state of Christendom is intolerable? Let me quote the very serious words of an eminent presbyterian theologian:[1]

"If it be the duty of the Church to represent her Lord among men, and if she faithfully performs that duty, it follows by an absolutely irresistible necessity that the unity exhibited in His person must appear in her. She must not only be one, but visibly one in some distinct and appreciable sense—in such a sense that men shall not need to be told of it, but shall themselves see and acknowledge that her unity is real. No doubt such unity may be, and is, consistent with great variety—with variety in the dogmatic expression of Christian truth, in regulations for Christian government, in forms of Christian worship, and in the exhibition of Christian life. It is unnecessary to speak of these things now. Variety and the right to differ have many advocates. We have rather at present to think of unity and the obligation to agree. As regards these, it can hardly be denied that the Church of our time is flagrantly and disastrously at fault. The spectacle presented by her to the world is in direct and palpable contradiction to the unity of the person of her Lord; and she would at once discover its sinfulness were she not too exclusively occupied with the thought of positive action on the world, instead of remembering that her primary and most important duty is to afford to the world a visible representation of her Exalted Head. In all her branches, indeed, the beauty of unity is enthusiastically talked of by her members, and not a few are never weary of describing the precious ointment in which the Psalmist beheld a symbol of the unity of Israel. Others, again, alive to the uselessness of talking where there is no corresponding reality, seek comfort in the thought that beneath all the divisions

[1] Dr. Milligan *Resurrection of our Lord* pp. 199-202.

of the Church there is a unity which she did not make, and which she cannot unmake. Yet, surely, in the light of the truth now before us, we may well ask whether either the talking or the suggested comfort brings us nearer a solution of our difficulties. The one is so meaningless that the very lips which utter it might be expected to refuse their office. The other is true, although, according as it is used, it may either be a stimulus to amendment or a pious platitude; and generally it is the latter. But neither words about the beauty of unity, nor the fact of an invisible unity, avail to help us. What the Church ought to possess is a unity which the eye can see. If she is to be a witness to her Risen Lord, she must do more than talk of unity, more than console herself with the hope that the world will not forget the invisible bond by which it is pled that all her members are bound together into one. Visible unity in one form or another is an essential mark of her faithfulness. . . . The world will never be converted by a disunited Church. Even Bible circulation and missionary exertion upon the largest scale will be powerless to convert it, unless they are accompanied by the strength which unity alone can give. Let the Church of Christ once feel, in any measure corresponding to its importance, that she is the representative of the Risen Lord, and she will no longer be satisfied with mere outward action. She will see that her first and most imperative duty is to heal herself, that she may be able to heal others also."

This is strong pleading. And, if it be the case that we are bound to seek organic unity; if it be the case that the results of our past divisions, of our past individualism, are such as to satisfy us that there has been something fundamentally wrong about current conceptions of Christian liberty and Christian progress; if further it be the case that new moral and doctrinal perils, consequent upon the collapse of Christian discipline and accompanied with the 'shaking' of established institutions in all directions, are constantly pressing upon us the obligation to consider afresh the basis of Christian life and order,—all this coincides to give new force and meaning to the claims of the apostolic succession.

For it alone, embodying as it does the principle of the historical continuity of the Church, affords a possible basis of union : it alone, while on the one hand it cannot possibly be abandoned, and while the Churches which possess it cannot be asked[1] (if there be anything in this argument) to regard it as simply one of many permissible forms of church government, on the other hand is not, when taken in its true breadth and in all its possibilities of application, open to objection as if it were itself inadequate or unsatisfactory.[2]

(b) to recall episcopal Churches to their true principles.

Nor is it the case that in this matter the Anglican Church is simply asking for a cause to be decided all her own way; for she has herself—to say nothing of other portions of the Church—much to do to recall herself to her true principles. God's promise to Judah was that she should remember her ways, and be ashamed, when she should receive her sisters Samaria and Sodom: and that He would give them her "for daughters, but not by her covenant"[3] : and certainly, if it were granted to the English Church to become a centre for the reunion of separated communities on the basis of the apostolic succession, the words 'not by her covenant' would need to be brought to memory.

To take only one example of this out of several which suggest themselves. The principle of the

---

[1] As Dr. Milligan would I suppose ask them. Some words imply this, in the context from which I have quoted.

[2] I had occasion to point out before that episcopacy is a much wider principle than has sometimes been supposed by both its friends and its enemies, see p. 72 f.

[3] Ezek. xvi. 61.

apostolic succession involves the truth that the bishops of the catholic Church are clothed with a spiritual authority, and a corresponding responsibility, as the guardians of Christian truth and worship and discipline, an authority and a responsibility which they cannot alienate from themselves, or commit to the secular government, without treason to their great Head. God in fact has instituted two kinds of societies in the world—coincident but distinct—the ministers of each representing His authority in their own sphere: indeed in one aspect the record of Christian history is the record of the divine overruling of various attempts on the part of one of these two authorities to deny to the other its independent existence. The early Christian Church recognised without hesitation that 'the powers that be are ordained of God,' but on the other hand the secular power alarmed at the growth of the new spiritual society—the *imperium in imperio*—endeavoured to crush out the Church At a later epoch, when the balance of powers had changed, the great writers of the middle age acknowledged side by side the Holy Church and the Holy Empire, but in the climax of its might the papacy would not be satisfied with less than the annihilation of the independence of the State. Once more and for the last time, an attempt was made which is specially identified with the history of the English Church and race, so to emphasize the idea of a Christianized nation, that Church and State could be regarded as only different aspects of the same society. On the basis of such a theory, if the State pledged itself to the

Church's faith, the Church on her side might be content to merge her independent governmental authority in that of the State.

The logic of events falsified in turn each of these attempts to fuse the distinct spheres of 'the two empires.' If circumstances have made it absurd in England now to speak of the nation as committed to the catholic faith or of her national courts as 'spiritual,'[1] then circumstances have taught us also how dangerous it was for the Church to go even as far as she did, in alienating her power of independent action. In the future she must be content to act as first of all part and parcel of the catholic Church, ruled by her laws, empowered by her Spirit. And, if the bishops are to make an intelligible claim, they must make it as the responsible guardians by Christ's appointment and apostolic succession of the doctrine and discipline and worship of the Church catholic, ready to maintain at all cost, the inherent spiritual independence which belongs to their office.

If then this be the case, the English Church has to learn as well as to teach—to recover a principle as well as to maintain it. For it admits of no question that, for instance, the Established Church in Scotland, though it is presbyterian, has maintained more successfully than the Church of England with her catholic succession the spiritual independence of

---

[1] As Hooker pleaded (*E. P.* viii. 8. 9): "If the cause be spiritual, secular courts do not meddle with it: we need not excuse ourselves with Ambrose, but boldly and lawfully we may refuse to answer before any civil judge in a matter which is not civil, so that we do not mistake the nature either of the cause or of the court."

Christ's society.[1] We have to learn, then, as well as to teach.

But the object of this book was only to maintain a principle; and I should desire to have left before the minds of my readers the picture of a universal spiritual society, in which the apostolic succession of the bishops constitutes by divine appointment a visible link between different epochs, witnessing everywhere to that permanent element in human nature to which Christ's Gospel appeals,—that fundamental humanity, underlying all developments and variations, in virtue of which there becomes possible a real spiritual continuity between the generations, so that 'the heart of the fathers is turned to the children and the heart of the children to the fathers, lest God come and smite the earth with a curse.'

---

[1] See the remarkable decisions of the Judges of the Court of Session, quoted in the *Report of the Royal Commission on Ecclesiastical Courts*, 1883, vol. ii. p. 46.

APPENDED NOTES.

A.

DR. LIGHTFOOT'S DISSERTATION ON "THE CHRISTIAN MINISTRY."[1]

THE Church at large owes Dr. Lightfoot a debt of gratitude so (in the strictest sense of the term) incalculable—I do not say as Bishop of Durham, for that consideration would be out of place here, but as an historical critic of the very first order, as a defender of the faith, and as an interpreter of St. Paul—and, more than this, any would-be vindicator of the Christian ministry owes so great a debt to the scholar who has again set almost beyond the reach of cavil the genuineness of the Ignatian Epistles, that, in venturing to say a word in criticism of what he has written and confirmed with his mature approval,[2] one runs a great risk of incurring the charge both of arrogance and of ingratitude.

Yet there is no doubt that the Essay named above has caused a great deal of disquiet and confusion: it has been found an effective instrument in defence of 'Congregational principles' by their ablest advocate[3]: and, though all this may have been due in most part (as Dr. Lightfoot says) to its "partial and qualifying statements" being "emphasized to the neglect of the general drift of the Essay,"[4] it does seem to justify such misinterpretations (if I may so speak) by the great ambiguity of the position which it takes up.

This has recently been made all the more apparent by a statement of the author, that he recognises in Dr. Langen (the distinguished Old-Catholic divine) one who "gives an account of the origin of episcopacy precisely similar to his own, as set forth in this Essay" (i.e. the Essay now under discussion).[5] But Dr.

[1] See his *Epistle to the Philippians* pp. 181 f.
[2] See the Preface to the Sixth Edition (1881).
[3] R. W. Dale's *Manual of Congregational Principles*, appendix p. 216.
[4] Pref. to Sixth Edition.
[5] *Ignatius* i. p. 376 note [1].

Langen's account of the matter [1] is given in complete accordance with the principle of the apostolic succession as contended for above. He never speaks as if the Church created her ministry originally, or created subsequently a new office of the episcopate by elevation from below.[2] He speaks of the episcopate as always handed down from the Apostles, and simply recognises (whether rightly or no) that, having been originally held by all the presbyters, at least in the West, it subsequently was limited to one. It is obvious that the same facts may admit of being expressed under either phraseology, though not with equal regard to their real significance. I am not now concerned with the facts. My point here is only this, that Dr. Lightfoot's expression of complete agreement with Dr. Langen indicates that he ignores what to many people seems the question of primary importance, viz., *what principles regulated the devolution and development of the ministry.* The question is not one of archæology only, but of principle. The principles which find expression in church history are at least as important as the facts in which they are expressed. It is fatal to neglect either one or the other. Dr. Lightfoot's facts may be perfectly true, but he may still err by ignoring the spirit which was at work in them.

I venture then to point out the main defects (as they seem to me) in this celebrated Dissertation.

(1) First, then, the Dissertation seems to be misleading by giving countenance to a popular confusion of thought, of great importance in religious matters. Men confuse two quite different antitheses. There is the antithesis of what is essential and what is unessential; there is the antithesis of means and ends. In religion the latter antithesis is of vital importance. There is only one *end* in religion. That is the actual restoration of man into the image of God, and therefore into unimpeded fellowship with God. To this end all else is a means—all sacraments and means of grace, all spiritual discipline and effort; amongst other instrumentalities the ministry. Dr. Lightfoot is therefore perfectly right in warning us against "exalting means into ends" (p. 184).

But he appears to countenance a misleading confusion between *means* and *unessentials.* "It was against this false principle," he says, "that [the Apostles] waged war; the principle which exalted the means into an end, and gave an absolute intrinsic value to

---

[1] *Geschichte der römischen Kirche* i. p. 95 f.

[2] *Dissert.* p. 196 : "The episcopate was formed . . . out of the presbyteral order by elevation."

subordinate aids and expedients. These aids and expedients, for his own sake and for the good of the society to which he belonged, a Christian could not afford to hold lightly or neglect. But they were no part of the *essence* of God's message to man in the Gospel." Here Dr. Lightfoot implies that in recognising anything to be a means, not an end, we are recognising it, at the last resort, as *not of the essence*. He is not, of course, using *essence* in any metaphysical sense, but in such sense as that what is essential, is equivalent to what is necessary, to what is of *primary* authority and importance. Are there not then such things as essential means? Do we say in the natural region that medicine and the ministry of healing are unessential because they are only means to an end beyond themselves—namely, health? No; they are essential means. Now, what is Christianity in the supernatural region? What did Christ send His Apostles to do? To announce the true end of human life—the true ideal on which our eyes must always be fixed? Most certainly; but not only—perhaps not chiefly—to do this. Their duty was at least as primarily to call people's attention to the means which God had devised 'that His banished should not be expelled from Him' (2 Sam. xiv. 14). Christ had established a kingdom or Church; and this, with its sacraments and its social obligations, was the divinely appointed—the essential or necessary—means to the great end. *Christianity is as much the establishment of a visible system of means for realizing the end of human life, as it is the divine announcement of what that end is.*

There are in Christianity, therefore, essential means—means, that is, not devised by men as the gradual outcome of their experienced needs, but ordained by Christ in anticipation of them. This, of course, Dr. Lightfoot would admit—though his language at times would suggest the false notion, on which enough has been said, that Christianity came into the world as a bare ideal (see pp. 181, 182). But at least he would admit that Baptism and the Lord's Supper were divinely appointed means 'generally necessary to salvation.'[1] Now these are social sacraments; they are parts of a social system; they involve the truth that Christ has instituted a 'kingdom of means,' a visible channel for His covenanted gifts of grace. Well then, if this be so, no new principle

---

[1] But, if this is so, then the proposition that "Christianity has no special sanctuaries" is at least misleading (p. 181). A Christian, to continue such, must participate in a sacramental 'breaking of bread,' which must be a local act, and which constitutes the place where it is celebrated, without more ado, a local sanctuary.

will be involved, supposing the evidence goes to show that Christ instituted a ministry of truth and grace in His kingdom, intended to be a permanent link of continuity and bond of unity in it. This ministry becomes one of the 'means which God devised.' But, strangely enough, the question is never faced: did Christ institute a ministry in the persons of His Apostles, and did they perpetuate it? Dr. Lightfoot says: "it became necessary to appoint special officers;" "it became necessary to provide for the emergency by definite officers" (p. 184). Was the Church ever without special officers constituted by divine appointment in the Apostles? Was not the household divinely planned so as to include commissioned stewards?

I cannot see how Dr. Lightfoot, accepting the Gospels, the Acts, and the Pastoral Epistles, can answer in the negative. But what I am calling attention to here is simply that he has not put the clear issue before us. He speaks in the earlier part of his Essay as if all the means for realizing the great ideal of humanity presented to us in Christ were left to man's devising, and were therefore matter only of spiritual expedience. But he is pledged to admit 'necessary means,' at the least in the two sacraments; and these spoil his whole theory. They involve the institution by Christ of a kingdom of means. They force us to put another question to ourselves, and not that which he suggests to us, viz., *Granted a kingdom of necessary means, is a ministry among them?*

(2) Dr. Lightfoot repudiates strenuously and rightly certain falsely sacerdotal conceptions (pp. 181, 182). He also admits the existence in the Church of a priesthood rightly so called (pp. 182, 266, 627). Confessedly in this controversy a good deal is a matter of words; something has been said on it above, and something on its historical aspect will be said further on. But here again the fundamental questions are, in the Dissertation, hardly put to us. Did Christ institute a ministry of sacred things —call it a priesthood or not—in such sense that the members of His Church were bound to avail themselves of it, and by this very obligation were given a centre and bond of unity? Dr. Lightfoot is at liberty to call Ignatius and Irenaeus unsacerdotal (pp. 250, 252); he is at liberty to quote Ambrosiaster as "giving a singularly appreciative account of the relation of the ministry to the congregation" (p. 185 note [1]). But these writers would have answered this question with a most unhesitating affirmative; they undoubtedly believed in the necessary subordination of every one who would be a Christian to the episcopal ministry

which represented the divine authority in the Church by succession from the Apostles ; they would not have recognised as a brother any one who was separated from the Church of the bishops. We go back to the apostolic age. Here, again, any one is at liberty to note that the ministry is not called a priesthood; but he must recognise that there was a ministry, and that it had special powers. For could any Christian receive the gift of the Holy Ghost except by the laying-on of apostolic hands ? Could any zealous Cretan become a presbyter except by Titus' ordination ? The sort of 'un-sacerdotalism,' which nevertheless makes an exclusive claim for an ordained ministry, is not what is wanted by anti-sacerdotalists of our day. Thus, as we read this portion of Dr. Lightfoot's Essay, we feel constantly drawn 'to move the previous question.' Was there ever a time in church history when men, who deserted the authoritative ministry and set up one of their own outside the due succession, would have been regarded as still within the covenant ? Was it ever a recognised principle in the Church that an unordained Christian at the last resort could celebrate the Eucharist ? I shall endeavour to answer these questions in the ensuing chapters. My present object is not to discuss the facts so much as to point out where, I think, Dr. Lightfoot tends to ignore the primary questions at issue.

B.

THE EARLY HISTORY OF THE ALEXANDRIAN MINISTRY.

(See pp. 137-144.)

JEROME'S statement (*Ep.* cxlvi *ad Evangelum*) is as follows: "Alexandriae a Marco evangelista usque ad Heraclam et Dionysium episcopos presbyteri semper unum ex se electum in excelsiori gradu collocatum episcopum nominabant, quomodo si exercitus imperatorem faciat aut diaconi eligant de se quem industrium noverint et archidiaconum vocent. Quid enim facit excepta ordinatione episcopus, quod presbyter non faciat ? "

These are his words. The parallel found in the military election might suggest a doubt as to his meaning, but the illustration from the election of an archdeacon seems plain. So at least thought the author of the *de Divinis Officiis* (wrongly attributed to Alcuin), who quotes Jerome's words and comments thus: "Archidiaconus eandem consecrationem habet quam ceteri diaconi, sed electione fratrum praeponitur" (ap. Hittorp. p. 74); so also Amalarius, bishop of Treves, c. A.D. 820, *de Eccles. Off.* ii. 13 (ap. Hittorp. p. 166): "Archidiaconi consecratio nobis notissima est: archidiaconus eandem consecrationem habet quam ceteri diaconi, sed electione fratrum praeponitur." They both treat this state of things at Alexandria as an instance of a substantial original identity in the office of bishops and priests, indicated by the same officers being called in the New Testament by either name. This comes to them from Jerome and Ambrosiaster, whom they quote.[1]

In Greek writers we get no hint of what Jerome mentions. We learn indeed from Epiphanius that "all the churches [or congregations] belonging to the catholic Church in Alexandria were under one archbishop, and presbyters were appointed over these separately to supply the ecclesiastical necessities of the inhabitants who lived in the neighbourhood of each church" (*Haer.* lxix. 1). Thus in his day the presbyters at Alexandria had the relative independence of later parish priests.[2] Of anything beyond this in the past we get no hint.

But an Arab historian is quoted to confirm Jerome. Sa'id Ibn Batrik, Melkite patriarch of Alexandria from A.D. 933-943—who took the Greek name of Eutychius (though he does not appear to have known Greek) and wrote annals in Arabic from the creation down to his own time—makes the following statements:[3]

"Mark the evangelist appointed, with Hananias the patriarch, twelve presbyters to be with the patriarch, so that when he died they should choose one of the twelve presbyters, and the other eleven should lay their hands on his head and bless him, and make him

---

[1] See further App. Note F, and above, p. 171 f.

[2] This is all that Epiphanius says. Is it fairly represented by Dr. Bigg's "Even in the time of Epiphanius they exercised a sort of episcopal jurisdiction" (*B. L.* p. 40)? It is the existence of these 'parishes' in the Alexandrian 'diocese' which accounts for Eusebius' language in *H.E.* v. 22: τῶν κατ' Ἀλεξάνδρειαν παροικιῶν τὴν λειτουργίαν ἐγχειρίζεται Δημήτριος, and iv. 35: τῶν κατ' Ἀλεξάνδρειαν ἐκκλησιῶν τὴν ἐπισκοπὴν Διονύσιος ὑπολαμβάνει. But he uses the first phrase in a more doubtful sense of Irenaeus in v. 23.

[3] A portion of the annals was edited first by Selden, under the title *Eutychii Aegyptii Patriarchae Orthodoxorum Alexandrini Ecclesiae suae Origines*, in 1642, in the interests of presbyterianism. He was replied to by a Maronite Father, Abraham Ecchellensis, in his *Eutychius Vindicatus*, 1661; also by Pearson in the *Vindiciae Ignatianae*, 1672. The *Annales*, or *Contextio Gemmarum*, is published in a Latin translation in Migne's *Patrol. Graec.* cxi. p. 907 f. The passages quoted above are from p. 982.

patriarch. Afterwards they should elect another eminent man and make him presbyter with themselves in place of him who had been made patriarch, that they might always be twelve. And this custom of the twelve presbyters of Alexandria appointing the patriarch out of themselves continued till the time of the patriarch Alexander, who was of the 318 [i.e. Fathers of Nicaea]; he forbade the presbyters henceforth to appoint the patriarch. He also ordered that when the patriarch was dead the bishops should assemble and appoint a patriarch." He also removed the restriction to elect from among the twelve presbyters. "Thus ceased the ancient custom of appointing the patriarch from among the presbyters and the power of appointing the patriarch came to belong to the bishops."

"From the time of Hananias to the time of Demetrius, the eleventh patriarch of Alexandria (A.D. 189 to A.D. 231-2), there was no bishop in the territory of Egypt. Nor had the patriarchs who were before him appointed a bishop. When Demetrius was made patriarch he appointed three bishops, and he was the first patriarch of Alexandria who appointed bishops. When he was dead Heraclas was appointed in his place, who appointed twenty bishops."

It will be noticed that Eutychius

(1) supports Jerome's statement, but specifies *twelve* presbyters, and adds that the presbyters *laid on hands*, which Jerome does not say:
(2) makes the arrangement last till Alexander's time, which again contradicts Jerome and is manifestly false:
(3) speaks of 'the patriarch,' which is of course an anachronism:
(4) adds information which, if true, would be very important, viz., that there was only one bishop in Egypt up to the days of Demetrius, who added three, and Heraclas, who increased them to twenty.

We cannot tell whence this writer derived his information. I think, however, that the following reasons are sufficient to prevent our attaching any weight to what he says:—

(1) He is so ignorant of the period to which he assigns the 'ecclesiastical revolution' caused by the creation of the Egyptian episcopate, that he actually is unaware of the existence at that time of infinitely the most important man of the age—Origen. When he comes to deal with the fifth Council he writes thus[1]: "There was in the time of Justinian a bishop of Manbag (episcopus Manbagensis), by name Origen, who taught metempsychosis, deny-

[1] ap. Migne *l.c.* p. 1073.

ing a resurrection. There was also Ibas, bishop of Edessa (Rohensis), Thaddaeus, bishop of Massisa (Massisensis), and Theodoret, bishop of Ancyra, who asserted that the body of our Lord Christ was phantastic and nothing real." This will suffice as a specimen of his historical knowledge. Pearson enlarges on his ignorance and blunders (*Vindic. Ignat.* part I. p. 294 f.).

(2) But it may be answered that however ignorant of the Greek church writers, and of church history generally, he may have had access to Alexandrian traditions. Have we reason then to think that his statements represent ancient Egyptian tradition? I think not. Partly because Jerome, had he known what Eutychius relates, would not have kept silence about it. But also—and this is more important—because Severus, bishop of Asmonaei in Egypt,[1] who wrote a history of the Alexandrian patriarchs[2] in the same century as Eutychius (c. A.D. 978) and professes to have consulted Greek and Coptic remains in the monastery of St. Macarius, knows nothing of what Eutychius relates and gives a great many details about the election of early patriarchs quite inconsistent with the supposed position of the twelve presbyters and involving the existence of other bishops. Renaudot complains (*Hist.* p. 23) of Severus' ignorance and doubts his knowledge of Greek, but at least he knows more of the period of Demetrius than Eutychius does. He abuses Origen out of all reason; but he knows his period and his fame as a scholar and writer. Now Severus makes St. Mark consecrate *a bishop, three presbyters, and seven deacons*, and then proceed into Pentapolis and consecrate in many places bishops, priests, and deacons (Renaudot *Hist.* p. 4). He represents Cerdo (the third bishop), as having been elected by bishops and priests with the faithful laity and that too by lot (*ib.* p. 14), and Primus (the fourth) as chosen out of the "orthodox people" not from among the presbyters (p. 15), and Claudian (the eighth) as elected by the people with the bishops (p. 17).[3] Thus the complete disagreement of the more

---

[1] Fabricius *Bibl. Graec.* ix. p. 349: "Asmonaeorum episcopus" (?=Ashmuneim).

[2] Condensed by Renaudot into a Latin version *Historia Patriarcharum Alexandrinorum*.

[3] Apparently he speaks of the election of Agrippinus the tenth patriarch in these words, as rendered by Renaudot in Latin (*Coll. Lit. Orient* i. p. 381): "convenisse populum et manus imposuisse illi atque illum ordinavisse patriarcham et in sede d. Marci collocavisse." Renaudot thinks this phrase in Severus makes it possible that Eutychius only meant to imply that the eleven presbyters 'got hands laid upon the new patriarch.' This, however, is improbable.

credible Severus with the statements of Eutychius seems to deprive them of the claim to represent a valid tradition.[1]

(3) Eutychius' information about the absence of bishops in Egypt till the times of Demetrius and Heraclas seems inconsistent with what we know of the history of the period. Photius records,[2] on the authority of Pamphilus, the author of an *Apology for Origen*, the following facts: "Demetrius' love is turned [by Origen's ordination] into hatred.... Moreover, a synod of bishops and some presbyters is gathered together against Origen. And they, as Pamphilus says, vote that Origen should be banished from Alexandria and neither live there nor teach, but that he should not be deposed from the honour of the presbyterate. But Demetrius, with some Egyptian bishops, removed him also from the priesthood, those who had formerly supported him subscribing this decree." Now Pamphilus was an enthusiastic disciple of Origen, and if this synod of bishops who overrode the mixed synod of bishops and presbyters had been a new thing created simply by Demetrius and lacking altogether in constitutional authority, it is very unlikely that we should not have been told so. Nay more, we should surely have been able to catch in Origen's own language about bishops subsequently some tone of disparagement, some hint of novel claims made in the name of episcopal authority; but all his language quoted on pp. 140, 141, dates from the period after his expulsion and deposition.[3] Dr. Bigg speaks of the patriarchate of Demetrius as involving "the bustle and excitement of a revolution," and he alludes to "a usurpation which lay heavy on the priests."[4] Now Demetrius died in 231; this "usurpation" was carried further, according to Jerome, in the episcopates of his successors by the abolition of the old method of appointing bishops. Yet Origen, writing about A.D. 249, speaks of the Alexandrian, among other Churches, as characterized by mildness and stability ($\pi\rho\alpha\epsilon\hat{\imath}\alpha$ $\kappa\alpha\grave{\imath}$ $\epsilon\grave{\upsilon}\sigma\tau\alpha\theta\acute{\eta}s$, *c. Cels.* iii. 30), and

[1] It may be said that still later historians, Georgius Homadius (El-Makin), an Arab Christian who died in 1273, and the Sheikh Taqi-ed-Din El-Maqrizi (fourteenth century—translated by Rev. S. C. Malan in *Original Documents of the Coptic Church*), support Eutychius in different degrees. But the former is said to be "made up out of Eutychius" (this portion of El-Makin is not edited), and El-Maqrizi undoubtedly depends upon him. "A gifted man," he describes him, "who wrote a useful history" (Malan's translation p. 87).

[2] Photius *Bibliotheca* cod. cxviii ap. Migne *Patrol. Graec.* ciii. p. 397. Pamphilus was martyred in A.D. 309. The book was completed by his friend Eusebius, bishop of Caesarea.

[3] The Homilies date from A.D. 245 and after.

[4] *B. L.* p. 100: "the *Stromateis* were written during the patriarchate of Demetrius *amid the bustle and excitement of a revolution*;" and p. 119.

thinks apparently that the fault Celsus is most likely to find in bishops and clergy is a want of zeal.[1]

(4) Eutychius' information seems inconsistent with a document which appears to let in light upon the very early days of Egyptian church history. The document known as the *Apostolical Church Ordinances* (which is to be distinguished both from the *Apostolical Constitutions* and from the *Apostolical Canons*) is the beginning of the canon law of the Egyptian Church. Its history indicates Egypt as its source, and Harnack, its last editor, rightly remarks that it has a provincial origin.[2] It is a composite document, and appears to contain fragments of very different epochs; some chapters (16-21) on the election of bishops, on presbyters, readers, deacons, and widows, seem to come from very early days.[3] The chapter on the election of a bishop is very curious: "If there be a paucity of men, and anywhere the number of those able to vote for a bishop *be less than twelve*, let them write to the neighbouring Churches, according to where it happens to be, that three chosen men having come from thence, and having put to the test him who is worthy—namely if any one have a good report of the heathen, if he be sinless, if he be a lover of the poor, if he be temperate, not a drunkard, not a fornicator, not covetous, nor a railer, nor a respecter of persons, nor such like things: it is good that he should be unmarried, or if not, a husband of one wife, educated, able to interpret the Scriptures, or if unlearned, meek in character, and let him abound in love towards all, lest the bishop come to be convicted in any matter by the multitude."[4] Here we have popular election, the possibility of illiterate bishops, heathen surroundings, and every thing that points to early days

---

[1] It should be remembered too that in Athanasius' day there were, as he tells us, about a hundred bishops (ἐγγὺς ἑκατόν) in Egypt, Libya, and Pentapolis (*Apol. c. Ar.* 71). The growth from four when Heraclas acceded (A.D. 232) to one hundred when Athanasius wrote (c. A.D. 350) would have been extremely rapid.

[2] *Texte und Untersuch.* band ii, heft 2, p. 193 f. and heft 5, p. 6.

[3] At latest, Harnack says, "the first third of the third century" (heft 2, p. 212). The remarkable position of the 'reader' *above the deacon* to which Harnack calls attention has also to be noticed.

[4] c. 16: . . . ἐὰν ὀλιγανδρία ὑπάρχῃ καὶ μήπου πλῆθος τυγχάνῃ τῶν δυναμένων ψηφίσασθαι περὶ ἐπισκόπου ἐντὸς δεκαδύο ἀνδρῶν, εἰς τὰς πλησίον ἐκκλησίας, ὅπου τυγχάνει πεπηγυῖα, γραφέτωσαν, ὅπως ἐκεῖθεν τρεῖς ἄνδρες παραγενόμενοι δοκιμῇ δοκιμάσαντες τὸν ἄξιον ὄντα, εἴ τις φήμην καλὴν ἔχει ἀπὸ τῶν ἐθνῶν, . . . καλὸν μὲν εἶναι ἀγύναιος, εἰ δὲ μή, ἀπὸ μιᾶς γυναικός· παιδείας μέτοχος, δυνάμενος τὰς γραφὰς ἑρμηνεύειν· εἰ δὲ ἀγράμματος, πραὺς ὑπάρχων . . . μήποτε περί τινος ἐλεγχθεὶς ἐπίσκοπος ἀπὸ τῶν πολλῶν γενηθείη.

and out-of-the-way communities. This makes it all the more noticeable that there is to be a bishop elected even *in communities where there are not twelve voters*. This is better evidence than Eutychius can offer!

On the whole, then, I think it is absurd to take Eutychius as an authority in the way in which some modern writers—notably Dr. Bigg—have done. I believe the evidence would suggest

(1) a wide-spread episcopacy in Egypt generally, as elsewhere, even in the smallest communities:

(2) a large degree of popular influence in the election down to the Nicene age:

(3) a special state of things in the 'diocese' of Alexandria, resembling the later parochial system and giving larger powers to the presbyters in charge of churches than was customary elsewhere:

(4) that we have no ground for accepting Eutychius' information about the college of twelve presbyters at Alexandria (the number twelve may derive in some way from the canon of the *Ch. Ordinances* just quoted, misunderstood in the light of later arrangements in less democratic days; or it may be due indirectly to the same causes which led to the selection of the number twelve for the presbyters ordained by St. Peter in the Clementines):

(5) that in the absence of any trustworthy support from Eutychius, there is no strong case for accepting Jerome's statement about the substantial identity of bishops and presbyters in early days at Alexandria, in such sense that no episcopal ordination, but only presbyteral appointment, was required to make a presbyter bishop. If there were many bishops in Egypt, the supposed ground for this exceptional system is gone.

C.

RITES AND PRAYERS OF ORDINATION.

(*See pp.* 144-149 *and* 177-181.)

A. GREEK RITES OF ORDINATION.

A rite in a MS stated by Morinus to be of the ninth century (*de Sacr. Ord.* p. ii. p. 64 f.) is to the following effect:—

(*a*) *For a bishop.* The archbishop reads the declaration of his election: "the Divine Grace . . . appoints such an one, the well-beloved presbyter, to be bishop."[1] This he reads "holding his hand upon the head of him who is being ordained." Then, after the Kyrie Eleison, "the archbishop lays the Gospel on his head and neck (while other bishops stand by and touch it), and, laying his hand on him, prays thus." In the prayer he invokes God as having ordained, through his Apostle St. Paul, divers orders for the ministry of His holy mysteries at His altar—apostles, prophets, teachers—and prays Him that the person now elected to pass under the yoke of the Gospel and under the high-priestly dignity, through the laying-on of his and his assistants' hands, by the descent and power and grace of the Holy Spirit, may be strengthened with His holy unction, like prophets and kings and high-priests of old, and made a blameless high-priest and intercessor for his people.

Afterwards, intercessions follow, during which the archbishop keeps his hand on the head of him who is being ordained ($\tau o\hat{v}$ $\chi\epsilon\iota\rho o\tau o\nu o\upsilon\mu\acute{\epsilon}\nu o\upsilon$) and prays thus: "O Lord God, who, because the nature of man cannot bear the essence of the Godhead, hast in Thy economy appointed us teachers of like passions with ourselves, occupying Thy seat, to offer Thee sacrifice and offering on behalf of all Thy people, do Thou, O Lord, make this man who has been made ($\dot{a}\nu a\delta\epsilon\iota\chi\theta\acute{\epsilon}\nu\tau a$) a steward of the grace of the high-

---

[1] This is the $\dot{a}\nu\acute{a}\rho\rho\eta\sigma\iota s$ $\iota\epsilon\rho\acute{a}$ (Dionysius ap. Morinus *de S. O.* p. ii. p. 57). It was made in the case of each order, and means that the consecrator ($\iota\epsilon\rho o\tau\epsilon\lambda\acute{\epsilon}\sigma\tau\eta s$) is the *interpreter of the divine election* and does not act by the impulse of his own favour ($\iota\delta\acute{\iota}\dot{a}$ $\chi\acute{a}\rho\iota\tau\iota$). This emphasis on the choice of divine grace is common to all (apparently) the oriental rites of ordination.

These rites are given in Morinus *de Sacr. Ord.* pars ii. For the COPTIC, see pp. 507-8 (as in the *Apostolical Constitutions* and the Latin rites, the presbyters are compared to the seventy elders); for the JACOBITE, pp. 482 f. (it contains directions for impressive solemnity of manner in the consecrating bishop—"manus deprimit tremulas . . . oculis desuper cum timore aspicientibus"—pp. 484, 487); for the MARONITE, pp. 404 f. In these last the idea of succession by laying-on of hands is strangely traced from God on Mount Sinai, through Moses and Aaron, to John the Baptist, from John the Baptist to Christ, from Christ to His Apostles; cf. Ephraem Syr. *Opp. Syr.* ii. p. 448 [ed. Rom. 1740]. The hierarchy of earth is compared, as by Clement, to the grades of angelic glory. There are distinct rites for the ordination of chorepiscopus, bishop, and patriarch. The prayer for the chorepiscopus speaks of the "imposition of the Divine Hand" (p. 416) but the ritual direction for the laying-on of hands is only given in the case of the patriarch (p. 429). The NESTORIAN rites are on pp. 452 f. They contain prayers for the gifts of miraculous power—to heal the sick, and generally (pp. 457-465). Throughout all these rites there is the same general conception of the sacerdotal offices—the same conception of laying on apostolic hands, with accompanying prayer, with a view to the obtaining of the grace qualifying for the distinct orders of the ministry.

priesthood, an imitator of Thee, the true Pastor, laying down his life for the sheep, being a guide of the blind, a light of those in darkness, an instructor of the ignorant, a light of the world, that having prepared the souls committed to him in this life, he may stand without shame at Thy judgment seat." Then the archbishop puts the book of the Gospels upon the altar, and the 'omophorion' on him who has been ordained (τῷ χειροτονηθέντι), and kisses him, and mounts with him to the common throne (σύνθρονος).

(b) *For a presbyter.* "The archbishop makes three signs of the cross upon his head and, having his hand laid upon him, prays thus:" he invokes "the Ancient of days (ὁ πάσης κτίσεως πρεσβύτατος ὑπάρχων) who has dignified with the name of presbyter those who are thought worthy in this grade (βαθμός) to minister (ἱερουργεῖν) the word of His truth"; and prays Him to bestow on the present chosen person "this great grace of His Holy Spirit," that he may walk worthily of the holy priestly honour committed to him.

Then intercessions follow, the archbishop holding his hand on the head of "him who is being ordained" and praying that God will fill him, whom He has thought worthy to undertake the office of presbyter, with His Holy Spirit, "that he may stand blamelessly at His altar, and preach the Gospel of His salvation, and minister (ἱερουργεῖν) the word of His truth, and offer Him gifts and spiritual sacrifices, and renew His people by the laver of regeneration."

Then he gives him the appropriate dress and kiss, and later on associates him with himself in the service of the altar.

In a later office (p. 112), the bishop gives the just ordained presbyter the consecrated bread with the words: "Receive this deposit, and guard it to the coming of our Lord." In general, with some ritual additions, the rite is unchanged. In the rite of the ordination of a bishop there is a long declaration of faith (p. 120 f.) and the giving of the pastoral staff, but no substantial change in the idea of the service or alteration in the rite and prayer. See Daniel *Codex Liturgicus* iv. pp. 556-563.

B. LATIN RITES OF ORDINATION.

There is an excellent account of these rites s.v. ORDINAL in the *Dict. Chr. Ant.* by Dr. Hatch; and they are described at length with elaborate references s.v. ORDINATION. The most recent and exact account of the MSS of the sacramentaries, is M. Delisle's *Mémoire sur d'anciens sacramentaires* [Paris, 1886]. We have

(1) Early accounts of the rite of ordination without prayers.

Cf. Martene *de Ant. Eccl. Rit.* [Antwerp, 1736] ii. pp. 86 f. (Ordo i), 151 f. (Ordo ix—given in part ap. Hittorp. *de Div. Cath. Eccl. Off.* p. 88); Muratori *Lit. Rom. Vet.* [Venice, 1748] i. p. 515 (the preface to the prayer of benediction).

(2) Early prayers of benediction without accompanying rites. Cf. Muratori *l.c.* i. p. 421 f. (Leonine), ii. p. 358 f. (Gregorian), i. pp. 513 f. and 622 f. (Gelasian).

(3) Early rites with benedictions. Cf. Muratori ii. pp. 406 f., 415 f.; Morinus p. ii. pp. 261-341 (Missale Francorum, etc.).

i. *Ordination of presbyters.* This begins with a presentation of the ordinand to the bishop: an address to the people, solemnly asking their assent: sometimes an examination of the ordinand: a declaration of election by the bishop, and a request for common prayer—"commune votum communis oratio prosequatur." Then follows the ordination—the presbyters with the bishop laying on hands. Of the following prayers the first is in all the forms:

(*a*) A collect (*Oratio*) for the outpouring of the "benediction of the Holy Spirit and the virtue of sacerdotal grace" upon him who is "offered for consecration."

(*b*) The *Consecratio.* God is invoked as the harmonious dispenser of all the distinctive grades and offices in the world, "unde sacerdotalis gradus et officia Levitarum sacramentis mysticis instituta creverunt"; special commemoration is made of His having ordained to offices of assistance in His kingdom at every stage "men of a second order and dignity" (sequentis ordinis, secundae dignitatis): to assist Moses, the seventy elders: to supplement Aaron's priesthood, that of his sons: to accompany the Apostles, "teachers of the faith," so that they filled the whole world with these "second preachers" (that is, apparently, the seventy). So God is implored to give His bishops now—as in their greater weakness they need it the more—the supplementary ministry of the presbyters, and, in particular, to give "to this His servant the dignity of the presbyterate, to renew in his heart the Spirit of holiness, that he may receive and hold from God the gift of second worth (secundi meriti munus), and by the example of his conversation set the standard of conduct (censuram morum insinuet), so that he may be the worthy assistant of the bishop (probus, or, providus nostri ordinis cooperator)." These prayers are in the Leonine Sacramentary (which seems to be the earliest that remains, and the Verona MS of which is assigned by Delisle, *Mémoire etc.* p. 65, to the seventh century) and in the Gregorian.

Note C. 367

(c) In the Gelasian MS (end of seventh or beginning of eighth century, Delisle *l.c.* p. 68), the Missale Francorum (end of seventh or beginning of eighth century, Delisle *l.c.* p. 72), and many later missals, we have after the *Consecratio* an invitation to prayer, entitled *Consummatio Presbyteri*, for the "sacerdotal gifts of the Holy Spirit" on the new presbyter. This is followed by the prayer, called *Benedictio*, that he may be all an elder ought to be, in meditation of God's law, in faith, in teaching, in life: "that he may keep pure and undefiled the gift of God's ministry, and in the service of His people may, by the body and blood of His Son, by undefiled benediction, be transformed into inviolable love and into a perfect man."[1] Then (in the Missale Francorum) there is a *Consecratio Manus*—an unction of the presbyter's hands with a prayer, "ut quaecunque benedixerint benedicta sint, et quaecunque sanctificaverint, sanctificentur."

In all this there is no mention of *offering sacrifice*, or of *absolution*. The presbyter is viewed as the assistant of the bishop. But gradual alterations in the ordination of priests tend to emphasize their special sacerdotal functions, and thus to give them a more independent priesthood. Thus, as an accompaniment to the vesting in the chasuble, a benediction—"ut offeras placabiles hostias pro peccatis atque offensionibus populi omnipotenti Deo"—appears in the Codex S. Eligii (ninth or tenth century; Morinus p. 270, Delisle p. 175). So in the Anglo-Saxon MS of eleventh century (Morinus p. 282 f.), which also adds in the *Consecratio Manus*— "ad consecrandas hostias quae pro delictis atque negligentiis populi

---

[1] This is perhaps the earliest form of this prayer, the varieties of which are remarkable. This form is from an Anglo-Saxon missal in Morinus *l.c.* p. 282 f. "ut purum atque immaculatum mysterii [? ministerii] donum custodiat, et per obsequium plebis tuae corpore et sanguine filii tui immaculata benedictione transformetur ad inviolabilem charitatem et in virum perfectum, in mensuram aetatis plenitudinis Christi [? et] in die iusti et aeterni iudicii . . . Spiritu sancto plenus appareat." This MS is dated by Delisle, p. 220, at the beginning of the eleventh century. In a Corbey MS of the tenth century (Morinus p. 304, Delisle p. 189) we have the same form, but with an insertion—which spoils the sense—of vel corpus before corpore. This indicates an approximation to the form of the prayer as it occurs in the Gelasian and Frankish missals, in which it is a prayer for the transformation not of the priest but of the elements: "ut per obsequium plebis tuae corpus et sanguinem filii tui immaculata benedictione transformet, et inviolabili charitate in virum perfectum, . . . S.s. plenus persolvat:" or, still more clearly (Morinus p. 319) "et per obsequium plebis tuae panem et vinum in corpus et sanguinem filii tui . . . transformet."

offeruntur;" cf. a Sens MS (tenth century, *ib.* p. 294 f.) and the Codex Ratoldi (tenth century, *ib.* p. 298 f.). In a (?) twelfth century MS (*ib.* p. 329 f.) appears the *porrectio instrumentorum* with "Accipe potestatem offerre sacrificium Deo missamque celebrare et tam pro vivis quam et pro defunctis." Lastly in thirteenth century MSS (Morinus pp. 338, 340) we have the "Accipe Spiritum sanctum; quorum remiseritis peccata etc."

On the newly ordained presbyters concelebrating with the bishop, see Morinus *l.c.* p. iii. ex. viii. 1. 1 f.

ii. *The ordination of a bishop.* In Martene's Ordo i (*l.c.* ii. p. 87) we have provisions for securing that the bishop has been duly elected "a populo civitatis," and for his examination in respect of morality, discipline, etc., both in private and in public, and for his due presentation. All this precedes the ordination by the interval of a day. Commonly a public examination of him who was to be ordained, in respect of doctrine and morality, took place at the time of the ordination (see Morinus p. ii. p. 275).[1] This is followed by a declaration of election, and the ordination.[2]

---

[1] The examination in doctrine and morals is enjoined in the so-called Canons of the 4th Carthaginian Council in A.D. 398 (which really are 104 canons, collected from East and West some time before the sixth century, and described as "secundum Gallorum institutiones" in the Ordo Romanus ap. Hittorp. p. 97).

In the Missale Francorum which gives one of the earliest rites, we find first an *Exhortatio ad populum* to choose a worthy successor to the pastoral office: the election is to be "testimonio presbyterorum et totius cleri et consilio civium ac consistentium," and the elected is to be "natalibus nobilis, moribus clarus, religione probus, fide stabilis, ... tenax in cunctis quae sacerdoti elegenda sunt." Then follow prayers for God's assistance and the effusion on those to be ordained of sacerdotal grace. After this the people are exhorted to pray God, who has established a propitiation for Himself and sacrifices and sacred rites (qui placationem suam et sacrificia et sacra constituit), to fill the high-priest with the due plenitude of honour and grade, with spiritual gifts, and wealth of sanctification, and especially with humility, that as a ruler he may make himself low and be among his flock as one of themselves (quasi unus ex illis), trembling always for the account for souls which he must give; also that he may be made fit for all sacred rites by the supreme benediction, the utmost that man can give (universis sacris sacrandisque idoneus fiat sub hac quae est homini per hominem postrema benedictio).

[2] The Canons of the 4th Carthaginian Council may have introduced into the West the eastern custom at the ordination of a bishop, i.e. the holding the book of the Gospels over his head. (See quotations in Bingham *Antiq.* ii. 11. 8 from *Apost. Const.*, Chrysostom, pseudo-Dionysius.) In the western collection of canons it assumes this form (c. 2): "Episcopus cum ordinatur, duo episcopi ponant et teneant evangeliorum codicem super caput et cervicem eius et, uno super eum fundente benedictionem, reliqui omnes

Note C. 369

The most original and constant accompanying prayer seems to be (a) a collect, as in the ordination of a presbyter, for the infusion of "sacerdotal grace, the virtue of the divine benediction," followed by (b) the *Consecratio*. In this God is invoked as having instituted all the symbolism of the old priesthood; because all that was there symbolized by outward decoration is to be realized in our priesthood by spiritual endowment; it is no longer the "honor vestium," but the "splendor animarum." Therefore He is implored to grant "ut quicquid illa velamina in fulgore auri, in nitore gemmarum et multimodi operis varietate signabant, hoc in horum moribus clarescat." Then there is a prayer that 'the unction of the Spirit (accompanying, as other MSS specify, the symbolic external unction) may flow down abundantly upon those who are being ordained, "ut tui Spiritus virtus et interiorum ora repleat et exteriora circumtegat"; that they may be endowed with faith, love, peacefulness; [that they may be true evangelists; that they may have the ministry of reconciliation, in word and in the power of signs and wonders (signorum et prodigiorum); that their preaching may have power; that God will give them the keys of the kingdom of heaven, and they may use them rightly, "to edification and not to destruction"; that what they bind on earth may be bound in heaven, etc.; that whose sins they retain may be retained, and whose sins they remit may be remitted; that whom they bless may be blessed, and whom they curse may be cursed; that they may feed and perfect their flock; that they may have all zeal and right judgment;] that God may give them the episcopal see (cathedra) for ruling His Church, be to them authority and power and strength, and multiply His blessing upon them.' The part of the prayer enclosed in brackets [ ] is in the Gelasian Sacr. (Murat. *l.c.* i. p. 625) and in the Missale Francorum (Morinus *l.c.* p. 266), but not in the Leonine (Murat. *l.c.* i. p. 422) or Gregorian Sacr. (*ib.* ii. p. 358). Omitting this part of the prayer, we have in the whole rite no *specification* of the special function of sacrifice or of the power of the keys.

episcopi, qui adsunt, manibus suis caput eius tangant." So it passed into western writers and missals; cf. Amalarius *de Eccl. Off.* ii. 14 ap. Hittorp. p. 167: "Dicit libellus, secundum cuius ordinem celebratur ordinatio apud quosdam, ut duo episcopi teneant evangelium, etc." It occurs in the Missale Francorum (Morinus *l.c.* p. 261), and in the Ordo Romanus (ap. Hittorp. p. 100). But it is omitted in one form given in the Ordo (ib. p. 96); and we find (pseudo) Albinus Flaccus, *de Div. Off.* ap. Hittorp. p. 74, protesting thus: "illud vero (here follows the canon) non reperitur in auctoritate veteri neque nova, sed neque in Romana traditione."

Later on there are a number of additions to the rite, connected with the giving of the ring, pastoral staff, etc. The enthronization of the bishop would probably have formed part of the rite from the beginning; see Martene's Ord. i and ii (*l.c.* ii. pp. 88, 90).

D.

I. CANON XIII OF ANCYRA.
II. CHOREPISCOPI.

(*See pp.* 152, 153.)

I. THIS canon is now commonly quoted (see Dr. Lightfoot *Dissert.* p. 232) in this form: χωρεπισκόποις μὴ ἐξεῖναι πρεσβυτέρους ἢ διακόνους χειροτονεῖν, ἀλλὰ μὴν μηδὲ πρεσβυτέροις πόλεως χωρὶς τοῦ ἐπιτραπῆναι ὑπὸ τοῦ ἐπισκόπου μετὰ γραμμάτων ἐν ἑκάστῃ παροικίᾳ—"It is not allowed to country bishops to ordain presbyters or deacons, nor even to city presbyters, except permission be given in each parish by the bishop in writing." In this form it recognises implicitly *the power of presbyters to ordain under certain circumstances.* But is this the right reading? We have three sources of evidence: (*a*) the MSS; (*b*) the Versions; (*c*) the Greek Collections of the canons.

(*a*) The MSS give apparently little support to the above reading of the second part of the canon. Pitra (*Iur. Eccl. Graec. Hist. et Mon.* p. 450) speaks of the reading ἀλλὰ μὴν μηδὲ πρεσβυτέρους πόλεως as the "vera canonis scriptura stabilita ex optimis codicibus." Thus, according to the best supported reading, the canon would say: "It is not allowed to country bishops to ordain presbyters or deacons, but neither, of course (are they allowed to ordain) city presbyters, except permission be given in each parish by the bishop in writing."[1]

[1] There is no satisfactory critical edition of the canons. Meanwhile it may be worth mentioning that I have examined the MSS in the Bodleian Library at Oxford, in the Laurentian at Florence, and in the Ambrosian at Milan.

Of the nine Bodleian Greek MSS seven read πρεσβυτέρους, viz. four of the 11th cent. (Barocc. 185, 196, Laud. 39, Misc. 206) and three of later date; the remaining two read ἐπισκόποι (Barocc. 26, saec. xi) and ἐπισκόπους (Misc. 170, saec. xiv) At Florence Laur x. 10 (saec. xi) has πρεσβυτέρους, but x. 1 (saec. xiii, careless and with many errors) πρεσβυτέροις. At Milan, however, in the Ambrosian two MSS from Magna Graecia, F 48 sup.

Note D.

(*b*) The VERSIONS are very ambiguous; (1) The SYRIAC version (made in the city of Mabug, A.D. 501, and preserved in a Nitrian MS of the first half of the sixth century, now in the British Museum)[1] supports, as quoted above p. 153, without doubt the reading πρεσβυτέρους. The canon in this version, which has not been edited, was kindly translated for me by Dr. Höning of the British Museum. I have since seen an independent translation to the same effect. (2) The LATIN versions are the real support of the reading πρεσβυτέροις. Thus the version of Dionysius Exiguus generally appears thus: "Chorepiscopis non licere presbyteros aut diaconos ordinare; sed nec presbyteris civitatis sine praecepto episcopi vel litteris in unaquaque parochia [aliquid imperare, nec sine auctoritate litterarum in unaquaque parochia aliquid agere]." Here the words "aliquid agere" or "aliquid imperare" seem introduced to give the canon a meaning applicable to presbyters. Similar qualifications are introduced in the versions of Fulgentius Ferrandus (*Brev. Can.* 79, 92) and Isidore Mercator; cf. the *Prisca* in Justellus *Bibl. Iur. Can. Vet.* i. p. 279, but others are without any addition, see Justellus *l.c.* p. 120. On the other hand an interesting MS at Milan of the version of Dionysius supports the reading πρεσβυτέρους thus: "Chorepiscopis non licere presbyteros aut diaconos ordinare sed nec presbyteros civitatis suae sine praecepto episcopi vel litteris in unaquaque parochia."[2] A Bodleian MS (Laud. Misc. 421, saec. xi) also has "presbyteros" corrected to "presbyteris."

(saec. xii) and E 94 (saec. forte xiii), read πρεσβυτέροις. From Rome Pitra cites only one MS (Vallicell.) for πρεσβυτέροις and one (Vat. 1) for ἐπισκόποις. It would thus appear that the MS authority for πρεσβυτέρους is very weak: as good a case might be made out on the MSS for ἐπισκόποις.

It is however possible that the test of the best MSS may be the preservation of the undoubtedly right readings of (*a*) βδελύσσοιντο in can. 14 and (*b*) περισχεθέντας in can. 3. Now of these (*a*) occurs in all the MSS mentioned above which have either ἐπισκόποις [-ους, -οι] or πρεσβυτέροις, but only in Bodl. Seld. 48 among those I have looked at which read πρεσβυτέρους, with apparently some referred to by Pitra: (*b*) is read in most of the same MSS, viz. Barocc. 26, Misc. 170, F 48, E 94, but also in Barocc. 158 which has πρεσβυτέρους.

The reading ἐπισκόποις would be more intelligible if coupled with the reading ἑτέρᾳ in place of ἑκάστῃ (as in Photius' *Syntagma*), but no MS which supports ἐπισκόποις reads also ἑτέρᾳ.

[1] See Wright's *Catalogue of Syriac MSS in the Brit. Mus.* p. 1032ᵃ.

[2] This MS (C 256 inf.) was beautifully copied under the orders of a bishop John of Bergamo ("Episc. Pergamensis" = ? John B. Milani, 1592-1611) from a very ancient MS, "vetustate paene consumptus," which was at that time in the archives of his see.

(c) Of the GREEK COLLECTIONS of the Canons, John of Antioch (6th cent.) in his *Collectio Can.* tit. 21 (given in Justellus) reads πρεσβυτέροις; Photius (9th cent.) in his *Syntagma Can.* (ap. Migne *Patrol. Graec.* civ. p. 552) ἐπισκόποις—but the Lat. trans. gives presbyteros. Balsamon and Zonaras (12th or 13th centuries) in their commentaries support πρεσβυτέρους.

The confusion is manifestly great. It must be borne in mind that the bishops at Ancyra expressed themselves frequently in very obscure Greek; see, for example, cc. 14 and 17. On the whole the reading which seems to have best support in MSS and versions taken together is that given by Routh *Rel. Sacr.* iv. p. 121 (cf. 144 f.): χωρεπισκόποις μὴ ἐξεῖναι πρεσβυτέρους ἢ διακόνους χειροτονεῖν, ἀλλὰ μὴν[1] μηδὲ πρεσβυτέρους πόλεως χωρὶς τοῦ ἐπιτραπῆναι ὑπὸ τοῦ ἐπισκόπου μετὰ γραμμάτων ἐν ἑκάστῃ παροικίᾳ. One is inclined to wonder whether the original canon did not run χωρεπισκόπους μὴ ἐξεῖναι πρεσβυτέρους . . . χειροτονεῖν, ἀλλὰ μὴν μηδὲ πρεσβυτέρους πόλεως . . . This would have been intended to convey the same meaning as the reading last quoted (i.e. πρεσβυτέρους πόλεως would be an accus. after χειροτονεῖν), but the ambiguity of the construction would account for the confusion of the versions and MSS, and for the mistake of the Latin translators in making presbyteris correspond to chorepiscopis; and, as was said above, the fathers of Ancyra certainly expressed themselves in other cases with very great ambiguity. χωρεπισκόπους has, however, no MS support.

II. CHOREPISCOPI were country bishops ordained to supervise the scattered flock in rural districts—"vicarii episcoporum," as Isidore of Seville calls them. We begin to hear of them in the East as established institutions early in the fourth century: first in the canon of Ancyra just discussed. Later they had a great development in the West also. The tenth canon of Antioch, A.D. 341, indicates (a) that they might be ordained by the *one* bishop, alone, who presided over the adjacent town church; (b) that they might ordain to the minor orders, but not to the diaconate or presbyterate without the leave of the bishop under whom they served. It limits their power thus: εἰ καὶ χειροθεσίαν εἶεν ἐπισκόπων εἰληφότες, i.e., as Dionysius Exiguus adds in his trans. "ut episcopi consecrati sunt." We find them present at councils voting and signing, presumably with the assent of their superior bishops; see Bingham *Ant.* ii. 14. 10; Morinus *de Sacr. Ord.* p. iii. ex. iv. 1. 12. Athanasius classes them with bishops in *Apol. c. Ar.* 85: "Mareotis

---

[1] For the use of μήν cf. Conc. Neo-Caesar. c. 13.

Note D. 373

is a district (χώρα) of Alexandria, and there has never been in the district (χώρα) a *bishop or chorepiscopus*," but only presbyters subject to the bishop of Alexandria. An ordination by a chorepiscopus is recorded in *Hist. Lausiac.* cvi, ap. Migne *Patrol. Lat.* lxxiii. p. 1193. Isidore, *de Eccl. Off.* ii. 6, describes them thus: "Chorepiscopi, id est vicarii episcoporum, iuxta quod canones ipsi testantur, instituti sunt ad exemplum lxx seniorum tanquam sacerdotes propter sollicitudinem pauperum.[1] Hi in vicis et villis instituti gubernant sibi conmissas ecclesias, habentes licentiam constituere lectores, subdiaconos, exorcistas. Presbyteros autem et diaconos ordinare non audeant praeter conscientiam episcopi in cuius regione praeesse noscuntur. Hi autem a solo episcopo civitatis cui adiacent ordinantur."

Later, in the awful collapse of discipline which characterized the Frankish kingdom, they were indefinitely multiplied: "wandering bishops ordained wandering clergy, and neither bishops nor clergy were easily brought to acknowledge a superior."[2] Isidore speaks bitterly of this state of things (*de Eccl. Off.* ii. 3): "Duo sunt genera clericorum: unum ecclesiasticorum sub regimine episcopali degentium: alterum acephalorum . . . quem sequantur ignorantium. Hos . . . solutos atque oberrantes sola turpis vita complectitur et vaga . . . quorum quidem sordida atque infami numerositate, satis superque nostra pars occidua polluitur."[3] Hence at the restoration of discipline, which marks the age of Charles the Great,[4] the chorepiscopi were the subjects of strong animadversion. Their usurpation of authority led to a disparagement of their original position. Papal decisions—not however that of Pope Nicholas, A.D. 864—pronounced them *mere presbyters.* Hence later Roman Catholic writers, e.g. Morinus, and others[5] have argued in this sense. The papal authority constitutes their real argument— "efficacissimum argumentum," as says Morinus. However, he also argues—(i) That they are compared to the seventy elders, which

---

[1] Cf. Conc. Neo Caes. c. 14. Rabanus Maurus (*de Inst. Cler.* i. 5 ap. Hittorp. p. 315) adds: "ne eis [sc. pauperibus qui in agris et villis consistunt] solatium confirmationis deesset."

[2] Hatch *Growth of Church Institutions* p. 159.

[3] Morinus (*l.c.* c. 5 § 4) finds in the circumstances of his own day a parallel to the ancient appointment of chorepiscopi in a way which led to their abuse: "ut nunc, in Germania potissimum, ditissimi et principes illi episcopi titularibus episcopis [utuntur] . . . qui pauca mercede contenti dioecesis onera ferunt, quamdiu veri episcopi Endymionis somnum dormiunt."

[4] Hatch *l.c.* p. 28 f.

[5] See Bingham *l.c.* §§ 2, 3.

is the comparison appropriated to *presbyters*.¹ Yes: to presbyters as *assistants*. This is the point of the comparison, and it holds for chorepiscopi also. Further, it is well known that the Old Testament analogies are loosely applied. (ii) That ordinations of *bishops* by one bishop were not tolerated, while chorepiscopi were so ordained. Yes: this, however, was a matter of provincial discipline—to secure the assent of the provincial bishops. But the chorepiscopi were an inferior sort of bishops with only a local, not a provincial or catholic, position. Morinus, however, does not hold them to have been presbyters pure and simple but a sort of middle order: "non sunt presbyteri simplices, sed inter episcopatum et presbyteratum media dignitas" (*l.c.* c. 5. § 12).

The view given above of the position of the chorepiscopi may be described as the ordinary view. It seems to be the only one supported by the evidence. Dr. Lightfoot, in his *Dissert.* p. 233, represents them as a survival of the original presbyter-bishops, but this theory has no evidence except such as is derived from the misread canon of Ancyra. The eastern chorepiscopi of later days were confessedly only presbyters. Further information (with reference to their privileges, uses, etc., and their suppression) can be found in Bingham *l.c.*; Morinus *l.c.*; and *Dict. Chr. Biog.* s.v.

E.

SUPPOSED ORDINATIONS BY PRESBYTERS IN EAST AND WEST.

(*See pp.* 161, 164.)

EASTERN CHURCH.

THE only case of such an ordination alleged in the East is that of Paphnutius. Dr. Hatch (*B.L.* p. 108, n.⁵², 1st edition only) spoke of this formerly as "the clearest case ... maintainable on the evidence." But it will not at all bear examination. Cassian, writing his Memoirs of oriental hermits at Marseilles about A.D. 422, tells us that the presbyter-abbot Paphnutius, "promoted" one of his companions on account of his conspicuous virtue, first to the diaconate, and then to the presbyterate (*Collat.* iv. 1: "a Paphnutio presbytero ... [Danielis] ad diaconii est praelatus officium ... eum presbyterii honore provexit

¹ See Morinus *l.c.* c. 2, §§ 6-11.

Note E.   375

[Paphnutius]"). This is taken to mean that he ordained him, and Cassian is supposed to mention it without surprise.

But (1) it is most improbable that Cassian, writing when and where he did, should mention such an act as if it were nothing surprising. He himself was in intimate relations with bishops in the West and knew well the difference between a monk and an ecclesiastical officer. See xi. 2 and his dedication to bks. i and xi.

(2) We have other evidence of the sense in which an abbot could promote to church offices. He could do it in the same sense as persons in power of any sort in the Church, as, for instance, a Prime Minister or patron of our day. He could *get him ordained at his nomination.* So we have a provision in the rule of St. Benedict (cap. 62) for abbots selecting worthy monks and getting them ordained. It should be noticed that this power of 'nominating' seems to have been a special privilege of the Alexandrian clergy; see Socr. *H. E.* i. 9 (the synodal letter from the Council of Nicaea to the Church of Alexandria) προχειρίζεσθαι ἢ ὑποβάλλειν ὀνόματα.

(3) The narrative of the abbot Ammonius, a friend of the older Athanasius (*Hist. Laus.* xii, ap. Migne *Patrol. Lat.* lxxiii. pp. 1103-4), shows how utterly distinct, in the minds of Egyptian monks, was the conception of a bishop from that of an abbot; an attempt was made to induce Ammonius to be *ordained bishop* and he resisted to death. The same broad distinction appears in Athanasius' letter to Dracontius.

(4) We are then bound to interpret the words in the present passage in the sense of 'nomination,' if they will admit of it. And they will do so without any difficulty. Instances are frequent in which influential laymen are said even to 'ordain' church officers, where there can be no doubt that what is meant is to appoint or get ordained; the laity of Oxyrinchus in Arian days " *episcopum sibi per tunc temporis episcopos catholicos ordinavit* " (*Marcell. et Faust. Lib. Prec.* ap. Migne *Patrol. Lat.* xiii. p. 101); again, without any explanation, Gregory of Tours *Hist. Franc.* viii. 22 : "Rex pollicitus fuerat se nunquam ex laicis episcopum ordinaturum." Otto III says "Sylvestrum papam elegimus et . . . ordinavimus et creavimus" (Gieseler *E. H.* Eng. trans. ii. p. 358, n.[28]). St. Cyprian, as will be seen, uses constituo and facio in the sense of procuring the appointment; cf. Bright *Early Eng. Ch. History* p. 134, from whom most of these instances are taken.

(5) It must be borne in mind that supposing Paphnutius had attempted to ordain any one in the ecclesiastical sense, he would have done what, in the patriarchate of Alexandria, had been

already (in Colluthus' case) pronounced null and void, and Daniel by the decision of the synod would have been regarded as a layman. But, as we have said, there is no reasonable case to be made out for his having done so.

WESTERN CHURCH.

1. The presbyter Novatus is said to have ordained Felicissimus deacon, and it is contended (Hatch *B. L.* p. 110, n.⁵²) that St. Cyprian did not regard the act as *invalid*. What is the state of the case? "He appointed Felicissimus deacon (Felicissimum diaconum constituit)," St. Cyprian says (*Ep.* lii. 2), and there is, it is urged, "nothing in the context to support the view that he uses the word in the unusual sense of 'procured the appointment.'" Is there nothing? St. Cyprian goes on to say that the same Novatus, when he left Africa and got to Rome, made Novatian a bishop. He uses the same word in both cases: "qui istic adversus ecclesiam diaconum fecerat illic episcopum fecit." He made Felicissimus a deacon, we may presume, in exactly the same sense as that in which he made Novatian a bishop. And in what sense did he do that? We know from the contemporary letter of Cornelius, the outraged bishop of Rome (ap. Euseb. *H. E.* vi. 43): "he [Novatian] compelled three bishops, boorish and most foolish men, ... to give him the episcopate by a shadowy and vain imposition of hands." Cf. Cyprian *Ep.* xlix. 1: "ei manum quasi in episcopatum imponi." Novatus then made Novatian a bishop and Felicissimus a deacon in this sense, that he *got them made* such by people, who, however "boorish" or "foolish," were none the less bishops (unless indeed Felicissimus was a deacon before, which is possible; see s.v. *Dict. Chr. Biog.*).

2. Dr. Hatch alleges in the same note that presbyter-missionaries in the middle ages ordained under exceptional circumstances of necessity, e.g. St. Willehad and St. Liudger, of the eighth century, are both in their lives said to have "constituted Churches and ordained presbyters over them"; see Pertz *Monumenta Hist. German.* ii. pp. 381, 411: "ecclesias [Willehadus] coepit construere ac presbyteros super eas ordinare." In both cases, however, a little investigation makes it plain that ordinare is used in the sense of 'appointing,' as it is used of secular persons (see just above). In the case of Willehad, his biographer tells us he remained a presbyter too long, because it was feared that the lawlessness of the Frisians would not tolerate the authority of a bishop. He therefore continued "cuncta potestate praesidentis

Note E. 377

ordinans—secundum quod poterat," i.e. up to a presbyter's power. Afterwards Charles the Great had him made bishop, "consecrari fecit." Then he redoubled his efforts and went about "confirmans populum qui olim baptizatus fuerat." He could not therefore *confirm* till he was made bishop. Is it likely then that he could *ordain*? In ruling Churches and appointing presbyters, however, he had only been doing what many 'ruling presbyters' in the mission field have done since, and are doing. In the case of Liudger, we are told that he was kept from being consecrated bishop by a sense of *unworthiness* and tried to get some one else consecrated in his place. Here then was not even a case of necessity, if such could be admitted, for a presbyter ordaining. The word is clearly used in his case, as in Willehad's, for 'appointing,' and both cases fall together. Both missionaries come in a close relation to the see of Rome and its strict discipline.

3. Dr. Hatch says further: " Ordination by other than a bishop, with the permission of the pope, is allowed even by the schoolmen and canonists, although the question is discussed among them whether the pope's licence can extend to the conferring of all orders, or should be limited to orders below the presbyterate" (*l.c.* p. 110, n.[52]). Now there need be no question here of orders below the presbyterate. What the matter comes to is this: a few mediaeval canonists (see opinions quoted in Morinus *de Sacr. Ord.* p. iii. ex. iii. 1-5 f.) maintained the theory that the papal licence could enable a presbyter validly to confer his own order (and even a confirmed Christian his own confirmation). But (*a*) this was a mere abstract question; there is no instance of a pope having attempted to give such a licence. And (*b*) Dr. Hatch's "even" is singularly out of place; this was an instance of papalism overriding catholicism. The men who made these claims on behalf of the pope were least of all maintainers of ancient discipline or liberty; they would have made almost any claim on his behalf. St. Thomas Aquinas says, *in Lib. iv. Sent.* dist. 25. qu. 1. art. 1: "Papa, qui habet plenitudinem potestatis pontificalis, potest committere non episcopo ea quae ad episcopalem dignitatem pertinent, dummodo illa non habeant immediatam relationem ad verum corpus Christi. Et ideo ex eius commissione aliquis sacerdos simpliciter potest conferre minores ordines et confirmare, non autem aliquis non sacerdos; nec iterum sacerdos maiores ordines, qui habent immediatam relationem ad corpus Christi, supra quod consecrandum papa non habet maiorem potestatem quam simplex sacerdos."

F.

THE THEORY OF THE MINISTRY HELD BY AMBROSIASTER, JEROME, ETC.

THE position explained above (pp. 171-176) is to be here justified by quotations.

I. AMBROSIASTER. (a) *His theory of ordination and the priesthood.* *in* 1 *Tim.* iv. 14 : " Gratiam dari ordinationis significat [Paulus] per prophetiam et manuum impositionem. . . . manus vero impositiones verba sunt mystica quibus confirmatur ad hoc opus electus, accipiens auctoritatem teste conscientia sua ut audeat vice Domini sacrificium Deo offerre." Cf. the reason why Christian "levitae et sacerdotes" should abstain from the indulgences of marriage (*in* 1 *Tim.* iii. 13); "Dei antistes" (*in* 1 *Tim.* v. 19); "in huius persona totius populi salus consistit" (*in* 1 *Tim.* vi. 16); "vicarius Christi" (*in* 2 *Tim.* i. 9); "actores Dei" (*in* 1 *Tim.* iii. 13). He does indeed hold that the original church arrangements were freer than those which prevailed subsequently. "When Churches had been established in all places and officers appointed, arrangements were made different from those with which things had begun. At first all used to teach and all to baptize, on whatever days and at whatever time there was opportunity. . . . So that the people might increase and be multiplied, all at the beginning were allowed to preach the Gospel and baptize and explain the Scriptures in Church; but when the Church embraced all places, places of meeting [conventicula] were established and rulers [rectores] and other offices in the Churches appointed, that none of the clergy who had not been ordained to it should venture to take to himself an office which he knows not to have been committed or granted to him."[1] There is thus a difference between modern and ancient arrangements. But even this very primitive practice of the earliest beginnings of the Church did not mean an indiscriminate condition of things. Even in the earliest days, we are told in the same passage, there were apostles, prophets, evangelists (who 'are deacons and not priests') and so on. Nor does he include among the things permitted to all, even for a time, the sacerdotal functions of sacrifice or laying-on of hands.[2]

[1] *in Eph.* iv. 11, 12.

[2] He uses the general Christian priesthood only as a ground for the position that all Christian people *can become priests* (i.e. in the ministry): "In

(b) *His recognition of the divine authority of the episcopate and of the principle of succession.* "In episcopo omnes ordines sunt, quia primus sacerdos est, hoc est, princeps est sacerdotum et propheta et evangelista et cetera adimplenda officia ecclesiae in ministerio fidelium" (*in Eph.* iv. 11); "in episcopo omnium ordinationum dignitas est" (*in* 1 *Cor.* i. 17); "et quia ab uno Deo Patre sunt omnia, singulos episcopos singulis ecclesiis praeesse decrevit" (*in* 1 *Cor.* xii. 28); "Paulus et Timotheus utique episcopi erant" (*in Phil.* i. 1); Archippus was a bishop (*in Col.* iv. 17); the Apostles were bishops (*in Eph.* iv. 11, *in* 1 *Cor.* xii. 28). St. Paul is so exact in his directions in the Pastoral Epistles not from anxiety for Timothy, but on account of his successors, that they might observe the ordination of the Church, and that they too, who in their turn hand on the form to their successors, might begin from themselves, i.e. in spiritual discipline (*in* 1 *Tim.* vi. 16). Whatever changes were made were made under the authority of an (apostolic) council: "immutata est ratio prospiciente concilio."[1]

(c) *His theory of the original identity of bishops and presbyters.* "Timotheum presbyterum a se creatum episcopum vocat [sc. Paulus], quia primi presbyteri [i.e. chief presbyters] episcopi appellabantur, ut recedente eo sequens ei succederet. Denique apud Aegyptum presbyteri consignant, si praesens non sit episcopus. Sed quia coeperunt sequentes presbyteri indigni inveniri ad primatus retinendos, immutata est ratio prospiciente concilio, ut non ordo sed meritum crearet episcopum multorum sacerdotum iudicio constitutum, ne indignus temere usurparet et esset multis scandalum" (*in Eph.* iv. 12). Here it is implied that at one period the difference of presbyter and bishop was not one of 'order' but only of selection. Again, when he has to account for St. Paul passing from the bishop to the deacon (1 Tim. iii. 10), he writes thus: "Quare, nisi quia episcopi et presbyteri una ordinatio est? Uterque enim sacerdos est, sed episcopus primus est, ut omnis episcopus presbyter sit, non tamen omnis presbyter episcopus; hic enim episcopus est, qui inter presbyteros primus est. Denique Timotheum presbyterum ordinatum significat; sed quia ante se alterum non habebat, episcopus erat. Unde et quemadmodum episcopum ordinet, ostendit; neque enim fas erat aut licebat, ut inferior ordinaret maiorem; nemo enim tribuit, quod non accepit." A little further, on ver. 13: "Nunc autem septem diaconos esse

lege nascebantur sacerdotes ex genere Aaron Levitae; nunc autem omnes ex genere sunt sacerdotali . . . ideoque ex populo potest fieri sacerdos" (*l.c.*).

[1] Cf. Lightfoot *Dissert.* p. 203, n.[5]

oportet et aliquantos presbyteros, ut bini sint per ecclesias, et unus in civitate episcopus."

Take this language altogether, and I think we shall draw the conclusion that the commentator did indeed minimize the distinction of grade within the sacerdotium. But I do not think we have any reason to suppose that he would have regarded the presbyters of his own day as possessing, under any circumstances, the power which the earliest presbyters possessed; because the *ordinations in his own day were distinct*, and the presbyter who attempted to lay on hands would do what is, in his words (*in Eph.* iv. 11), "praesumere officium quod sciret non sibi creditum vel concessum."

II. I need not dwell on the AUTHOR OF THE QUAESTIONES. He only (*Qu.* ci) applies the language of the commentator, which he borrows, to castigate in the spirit of Jerome the Roman deacons. He says: "in Alexandria et apud totam Aegyptum, si desit episcopus, consecrat presbyter." There is another reading however consignat, as in the commentaries. Whichever word is used the reference is to *confirmation*; cf. Isidor. Hispal. *de Eccl. Off.* ii. 25 "unctione chrismatis consecrari" (of those who are confirmed), and see s. v. in Ducange *Gloss. Med. et Inf. Latin.* Consigno is the regular word for confirmation, but is never used for ordination.

III. JEROME repeats the theory of the commentator, adding to it the remark discussed above about the Alexandrian election to the episcopate.

(*a*) *His sacerdotalism.* Jerome is a great sacerdotalist. He believes indeed in the priesthood of the laity (*adv. Lucifer.* 4 : "sacerdotium laici, id est baptisma"), but not in such sense as militates against even an extreme sacerdotalism (*ib.* 21). Twice in his works the idea occurs—"a priest can intercede for a layman, but, if a priest falls, who can intercede for him?" (*ib.* 5, *Ep.* xiv *ad Heliodorum* § 9.) Again and again he dwells on the sacerdotal authority and sacrificial function.

(*b*) *His recognition of the apostolic authority of the episcopate.* "Ecclesia multis gradibus consistens ad extremum diaconis, presbyteris, episcopis finitur" (*adv. Lucifer.* 22); "quid facit excepta ordinatione episcopus quod presbyter non faciat? omnes [episcopi] . . . apostolorum successores sunt" (*Ep.* cxlvi *ad Evangelum*). The present *monepiscopal* constitution is attributed to (apostolic) decree (on Titus i. 5): "in toto orbe decretum est." The Apostles are represented as ordaining bishops and priests: "quod fecerunt et apostoli, per singulas provincias presbyteros et episcopos ordinantes" (*in Matt.* xxv. 26).

(c) *His theory of the original identity of bishops and presbyters.* This he (*Ep.* cxlvi *ad Evangelum*) proves from the language of Scripture, and continues: "quod autem postea unus electus est qui ceteris praeponeretur, in schismatis remedium factum est; ne unusquisque ad se trahens Christi ecclesiam rumperet." Then follows the passage about Alexandria, and the conclusion just quoted, "quid facit, excepta ordinatione etc.?" So to the same effect *in Tit.* i. 5: 'Idem est presbyter qui episcopus. At first communi presbyterorum concilio ecclesiae gubernabantur; then factions arose, 'I am of Paul,' etc. On this account in toto orbe decretum est ut unus de presbyteris electus superponeretur ceteris. He would therefore have the bishops in his own day recognise that se magis consuetudine quam dispositionis dominicae veritate presbyteris esse maiores.' Of course this is strong language. St. Jerome does not measure words when his temper is up, as it was with bishops. But even so I do not think it can be fairly taken to mean that Jerome ever held a *presbyter of his own day* to be the same as a bishop, even in an extreme case. The conclusion he draws in the text is only that bishops should govern the Church 'in commune, i.e. with the co-operation of the presbyters, in imitation of Moses, who, when he had it in his power to rule the people alone, chose seventy elders to judge the people with him.' Once again he says, in the *Dial. adv. Lucifer.* 9: "Ecclesiae salus in summi sacerdotis dignitate pendet: cui si non exsors quaedam et ab omnibus eminens detur potestas, tot in ecclesiis efficiuntur schismata quot sacerdotes." He still makes the distinctive powers of the bishop to have had their origin in moral necessities, but those necessities were paramount, and the result of the change involved in the limitation of the episcopate is one that cannot be reversed.

IV. LATER LATIN WRITERS. Certainly it was in the sense of an original, not of a present, identity of the episcopate and the presbyterate, that St. Jerome's influence and authority impressed his view on late Latin authors.[1] It is desirable to illustrate this by quotations.

ISIDORE OF SEVILLE, c. A.D. 630, in his *de Eccl. Off.* ii. 7 (ap. Hittorp. p. 22) quotes St. Paul to show "presbyterum etiam sub episcopi nomine taxari"; he says "secundus et paene coniunctus

---

[1] St. Augustin admitted, at any rate by implication, the change of nomenclature, *Ep.* lxxxii *ad Hieron.* § 33: "Quamquam secundum honorum vocabula quae iam ecclesiae usus obtinuit episcopatus presbyterio maior sit, tamen in multis rebus Augustinus Hieronymo minor est."

gradus [sc. presbyterorum] est." On the other hand he clearly distinguishes the orders (ii. 26): "Presbyteri, licet sint sacerdotes, pontificatus tamen apicem non habent. Hoc autem solis pontificibus deberi, ut vel consignent vel paracletum Spiritum tradant, quod non solum ecclesiastica consuetudo demonstrat, verum et superior illa lectio apostolorum [i.e. Acts viii. 14 f.]" Cf. also ii. 5, which is quite clear, and makes only bishops in the later sense the successors of the Apostles.

(Pseudo) ALBINUS FLACCUS, 9th century, in the *de Div. Off.* (ap. Hittorp. p. 72) distinguishes the powers of bishop and presbyter. He goes on to say that formerly the names were used indiscriminately, i.e. in the New Testament, "sed postmodum utili satis provisione constitutum est, ut hoc nomen [i.e. episcopus] solis pontificibus tribuatur, quorum maioris gradus excellentia crescat et minor ordo mensurae suae limitem recognoscat, sitque differentia in vocabulis sicut praecelsior locus honoris." This means, I think, that there had always been a difference of *grade* which produced a distinction of name. He afterwards (p. 74) quotes Jerome's account of the early Alexandrian mode of electing a bishop.

AMALARIUS, bishop of Treves, 9th century, in his *de Eccl. Off.* ii. 13 (ap. Hittorp. p. 165), holds about the same language, i.e. he recognises community of names in New Testament, and quotes Jerome on the Epistle to Titus and on the Alexandrian election of bishops. But he also assumes an original distinction of office, and makes the successors of the Apostles take from the lower grade its name of 'bishop,' because they would not arrogate to themselves the title of apostles; so that those were called bishops "qui et ordinationis praediti potestate."

RABANUS MAURUS, 9th century, quotes Jerome and Isidore and recognises the original community of names in New Testament— "sub episcoporum nomine presbyteros complexus est [Paulus]"— but keeps the distinction of offices clear (*de Inst. Cler.* i. 4. 6, ap. Hittorp. pp. 313, 315). He makes eight *gradus* in the Church, the chief being bishop, priest, and deacon, and three *ordines*— clergy, laity, and monks.

Gieseler, *Eccl. Hist.* § 30 [Eng. trans. i. p. 88], quotes a remarkable expression of Jerome's position from BERNALDUS OF CONSTANCE, c. A.D. 1088. He affirms that presbyters actually had "antiquitus" [i.e. presumably in the apostolic age] episcopal powers, and this as a matter of certainty—"habuisse non dubitantur." He goes on: "Postquam autem presbyteri ab episcopali excellentia cohibiti sunt, coepit eis non licere quod licuit, vide-

Note F. 383

licet quod ecclesiastica auctoritas solis pontificibus exequendum delegavit."[1]

Gieseler gives other mediaeval references: but the effect of his whole note is to produce an erroneous impression. It is not the case that the ancient Church in general made little distinction between bishops and presbyters; that this mode of thought survived more or less into the Middle Ages; and that it was finally suppressed by the theology of Trent, while the Protestants returned to the ancient doctrine. I hope I have shown that this is not the case. The fact is that mediaeval writers who minimized the distinction of bishops and presbyters did so either to exalt the dignity of the sacrificial priesthood which is common to both, or in simple deference to Jerome's authority, or with the intention of magnifying the papal prerogative (see App. Note E, p. 377).

G.

THE LAYING ON OF HANDS.

It is plain that the conclusions arrived at on pp. 183-200 depend mainly on the question whether we have evidence to justify the statement that the ministers of the Church were from the first solemnly ordained by laying-on of hands and that a special gift of the Holy Ghost was believed to accompany the ceremony. The following is a summary of the evidence on this point.

Assuming the historical trustworthiness of the Acts and the Pastoral Epistles, we have evidence that the laying-on of apostolic hands was the method of imparting the gift of the Spirit. It was also, as a natural consequence, the method of ordination to church office. So the seven are ordained, Acts vi. 6 προσευξάμενοι ἐπέθηκαν αὐτοῖς τὰς χεῖρας. So St. Paul and St. Barnabas have hands laid on them by the prophets of Antioch, Acts xiii. 3 νηστεύσαντες καὶ προσευξάμενοι καὶ ἐπιθέντες τὰς χεῖρας αὐτοῖς ἀπέλυσαν. So St. Paul, in company with the presbytery, ordained Timothy (1 Tim. iv. 14; 2 Tim. i. 6), and he writes to him that he "stir up the gift that is in him by the laying-on of hands." He also implies that Timothy will use the same ceremony in ordaining other clergy (1 Tim. v. 22). Thus, as in the case of baptism, the Church gave a new meaning, a new reality to an old Jewish rite.

[1] Cf. also Morinus *de S. Ord.* p. iii. ex. iii. 2. 8 f.

It was not likely that a practice which had this apostolic sanction would become disused. Ordination or appointment is, of course, constantly mentioned without any specification of the method in the early Church as amongst ourselves.[1] But we have in each century quite enough evidence to assure us of what the method was.

Thus in the second century the Ebionite Clementines represent St. Peter as ordaining bishops, and by implication priests and deacons, by laying-on of hands (*Hom.* iii. 72, with the prayer that God would give the bishop the authority to bind and loose aright; *Recog.* iii. 66 ; *Ep. Clem.* 2, 19).

In the third century we have evidence that Origen was so ordained : ἐπὶ τὴν Ἑλλάδα στειλάμενος τὴν διὰ Παλαιστίνης, πρεσβυτερίου χειροθεσίαν ἐν Καισαρείᾳ πρὸς τῶν τῇδε ἐπισκόπων ἀναλαμβάνει (ap. Euseb. *H.E.* vi. 23) ; and he implies that this was the method by which bishops were consecrated in his day (see above, p. 140). Cyprian, as will be seen, assures us that this was the method of episcopal ordination in Africa, and Novatian's schismatical ordination lets us see that it was so also at Rome.

We need not give many later instances. The witness of the *Apostolical Constitutions,* of Gregory (in his account of Basil's death-bed), of Basil himself, and of Lucifer and others, in the West, has been quoted already (pp. 149, 158, 170, 172, 191 n.[2]). When Chrysostom, still later, is explaining the expression ἐπέθηκαν αὐτοῖς τὰς χεῖρας in Acts vi. 6 (*Hom.* xiv. 3), he says : "This is the χειροτονία : the hand of the man is laid upon the other ; but all the working is of God, and His hand it is which touches the head of him who is ordained, if he be ordained aright." Jerome too interprets χειροτονία in Latin as "extentus digitus," and explains it as "ordinatio clericorum quae non solum ad imprecationem vocis sed ad impositionem impletur manus " (*in Isai.* lviii. 10).

In none of these cases is there any controversial stress laid on the rite. It is simply assumed as the Church's method of ordination.

It has been affirmed, however, by Dr. Hatch that the rite was not universal, and argued that "it is impossible that, if it was not universal, it can have been regarded as essential" (*B. L.* p. 134). Let us consider, then, the supposed cases in which it is absent.

---

[1] Thus, e.g., Theodoret, who had, as we shall see, very clear ideas as to the method and effect of ordination, speaks simply of a bishop bringing a man to the altar and 'enrolling him in the priesthood' without his knowing it; elsewhere, in a similar case, he describes *how* it was done (*Relig. Hist.* xiii, xix).

Note G. 385

1. "Nor is the rite mentioned in the enumeration which Cyprian gives of the elements which had combined to make the election of Cornelius valid: it was of importance to show that no essential particular had been omitted, but he enumerates only the votes of the people, the testimony of the clergy, the consent of the bishops." This is not the case. It is quite true that Cyprian is emphasizing the due *election* of Cornelius by the community to prove that his consecration was not 'done in a corner.' But while he says [1]: "factus est Cornelius *de* Dei et Christi eius iudicio, *de* clericorum paene omnium testimonio, etc.," he also says just before: "factus est episcopus *a* plurimis collegis nostris qui tunc in urbe Roma aderant." Cornelius was made a bishop *by* other bishops *on the basis of* a due election. How then was he made? By laying-on of hands, no doubt. That this was the recognised method in the contemporary Roman Church we have indisputable evidence, for Novatian, Cornelius' rival, had to get himself so consecrated. So Cornelius himself tells Fabian of Antioch: " He compelled certain boorish and ignorant bishops to give him the episcopate with a laying-on of hands which was shadowy and vain" (because it was uncanonical).[2] In a letter of Cyprian's too, where he is explaining why the presence and assent of the people and the bishops is necessary to a duly conducted episcopal consecration, he says: "All this took place in the ordination among you of our colleague Sabinus, so that it was by the vote of the whole brotherhood, and the judgment of the bishops, that the episcopate was given him *and hands laid upon him* in Basilides' room."[3] To "lay on hands" is a synonym for to give the episcopate.

2. "In entire harmony with this [omission of the laying-on of hands] is the account which Jerome gives of the admission to office of the bishop of Alexandria: after the election the presbyters conduct the elected bishop to his chair: he is thereupon bishop *de facto*." Quite so. This is Jerome's account of it. And because this is all that he thinks occurred, he and those who follow him would not describe it as a distinct ordination. There was, they say, originally only one ordination to the priesthood, i.e. that which made a man a presbyter, after which he became a bishop by mere nomination.

---

[1] *Ep.* lv. 8.

[2] ap. Euseb. *H. E.* vi. 43. See also Cornelius' letter to Cyprian (*Ep.* xlix. 1): the confessors said they had been deluded "ut paterentur ei manum quasi in episcopatum imponi."

[3] *Ep.* lxvii. 5.

3. "In a similar way Synesius, *Ep.* 67, p. 210, by his use of the phrase ἀποδεῖξαί τε καὶ ἐπὶ τοῦ θρόνου καθίσαι, appears to consider the announcement of election, followed by enthronization, as the constitutive elements of the ordination of a bishop" (*l.c.* p. 134 n.[45]). ἀποδεῖξαι often means '*to make*' in Greek; and if Dr. Hatch had read the previous letter he would have seen that it means '*to make by laying-on of hands.*' See p. 206, where it is said that one ὑπὸ τῶν ἐκείνου χειρῶν ἐπίσκοπος ἀνεδείχθη τῆς Βιθυνῶν Βασινουπόλεως.

4. Dr. Hatch quotes (pseudo) Albinus Flaccus as denying that the laying-on of hands was the traditional mode of making a bishop of Rome; the passage is given in App. Note C, p. 369 n. What the author must mean is to depreciate the authority in the West of the *imposition of the book of the Gospels*. And whatever he means, we can check him. Isidore of Seville, who is several centuries earlier, says: "Quod vero per manus impositionem a praecessoribus Dei sacerdotibus episcopi ordinantur, antiqua institutio est" (*de Eccl. Off.* ii. 5); and refers the rite back to patriarchal and apostolic days. We have also the evidence of Lucifer and of the practice of the Roman Church in Cornelius' time.

5. "There is the remarkable fact that the passage of the *Apostolical Constitutions* which describes with elaborate minuteness the other ceremonies with which a bishop was admitted to office, says nothing of this" (p. 133). I have taken this point last because it introduces a new aspect of the question. The passage (quoted above p. 146 f.) describes a solemn ceremony, by which a man in virtue of consecration from above becomes something he was not before. The rites mentioned are the laying upon his head of the book of the Gospels with a solemn prayer which specifies the sacerdotal character of the office he is being ordained to. He who is described in the process as 'being ordained,' is 'ordained' at the end.[1] Here, then, there is no question of the sacramental character of ordination: the only question is whether the laying-on of hands is in all cases the essential 'matter' or rite. A man might heartily hold the whole doctrine of ordination and still be unwilling to believe, supposing he found, e.g. that in a particular Church orders had been administered by 'spiration,' that the administration had been invalid. This is, as it were, a further ecclesiastical question. Still it seems most improbable that the ceremony of laying-on of hands specified in the *Apost. Const.* in the case of the deacon and

[1] Cf. similar uses of the words χειροτονούμενος, χειροτονηθείς in the later Greek ordination rites, pp. 364-5. The rites described in the *Apostolical Constitutions* are, it should be remembered, more or less imaginary.

the presbyter is intentionally omitted in the case of the bishop. The same book contains a passage which is sufficient to disprove this (viii. 46): ἴστε γὰρ πάντως ἐπισκόπους παρ' ἡμῶν ὀνομασθέντας καὶ πρεσβυτέρους καὶ διακόνους εὐχῇ καὶ χειρῶν ἐπιθέσει, τῇ διαφορᾷ τῶν ὀνομάτων καὶ τὴν διαφορὰν τῶν πραγμάτων δεικνύοντας· οὐ γὰρ ὁ βουλόμενος παρ' ἡμῖν ἐπλήρου τὴν χεῖρα [i.e. was consecrated] . . . ἀλλ' ὁ καλούμενος ὑπὸ τοῦ θεοῦ—"bishops and presbyters and deacons were appointed by prayer and the laying-on of hands." Presumably, therefore, in the rite as described the laying-on of hands is implied in the word χειροτονεῖν. The word was supposed, in the fourth century at least (see quotations from Jerome and Chrysostom just given), to have that implication.[1] Also, it should be noticed, 'manual acts' are often omitted in early sacramentaries. Thus in the *Apost. Const.* themselves the laying-on of hands, in connection with the unction of confirmation, is both specified and omitted in the same chapter (vii. 44). So the directions for the manual act of laying on hands is omitted in some of the accounts of the rite of ordination in the Ordo Romanus; e.g. ap. Hittorp. p. 31 we have simply "consecrat illos," although a late date is indicated by the mention of the incense being blessed, the introits, the litany, the vestments; cf. *ib.* p. 107. On the other hand it is specified in an 'ordinal' which Dr. Hatch (*Dict. Chr. Ant.* s.v.) thinks represents one of the earliest remaining western types (Hittorp. p. 88; Martene, Ordo ix, *Ant. Eccl. Ritus* ii. p. 151). It is not specified in Martene's Ordo i (*l.c.* p. 86 f.), nor in a very brief order in Muratori *Lit. Rom. Vet.* i. p. 512 f., nor in the Maronite rite (in Morinus *de S. Ord.* p. ii. p. 419 f.). It is only later that 'ritualia,' giving complete rubrical directions, are written.

Now what was the significance attached to this laying-on of hands?[2]

---

[1] *Apost. Const.* viii. 28 distinguishes χειροθετεῖν, i.e. to give certain benedictions of penitents, from χειροτονεῖν = 'to ordain.' χειροτονεῖν is a technical term for one special sort of laying-on of hands.

[2] Dr. Hatch has endeavoured to minimize it (*B.L.* p. 135 and *Dict. Chr. Ant.* ii. p. 1508). Jerome no doubt says that the value of the outward rite lay, in one respect, in its preventing the possibility of people being ordained without their knowing it: "ordinatio clericorum non solum ad imprecationem vocis sed ad impositionem impletur manus, ne scilicet, ut in quibusdam risimus, vocis imprecatio clandestina clericos ordinet nescientes" (*in Isai.* lviii. 10)— a function which it fulfilled but imperfectly, as we know from some curious stories of Theodoret (*Relig. Hist.* xiii, xix). But it was much more than this to Jerome, as we have seen; the whole rite made a man a priest, with

It was conceived of as giving ministerial authority, and not only authority, but something which accompanied the authority—a gift of special grace empowering a man for its exercise.

Thus, in the fifth century, Theodoret, bishop of Cyrus, the literalist interpreter of a temper which Dr. Newman characterizes as 'English,' no less than the mystic writer who passes for Dionysius, believed that the laying-on of hands conveyed a specific grace of order. He believed this even when the rite was administered to a man without his knowledge. He records (*Relig. Hist.* xix) how a bishop, wishing to ordain a recluse, got into his cell by surreptitious means and "laid his hand on him and performed the prayer and then spoke at length to him and made plain to him the grace which had come upon him." He regarded the grace as given by the laying-on of hands in virtue of the prayer which invoked the Spirit. "We ought," he says, commenting on 1 Tim. v. 22, "first to examine the life of the man who is being ordained, and so to invoke upon him (καλεῖν ἐπ' αὐτόν) the grace of the Spirit."

In the fourth century we have found St. Gregory of Nazianzum conceiving with great richness of thought of the effect of ordination; and speaking of St. Basil on his deathbed as "*giving his hand and the Spirit*[1] in ordination of the most genuine of his followers." So St. Basil himself, speaking of those who had left the Church, says: "they had no longer the grace of the Holy Spirit upon them; its communication failed when the succession was broken off (τῷ διακοπῆναι τὴν ἀκολουθίαν). For those who first went into schism had their ordinations from the fathers, and *through the laying-on of their hands they had the spiritual gift*; but those who broke off, having become laymen, had neither the authority to baptize nor to ordain, being no longer able to impart to others the grace of the Holy Spirit, from which they had themselves fallen."[2] We

---

sacerdotal powers and authority. St. Augustin also says (*de Bapt.* iii. 16. 21): "Quid est aliud [manus impositio] nisi oratio super hominem?" But he is not speaking of ordination. The laying-on of hands in ordination did, according to Augustin, as we shall see, "impose a sacrament" which was indelible. The pseudo-Dionysius sees in the laying-on of hands more than "fatherly sheltering and subjection to God": it ἐμφαίνει τὴν τελεταρχικὴν σκέπην, ὑφ' ἧς . . . ἕξιν καὶ δύναμιν ἱερατικὴν δωρουμένης, κ.τ.λ. (ap. Morinus *de S. Ord.* p. ii. p. 58.)

[1] The early Church did not use the imperative formula, 'Receive the Holy Ghost.' St. Augustin certainly implies this (*de Trin.* xv. 26). But no more is implied in this formula than in saying 'I baptize,' or (as St. Gregory in this case) 'he gives the Holy Spirit.' [2] *Ep.* clxxxviii.

have already heard St. Athanasius explaining to the recalcitrant Dracontius, that in being ordained he had received a grace of the Spirit, which was in him whether he liked it or no, and for the exercise of which he was responsible. The prayer for the ordination of a bishop in the *Apostolical Constitutions* runs: "Thyself [O God], now by the mediation of Thy Christ, *pour out through us* [the ordaining bishops] *the power of Thy ruling Spirit*" (δι' ἡμῶν ἐπίχεε τὴν δύναμιν τοῦ ἡγεμονικοῦ σου πνεύματος, viii. 5). St. Peter in the Clementine Homilies is represented as laying-on hands and invoking for him who is being made bishop the authority to bind and loose aright (*Hom.* iii. 72; cf. *Ep. Clem.* 2).

When we turn to the West we find a similar set of conceptions attached to the ordination of the clergy. The author of the *Quaestiones in Vet. et Nov. Test.* speaks thus (*Qu.* xciii): "When the Lord is said to have breathed on the disciples a few days after His resurrection and to have said 'Receive ye the Holy Ghost,' He is understood to have been conveying ecclesiastical power (ecclesiastica potestas collata intelligitur esse): and because it really belongs to ecclesiastical authority (ad ius ecclesiasticum), He adds 'Whose sins ye retain,' etc. This inbreathing of Christ is a certain grace, which by succession is infused into those who are ordained (per traditionem infunditur ordinatis), by which they are made more acceptable." He then quotes St. Paul's words to Timothy (1 Tim. iv. 14) and explains that this outward act of Christ was enacted "ut ex eo traditioni ecclesiasticae Spiritus sanctus infusus credatur." The contemporary Ambrosiaster, writing also from Rome, speaks more definitely (see App. Note F) of the "grace of ordination" as attached to the laying-on of hands. "He only," says Lucifer (*de S. Athan.* i. 9), "can be *filled with the virtue of the Holy Spirit for the governing of His people, whom God has chosen, and on whom hands have been laid by the catholic bishops*, as Moses' hand was laid upon Joshua." We have seen that St. Cyprian understood by ordination the laying-on of hands and that he regarded ordination, when rightly administered in the Church, as bestowing sacerdotal authority. Before Cyprian, the great theologian Hippolytus uses the following language as to the relation of the Holy Ghost to the ministry (*Ref. Omn. Haer.* prooem.): "No other will refute these errors save the Holy Ghost given in the Church, which the Apostles first received and then imparted to right believers; and forasmuch as we are their successors, sharing the same grace and high priesthood and teaching and accounted guardians of the Church, we shall not suffer our eyes to sleep."

Irenaeus also regards church officers as endowed with special spiritual gifts; he speaks of "the presbyters who hold the succession from the Apostles, who with the succession of the episcopate have received the sure gift of truth (charisma veritatis) according to the good pleasure of the Father" (iv. 26. 2). "God, says St. Paul, hath put in the Church first apostles, secondly prophets, thirdly teachers; where, then, the gifts of the Lord have been put, there we should learn the truth" (iv. 26. 5). Lastly, though Clement does not, any more than Irenaeus or Hippolytus, allude to the ceremony of ordination, he connects the mission of the ministry with that one mission by which "Christ is from God, and the Apostles from Christ" (c. 42). Such, then, is the continuous conception of churchmen in respect of the grace of ordination and the rite of laying-on of hands; and it has its origin in the simple and decisive expressions of the New Testament.

H.

MONTANISM.

(See pp. 207-213.)

THE true nature of Montanism seems to emerge very clearly from an examination of the ancient writings bearing on it, which are not of very considerable bulk. They are mainly—(i) the anti-Montanist writers of the second, or early third, century, quoted by Eusebius *H. E.* v. 16-19; (ii) Didymus *de Trin.* especially iii. 41; (iii) Epiphanius *Haer.* xlviii (both these writers drawing on more ancient sources); and (iv) the Montanist writings of Tertullian, its chief western advocate. There are also important references in Hippolytus *Ref. Omn. Haer.* viii. 19; and pseudo-Tertull. *de Praescr.* ad fin. Other references are collected, and all the sources analysed, in Bonwetsch's admirable *Gesch. des Montanismus* § 1; cf. also Harnack *Dogmengesch.* i. pp. 318-330; and *Dict. Chr. Biog.* s.v. MONTANUS (Dr. Salmon).

From these authorities it appears—

1. That the primary claim of Montanus and his followers was that of supernatural inspiration. Montanus claimed to be a passive organ through which Almighty God spoke—apparently even to be Almighty God, in the sense that his voice was God's voice. A similar claim was made by his prophetesses, Prisca (Priscilla) and

Maximilla. In this consisted the New Prophecy (Epiphan. *Haer.* xlviii. 11, 12; Didymus *de Trin.* iii. 41; and the anonymous presbyter ap. Euseb. *H.E.* v. 16).[1] The inspired utterances of these first Montanist prophets were collected and reckoned by the Montanists as additional scriptures (συντάττειν καινὰς γραφάς, Euseb. *H.E.* vi. 20); Tertullian constantly quotes them as inspired oracles (see *de Exh. Cast.* 10; *de Res. Carn.* 11; *de Fuga* 9, 11; *de Pud.* 21; *adv. Prax.* 8, 30; *adv. Marc.* iii. 24). If the highest sort of inspiration was supposed to belong to these prophets only (and the Fathers taunt them with the cessation of the gift), yet "revelations" continued in the society. Tertullian quotes, to prove the materiality of the soul, the visions of a "spiritual" sister who "had the gift of revelations" (*de An.* 9). As claiming inspiration, the Montanists claimed to be in a prophetic succession. They claimed to succeed to the ancient prophets and to those of the new covenant (ap. Euseb. *H. E.* v. 18).[2] They argued that their inspiration was only a new instance of an old phenomenon (see the Montanist preface to the Passion of Perpetua and Felicitas, and note especially "things of later date are to be esteemed of more account," and the conclusion of the account). The Church judged them on their claim. She 'tried the spirits,' and decided that this was a case not of supernatural inspiration but of false prophecy, or even demoniacal possession. As thus judged and condemned, they were excommunicated by the Asiatic Churches, and the orthodox held them in such horror that under persecution they would not even die with them (ap. Euseb. *H.E.* v. 16 ad fin.). They were afterwards excommunicated at Rome also (see esp. *Dict. Chr. Biog.* iii. pp. 936, 944).

The arguments used against the Montanist claims seem to have been

(*a*) that the prophetic gift failed with the death of the first claimants to it (ap. Euseb. *H. E.* v. 17):

(*b*) that their prophecies of wars and revolutions and the speedy end of the world did not come true (ap. Euseb. *H. E.* v. 16, and Epiphan. *l.c.* § 2):

---

[1] The claim to speak with the voice of the Father, the Son, and the Holy Ghost indiscriminately, carried with it, according to Didymus, a confusion of the Divine Persons (*l.c.* and elsewhere). Epiphanius, however (*l.c.* § 1), says the Montanists were orthodox. The pseudo-Tertullian draws a distinction in this respect between two sects. Tertullian makes their orthodoxy emphatic.

[2] There is perhaps no reason to make this claim an afterthought, with Harnack *Dogmengesch.* i. p. 323.

(c) —the earliest and most important argument—that whereas prophecy in the Church was *rational* and the prophet *intelligent and conscious*, Montanist prophecy was, on their own showing, an irrational frenzy : cf. ἐν κατοχῇ τινὶ καὶ παρεκστάσει ἐνθουσιᾷν ... ὡς ἐπὶ ἐνεργουμένῳ καὶ δαιμονῶντι ... τὸ βλαψίφρον πνεῦμα ... λαλεῖν ἐκφρόνως ... ἀμετροφώνους προφήτας (ap. Euseb. *H. E.* v. 16, 17); cf. the title of (?) Alcibiades' anti-Montanist work, τοῦ μὴ δεῖν προφήτην ἐν ἐκστάσει λαλεῖν; Epiphan. *l.c.* §§ 3-7 ; and Tertullian's expressions "ecstasis ... excessus sensus et amentiae instar," "amentia ... spiritalis vis qua constat prophetia" (*de. An.* 45, 21, *adv. Marc.* iv. 22).

It was, then, mainly on account of its irrational, ecstatic, and therefore unchristian, pagan character that Montanism was rejected.[1] The point to observe is that the Church judged it on its claim. It claimed to be a new, special, supernatural inspiration, and the Church decided, not that such inspiration had ceased with the Apostles, but that *these people were not divinely inspired*. The Church had contained men and women recently whom it recognised as prophets, such as Quadratus and Ammia. It would not recognise Montanus and Maximilla on account of the character of their supposed 'gifts.' The Montanists *acknowledged their novel character* (see Epiphan. *l.c.* § 8 οὐχ ὅμοια τὰ πρῶτα χαρίσματα τοῖς ἐσχάτοις— a Montanist saying). No doubt this repudiation of Montanist prophecy inclined the Church to regard the prophetic gift as having altogether ceased. See Epiphan. *l.c.* § 3. Irenaeus, like Justin, speaks of prophecy as continuing in the Church: "we hear of many brethren in the Church having prophetic gifts" (ii. 32. 4, v. 6. 1); cf. Justin *Dial. c. Tryph.* 82 : παρὰ γὰρ ἡμῖν καὶ μέχρι νῦν προφητικὰ χαρίσματά ἐστιν. The Muratorian fragment, on the other hand, speaks of the "completus numerus" of the prophets; and Origen puts them almost wholly in the past, *c. Cels.* vii. 8 ἴχνη ἐστὶν αὐτοῦ [the prophetic spirit] παρ' ὀλίγοις. Alcibiades, against the Montanists (ap. Euseb. *H. E.* v. 17), speaks of prophecy "as remaining in the whole Church until the second Coming," but in what sense is not plain. In any case that supernatural prophecy had ceased was not a principle; it was an experience. See on this the account Tertullian gives of the rejection at Rome of the Montanist prophecy (*adv. Prax.* 1). If the Montanists

---

[1] As a matter of fact Montanus probably brought his idea of inspiration from his Phrygian paganism. He had been a pagan priest (Didymus *l.c.* § 3); Jerome seems to imply a priest of Cybele 'semivir' (*Ep. ad Marcell.* xli). On the purely pagan character of 'ecstasy' see Bonwetsch *l.c.* pp. 65, 66.

taunted the Church with rejecting prophecy, the Church replied: 'we do not believe you are inspired.'

2. Their prophecy claimed to be 'new' in a special sense. The Montanists claimed (says Didymus) "*that their leader had come, and had the completeness of the Spirit.*" The Spirit promised by Christ had come in him. The age of the Spirit, through the Montanist revelations, had superseded the hitherto imperfect Church. Didymus is at pains to prove, as against them, that Montanus could not be greater than the Apostles: that the Apostles had had the Spirit in His completeness from Christ, and had imparted Him by laying-on of hands to the Church (*l.c.* § 2).[1] Their claim finds very complete expression in Tertullian (see above, p.209 f.). If he also claims that Montanism is a "restitutio" (*de Monog.* 4), this is only in the sense that it restores a severity of discipline about second marriages, which *the Apostles had allowed to remain relaxed*, owing to human weakness: it restored, that is to say, the primeval severity of the divine intention, but it was even here an advance on apostolic Christianity. See, on this *new* character of Montanist illumination, Harnack *l.c.* pp. 319-323, and Bonwetsch, esp. *Die Prophetie in apost. u. nachapost. Zeitalter* in *Zeitschr. f. k. Wissenschaft u. k. Leben*, heft viii and ix, 1884.

3. However true it may be that some at least of the Montanist claimants to prophetic inspiration were self-seeking charlatans (see Apollonius ap. Euseb. *H. E.* v. 18), there is no reason to doubt that Montanism was really, even at first, *a movement in the direction of ascetic puritanism.* No doubt the establishment of the new Jerusalem in the "little Phrygian cities of Pepuza and Timius," where Montanus "would have gathered together" the children of the new dispensation "from all sides," was one of the many attempts which church history records to found a 'pure Church.' There the elect expected to behold the 'Jerusalem which is above' descend from heaven (Epiphan. *l.c.* § 14). It was mainly the puritan rigorism of Montanism, with its special fasts ($\nu\eta\sigma\tau\epsilon\iota\hat{\omega}\nu$ $\nu o\mu o\theta\epsilon\sigma\acute{\iota}a$ is a feature noticed by Apollonius ap. Euseb. *l.c.*) and ascetic restrictions on marriage, that commended it to the impatient zeal of Tertullian. There was no doubt a tendency to worldliness, a 'Verweltlichung,' in the Church of the third and fourth centuries, just so far as she was allowed to live at ease, which accounts for, and in part excuses, if it cannot justify, the

---

[1] The Montanist claim is expressed otherwise thus: "in apostolis Spiritum sanctum fuisse, Paracletum non fuisse" (pseudo-Tertull. *de Praescr.* 52).

outbreaks of puritan fanaticism which the history of the Church in those centuries bears repeated witness to.

4. If men making a claim to inspiration would inevitably, in any case, have a tendency to look down upon church officers who made no such profession, much more were the *repudiated and excommunicated* Montanist claimants put into the most marked *hostility to the Church*. Their belief in the new dispensation of the Spirit tended to make them regard the Church as antiquated; in their puritanism they would have regarded her as corrupt, perhaps as unchurched by corruption; their expectations of an immediate παρουσία made them disparage her organization, which aimed at permanence.[1] Thus they would have every motive for setting "the Church of the Spirit" against "the Church of the bishops," for setting personal inspiration against official authority, and ascetic severity against sacerdotal claims. As a fact their ascription of the power of absolution to spiritual men—in opposition to church officers—is a feature hinted at by Apollonius: "who forgives sins [amongst you Montanists]?" he asks in ridicule, "does the prophet forgive the thefts of the martyr, or the martyr the covetousness of the prophet?" In Tertullian this feature appears more prominently; see p. 209 f.

I.

PROPHECY IN THE CHRISTIAN CHURCH.

(See pp. 240, 241, 249, 250.)

THE words of Jesus Christ, "all the prophets and the law prophesied until John," are clearly not to be understood as excluding prophecy from His kingdom. If His own language is not without ambiguity,[2] yet in the apostolic writings the evidence is abundant. There are prophets in the Church who rank only next to apostles: see Eph. iv. 11, iii. 5, ii. 20, 1 Cor. xii. 28, Acts

---

[1] See especially Bonwetsch *Montanismus* p. 139: "Allem dem entgegenzutreten, wodurch die kirchlichen Verhältnisse eine dauerndere Gestalt zum Zweck des Eingehens in eine längere geschichtliche Entwicklung erhalten sollten." This was modified in later Montanism.

[2] But see St. Matt. vii. 22, x. 41: elsewhere He speaks of false prophets (vii. 15, xxiv. 11) or Old Testament prophets (St. Luke xi. 49-51) or couples prophets with "wise men and scribes" so that the language becomes analogical (St. Matt. xxiii. 34, cf. x. 41).

Note I. 395

xiii. 1, xiv. 4, and xv. 32. We should gather that not all persons who received at one moment or another the gift of prophecy, as in Acts xix. 6, would have ranked as prophets. The prophet would have been a person who *habitually* possessed the prophetic inspiration.[1] There was an abundance of the prophetic gift in the Corinthian Church (1 Cor. xiv. 29-36), but if the prophets appear here as members simply of the local community, speaking generally they belong to the general, as opposed to the local, ministry and rank with apostles and evangelists and teachers (see esp. Eph. iv. 11, iii. 5, ii. 20, and Acts xiii. 1, where Barnabas and Saul rank amongst prophets and teachers).

We get a clear idea of the characteristics of Christian prophecy.

1. In marked contrast to the idea of a prophet in Plato and in Philo,[2] St. Paul insists that the Christian prophet is no unconscious, passive instrument of the Spirit. Prophecy is rational and subject to the will of the prophet in a remarkable manner, see 1 Cor. xiv. and especially verse 32: "the spirits of the prophets (cf. Apoc. xxii. 6) are subject to the prophets," also Rom. xii. 6, and Acts xxi. 4, 11, where St. Paul seems to regard prophetic utterances as misdirected in intention though true in fact. St. Paul indeed on one occasion was the subject of something like an ecstasy. But it afforded no material for his public ministry; it was a blessing only for his own spirit, and is not mentioned for fourteen years (2 Cor. xii. 2-4). St. John's Apocalypse is a special form of prophecy of most direct inspiration (cf. Apoc. i. 3, 10, iv. 2, xxii. 7, 10, 18, 19), but St. John clearly retains his consciousness and personality throughout the revelations made to him, and the function of prophecy is generally defined as "the testimony of Jesus" (xix. 10) and regarded as continuing into the new covenant (xi. 18, xviii. 20).

2. The Christian prophet is no individual oracle. He is one of a body, and his gift exists for the good of the whole body. Accord-

---

[1] So Meyer on 1 Cor. xiv. 31, and Bonwetsch *Die Prophetie in apost. u. nachapost. Zeitalter* in *Zeitschr. f. kirchl. Wissenschaft u. k. Leben*, 1884, heft viii, p. 413, and ix, on whom this note is largely based. It should also be noticed that the existence of these distinctive prophets is not inconsistent with the gift of prophecy being given to the whole Church, see Acts ii. 17, 18.

[2] See Bonwetsch *l.c.* p. 415. He gives excellent references showing how essential to the idea of prophecy in these writers is its ecstatic character: οὐδεὶς ἔννους ἐφάπτεται μαντικῆς ἐνθέου (Plat. *Tim.* 72a), ἐξοικίζεται ἐν ἡμῖν ὁ νοῦς κατὰ τὴν τοῦ θείου πνεύματος ἄφιξιν (Philo *Quis Rerum Divin. Haer.* i. 511). It was because Montanist prophecy was of this irrational, ecstatic character that the Church rejected it.

ingly it is subordinated to the regulative authority in the body, in the interest of order: see 1 Cor. xii, and xiv. 4, 5, 12, 17, 29-33, 40. Our Lord had directed that prophets were to be known by their moral fruits (St. Matt. vii. 15, 16). St. John also directs that utterances claiming inspiration should be tested by the rule of faith (1 John iv. 1-3, 2 John 7-11, cf. 1 Thess. v. 19-21).

3. We should gather from the Acts that Christian prophets foretold, like Agabus; see Acts xi. 28, xxi. 11. So St. Peter exercises prophetic power (Acts v. 3-10) and the Spirit guides the Apostles on critical occasions by specially communicated directions or prohibitions (Acts x. 19, xiii. 2, xvi. 6, xx. 22, 23, xxiii. 11, xxvii. 23). It is also the prophetic function to exhort and confirm and edify (Acts xv. 32 παρεκάλεσαν, ἐπεστήριξαν, cf. 1 Cor. xiv. 3 οἰκοδομή, παράκλησις, παραμυθία). Further in Acts xiii. 1-3, prophets (and teachers) appear as ministers of the Church's worship, and as sharing the apostolic function of laying on hands in the case of Saul and Barnabas. On this occasion the laying-on of hands recognised, rather than gave, apostolic commission, but it is probable that those who could enact the rite on this occasion could have done so under more ordinary circumstances, for ordination or confirmation. It falls in with the 'liturgical' function of prophets, that St. Paul implies that there were such things as inspired prayers as well as inspired exhortations. There is a praying and praising which is by both the spirit and the reason, a 'eucharist' to which the private Christian can say his Amen with an intelligent assent, and which is none the less 'in the spirit' (1 Cor. xiv. 15, 16).[1] So in the Pastoral Epistles St. Paul speaks of prophecy, both as having pointed out Timothy for his ministry (1 Tim. i. 18), and also as the instrument through which, in the form presumably of an inspired prayer or declaration uttered by the Apostle, when he laid hands on his head in association with the presbyters, Timothy received his pastoral charisma (1 Tim. iv. 14, 2 Tim. i. 6).

The gift of prophecy continued as a recognised endowment of the Church into the second or third centuries. Certain people were recognised as prophets, e.g. Ignatius, Polycarp, and Quadratus, already referred to (cf. Euseb. *H. E.* v. 1. 49 on Alexander the Phrygian). As in the apostolic Church there had been prophetesses, so too they had their late representative in Ammia at Philadelphia (Euseb. *H.E.* v. 17). St. Irenæus, besides denouncing false prophets (*adv. Haer.*

---

[1] In 1 Cor. xiv. 15, πνεύματι must I think mean 'spirit only,' i.e. an unintelligible tongue, as opposed to 'spirit and reason,' i.e. a prophetic prayer.

iv. 33. 6), protests against those who would banish prophecy from the Church under pretence of exposing such pretenders (iii. 11. 9 : "propheticam . . . gratiam repellunt ab ecclesia ") and witnesses like Justin Martyr to the continuance of prophetic gifts in his day (ii. 32. 4, v. 6. 1 ; Justin *c. Tryph.* 82). Even an opponent of the false prophets of Montanism recognises that prophecy must continue in the whole Church to the end (ap. Euseb. *H. E.* v. 17). The Montanist prophets were rejected by the Church specially on account of the ecstatic and irrational character of their supposed gifts. Their rejection involved no slight at all on the gift of prophecy and no denial of its claims. As a matter of fact, however, the genuine gift seems to have become exceedingly rare; Origen speaks of slight traces of it remaining to his time (*c. Cels.* i. 46, vii. 8).

The documents of the subapostolic age are of special interest for this subject—the *Didache* and the *Shepherd* of Hermas. In the *Didache*, the true prophet is distinguished from the false 'by his fruits,' i.e. by his genuine poverty and disinterestedness and by his orthodoxy. So far he is subject to the testing of the Church. But when once his true prophetic inspiration is accepted, it becomes a sin against the Holy Ghost to judge him; see xi. 1, 2, 7-13. The remarkable features in the prophets of this document is that, like those at Antioch in the Acts, they become, wherever they appear, the chief ministers of worship, no less than of teaching, and hold, with the less defined figures of apostle and teacher, the first rank in the church hierarchy. The *Didache* is, as was said, the last document in which prophets appear clothed with this higher dignity. Prophetic bishops take the place of episcopal prophets. There is not, however, as has been pointed out elsewhere (p. 259), any reason to think that the latter ever held their quasi-apostolic position in the Church on the mere ground of their prophetic gifts, without ordination.

In the *Shepherd*, Hermas appears as the recipient of veritable visions which are to be communicated to the Church. If thus he is to be considered as a true prophet,[1] he gives us also a vivid picture of the false prophet inspired of Satan (*Mand.* xi). His characteristic is self-seeking and ambition. He is represented sitting on a 'cathedra,' answering the questions of those who come to consult him. No spirit given from God, says Hermas, is thus questioned, but speaks of itself according to the divine power given. The spirit which is questioned and answers according to

[1] See Salmon's *Introd.* p. 577 f.

the lusts of men is earthly and devilish. Again, in order to secure reputation, the false prophet isolates himself and prophesies in a corner, whereas the true prophet only speaks (where the pretender is dumb) in the congregation of just men. Again, the false prophet is ambitious of ecclesiastical preferment, he desires the 'chief seat,' while the true prophet is humble and meek. Again, the false prophet requires to be paid before he will speak. Thus the true and false prophets are to be distinguished by their conduct.

It is clear that at the time of the *Shepherd* the prophet did not hold anything like the position which he held in the *Didache*. No doubt the abundance of pretenders to inspiration made it plain that prophecy, even if an abiding endowment of the Church, was a rare one and not intended for the Church to depend upon for a supply of her chief ministers. In the *Apostolical Constitutions* we have a clear intimation of the transitory character of the miraculous 'charismata' of the early Church, and of prophecy among them. The Apostles are there represented as declaring that in contrast to the fundamental spiritual gift which is the essence of Christian life miracles were only vouchsafed in view of the conversion of the world and would become superfluous when all were Christians: accordingly those who possess the exceptional gifts are warned not to exalt themselves on that account over the church rulers, and the exorcist, in spite of the gift of healings which marks him for his special office without any ordination, is yet required to be ordained in the usual way, "if there be need that he should become a presbyter or bishop." See *Apost. Const.* viii. 1 and 26.

The earlier functions of the prophet passed in a certain sense, as has been pointed out (p. 284), to bishops and readers. Ambrose, we may further note, regards interpreters of the Scriptures as their representatives in his day.[1]

---

[1] See Cornelius a Lapide in Eph. iv. 11.

K.

THE ORIGIN OF THE TITLES 'BISHOP,' 'PRESBYTER,' 'DEACON,' WITH REFERENCE TO RECENT CRITICISM.

I. The purpose of this note is, first, to offer evidence for what has already been advanced on this subject in the text (pp. 253, 263-4).

(a) The title PRESBYTER is derived confessedly from the organization of the Jews,[1] but in order to show that the Christian organization was not imitated from the Jewish *as a whole*, it is necessary to give some account of what the Jewish organization was, as far as we know it, both in Jerusalem and in 'the dispersion.'[2]

It was fourfold. (1) There was the priestly organization for the purpose of the temple worship, with high-priests, priests, and Levites. This, however, did not of course exist anywhere except at Jerusalem.

(2) Representing the traditional religious learning amongst the Jews, we find, both in Jerusalem and in the dispersion, the recognised order of the scribes, who may be said to have taken the place of the prophets. Their name occurs commonly in the Jewish inscriptions found at Rome.

(3) For the purposes of the synagogue worship, both in Jerusalem and throughout the Jewish world, there was a ἀρχισυνάγωγος, with his ὑπηρέτης or clerk, or several ἀρχισυνάγωγοι (see Acts xiii. 15; cf. St. Mark v. 22, where however the reference may be to the rulers of different synagogues; for the ὑπηρέτης see St. Luke iv. 20). The 'ruler of the synagogue' selected and regulated the readers or preachers.

(4) For judicial and disciplinary purposes there was a πρεσβυτέριον, or body of πρεσβύτεροι, of whom we hear often in the New Testament (e.g. St. Luke xxii. 66, Acts xxii. 5) as constituting the

---

[1] However, as the reverence for age is universal, so we have not only the ancient Greek γερουσία, but a later use of πρεσβύτεροι for members of a γερουσία, at least in Asia Minor. See Hatch *B.L.* pp. 65, 66.

[2] The following account is largely derived from Schürer *Die Gemeindeverfassung der Juden in Rom in der Kaiserzeit*, Leipzig, 1879. His results have been verified by Kühl in *Die Gemeindeordnung in den Pastoralbriefen*, Berlin, 1885, p. 117.

sanhedrin. Apparently, however, this name was not much used except at Jerusalem: Schürer does not find the name in his Roman inscriptions.[1] In the Jewish communities at Rome[2] we have ἄρχοντες, or 'rulers' (in St. Matt. ix. 18 however ἄρχων = ἀρχισυνάγωγος, ‖ St. Luke viii. 41, St. Mark v. 22; and see Acts iv. 5, 8), presided over by a γερουσιάρχης, who was *primus inter pares*. These presidents are called πρωτεύοντες τῆς γερουσίας by Josephus *Bell. Iud.* vii. 10. 1 (= *maiores* or *primates*). The ἄρχοντες seem to have been elected annually[3]; cf. pseudo-Chrysostom *Opp.* [ed. Paris, 1588] ii. p. 1086. These four organizations were essentially distinct, though it might happen that the presbytery at Jerusalem might consist of "high-priests and scribes," as in St. Luke xxii. 66 (but on the other hand see Acts xxii. 5), or that an ἄρχων at Rome might also be an ἀρχισυνάγωγος (as in Schürer's inscriptions 19, 42), or a priest an ἄρχων (inscr. 5). Besides these officers we hear also of the title of 'father' or 'mother of the synagogue' being given to persons of age or influence.

This sketch of the Jewish fourfold organization will suffice to show within what limits the Christian Church can be described as having borrowed from it. The important points to notice are two.

First, that the Christian Church borrowed none of the Jewish titles except that of 'presbyter.' Epiphanius indeed mentions (*Haer.* xxx. 18) that the Ebionites used the title ἀρχισυνάγωγος, but this is an instance of reversion, for there is no evidence for the

[1] These Roman inscriptions belong apparently to the third or fourth century A.D. The word πρεσβύτερος occurs once among the Hebrew inscriptions found at Venosa, in South Italy, perhaps of the sixth century and later: see a paper of Ascoli in the *Atti del IV Congresso dei Orientalisti*, Florence, 1880, vol. i. pp. 239 f.; esp. p. 281 note 2, 292 and 350. Kühl, *l.c.* p. 117, discounts this on account of its date. Also the more frequent occurrence of the female form πρεσβυτέρη (*sic*) indicates that it has no longer its official meaning. Ascoli says, "piuttosto dev' esser titolo d'onoranza, che non di vera dignità, poichè gli sta accanto la πρεσβυτέρα." There is, however, one instance of the use of the term out of Jerusalem in an inscription at Smyrna; see *C.I.G.* 9897.

[2] At Alexandria, it should be noticed, the Jews formed one community under one Gerusia. At Rome, on the contrary, they constituted a number of separate communities (or 'colleges' in the eye of the State); each had its own synagogue and officers. The Christians in Rome, before they were organized into a Church, seem to have formed a number of separate congregations (see Rom. xvi. 5, 14, 15).

[3] It is said that they often held office for life, and that on this account an archon came to be known as διάβιος (*diabius*), but Ascoli denies this latter assertion, and regards the word as an exclamation or condensed prayer, see *l.c.* p. 344.

use of the title in the Christian Church. Lucian again, the pagan, speaks of Peregrinus as προφήτης καὶ θιασάρχης καὶ ξυναγωγεύς of the Christians, but this last title, no more than the second, was recognised in the Church. The Christian place of meeting is called a συναγωγή by St. James (ii. 2). This, however, is the only case in which it is used in the Christian Church in the specific Jewish sense: see, for its use in the more general sense of a gathering, Ignatius *ad Polyc.* 4 and Lightfoot's note, Hermas *Mand.* xi. 9, Heb. x. 25. Epiphanius also (*l.c.*) mentions that the Ebionites used the term, and the author of the *Testament of the Twelve Patriarchs* endeavours to give his work a Jewish colouring by speaking of Christian Churches as "synagogues of the Gentiles," and their ministers as "archons" (*Benj.* 11). The Christian 'council' is also called a συνέδριον in Ignat. *ad Philad.* 8, *ad Magn.* 6, *ad Trall.* 3, but, as is noted below, in the way of metaphor.

Secondly, that the Christian Church had only one gradually developed organization. It is true that this organization embodied various principles—the principle of authority and rule, the veneration due to age, the power derived from inspiration or spiritual gifts, and the devolution of special tasks on special executive officers, owing to the natural exigencies of organization.[1] It is true also that amongst the Jews the same person might be at once a scribe, a ruler of the synagogue, and a presbyter—that is, the distinct organizations might be represented by the same person. Still it remains the case that all our evidence goes to show that the Christian Church had only one organization, while the Jews, with their temple, schools, synagogue, and sanhedrin, had four. All the functions and powers of the Church were, in fact, summed up at first in the Apostles, and were gradually imparted under their authority and leading to different officers, who shared the same ministry in distinct grades. Thus, if the function of *worship*, which in the Christian Church formed the spiritual counterpart of the temple λειτουργία, was (as Harnack says [2]) "the primary function" of the episcopate—if it was the bishop's office to "offer the gifts" (Clem. *ad Cor.* 44), yet they certainly in this respect only share the λειτουργία of the prophets and teachers (*Did.* xv. 1), and these prophets and teachers are in the Acts specially brought before us

---

[1] See Harnack *Texte u. Untersuch.* b. ii, h. 2, p. 146 f. He calls these principles the aristocratic, the patriarchal, the spiritual, and the administrative.

[2] *Dogmengesch.* i. p. 155; cf. *Expositor*, May 1887, pp. 340-342. He includes the *deacon* also. The matter is discussed below.

as fulfilling this function of worship (Acts xiii. 2). Prophets, in fact, and of course apostles, were ministers of worship, as well as 'ministers of the word' and governing authorities. Then, again, with reference to this function of *teaching*. It belongs primarily to apostles and prophets and teachers or evangelists, but it is shared also by the 'bishops' or 'presbyters' (1 Thess. v. 12, 1 Tim. iii. 2, v. 17, Tit. i. 9, Acts xx. 29, 30; the local 'pastors' are called 'teachers' in Eph. iv. 11). Once again, if the presbyterate as derived from Judaism held the *judicial* function, yet in the Christian Church the Apostles are the chief ministers of discipline (cf. 1 Cor. v; Acts xv), and the presbyters, as will be shown, were also bishops, and, as such, teachers and leaders of worship; they share, in fact, the whole apostolic pastorate (1 Pet. v. 1, 2), and in St. James's Epistle they perform a function which involves a spiritual ministration (James v. 14); later, when they are distinct from the bishop, they sometimes indeed appear as the special ministers of discipline, as in the Ebionite Clementines (*Ep. Clem.* 7-10; *Hom.* iii. 67, 68), but even so under the bishop (*Ep. Clem.* 2, 3, 6; *Ep. Petr.* 4), and not to the exclusion of the deacons (*Ep. Clem.* 12; *Apost. Const.* ii. 44, 57, viii. 28). Finally, if the *administration of alms* was in some special sense a function of the diaconate in its original idea, yet it does not cease to be part of the apostolic office to organize almsgiving (see Gal. ii. 10, 2 Cor. viii, etc.), nor should it surprise us to find it specially mentioned in connection with the presbyterate (Acts xi. 30; Polycarp *ad Phil.* 6, 11; cf. *Ch. Ordinances* c. 18), though when the presbyterate came to be the name for a distinct office from the episcopate, the function of the administration of alms came to belong generally to the bishop, with the assistance of the deacon.

(*b*) The title EPISCOPUS was common among the Greeks. In Attic it is used for a commissioner "appointed to regulate a new colony or acquisition" whom the Spartans would have called a 'harmost.' Among writers of the period of the empire, it is used by Arrian for the inspectors employed by Indian kings; by Appian for a commissioner appointed by Mithridates in Ephesus[1]; by Dionysius of Halicarnassus for the inspectors of agriculture whom Numa Pompilius is supposed to have instituted.[2] It is used also in inscriptions of the Haurân (a district of the ancient Bashan) for

---

[1] For refs. see Lightfoot *Philippians* p. 95.
[2] Dion. Hal. *Ant. Rom.* ii. 76 : διεῖλε τὴν χώραν ἅπασαν εἰς τοὺς καλουμένους πάγους καὶ κατέστησεν ἐφ' ἑκάστου τῶν πάγων ἄρχοντα ἐπίσκοπόν τε καὶ περίπολον τῆς ἰδίας μοίρας.

civic officers who seem to represent the "agoranomi," "qui praesunt pani et ceteris venalibus rebus quae civitatum populis ad quotidianum victum usui sunt" (so Charisius, a jurisconsult of Constantine's time, explains their office, *Digest* l. 4 18); and also for 'committees' appointed to superintend any work, see Le Bas et Waddington *Inscriptions Grecques et Latines*, 1990, 2330, 2308. This last commemorates the restoration of a conduit and temple in Conmodus' time at Soueida ἐπισκοπούσης φυλῆς Σομαιθηνῶν. It seems also to be used for the officer of a guild, though his functions are not clear.[1] MM. Le Bas and Waddington remark (tom. iii. p. 474):
"il est intéressant de rencontrer si près du berceau du christianisme le mot ἐπίσκοπος appliqué à un fonctionnaire civil. C'est là, peut-être que les apôtres l'ont pris pour le donner aux premiers surveillants et directeurs des communautés chrétiennes."

So far then we have seen cause at least to recognise that there was a wide use of the term ἐπίσκοπος in Greek of the imperial period, and especially in Syria, for an administrative officer, which must clearly have suggested or facilitated the Christian use of the term. On the other hand the word had a use in the Old Testament (LXX). "In the LXX," says Dr. Lightfoot,[2] "the word is common. In some places it signifies 'inspectors, superintendents, taskmasters,' as 2 Kings xi. 19, 2 Chron. xxxiv. 12, 17, Is. lx. 17; in others it is a higher title, 'captains' or 'presidents,' Neh. xi. 9, 14, 22. Of Antiochus Epiphanes we are told that when he determined to overthrow the worship of the one true God, he 'appointed commissioners (ἐπισκόπους, bishops) over all the people,' to see that his orders were obeyed (1 Macc. i. 51, comp. Joseph. *Ant.* xii. 5. 4: in 2 Macc. v. 22 the word is ἐπιστάτας). The feminine ἐπισκοπή, which is not a classical word, occurs very frequently in the LXX, denoting sometimes the *work*, sometimes the *office*, of an ἐπίσκοπος. Hence it passed into the language of the New Testament and of the Christian Church." Dr. Sanday quotes this passage,[3] and adds: "If ἐπισκοπή had its origin in the usage of the LXX, is it not reasonable to derive ἐπίσκοπος from the same source?" He argues in favour of this position with great force, and calls attention to

[1] Hatch *B.L.* pp. 37, 38, note. The matter is not of great importance. Dr. Lightfoot calls the evidence "slight" (*Dissert.* p. 194). So also Kühl pp. 93-96. Sanday, *Expositor*, Feb. 1887, pp. 98-100: "I confess that I cannot quite satisfy myself as to the evidence which has been adduced to show that this was a standing title for the financial officer of the clubs or guilds." Salmon, *Expositor*, July 1887, p. 19: "The proof offered is extremely meagre."

[2] *Philippians* pp. 95, 96.

[3] *Expositor*, Feb. 1887, p. 102.

the fact that Clement of Rome refers back the institution of Christian bishops to the authority of Isaiah.[1] It should be added that St. Peter speaks of Judas' apostolate with reference to Ps. cix. 8, as an ἐπισκοπή (Acts i. 20). On the whole, if contemporary secular usage had a good deal to do with the use of the term 'episcopus' in the Christian Church, it is probable that Old Testament usage had at least as much influence. Obviously the two influences are very likely to have combined. The name has no more definite meaning than that of 'superintendence.' On being adopted by the Apostles, it would have gained from the first a new colour from the spiritual character of the supervision which the Christian communities required:[2] the Christian presbyters were charged by St. Paul to "take heed unto themselves, and to all the flock, in the which the Holy Ghost had made them bishops, to feed [rule] the Church of God, which He purchased with His own blood."

(c) The title DEACON (Phil. i. 1) does not seem to have been derived from any Jewish or pagan source, but to have been a natural application of the more general idea of ministry to the wants of others, so specially characteristic of Christianity; see St. Luke xxii. 26, 27.

(d) The titles 'presbyter' and 'episcopus' were used interchangeably for the same officers; see esp. Acts. xx. 17, 28, Titus i. 5, 7.[3] At the same time it is natural to suppose that the title 'presbyter' would have seemed more natural in Jewish communities, and the title 'episcopus' among Gentile Christians. Thus in fact St. James and probably St. Peter (see *varr. lectt.* on 1 Pet. v. 2), uses only the former title. But the distinction cannot be pressed. The Jewish *Didache* knows only the title ἐπίσκοπος (xv. 1). On the other hand the officers at Ephesus are known as presbyters as well as 'episcopi' (Acts xx. 17; 1 Tim. v. 17, 19; cf. Acts xiv. 23). It is natural also to suppose that the term ἐπίσκοπος was more definitely the title of an office, while πρεσβύτερος with its vaguer application to the dignity of age (cf. 1 Pet. v. 1-5; Clem. *ad Cor.*

---

[1] Is. lx. 17, quoted by Clem. *ad Cor.* 42 as καταστήσω τοὺς ἐπισκόπους αὐτῶν ἐν δικαιοσύνῃ καὶ τοὺς διακόνους αὐτῶν ἐν πίστει. It is quoted also by Irenaeus with a similar purpose, but from the LXX, without alteration.

[2] Dr. Sanday inclines to think the superintendence was of persons, and specially of deacons: the bishop, that is, was the superintendent of deacons. cf. *Expositor*, Feb. 1887, p. 100. But see Acts xx. 28. He also suggests (with Kühl) that, as the verb διακονεῖν preceded the title διάκονοι, so the verb ἐπισκοπεῖν may have preceded the title ἐπίσκοποι. But there is no evidence of this.

[3] See Dr. Lightfoot's note, *Philippians* p. 95 f.

i. 3; Polycarp *ad Phil.* 5, 6; in all which cases it is put in contrast to youth[1]) represented rather a position of respect. Thus Theodore of Mopsuestia, while he acknowledges that 'presbyter' and 'episcopus' are used interchangeably, yet justifies the use of the 'presbytery' in 1 Tim. iv. 14 (as he thinks) for ὁ τῶν ἀποστόλων σύλλογος with these words: πρεσβυτέριον αὐτὸ ὀνομάσας ἀπὸ τοῦ ἐντίμου. This, he explains, was rather a title of respect as amongst the Jews, while presbyters were called bishops ἀφ' οὗπερ μετῄεσαν καὶ ἔργον, τῷ μάλιστα πᾶσιν ἐπισκοπεῖν (in 1 Tim. iii. 3, Swete ii. p. 120). But this distinction again admits of being pressed very little way. All the evidence goes to show that the presbyterate was a definite office to which the Apostles appointed men (Acts xiv. 23) and that the presbyter was also called a bishop.

(*e*) The presbyter-episcopi exercised a pastorate of souls (1 Peter v. 2, Acts xx. 28). They shared with the Apostles the stewardship of God (Titus i. 7). They took their share in teaching and admonishing (1 Thess. v. 12, etc.; though there may perhaps have been some who did not teach, 1 Tim. v. 17). They administered sacraments and sacramental rites (Clem. *ad Cor.* 44, *Didache* xv. 1, James v. 14). They also administered discipline and, in part at least, charity. In fact they were, under the Apostles and apostolic men, the spiritual 'presidents' of the Churches.

II. In view of this positive position we have now to examine the recent speculations[2] especially connected with the names of Dr. Hatch and Professor Harnack.

(*a*) Dr. Hatch lays stress upon the fact noticed above that the Jewish communities possessed distinct organizations from different points of view, the presbyterate constituting the organization for the purpose of discipline. He supposes the Christian Church to have derived from Judaism not only the title of the presbyterate, but also its functions, unchanged. "It may be gathered," he says (*B. L.* pp. 57-62), "from the Talmud that out of the elders or chief men of every community a certain number had come to be officially recognised, and that definite rules were laid down for their action. Side by side with the synagogue of a town, but

---

[1] But the presbyters in all these cases are also definite officers; cf. the term κλῆροι (= 'allotted charges') in 1 Pet. v. 3.

[2] The earlier speculations to which Baur gave the chief impulse have been noticed above, p. 250 note[1]. They were connected primarily with the question of the authenticity of the Acts and the Pastoral Epistles, and the general theory of the Tübingen school which is bound up with this question. They treated the development of the ministry only secondarily.

distinct from it, was the συνέδριον or local court. The former was the general assembly, or 'congregation' of the people: the latter was the 'seat' of the elders." So in the Christian Church "there is a strong presumption that the officers who continued to bear the same names in the same community exercised functions closely analogous to those which they had exercised before; in other words, that the elders of the Jewish communities which had become Christian were, like the elders of the Jewish communities which remained Jewish, officers of administration and of discipline." This derivation of functions from Judaism to Christianity was facilitated in Dr. Hatch's view, as this quotation will have shown, by the very gradual transition which he supposes to have taken place from the older Jewish to the Christian religion. "When the majority of the members of a Jewish community were convinced that Jesus was the Christ, there was nothing to interrupt the current of their former common life. There was no need for secession, for schism, for a change in the organization. The old form of worship and the old modes of government could still go on. The weekly commemoration of the Resurrection supplemented, but did not supersede, the ancient sabbath. The reading of the life of Christ and of the letters of the Apostles supplemented, but did not supersede, the ancient lessons from the prophets, and the ancient singing of the psalms. The community as a whole was known by the same name which had designated the purely Jewish community. It was still a παροικία—a colony living as strangers and pilgrims in the midst of an alien society. . . . The same names were in use for the court of administration and for the members of that court: and even the weekly court-days remained the same."[1] Thus the Jewish Christian communities derived from the Jewish a presbyterate of men of age and gravity, for purposes of "administration and discipline." The origin of the episcopate was

---

[1] The general idea of this paragraph will be criticised further on. Here a few details need notice. (1) There is no evidence quoted of a Jewish community of 'the dispersion' calling itself a παροικία. The Jewish instance of the word quoted p. 61 n.[15] is from the LXX and refers to the captivity. All the other instances given are Christian.

(2) The Christian presbyterate is compared to the συνέδριον τῶν ἀποστόλων in *ad Magn.* 6; so in *ad Trall.* 3, ὡς συνέδριον θεοῦ καὶ ὡς σύνδεσμον ἀποστόλων; in *ad Philad.* 8 it is called the "synedrion of the bishop." But in none of the cases is the presbyterate called the sanhedrin in the Jewish sense, officially, still less so by the "Fathers of the fifth and sixth centuries."

(3) There is no reference given for the weekly court-days remaining the same.

different. "The officers of administration and finance [in the contemporary non-Christian associations] were chiefly known by one or other of two names"—ἐπιμελητής or ἐπίσκοπος.[1] This latter title then was borrowed to express the administrative officer of the Christian communities, or, as the primary administration is supposed by Dr. Hatch to have been financial, so the primary function of the primitive 'bishop' was financial administration.[2] On this point Dr. Hatch's theory was modified by Prof. Harnack in his *Analecten* to his German translation of Dr. Hatch's work, and Dr. Hatch himself now explains that he "is wrongly supposed to 'lay any exclusive or even especial stress upon the financial character of the ἐπίσκοποι."[3] The presbyterate was, then, a disciplinary board derived from Judaism, the episcopus was an administrative officer, derived from the contemporary guilds.

This theory of Dr. Hatch was developed by Prof. Harnack, and while the former in his *Bampton Lectures* had taken up no decisive position about the genuineness of the Pastoral Epistles and Acts, the latter boldly declares all these documents to belong to the second century (with the Epistle of St. James), and in developing his theory is at pains to explain that it is intimately bound up with the critical position. Having thus given himself free scope for writing on the *origines* of the ministry by having abolished almost all the evidence, he supposes that the office of the episcopus was originally quite distinct from that of the presbyter, and that there was a partial fusion, followed again by a fresh separation in the monarchical episcopate of later days.[4]

[1] *B. L.* p. 36 f.
[2] *B. L.* p. 39: "in their special capacity as administrators of church funds they were known by a name which was in current use for such administrators."
[3] See Dr. Hatch's explanation in *Expositor*, Feb. 1887, p. 99, note [1], and his communication to Dr. Harnack's *Dogmengesch.* i. p. 155, note [1]. This latter may indicate that he would not (since the discovery of the *Didache*) differ from Harnack that the "episcopi and diaconi were primarily officers of worship"; cf. *Expositor*, May 1887, pp. 339-342; *Texte u.s.w.* l.c., p. 144. This explanation of Dr. Hatch's renders unnecessary a good deal of criticism (as by Kühl and others). It also makes it difficult to see the point of his arguments and references on pp. 47, 48.
[4] See Harnack, in *Expositor*, l.c. His theory is explained by Dr. Sanday, *Expositor*, Jan. 1887. Dr. Hatch on the other hand says that "the weight of evidence has rendered practically indisputable" the identity of presbyters and episcopi in the N. T. (*B. L.* p. 39). Dr. Sanday calls this "something that looks a little like a concession to the older view" (*l.c.* p. 12). It seems to me inconsistent with the episcopi and presbyters representing different organizations. With reference to this view as carried out by Harnack with "more uncompromising logic," it would appear that the evidence of such

(b) Dr. Hatch, regarding the functions of presbyters as judicial or disciplinary and those of the episcopus as administrative in an almost secular sense, treats the local officers of the Christian Churches as originally hardly 'spiritual' persons : 'the ministration of the word and sacraments' was a later conception of the presbyterate.[1] He also supposes that their office was only temporary. Here again, however, Prof. Harnack modifies the idea, maintaining that the episcopate and diaconate, as distinct from the presbyterate, ranked as *charismatic*, and were therefore "almost free from control."[2]

It will be seen at once that this position as carried out by Prof. Harnack rests upon the repudiation of the Acts and the Pastoral Epistles as representing authentic history and the mind of St. Paul. Enough has been said earlier in this note on the identification of the presbyters and the bishops, and on the 'spiritual' functions of the presbyter-bishops. It should however be pointed out further with reference to other parts of Dr. Hatch's theory, that :—

1. The title 'presbyter' was chiefly, if not exclusively, in use amongst the Jews of Jerusalem, and its use in the Churches would therefore indicate not the gradual organization of Christian communities side by side with the Jewish, and on their model, all over the empire—in which case we should have had Christian *archons*—but the derivation of the Christian communities from Jerusalem as a centre.

2. Though the Christianity represented on one level by St. James and on a much lower level by the *Didache* may be described as a gradual transition from the old to the new covenant, this was not an ordinary position. Not only the Epistle to the Thessalonians

passages as Acts xx. 28, Titus i. 5, 7 (whenever written), and of Clem. *ad Cor.* 44, was enough to overthrow it. No passage can be produced in which there are signs of a distinction being drawn between presbyters and episcopi, existing together, till the later distinction of the monarchical episcopate. Nor, in view of Polycarp *ad Phil.* 5 ὑποτασσομένους τοῖς πρεσβυτέροις καὶ διακόνοις, can the connection of the title diaconus with that of episcopus be pressed as if the deacons were in no relation to the presbyters. It is probably an accident that we do not hear more of presbyters and deacons in conjunction. Later no doubt the deacon was attached specially to the monarchical bishop, but still the clergy are often described as presbyters and deacons, as e.g. by Clem. Alex. in *Strom.* vi. 13.

[1] *B. L.* pp. 72-82.

[2] *Analecten zu Hatch* p. 234, note [1]; but in *Expositor,* May 1887, p. 333, he speaks of Clement as first maintaining the lifelong character of the episcopate.

Note K. 409

and the Acts of the Apostles, but that most Jewish of New Testament documents, the Apocalypse, witness to the marked hostility of the Jews to the Christians, and therefore to the marked separation of the Christian communities.[1] The Jews of Palestine "expelled" the Christians, says St. Paul, and where this did not occur, the process is described by Dr. Lightfoot as a secession resulting in the establishment of a separate synagogue. There was no process of 'continuity without a break.'

3. The evidence for 'episcopus' as an officer of contemporary guilds is exceeding slight. For this statement I need not add to the references given above, except to mention that Harnack seems to agree as to the inadequacy of the evidence:[2] "Inquiries about the place or character of such an office in civil constitutions do not afford any solution of the problem. No other meaning can be given to the word than that of 'overseer'; but what sort of oversight such overseers exercised cannot be more precisely determined."

4. Dr. Hatch underrates strangely the intense consciousness of the Christians, especially of the Christian Apostles who organized the Churches, that 'all things had become new.' Whatever elements of organization or practice the Christian Church may have derived from external sources, Jewish or even pagan, they were fused at once by the 'one Spirit' into the 'one body,' and gained with immense rapidity a quite new set of associations. Christian institutions must be interpreted from within as the Christians understood them. It is by a simple application of this principle, in contrast to Dr. Hatch's method, that Harnack reaches the speedy conclusion that "bishops were originally the directors of the worship, the offerers κατ' ἐξοχήν. They are called overseers insomuch as they direct or superintend the assembly met for worship. Out of this function all others have been necessarily

---

[1] So even in the *Didache* (viii. 1) we have the suggestive direction: "Let your fasts be not with the hypocrites; for they fast on the second and fifth days of the week, but do ye fast on the fourth and the preparation day (Friday). Neither pray ye as the hypocrites." The language of the Apocalypse is also very noticeable, see ii. 9; "the blasphemy of them which say they are Jews and are not, but are a synagogue of Satan." Cf. 1 Thess. ii. 15, on the hostility of the Jews of Judaea, "who both killed the Lord Jesus and the prophets and drove out us." See Dr. Lightfoot *Philipp.* p. 190, and a criticism of Dr. Hilgenfeld in *Zeitschr. f. wissensch. Theol.* 1886, p. 5: "solcher Uebertritt ganzer oder fast ganzer jüdischer gemeinden zum Christus-Glauben wird sehr selten vorgekommen sein."

[2] *Expositor* l.c. p. 339.

developed."[1] Probably if Prof. Harnack gave the weight he should to some documents of the New Testament, he could somewhat modify the decision, so far as to extend the original oversight of the bishop to all the concerns of the flock. But at least it is a decision based primarily on an investigation of what Christians thought of their own institutions, and the result is therefore the exaltation to the first place of the spiritual function. Dr. Hatch, by his method of giving exaggerated weight to external associations and connections and ignoring the primary evidence from within, as he despiritualizes the episcopate, so he does the same for the Eucharist. He rightly deduces the connection of the bishop with the Eucharist from such passages as Justin Martyr *Apol.* i. 67, and Ignatius *ad Smyrn.* 8,[2] but the nature of the Eucharist may also be gathered from these passages, and how subordinate a place does charitable relief hold in it by comparison to its great spiritual functions. How could it be otherwise when St. Paul wrote of it as in 1 Cor. xi. 17-34?

Dr. Hatch's references, one may notice, do not always suggest the idea in the text. For example, in support of the secular idea of the eucharistic administration, he remarks that the offerings made by those who were present at that service at first seem to have been of various kinds; but afterwards a rule was made limiting them to bread and wine or corn and grapes (*Apost. Can.* 3); and still later, those which were not consumed at the time were divided in fixed proportions among the clergy (*Apost. Const.* viii. 31). But the canon he refers to is suggestive of a view of the Eucharist very different from what he is emphasizing; it runs thus: "If any bishop or presbyter, otherwise than our Lord has ordained concerning the sacrifice, offer other things at the altar, as honey, milk, or strong beer instead of wine, any necessaries or birds or animals or pulse, otherwise than is ordained, let him be deprived; excepting grains of new corn, or ears of wheat, or bunches of grapes in their season. For it is not lawful to offer anything besides these at the altar, and oil for the holy lamp, and incense in the time of the divine oblation. But let all other fruits be sent to the house of the bishops as first fruits to him and the presbyters."

[1] *Expositor* l.c. p. 342.
[2] *B. L.* p. 40 note [32] and pp. 79, 80. See in criticism Hilgenfeld *l.c.* p. 16 f.

L.

THE TEACHING OF THE TWELVE APOSTLES.

(*See p.* 276.)

This document was discovered in a MS in Constantinople and given to the world in 1883 by Bryennius, the Patriarch of Nicomedia.[1]

It may be conveniently divided into the following parts:—

1. Rudimentary moral instructions about *the two ways* of life and death, as an address to catechumens just about to be baptized (cc. i-vi).[2]
2. Instructions to a community of Christians, addressed as a whole, about the proper method of baptizing, the Christian fasts, the use of the Lord's Prayer, and the celebration of the Eucharist (cc. vii-xi).
3. Further instructions about 'apostles' and 'prophets,' in their relation to the local Church, about the Sunday service, and about the election and functions of the local ministry of bishops and deacons (cc. xi-xv).
4. A final section about the second coming of Christ (c. xvi).

The first section is a primitive version of the *Two Ways*, a piece of moral instruction, perhaps originally Jewish, which appears in a great variety of early Christian writings,[3] and this is the only part

[1] For further information about this discovery also see Dr. Schaff *The Oldest Church Manual*.

[2] Of this portion, however, it may now be taken for proved that the passage from i. 3 εὐλογεῖτε to ii. 1 τῆς διδαχῆς is a later interpolation. The document in its interpolated form, or rather, perhaps, that on which the interpolation is based, is early enough to be known to Hermas, see Schaff *l.c.* p. 233. But the Latin fragment of the *Didache* (Schaff p. 219) and the *Church Ordinances* of Egypt (a document based on the early portion of the *Didache*, and showing acquaintance with the rest, see Schaff *l.c.* p. 237 f. and cf. c. 12 with *Did.* x. 3) show that this passage was wanting in its earliest form; cf. Dr. Taylor *The Teaching of the Twelve Apostles* pp. 19-22; Dr. Warfield in the *Bibliotheca Sacra*, Jan. 1886, p. 115 f. That these earlier chapters are a baptismal address is shown by the first words of c. vii ταῦτα πάντα προειπόντες βαπτίσατε; see Warfield *l.c.* p. 151.

[3] It is mentioned by Rufinus and Jerome under the titles of the *Two Ways*, or the *Judgment of Peter*. Dr. Krawutzcky of Breslau two years before Bryennius' publication had reconstructed this document from the uses of it by Christian writers almost in the words of the *Didache*. Harnack speaks of this as "a critical masterpiece, such as we can point to but few examples of

of the *Didache* which was permanently popular in at all its present shape.¹ In the second and third portions we recognise a primitive manual of church directions, most probably drawn also in part from a Jewish source, which are worked up into book vii of the *Apostolical Constitutions*. There is a writing mentioned by Eusebius as τῶν ἀποστόλων αἱ λεγόμεναι διδαχαί; there is also a διδαχὴ καλουμένη τῶν ἀποστόλων which Athanasius classes among "the books not admitted into the canon, but appointed by the Fathers to be read to those who are just coming to us and desire to be instructed in the doctrine of godliness"; but it is difficult to feel certain whether these references are to the *Didache* as we have it.²

The acquaintance with more than the earlier portion of our *Didache*, displayed apparently both in Barnabas' Epistle and in the *Church Ordinances*,³ would be enough to guarantee for it a very early date. But, in fact, the internal evidence does not allow us to doubt this. It is the work plainly of a Jewish Christian. He is conscious enough of his alienation from the Jews proper, whom he calls "the hypocrites,"⁴ and there is no sign of any insistence upon circumcision; but we must bear in mind that there was in the age preceding Christ's coming a widely spread school of liberalized Jews, who had come to regard their religion as "the school of the knowledge of God and of the spiritual life for the whole world"⁵; and a Jew of this sort who had accepted Christ as the Messiah and become a member of His Church as being the way of life and learnt ardently to desire His second coming to

in the history of literary criticism" (*Texte u.s.w.* b. ii. h. 1, 2. p. 208). Barnabas reproduces this *Two Ways*. "We are led to infer," says Dr. Taylor (*l.c.* p. vii), "that Barnabas in his Epistle surely drew, if not from our very *Teaching of the Twelve Apostles*, from a tradition or writing of which it has preserved the original form." Clement remarks "that the gospel and the apostles, like all the prophets, suggest the idea of two ways" (*Strom.* v. 5. 31, quoted by Warfield *l.c.* p. 139). It of course resembles the Choice of Heracles.

¹ For example the *Church Ordinances* shows acquaintance with, but does not use, the latter part, see Harnack *l.c.* ii. 230.

² See on this Salmon *Introd.* pp. 608, 613; cf. also p. 603, where he notices that in Rufinus' list of the canonical and ecclesiastical books, based on Athanasius, where the latter mentions the *Didache*, Rufinus speaks of the *Duæ Viæ*. It should also be mentioned that a legitimate doubt has been expressed, based on a calculation of the number of στίχοι, whether the *Teaching* mentioned by Nicephorus can be the whole of our manual, cf. Salmon *Introd.* p. 601; and on patristic refs. Schaff *l.c.* p. 114 f.

³ For Barnabas, see Schaff *l.c.* p. 227, and for the *Ch. Ord.* p. 238.

⁴ viii. 1, 2.

⁵ This is Athanasius' account of Judaism (*de Incarn.* c. 12). On the liberal Judaism of the Roman empire, see Harnack *Dogmengesch.* i. p. 73 f.

establish His kingdom—such a Christianized Jew, living or having lived under circumstances which made him acquainted with the vices of the Græco-Roman civilization,[1] must have been the author of our *Teaching*.

The moral instruction is of an intensely Jewish character. It is indeed not wholly Christian—not by any means on the level of the Sermon on the Mount, or of St. James who has so profound a grasp on the principles of the 'law of liberty.' It belongs rather to the enlightened synagogue than to the illuminated Church. "Whatsoever thou wouldst *not have done* to thee, neither do thou to another." "Thou shalt not hate any man, but some thou shalt rebuke, and for some thou shalt pray, and *some thou shalt love above thine own soul.*" "If thou hast, thou shalt give with thine hands as a ransom for thy sins." "Fast for those who persecute you." "Let your fasts not be with the hypocrites: for they fast on the second day and the fifth, but do ye fast on the fourth day and the Preparation [Friday]." "If thou canst bear the whole yoke of the Lord, thou shalt be perfect; but if thou canst not, what thou art able to do, that do. As regards food, bear what thou canst. But from that which has been offered to an idol, be greatly on thy guard. For it is the service of dead gods."[2] This impression of a Jewish tone about the moral teaching is deepened at every step of closer study.

Once again, the regulations given about baptism are thoroughly Jewish in character. In what sense? Not because they are minute regulations, but because baptism seems to be regarded, as a half-Christianized Jew might regard it,—as a *prescribed ordinance*, not as a means of grace. He seems to have no grasp at all of the sacramental principle. Baptism and (as we shall see) the Eucharist are ordinances of the Gospel, like prayer and fasting and alms-

[1] See the list of vices which characterize the way of death, c. v.
[2] This advice about 'bearing the yoke' and 'bearing the burden' of Jewish observance only up to a man's power, reveals the intensely Jewish atmosphere out of which it comes. It carries us back in its very language to the circumstances of the Apostolic Council (Acts xv. 10-28). Taylor has admirable remarks on the regulations about fasting (p. 58 f.), and on the whole passage about 'the two ways.' "There remains (when the interpolated portion is removed) little or nothing distinctively Christian in the first part of the *Teaching*." It is also very noticeable that in place of our Lord's spiritualizing of the law, which makes the inward sin of intention equivalent to the outward act of commission (St. Matt. v. 28), we have in c. iii a Jewish method of 'making a fence to the law,' which is a very different thing; "Be not lustful, for lust leads to fornication, etc." See Taylor, p. 23.

giving—nothing more.¹ The meagreness and inadequacy of the whole conception of the Eucharist strikes every one at once. It is fenced indeed by the preliminary requirement of baptism² and the injunction of previous public confession of sins³; it is regarded as the Christian sacrifice⁴ or thankoffering,⁵ in which is fulfilled the prophecy of Malachi about the "pure sacrifice" of the new covenant (xiv. 3), and which, it is probably implied, our Lord alluded to when He spoke of 'bringing our gift to the altar'⁶; it is also called spiritual food and drink (unless indeed these words refer to

---

¹ The mention of the Wednesday and Friday fasts, and of the threefold repetition of the Lord's Prayer, with the doxology (which, however, took the place of the Amen, and no more belonged to the Lord's Prayer than to any other prayer; see x. 5, and Taylor p. 67), is very interesting as carrying back these practices to such very primitive times. Indeed, the whole evidence of the *Teaching* goes to increase our belief in the early or Judæo-Christian origin of the ritual regulations of the Christian Church. Further, the regulations about baptism have a very high interest (1) As emphasizing that baptism "into the name of the Lord" is baptism performed "into the name of the Father, and of the Son, and of the Holy Ghost;" see ix. 5, vii. 1. (2) For the evidence of the use of 'trine affusion' in the earliest Church, vii. 3. (3) For the prescription of fasting for the baptizer and the baptized. This practice in the case of the baptizer did not apparently die out, as the commentators seem to think: see St. Chrysostom's answer to his accusers, *Ep.* cxxv. p. 668: καθελέτωσαν καὶ τὸν Παῦλον ὃς μετὰ τὸ δειπνῆσαι ὁλόκληρον τὸν οἶκον ἐβάπτισεν. He seems to mean that St. Paul baptized after eating, and that this would be an ecclesiastical offence. He is, however, forgetting the order of events in the original passage, Acts xvi. 33, 34; and the context possibly makes his meaning ambiguous. (4) For the bearing of these Judaic regulations on the history of infant baptism. The Christian Church would presumably have carried on the Jewish practice of infant baptism. See Taylor on the 'little proselytes,' pp. 55-58 (very suggestive on the theory of infant baptism); and Sabatier *La Didachè* pp. 84-88 : " L'Eglise, en donnant au baptême une signification nouvelle, ne s'écarta cependant pas beaucoup dans le principe de la discipline du baptême juif."

² ix. 5.

³ xiv. 1 : προ[σ]εξομολογησάμενοι τὰ παραπτώματα ὑμῶν, cf. iv. 14 : "In the Church thou shalt confess thy transgressions," i.e. before public prayer. This throws a strong light on the history of public confession in the Christian Church, see St. James v. 14-16, 1 St. John i. 9 (Westcott's note). It is noticeable that this injunction of confession "in the Church" is omitted in the later *Apostolical Constitutions* (vii. 14), or rather turned into "Thou shalt confess thy sins to the Lord thy God."

⁴ xiv. 1.

⁵ c. ix. "Eucharist" is clearly used technically. Thus the *Didache* throws back the date of the technical use of the word.

⁶ xiv. 2 : "Let no man who has a dispute with his fellow come together with you until they be reconciled [διαλλαγῶσιν, cf. St. Matt. v. 24], that your sacrifice be not defiled," seems to refer to the saying of our Lord.

Note L.   415

the *teaching* of Christ),[1] and is celebrated in definite anticipation of His second coming (x. 6): but the whole conception of it is more Jewish than Christian.[2] Sabatier says truly: "Our document cannot but surprise those who read for the first time its liturgy of the Eucharist. We have here a form without analogy anywhere. It separates itself much less from the Jewish ritual than from the Christian." "It is an ordinary repast just touched by a breath of religious mysticism, such as is the outcome of the importance which belongs, in Jewish and oriental idea, to repasts taken in common."[3] There is, in fact, nothing to recall to our mind our Lord's words in the institution of the Eucharist, of which, we must remark, we have the form given us in St. Paul's Epistle to the Corinthians, —nothing to recall to us St. Paul's language about the significance of the communion. It is a Jewish feast Christianized in a measure by the recognition of the Messiahship of Christ and the expectation of His second coming.

It must not indeed be supposed that the mere absence of later ritual would mean the absence of sacramental idea. This view has been combated already (pp. 178, 179). We find in some cases an

[1] x. 3. See Sabatier *l.c.* p. 104.

[2] See Salmon *Introd.* p. 607. Thus the Prayer of Thanksgiving over the bread is reproduced as a sort of 'grace before meat' in the pseudo-Athanasius *de Virginitate* 13; see Schaff *l.c.* p. 194. There is nothing in it to raise it above the level of such a use. There are, however, indications that these prayers in the *Didache* are really prayers for the Agape, and that the actual communion is meant to occur after x. 6. The word Eucharist may well include the Agape. Thus the cup in ix. 2 corresponds (cf. St. Luke xxii. 17) to the second paschal cup. The expression "after being filled" (x. 1) refers to the preliminary eating, and Dr. Taylor quotes a most suggestive parallel from Jewish language about the passover, *l.c.* p. 130: "The chagigah was eaten first that the passover might be eaten after being filled." Thus the occurrence of the Holy Communion after the Agape would rest upon a Jewish practice. Then the exclamations of *Did.* x. 6: "If any one is holy, let him come: if any one is not, let him repent," refer, as they naturally should, to the subsequent eating of the holy things. This again would explain the meaning of the rule (of xi. 9) that the prophet who "orders a table in the spirit" is, as a test of his disinterestedness, not to eat of it: he is not to eat of the Agape, not to "fill himself," and is, of course, to communicate at the subsequent Eucharist. This interpretation of the 'eucharistic' prayers would seem the most natural, I think, but for the immense difficulty for suggesting a reason for the silence about the Holy Communion, unless we can introduce the idea of reserve about 'the mysteries': cf. Taylor *l.c.* p. v. Perhaps, however, the difficulty is less great if these benedictions are based on formulas in use amongst the Jews at religious meals, as seems very probable; see Rendall *Theol. of Hebr. Chr.* p. 89 f.

[3] Sabatier *l.c.* pp. 109, 112.

absence of elaborate ritual coinciding with the fullest appreciation of the spiritual efficacy of a sacrament. In the *Teaching* it is the idea that is absent. This falls in further with the absence of grasp on the principle of the Incarnation. Of course Trinitarian doctrine is implied in the use of the Trinitarian formula of baptism,[1] but the author seems to be quite uninfluenced by the teaching of St. Paul, St. Peter, and St. John on the Incarnation and the Atonement and the Holy Spirit.[2] The Christology indeed is barely as full as

[1] Schaff maintains that the author of the *Didache* in the phrase "Hosanna to the God of David" (x. 6) refers to Christ as God. If the reading is right, however, it more probably refers to the Father. Nor does the "Lord" of xiv. 3 seem to refer to Christ as the Messiah of the Old Testament. It is a simple reference to the words of the original. It is not that the author is heretical, but he is inadequate.

[2] It is indeed well open to question whether he had any acquaintance with their writings:

(*a*) His supposed references to St. Paul are not at all convincing. *Did.* iii. 1: "Flee from evil and all that is like it" is a reference not to 1 Thess. v. 22, but to a Jewish saying (see Taylor, p. 24); v. 2: οὐ κολλώμενοι ἀγαθῷ οὐδὲ κρίσει δικαίᾳ does suggest Rom. xii. 9, but κολλᾶσθαι is a common word e.g. with St. Luke. Beside these, πνευματικὴ τροφὴ καὶ ποτός (x. 3) applied to the Gospel or the Eucharist does not suggest 1 Cor. x. 3, 4. The connection of the Church's unity with the unity of the bread in *Did.* ix. 4 is strikingly different from that in 1 Cor. x. 17, and the account of Antichrist in c. xvi shows great independence of St. Paul's treatment, though acquaintance with the idea that he is using.

(*b*) The reference in i. 4 to 1 Peter ii. 11 occurs in the interpolated portion (cf. also 4 Macc. i. 32).

(*c*) The supposed references to St. John seem on examination to be very unconvincing. The Vine of David (ix. 2) is the Church, not Christ, and suggests therefore ignorance of St. John xv. The phrase (x. 2) εὐχαριστοῦμέν σοι πάτερ ἅγιε, ὑπὲρ τοῦ ἁγίου ὀνόματός σου, οὗ κατεσκήνωσας ἐν ταῖς καρδίαις ὑμῶν [ἡμῶν] καὶ ὑπὲρ τῆς γνώσεως καὶ πίστεως καὶ ἀθανασίας ἧς ἐγνώρισας ἡμῖν διὰ 'Ιησοῦ τοῦ παιδός σοῦ is in fact a reference to Jerem. vii. 12 κατεσκήνωσα τὸ ὄνομά μου, and further suggests familiarity with the language used in the early chapters of the Acts, ii. 28 ἐγνώρισάς μοι ὁδοὺς ζωῆς, iii. 13 ὁ ἅγιος παῖς 'Ιησοῦς, cf. iii. 26, iv. 27-30, language which again is in direct reference to the Old Testament. St. John never uses ἀθανασία or γνῶσις. Indeed "Holy Father" is the only phrase which recalls St. John in his report of our Lord's Prayer, and our author is fond of the word ἅγιος. Altogether there is no reason to think he knew St. John's Gospel.

(*d*) Did the author of the *Didache* know either of the other Gospels? The Lord's Prayer and the baptismal formula would be an element in any tradition. Beyond these we have only a record of those 'sententious' sayings of our Lord, such as are most easily handed down in real tradition: οἱ πραεῖς κληρονομήσουσι τὴν γῆν, μὴ δῶτε τὸ ἅγιον τοῖς κυσίν, ἄξιος ὁ ἐργάτης τῆς τροφῆς αὐτοῦ (iii. 7, ix. 5, xiii. 2). The acquaintance with our Lord's eschatological discourses, shown in c. xvi, is very independent of the Gospels. He refers to

that of the early speeches in the Acts. Perhaps, however, we can best characterize the tone of the *Didache* by saying that it would represent the beliefs of a Jewish Christianity yet unleavened by the deeper 'teaching of the Apostles,' which was to follow that first earnest emphasis on the Messiahship of Jesus, of which the early chapters of the Acts give us the record.[1]

Of course there is teaching implied in the writing which is not given. Why should Christians "fast on Wednesday and Friday"? The answer to this question at least implies a record of historical facts about our Lord, though not more. Why should God be glorified "through Jesus Christ" (ix. 4)? Here is involved some doctrine of mediation. Why are Christians baptized into the name of the Son and the Spirit as well as of the Father? This must carry with it some teaching about the Persons represented by these Divine names. Thus there is a teaching implied which is not given, and apparently, we must add, not realized.

Our mind naturally goes back to those Jewish Christians to whom the Epistle to the Hebrews was written. Here were Christians who only half realized what their religion meant—who knew its 'first principles,'—those which a Jew could most easily realize—"repentance from dead works and faith toward God, the teaching of baptisms and of laying-on hands, and of resurrection

"the gospel of the Lord" (xv. 4), but it is doubtful whether it is a document. See, however, on the whole question, Taylor pp. 108-112.

[1] Certainly the connection of the *Didache* with the language of St. Peter's first sermons, and the phraseology of these chapters, is very striking. It is more than a coincidence of mere language.

(a) With ix. 2 'Ιησοῦς ὁ παῖς σου, cf. Acts iii. 13, 26, iv. 27, 30. See Clement's Epistle, c. 59. In *Mart. Polyc.* 14, as in the *Apost. Const.*, it has a new meaning; it is no longer *servant* as in the *Didache* (used alike of David and Jesus in the same clause), with reference to the 'servant of Jehovah' in Isaiah; it has got the meaning of 'Son'—'My beloved Son.' See Lightfoot on Clement, *in loc.*

(b) With x. 2 quoted above, and ix. 2, cf. Acts ii. 28., ἐγνώρισάς μοι ὁδοὺς ζωῆς.

(c) For the whole idea of the Acts, ii. 42 ἦσαν δὲ προσκαρτεροῦντες τῇ διδαχῇ τῶν ἀποστόλων. . . . τῇ κλάσει τοῦ ἄρτου καὶ ταῖς προσευχαῖς, cf. ix. 3, xiv. 1, τὸ κλάσμα, κλάσατε ἄρτον.

(d) With iv. 8 συγκοινωνήσεις δὲ πάντα τῷ ἀδελφῷ σου καὶ οὐκ ἐρεῖς ἴδια εἶναι, cf. Acts iv. 32 οὐδὲ εἷς τι. . . ἔλεγεν ἴδιον εἶναι. . . ἅπαντα κοινά.

(e) For the coupling of fasting and prayer, cf. Acts xiii. 3.

(f) With vi. 1-3, on 'bearing the yoke,' and 'guarding oneself from that which is offered to an idol,' cf. Acts xv. 10-28.

(g) 'The way' of life suggests the use of 'the way' in the Acts as a synonym for Christianity.

of the dead, and of eternal judgment." Is not the Christianity of this *Teaching* very much the sort of inadequate Christianity which the author of the Epistle to the Hebrews sought to lift into a complete realization of the divine majesty of Christ, of the mystery of His eternal high-priesthood and the Church's fellowship with Him and in Him? Not indeed that our document presents all the features of the Judaism which the author of that great Epistle had in view; there is no sign here of falling away, no craving after the "worldly" ritual of the old covenant; but the instruction given in the *Didache* embodies 'first principles' closely resembling those which the Hebrews had made their own: the belief in God and the moral duties of obedience and repentance which follow from that belief; the due and careful performance of the ceremonial and religious duties of religion and the reverence due to its teachers; the keen expectation of 'the end' and the coming of the kingdom, with the judgment and the resurrection.[1]

We have then to do with a Jewish Christian document of very early date. Sabatier would have us put it back as early as the middle of the first century, before St. Paul's Epistles, but it is perhaps more likely that its author escaped the influence of St. Paul by remoteness of situation rather than by priority in the date of his writing. In any case, we can with very great security date the *Didache* within the first century. Not only does its whole tone remind us of the Jewish cradle of Christianity, but other indications coincide with this. The Church's enemy is as yet simple imposture and self-seeking, and there are no traces of any prevalent heresy. Again, the state of the Christian ministry, which is discussed elsewhere, suggests a date long anterior to Ignatius.[2]

Have we any grounds on which to fix the district in which the *Didache* was written?

The suggestion of Alexandria or Egypt seems excluded by the physical features alluded to in the words "the bread scattered upon the mountains and gathered together."[3] On the other hand Dr. Taylor remarks (p. 116): "Sowing upon the mountains suits no

---

[1] Sabatier calls attention to the entire absence of any mention of women, as emphasizing its Jewish origin and early date (p. 153): "La plupart des documents d'origine juive ignorent la femme."

[2] See also Taylor, p. 118.

[3] ix. 4: thus the words ἐπάνω τῶν ὀρέων are omitted in the grace before meat for use in Egypt, which is referred to above as reproducing this prayer: this tends to dispose of Harnack's plea for Egypt (*l.c.* p. 26, proleg. pp. 25, 169).

place better than northern Palestine." It is however agreeable to Syria in general. Other indications point in the same direction. Thus, in vii. 2, there is a remarkable permission to baptize in warm water, where cold could not safely be used, and "it stands recorded in the Gemara that a fruitless attempt was made in the days of R. Jehoshua ben Levi (cent. ii-iii) to obtain dispensation from the practice of purificatory immersion in certain cases, in the interest of the women of Galilee, who were said to be afflicted with barrenness by the cold. But it was permitted to warm the water for the use of the high-priest on the Day of Atonement, if he was aged or delicate" (Taylor, pp. 54 f.). The Christian Judaism of the district appears here as granting to all what Pharisaic Judaism refused. Again, before the publication of this document, Drs. Westcott and Hort had declared that there "could be little doubt that the doxology [to the Lord's Prayer] originated in liturgical use *in Syria*,"[1] and that doxology appears in our manual as a substitute for the Amen in Jewish fashion at the end of the eucharistic thanksgiving, as well as the Lord's Prayer.[2]

We are inclined then to assign the document to Palestine or Syria, and should give the preference to an out-of-the-way district, such as that beyond the Jordan.

---

[1] *New Testament—Notes on Select Readings* p. 9. Harnack calls attention to the omission of ἡ βασιλεία before ἡ δύναμις καὶ ἡ δόξα. This omission occurs also in the Sahidic (Egyptian) version. This he thinks is a "subtle" indication of Egyptian origin (*l.c.* p. 26). But the same reading appears in Gregory of Nyssa. It was probably the original Jewish form.

[2] viii. 2, x. 5. It is hardly fair to quote the Aramaean *Maranatha* (x. 6) as an indication of Palestinian origin, in view of 1 Cor. xvi. 22. I suppose the produce of the land from which first-fruits are to be taken—cattle, flocks, corn, wine, oil—would suit most eastern countries.

ADDENDUM TO PAGE 389.

The tract de Aleatoribus—*just edited by Harnack* (Texte u. Untersuch. V. 1), *and by him assigned to Victor, bishop of Rome, c.* A.D. *195, but perhaps more probably by an African bishop* (? *writing before Cyprian*)—*contains the following passage illustrating the early conception of laying-on of hands* (c. 3) :—
"Since we bishops have through the laying-on of hands received the same Holy Spirit within the shelter of our breast, let us cause no sadness to Him who dwells with us—*quoniam episcopi idem* [? *eundem*] *Spiritum sanctum per impositionem manus cordis excepimus hospitio, cohabitatori nostro nullam maestitiam proponamus.*"

[Quite recently (see *Theologische Literaturzeitung*, Jan. 12, 1889) Wölfflin *Archiv für lat. Lexicographie*, v. heft 3, 4, pronounces an opinion, on purely linguistic grounds, that this tract is later than Cyprian's day, and probably by an African writer.]

INDEX.

ACHATIUS, Acts of bp. 212 n.
Aerius 160.
Albinus Flaccus 90 n.; (pseudo-) 181 n., 284 n., 358, 369 n., 382, 386.
Alexander Severus, 101.
Amalarius 284 n., 358, 369 n., 382.
Ambrose (St.) 241 n., 398; (pseudo-) 202 n.
Ambrosiaster: on orig. identity of bishop and presbyter 138 n., 171-176, 274 n., 307 n.; on the ministry 378-380.
Ammonius (abbot) 375.
Andrew (St.) in Asia Minor 288.
Anselm (St.) 163 n.
Apocalypse, angels of the 254.
Apost. Canons 189 n., 190 n., 192 n.; 410.
Apost. Constitutions, date of 145 n.; rites in 144-149, 386-387, 389; on the ministry 149-151; 160 n., 201 n., 284 n., 303, 319 n., 398.
Archippus 246 n., 379.
Arethas 255 n.
Aristides Philosophus 28.
Athanasius (St.) 136 n., 139, 142 n., 372, 412; on the episcopate 156; (pseudo-) 18 n., 204 n., 415 n.
Athenagoras 198.
Augustin (St.): on the Church 13 n., 19 n., 43, 59 n., 166 n.; on lay-priesthood 90 n.; on ordination 95, 191 n.. 193, 194, 388 n.; on councils 168 n.; on Peter's see 169 n.; 171 n.; 381 n.

BARNABAS (St.) 257, 259; 261; 262 n.
Basil (St.) 158 n.; 191, 194 n., 388.
Baur (C. F.) 245 n., 250 n.
Bede (Ven.) 52 n.
Bernaldus Constantiensis 382.
Bernard (St.) 163 n.

Bigg (Dr.) 90 n., 136 n., 204 n., 358 n., 361.
Bilson (Bp.) 73 n.
Boissier (M.) 31-35.
Bonwetsch (Prof.) 211 n., 394 n., 395 n.
Butler (Bp.) 11 n., 111.

CALLISTUS 188.
Cassian 374-375.
Chillingworth 108 n.
Chrysostom (St.): on ordination 104, 158-159, 384; on the orders 240, 241 n., 264 n.; (pseudo-) 400.
Church (Dean) 9, 43 n.
Church Ordinances 101 n., 284 n., 305 n., 362; 316 n., 412; date 362.
Clement of Alexandria: on the Church 20 n., 25, 26, 28 n.; Eucharist 79 n., 204 n.; ministry 135; traditions in 234 n., 249 n., 261 n., 273 n., 286; 325 n.
Clement of Rome 308; bp. 125, 324, 330; his letter 310-312; on the Church 23, 43 n.; Eucharist 226 n.; priesthood 199, 203; ministry 312-325, 390; 100, 188, 233 n., 281 n., 305, 404.
Clementines, The: date 129 n.; St. Peter appoints bps. 129; St. James in 130 n., 274 n.; on the ministry 130 n.; 154, 190, 219 n., 284 n., 303, 384, 389.
Colluthus 139.
Cornelius (of Rome) 376, 385.
Councils: Alexandria [A.D. 324] 139, 153.
Ancyra 152-153, 370-372.
Antioch 192 n., 372.
Arles [A.D. 314] 177, 193.
Capua [A.D. 391] 189 n.

Councils: Carthage [A.D. 256] 176;
    [A.D. 390] 177 n.
    ['Canons of iv Carthage'
    186 n., 368 n.]
    Elvira 177, 201 n.
    Neo-Caesarea 153 n.
    Nicaea 153-154, 189 n.,
    192 n., 202, 375.
    Orleans [A.D. 511] 192 n.
    Saragossa [A.D. 592] 192n.
    Seville [A.D. 619] 181 n.
    Toledo [A.D. 400] 177 n.;
    [A.D. 633] 191 n.
Cyprian (St.): on the Church 16, 53,
    55; tradition 68-69; ministry
    101, 104, 164-169, 190 n.; ordination 376, 385.

"DIDACHE:" date etc. 276, 411-419;
    on the Church 30n., 43n.; Eucharist
    79 n., 226 n., 315 n.; ministry
    101 n., 263 n., 277-285, 312 n.;
    priesthood 196 n., 199 n.; confession 254 n.; prophets 397.
Didymus 25 n.; 138 n.; 391 n., 393.
Dio Cassius 186 n.
Diognetum, Ep. ad. 29 n., 76 n., 88 n;
    278 n.
Dionysius the Areopagite 246 n., 307;
    (pseudo-) 144, 145 n., 146 n,
    364 n., 388 n.
Dionysius of Corinth 133-134, 246 n.,
    307, 308 n.
Dionysius Exiguus 371-372.
Dionysius of Halicarnassus 402.
Diotrephes 255.
Dracontius 156.

"ECCE HOMO" 36.
Epaphroditus 233 n.
Ephraem Syrus 5 n.; 161 n., 303 n.,
    364 n.
Epiphanius (St): on Alexandria 138,
    165 n., 358; the episcopate 159-161; 391 n.; 400, 401.
Eugenius IV 68 n.
Eusebius: on apost. council 274 n.;
    evangelists 283.
Eutychius 358-363.

FELICISSIMUS 376.
Firmilian (St) 155 n., 166 n.

GAIUS OF THESSALONICA 134n., 246n.,
    330 n.

Gieseler 375, 383.
Gladstone (W. E.) 77 n., 81, 109,
    116, 231-232 n.
Godet (Prof.) 7, 222 n., 229 n.
Gregory of Cappadocia 102.
Gregory the Great 158 n.
Gregory Nazianzen 157-158, 388.
Gregory of Tours 113, 375.

HADRIAN 29 n., 137.
Harnack (Prof.): on N. T. documents
    3 n., 4 n., 5 n., 233 n.; the Church
    28; ministry 165 n., 186 n., 188 n.,
    319 n., 407-410; Eucharist 226 n.;
    Ignatius 290 n.
Hatch (Dr.): on the Church 8 n.,
    9 n., 13, 49 n., 52, 53; ministry
    64, 164 n., 218 n., 303 n., 326 n.,
    405-410; ordination 183-185, 189 n.,
    374, 376-377, 384-387; baptism
    40; Montanism 207 n.
Hebrews, Ep. to the: witness as to
    church rulers 252 n., 323.
Hegesippus 127-128; 273-276, 307.
Hermas, The *Shepherd* of: its date
    330; on the Church 15 n., 21-2,
    54; ministry 313 n., 323, 331-333;
    prophecy 397.
Hilary the deacon 171 n., 201.
Hippolytus 165 n., 188 n., 199,
    284 n., 389.
Hoadley (Bp.) 49 n.
Holland (H. S.) 38 n., 44 n., 222.
Holtzmann (Dr.) 250 n., 257 n.
Hooker 10 n., 350 n.
Hugh of St. Victor 86 n.

IGNATIUS (St.) 290-292, 329; a prophet 280, 284, 300 n.; his letters
    289 n; on the Church 23-24, 53,
    55; Eucharist 79 n.; priesthood
    199, 202-203; ministry and episcopate 293-305, 274 n., 288, 328,
    406 n.
Irenaeus (St.) 116-118; on the Church
    15 n., 17-18, 20, 53, 55, 77;
    Eucharist 72, 78 n., 226 n.; priesthood 89 n.; episcopal successions
    119-125, 287, 307; ministry 244
    n., 264 n., 275 n., 284 n.; prophecy
    392, 396.
Ischyras 139.
Isidore of Seville: on priesthood 90
    n.; bishops and presbyters 181 n.,
    380, 381; chorepiscopi 373; other

Index. 423

orders 153 n., 178 n., 284 n.; ordination 386.
Isidore of Pelusium 97.

JAMES (St.): bp. of Jerusalem 128, 260, 273-274; in the Clementines 130 n., 274 n.; on 'presbyters' 252 n., 253.
Jerome (St.): on the Church 19 n., 166 n.; priesthood 84, 90 n., 201-202; episcopate 169 n., and presbyterate 219 n.; ordination 193, 384, 385, 387 n.; episcopate at Alexandria 137-142, 339, 357-363; original identity of bishops and presbyters 171-176, 274 n., 308 n., 380-381.
John (St.): 'presbyter' 244 n.; priest 284 n.; institutes episcopacy 286-287.
Judas Barsabbas 262 n., 323.
Jude (St.): his epistle 252 n.; his descendants 276.
Julius I (Pope) 102.
Junias 233 n., 251 n.
Justin Martyr: on the Church, 18, 29; Eucharist 79 n., 184, 198, 226 n.; priesthood 87-88, 284 n.; prophecy 392.

LANGEN (Dr.) 334, 354.
Laurentius Mellifluus 91-92.
Law (W.) 20 n., 42 n., 49 n., 99 n.
Leo (St.): on lay-priesthood 90 n.; ordination 102-103, 194-195.
Liberatus 142 n.
Liddon (Dr.) 83 n., 84, 318 n.
Lightfoot (Dr.): on the *Apost. Const.* 144 n.; deacons 264 n.; Ignatian letters 289; can. xiii of Ancyra 370; sacerdotalism 72 n., 84, 196 n., 305 n.; the ministry 353-357; history of episcopate 128, 134-135, 138 n., 247 n., 273 n., 275 n., 288, 307, 328 n., 329 n.
Liudger (St.) 376-377.
Lucifer of Cagliari 169, 170, 171 n., 389.

MACAULAY (Lord) 107.
Maurice (F. D.) 220.
Meletius 165 n., 192 n.
Melito 29 n.; 132.
Milligan (Prof.) 45 n., 254 n., 346-347.
Minucius Felix 30.

Möhler 69 n.
Montanism 207-213, 390-394.
Morinus: *de Sacr. Ord.* 68 n.; 'traditio instrumentorum' 68 n., 186 n.; on orders 115 n.; St. Jerome 172 n., 175 n., 176 n.; valid ordination 190 n., 191, 195; rites 363-369; chorepiscopi, 373-374.
Muratorian Canon 287, 288 n., 330 n., 392.

NOVATIAN schism 55 n., 164 n., 192 n., 376, 385.

OECUMENIUS 264 n.
Optatus of Milevis 169 n.
Ordo Romanus on presbyterate 181 n.
Origen 140, 361, 384; on the Church 19 n., 24 n., 26-28, 29 n.; ministry 140-142, 247 n.; priesthood 89 n., 155; prophecy 392, 397; *Shepherd* of Hermas 331 n.; traditions in 134 n., 275 n., 290 n.

PAPHNUTIUS 374-375.
Papias 132; 118 n., 244 n.
Paul (St.): witness of his epp. as to the Church 46-51; ministry 231-251; ordination 268-269.
Paulianist clergy 192 n.
Pearson (Bp.) 70 n.
Peter (St.): commission to 5 n., 222-226, 230; 'presbyter' 302 n.; at Antioch 306; appoints bishops, etc. 129; his primacy 167, 169, 224; evidence of his ep. on the ministry 252 n., 254.
Pfleiderer (Prof.) 5 n., 23 n., 49, 50.
Philip (St.) in Asia Minor 288.
Philip the Evangelist 241 n., 265.
Phoebe 238, 251 n.
Photius 361, 372.
Polycarp, bp. of Smyrna 20, 116-117, 125, 287, 326 n.; prophet 280, 284, 329 n.; his letter 326; its witness as to the ministry 305 n., 326-330, 333, 405, 408 n.
Polycrates 132-133, 196 n., 286, 288 n.
Potter (Abp.) 109.
Primus 127, 133.
Pusey (Dr.) 45 n.

"QUAESTIONES IN N. ET V. TEST." 171-176, 189 n., 380, 389; their author 171.

RABANUS MAURUS: on priesthood 90 n.; sacraments 183 n.; orders of the ministry 181 n., 284 n. 373 n., 382.
Raymund of Sabunde 337 n.
Reeves on Irish episcopate 162 n.
Renan (M.) 56 n., 256, 264 n.
Renaudot 360.
Rothe 19 n., 21 n., 274 n.
Rufinus 17 n., 411 n., 412 n.

SABATIER (M.) 256 n., 414 n., 415, 418.
Salmon (Dr.) 129 n., 164 n., 217, 277 n., 325 n., 331 n., 335 n.
Sanday (Dr.) 52 n., 211, 403-404 n., 407 n.
Severus of Asmonaei 360.
Silas (St.) 262 n., 323.
Socrates Eccles. 105, 192 n.
Sozomen 330 n.
Stanton (V. H.) 19 n., 41 n., 54, 343.
Stephen I (Pope) 95, 155 n., 166 n.
Strabo, Walafrid 90 n.
Symeon, bp. of Jerusalem, 274-275.
Symeon of Thessalonica 144, 146 n.
Synesius 386.

TAYLOR (Dr.) 225 n., 413 n., 415 n., 419.

Teaching of the Apostles (Syriac) 131 n., 219 n.
Tertullian: on the Church 13-16, 20 n., 29 n., 34, 119, 132 n.; sacraments 78 n., 178, 179, 258 n.; episcopal successions 125-127, 134, 287; priesthood 88 n., 202 n., 204-207; his Montanist views 207-213, 391-393.
Testaments of the Twelve Patriarchs 401.
Theodore of Mopsuestia 160 n., 336 n., 405.
Theodoret 189 n., 234 n., 336 n., 384 n., 388.
Theophilus of Antioch 29, 130.
Theophylact 224 n., 241 n.
Thomas Aquinas (St.) 91 n., 377.
Timothy (and Titus) 246-249, 262, 267, 287 n., 302 n., 323.
Todd on Irish bps. 162 n., 163.
Trent, Catechism of 115 n.

VALENS (of Philippi) 327 n.
Victor I (Pope) 20, 117.
Victorinus of Petau 90 n, 255 n.
Vitringa 35 n.

WESTCOTT (Dr.) 16 n., 229 n.
Willehad (St.) 376-377.

ZAHN (Prof.) 289 n., 300 n.

www.ingramcontent.com/pod-product-compliance
Lightning Source LLC
Chambersburg PA
CBHW071223230426
43668CB00011B/1282